Managing Human Resources for the Millennial Generation

A Volume in
Contemporary Human Resource Management:
Issues, Challenges, and Opportunities

Series Editor
Ronald R. Sims, *College of William and Mary*

Contemporary Human Resource Management: Issues, Challenges, and Opportunities

Ronald R. Sims, Series Editor

Managing Human Resources for the Millennial Generation

Edited by

William I. Sauser, Jr.
Auburn University

Ronald R. Sims
College of William and Mary

Information Age Publishing, Inc.
Charlotte, North Carolina • www.infoagepub.com

Library of Congress Cataloging-in-Publication Data

Managing human resources for the Millennial generation / edited by William
I. Sauser, Jr. and Ronald R. Sims.
    p. cm. — (Contemporary human resource management)
  Includes bibliographical references.
  ISBN 978-1-62396-052-0 (paperback) — ISBN 978-1-62396-053-7 (hardcover) —
ISBN 978-1-62396-054-4 (ebook) 1. Personnel management. 2. Generation
Y—Employment. 3. Young adults—Employment. 4. Intergenerational
relations. 5. Generation Y—Attitudes. 6. Organizational behavior. I.
Sauser, William I. II. Sims, Ronald R.
  HF5549.M31353 2012
  658.3—dc23

                                                            2012037274

Printed in the United States of America

CONTENTS

PART II: MILLENNIALS AND THE TRADITIONAL FUNCTIONS OF HUMAN RESOURCE MANAGEMENT

PART III: BEST PRACTICES FOR MANAGING HUMAN RESOURCES FROM THE MILLENNIAL GENERATION

PART IV: SPECIAL ISSUES AND CONTEXTS

PART V: CONCLUDING THOUGHTS

LIST OF TABLES AND FIGURES

TABLES

FIGURES

ACKNOWLEDGMENTS

We are indebted to George F. Johnson at Information Age Publishing, Inc. who provided a collective outlet for our ideas. A hearty round of applause and thank you to our top-notch group of contributors. Their collective wisdom as human resources management practitioners, academics and researchers becomes quite evident when reading through the impressive content of their chapters. We believe they have made a significant contribution to the overall human resources management and generational dialogue with their work, and we are indebted to them all as colleagues and friends. Without their efforts and insights, this book ceases to exist.

SIMS ACKNOWLEDGMENT

A very, very special thanks goes to my coeditor, William I. Sauser, Jr. and Herrington Bryce who continues to serve as my colleague, mentor and valued friend. The administrative support of the Mason School of Business at the College of William and Mary is also acknowledged.

Thanks and appreciation goes to Nandi, Dangaia, and Sieya who have supported me throughout my work on this book.

SAUSER ACKNOWLEDGEMENT

William Sauser is grateful for the fine work of his colleagues in the preparation of the chapters comprising this book, and the patience and skill of

Managing Human Resources for the Millennial Generation, pp. xiii–xiv
Copyright © 2012 by Information Age Publishing
All rights of reproduction in any form reserved.

the professionals at Information Age Publishing. He wishes especially to thank his friend and coeditor, Ronald Sims. "Ron, you never cease to amaze me with your energy, can-do attitude, and generosity. Thanks for including me in yet another of your exciting projects." William dedicates this book to his "one and only," his dear wife Lane.

CHAPTER 1

WHO ARE THE MILLENNIALS AND HOW ARE THEY CHALLENGING MODERN HUMAN RESOURCES MANAGEMENT?

Ronald R. Sims and William I. Sauser, Jr.

INTRODUCTION

The purpose of this book is to explore the talents, work styles, attitudes, and issues that members of the Millennial generation are bringing with them as they enter the workforce. The Millennial generation is a roughly 20-year cohort of young people whose "leading edge" members were born in 1982 and graduated high school in 2000 (thus giving this generation its name). As of this writing, these are the young adults who began entering college, the military, and the workplace during the present decade, and who will continue to do so for perhaps another decade more, when the "trailing edge" of this age cohort will give way to what some have termed the "20-20 Generation" (again based on the year members of this even newer cohort will begin graduating from high school).

Managing Human Resources for the Millennial Generation, pp. 1–20
Copyright © 2012 by Information Age Publishing

The Millennial generation has been exposed during their formative years to a unique variety of historical, cultural, economic, and technological changes that have shaped their particular attitudes and values, preferred social interaction styles, beliefs about what is proper in the workplace, and personal concerns and desires. Millennials are bringing their unique perspectives into their places of employment, where at times they clash with those of the older generations who are already established there. Members of this generation—the Millennials—are challenging human resource managers in many ways: How can talented Millennials best be recruited, selected, trained, developed, and retained? What management and coaching styles work best with them? What rewards are they seeking, and how do they expect these rewards to be earned, packaged, and distributed? How are their often extraordinary skills in the use of information and communication technology to be harnessed and used for the benefit of their employing organizations? How can their employers best cope with—and benefit from—this generation's distinct preference for social networking through today's marvelous new electronic devices? What changes will this generation bring to the way organizations are structured, workplaces are arranged, information is shared, and goods and services are produced and marketed? What will their jobs be like, and how will their careers unfold? What demands will they bring for reforms in the workplace? How will they balance work with other aspects of their life, and what demands might this desire for balance place on other employees? How responsive are Millennials to unionization, the environmental movement, and calls for public service? What organizational citizenship behaviors can their employers expect from them, and what workplace problems might they generate? These and many more are the questions human resource managers are even now asking themselves about Millennials as members of this large generation enter the ranks of the employed.

To address these questions we have invited a number of experts from a variety of viewpoints to prepare chapters for this book. As you will discern as you read their contributions, these experts do not always agree, nor do they always share the same perspective on the talents, values, and contributions the Millennials bring to the workplace. What our chapter authors *do* provide, however, is wisdom about the Millennial generation derived from careful research, observation of employers' "best practices," and considerable first-hand experience in working with and alongside these new entrants to the workplace. It is our hope that the ideas presented in the chapters that comprise this volume will inform your own perspective and shape your own ideas about how to work effectively with this new generation of employees.

Before we introduce in summary form the ideas presented in this volume, we believe it is important to provide some useful background information. What is a "generation" and what are some of the key characteristics of the focal generation of this book—the Millennials? What information can we find in existing literature about these individuals and how best to work with them? What recommendations have earlier writers provided? Let us now turn our attention to these questions.

THE MILLENNIAL GENERATION

Living Generations

A generation is a cohort of people who were born and came of age together during (roughly) a 20-year period of history. Twenty years is, of course, the approximate period of time between birth and early adulthood, when "the next generation" begins to come along. While each member of a generation is unique in many ways (and should be appreciated and understood as such), members of a generational cohort share common formative experiences that affect their outlook on life (Strauss & Howe, 1991). Such common formative experiences include historical and cultural events; music, movies, books, icons, heroes, villains, and slang; technological innovations; fashions and trends; and child-rearing and educational practices. According to William Strauss and Neil Howe, a pair of pioneering social commentators whose works (Strauss & Howe, 1991, 1997; Howe & Strauss, 1993, 2000) have shaped modern thought on generational differences, there are members of six generations currently living in the world. These generations and their birth years, according to Strauss and Howe, are G. I. (1901-1924), Silent (1925-1942), Boom (1943-1960), Gen-X (1961-1981), Millennial (1982-2002), and the post-9/11 children some have termed 20-20 (2003-present). It should be noted, of course, that other writers have used different names for these generations, and even different birth dates. Millennials are variously referred to by others also as "Generation Y" and "Generation Me."

Sadly, members of the G. I. generation (to whom we all owe a great debt of gratitude) are dying by the thousands every day, and most members of the Silent generation have now retired, though some still hold influential positions as owners, directors, and managers in business. The large Boom generation (the "Baby Boomers") have long dominated the workplace due to their sheer numbers, but Boomers (at least, those who can afford to do so in these difficult economic times) are retiring from the workplace by the thousands every day, making room for members of the smaller Generation X cohort to move into leadership positions. Millenni-

als—another very large generation—make up most of the current new entrants to the workforce, and they are bringing with them a set of attitudes, values, beliefs, and behavioral styles shaped by the events immediately preceding and following the year 2000. Some of those key events included the rise of computers, the Internet, "smart" phones, and social media; the ubiquitous presence of television, children's shows such as *Sesame Street,* and teen-focused dramas like *Beverly Hills 90210* and *The OC;* the deaths of Princess Diana and John Kennedy, Jr.; violent killings at Columbine High School; the Oklahoma City bombing; the dramatic terrorist events of 9/11; Enron and other corporate scandals; Hurricane Katrina; wars in Iraq and Afghanistan; and "The Great Recession." No wonder many of their parents displayed a protective childrearing style.

Characteristics of Millennials

Many have sought to characterize the Millennial generation, and books and articles about this intriguing group of persons abound. In *Millennials Rising,* Howe and Strauss (2000)—based on studies of this generation in their childhood—declared the Millennials to be *The Next Great Generation* (which is the subtitle of their book). Here is a quotation representative of their extreme optimism concerning this generation:

> As a group, Millennials are unlike any other youth generation in living memory. They are more numerous, more affluent, better educated, and more ethnically diverse. More important, they are beginning to manifest a wide array of positive social habits that older Americans no longer associate with youth, including a new focus on teamwork, achievement, modesty, and good conduct. Only a few years from now, this can-do youth revolution will overwhelm the cynics and pessimists. Over the next decade, the Millennial Generation will entirely recast the image of youth, from downbeat and alienated to upbeat and engaged, with potentially seismic consequences for America. (p. 4)

As this cohort began entering college, however, they began to acquire a less sanguine, more balanced reputation: special, sheltered, confident, team-oriented, achieving, pressured, and conventional (Williams, Beard, & Tanner, 2011). Here are a few insights quoted from Williams and colleagues (2011, pp. 44-45) describing the characteristics of Millennials in college today:

- Many of these young adults want to be recognized just for showing up and trying, and they're indignant or upset when that's not good enough at the university level.

- Many are unprepared for the realities of the college classroom. Many do not hesitate to challenge their professors when they do receive constructive criticism or don't receive A grades.
- Millennials possess high levels of trust and optimism. Faculty sometimes interpret their self-assurance as arrogance, a sense of entitlement, and an unrealistic belief that they can accomplish too much too soon.
- Millennials have strong team instincts and tight peer bonds; they rely on e-mail, texting, and social media like Facebook, Twitter, and YouTube to stay in constant touch with friends and family.
- Millennials are on track to become the best educated and best behaved adults in history. But since many of them have never worked outside the home, they frequently lack business etiquette and social skills.
- Millennials feel pressured to excel. They actively seek reactions and are lost without constant feedback, and the drive to succeed can cause them to cheat, plagiarize, and whine in the classroom.
- More comfortable with their parents' values than any previous generation, Millennials also have a high respect for teachers and institutions. At the same time, that conventionality leads Millennials to be less creative and take fewer risks in the classroom.

Susan Eisner (one of the authors whose work appears in this volume) began studying carefully the characteristics of Millennials as they began entering the workforce. In a 2005 article she summarized many of the traits and characteristics of this generation in the workplace. Here are a few of her observations (paraphrased):

- They are educated, experienced (beyond their years), sociable, technically skilled multitaskers with a good work ethic.
- They lack direction, focus, confidence, and interpersonal ("soft") skills.
- They expect to make decisions.
- They have a strong need to achieve.
- They are self-reliant, curious, energetic, and they ask questions.
- They distrust "job security."
- They dislike "face time."
- They dislike menial jobs (Eisner, 2005).

Here is how another experienced generational researcher, Rachel Burges (2011), describes this generation:

Millennials, born between 1983 and 2001, were raised by doting parents and awarded praise and trophies for just showing up. They suffer from no lack of self-esteem. Yet they are facing harsh economic realities thanks to the Great Recession. Unable or unwilling to find work, Millennials are enjoying a prolonged adolescence living at home and remaining untested. Still, the generation shows promise. Technologically savvy, Millennials are hyper connected through mobile devices, instant messaging and texting. The internet is second nature. Furthermore, as social libertarians in their outlook, they are comfortable with diversity in race, culture, and sexual orientation. Millennials are joiners: Early signs suggest they may engender a renaissance in civic participation and the rebuilding of social capital. (p. 9)

Millennial Values

Interestingly, Jean Twenge—herself a Millennial—disputes Burges' comments about Millennials' eagerness to participate in rebuilding social capital. She and her colleagues (Twenge, Campbell, Hoffman, & Lance, 2010; Twenge, Campbell, & Freeman, 2012) have conducted carefully constructed multigenerational studies of values over time using national survey data and have concluded that Millennials value leisure over work and extrinsic rewards (status, money, fame, image) over intrinsic rewards (self-acceptance, affiliation, community) and altruistic work values, such as helping others and societal worth. Twenge and colleagues (2012) provided these particularly pertinent conclusions as they contrasted Millennial values with those of members of the *Boom* and *Gen-X* cohorts:

> Concern for others (e.g., empathy for outgroups, charity donations, the importance of having a job worthwhile to society) declined slightly. Community service rose but was also increasingly required for high school graduation over the same time period. Civic orientation (e.g., interest in social problems, political participation, trust in government, taking action to help the environment and save energy) declined ... between GenX and the Millennials. Some of the largest declines appeared in taking action to help the environment. (p. 1)

In her popular book, *Generation Me*, Twenge (2006) describes (in the subtitle of the book) today's young Americans as "more confident, assertive, entitled—and more miserable—than ever before." She believes she knows why: Millennials have very high expectations formed in childhood that are unmet once early adulthood is reached. Here is her explanation:

> In many ways, the higher expectations of GenMe [Twenge's name for the trailing edge of the Millennial cohort] are rooted in our focus on the self. We've been told all our lives that we're special, so we think we deserve to be

famous and rich. We also have higher expectations for jobs and romantic partners, expecting fulfillment in all realms of life. It would be wonderful if these appetites could always be sated, but of course they can't. Not everyone can live in a huge house, and most people's jobs, by economic necessity, are not going to be fulfilling, at least not all of the time. You might be married to a great guy, but he's not going to be your perfect soulmate all the time. We focus so much on our individual wants, feeling empty inside, that depression is often the result. (Twenge, 2006, pp. 133-134)

Twenge (2006) believes that the "you can be anything you want to be" approach to childrearing and education that characterized the 1990s—while perhaps a well-intentioned effort to raise this generation's self-esteem—has actually *harmed* Millennials by setting them up for disappointment when they learn that the slogan simply is not true. If skills and abilities are lacking; if motivation, self-discipline, and persistence are not applied; if careful preparation (including appropriate education and training) are not part of the plan; and if "the breaks" just don't go your way, it is likely that you will *not* "be anything you want to be." Instead, Twenge believes the "follow your dream" ethos has led this generation to become narcissistic, focused only on the self. As a result of the way many of these "trophy children" were brought up and educated, they have become characterized with an unhealthy obsession with appearance and materiality, and an adolescence extended well beyond previous generational limits (see in particular her third chapter, "You can be anything you want to be," for Twenge's (2006, pp. 72-103) convincing evidence.

In *The Trophy Kids Grow Up*, Ron Alsop (2008) applies his *Wall Street Journal* reporting skills to a study of the Millennial generation. The resulting book is breezy, fact-filled, entertaining, and highly informative. Alsop shares Twenge's (2006) concerns about the formative years of the young Millennials, but also displays some of Howe and Strauss' (2000) earlier optimism. Here is his take on the newest entrants to the workforce, based on extensive interviewing and personal research:

> In my research, I found the millennials frequently written off as narcissistic, arrogant, and fickle. Although there is certainly some truth in such negative perceptions, the millennials also can be quite impressive in their ambitions and achievements. They are a generation of conflicting characteristics—self-absorbed but also civic minded, for instance. Keep in mind, however, that the traits ascribed to the millennials certainly don't apply to every member of that generation. They are common but not universal attributes. (Alsop, 2008, p. vii)

Our own personal experience, described a bit later in this chapter, comes closest to Alsop's (2008) perspective on the Millennial generation. We see both strengths and weaknesses, and certainly agree with Alsop's important caveat. In fact, while we believe it is very useful to consider generational differences among people, we believe that they are but one way of many in which persons can differ. Other important sources of diversity of ideas, values, and behavior include racial-ethnic differences; regional and cultural differences; socioeconomic differences; and age, gender, and ability differences. Our recommendation is always to manage—lead, coach, teach—the *individual*, not the stereotype.

Ideal Job Characteristics for Millennials

With tongue planted firmly in cheek, Alsop (2008, p. 211) describes the "ultimate dream job" for the Millennial generation thusly: "Well, it would definitely have to provide unlimited career opportunities, plenty of praise and rewards, flexible work hours, a casual and fun atmosphere, and, of course, a meteoric rise to the executive suite." In a more serious vein, Alsop (2008) provides these comments about Millennials and their preferred job characteristics:

- Highly accomplished and doted on by their parents, the trophy kids are arriving in the workplace by the millions. Employers are benefiting from their technology, multitasking, and teamwork skills, but bristling at their demands for flexible working conditions, frequent feedback and guidance, and rapid promotion (p. 21).

- A strong sense of entitlement is one of the most striking characteristics of the millennial generation. Young people have extremely high expectations about their jobs—everything from a desire for frequent performance feedback and fast promotions to a need for work-life balance and opportunities to perform community service (p. 47).

- Millennials gravitate toward employers with a culture of meritocracy. They want to advance as quickly as their achievements merit, and they absolutely detest any rigid timetables hampering their rise to the top (p. 47).

- Because of their great expectations, millennials are notoriously fickle and prone to job hopping. In fact, some employers consider retention a bigger challenge than recruiting this young generation (p. 48).

- To improve their retention rates, companies must work harder to keep millennials engaged in their jobs. That means clearly showing them the value and impact of their work, creating a collegial and team-oriented culture, and, above all, offering them a rich variety of opportunities to advance in their careers (p. 48).

- The millennial generation craves feedback, especially praise, from their bosses on a regular basis. It keeps them engaged and motivated—and strongly increases the odds of retaining them (p. 114).
- Millennials require special handling when their performance isn't up to par. Harsh criticism can provoke tears—or even a resignation (p. 114).
- Beyond performance reviews, millennials expect mentors, coaches, and training programs to help them develop their skills and to rise to higher levels in the organization (p. 114).
- "Work-life balance" is the mantra of the millennial generation. Unlike any generation before them, millennials are demanding that companies give them flexible working conditions so that they can have time for family and personal passions (p. 184).

Desires for flexibility, meritocracy, and retention programs; a collegial and team-oriented culture; opportunities for advancement; praise from supervisors; provision of mentors, coaches, and training programs; and work-life balance are certainly not unique to the Millennial generation. Efforts by human resource managers to provide these job characteristics will likely enhance employee retention across *all* the generations currently comprising the workforce. This is, however, a clear challenge to human resource managers that has risen in prominence with the arrival of Millennials in the workplace.

Eisner (2005) has provided a number of practical ideas for managers to employ as they seek to attract, develop, and retain Millennials. Some of them (paraphrased) are as follows:

- Manage them with a coaching style.
- Allow them to work with bright, creative people under the leadership of a seasoned mentor.
- Give them flexibility and voice.
- Provide access to coworkers and company information through technology.
- Assign project-centered work.
- Explain expectations from the outset.
- Describe the "big picture" and how they fit into it.
- Give them a sense of belonging.
- Create a sense of enjoyment and challenge.
- Speak candidly, avoid hyperbole, and use your sense of humor.

- Provide cultural awareness and transparency.
- Encourage teamwork and flexibility.
- Define roles and responsibilities clearly.
- Use task lists and timelines.
- Don't promise what can't be provided.
- Provide opportunities for socially responsible actions contributing to the greater good.
- Tailor spaces, processes, and practices to facilitate the exchange of ideas.

These and other ideas are developed by our team of authors in the chapters that follow. Before introducing some of these ideas in summary form, however, we'd like to provide some of our own personal observations about the members of the Millennial generation with whom we have been working for over a decade.

PERSONAL OBSERVATIONS

The authors of this chapter (and editors of this book) are both members of the *Boom* generation who have been teaching at the university level for 3 1/2 decades. We began our careers teaching "trailing edge" Baby Boomers, then saw our students transition into the Gen Y cohort, and—over the past decade—into members of the Millennial generation. We would like to share a few of our general observations about the Millennials with you, the reader. These observations are limited to the young adults we have worked with in our local settings, of course, and must be understood within the important caveat we emphasized above: Each individual—no matter which generation she or he represents—should be recognized and treated as such. Stereotyping of individuals is not appropriate, yet we believe there is merit in understanding some of the general characteristics of students from the Millennial generation we have observed first hand. Thus we offer these comments:

- They are indeed very technologically savvy—and their knowledge of technology greatly exceeds our own.
- Unfortunately, their constant use of IT and social media can become distracting. In fact, we find them to be easily distracted.
- They are also not very tolerant of others who do not share their IT skills.

- "Reverse mentoring" is a useful idea with these persons. Let them teach you a thing or two about technology, and show your appreciation.
- They seem eager to work, but expect their work—even at the start—to be interesting, challenging, and rewarding ... and can become frustrated when that is not the case.
- They don't like "busy work," lower level assignments, and "boring" tasks. The idea of "working your way up the ranks" seems foreign to many of them. They want to make an immediate impact.
- Maybe give them a challenge early in their career to see how they can handle it ... and mentor them along the way.
- They have grown up with diversity and are very comfortable with the concept of pluralism in the workplace.
- They are also very indignant about any lack of tolerance in the workplace. This is a big "turnoff."
- They do have a sense of social justice and are willing to take part in voluntary activities for the benefit of society.
- Their networking skills—especially using social media—are very strong. They have a world of information literally at their fingertips.
- Unfortunately, they are not always provided accurate information through the social media, and they do not always assess what they have heard critically.
- They expect immediate feedback on their work and their ideas. They expect their supervisors to give them this feedback via e-mail or text messaging.
- They do not typically enjoy "face to face" meetings. They prefer to do their communicating electronically.
- This may frustrate their older supervisors and coworkers.
- As a group they are much more casual in their communication styles. Their lack of formality can sometimes be interpreted by their elders as rudeness.
- They do not plan to stay in one job or organization very long. They expect to hold five or more (maybe many more) jobs during their lifetime.
- They do not tend to read instructions, nor do they follow written instructions very well. They prefer to ask questions and learn through trial and error.
- This makes them appear unstructured and very needy of direction and coaching. It can frustrate older managers and coworkers.

- They have a high sense of self-worth, and they expect "second chances" when they do not succeed on the first try.
- They are very interested in work-life balance and expect their employers to give them flexible schedules, time off, and lots of vacation time.
- They expect to be provided with the latest technology and are frustrated when asked to use "obsolete" equipment.
- They have grown up in an era of "planned obsolescence" and the "replace rather than repair" approach to equipment maintenance.
- They can be very valuable members of your work team if you use their eagerness, creativity, connectedness, technological skills, acceptance of diversity, and other positive traits to the advantage of your organization.
- Help them fit in and coach them well; give them a chance to prove their worth. Be patient and help them learn.

With that said, let us now preview the remaining chapters in this book to see how they develop and build upon the ideas presented in this brief introduction to the Millennial generation and the challenges they are bringing to the workplace.

THE CHAPTERS THAT FOLLOW

Here is the information you will encounter as you read the chapters that follow this introductory piece.

Characteristics and Values of the Millennial Generation

In Chapter 2, "Millennials Break Out as the Me Generation: Their Attitudes, Expectations and Fears," Daniel D. Butler and William I. Sauser, Jr. highlight the thoughts of a group of college-age Millennials (i.e., the "Me Generation") and their attitudes toward the world and concerns about entering the world of work, as revealed in surveys and focus group interviews. Before concluding the chapter with their own personal observations of Millennials in action Butler and Sauser share their thoughts about how human resource managers may use these insights for the mutual benefit of the "Me Generation" and their employing organizations.

In Chapter 3, "Millennial Work Expectations and Organizational Incentive Systems: 'Carrots' for the New Millennium," Daniel J. Svyantek,

Kristin L. Cullen, and Frances L.H. Svyantek highlight the point that the Millennial generation is popularly thought to "want it all and want it now:" These individuals see themselves as entitled to rewards which do not match their actual performance. Further, the authors note that the expectations of the Millennial generation contain a potential disconnect between reward and performance. Therefore, the task of motivating Millennials offers new challenges to organizations. Svyantek, Cullen and Svyantek first review the literature and provide a description of the expectations of the Millennial generation for extrinsic motivation in the workplace. Next, the chapter briefly addresses the basics of motivational theories. Then, the chapter explores the fit between current organizational incentive systems and the expectation for pay, benefits and advancement held by the Millennial generation and the proposals of work motivation theory. Finally, the authors propose organizational reward systems that they believe have the greatest match between the expectations of the Millennial generation and the motivating value of these systems, and offer organizations suggestions for developing incentive systems which will appeal to—and motivate—the Millennial generation to meet organizational goals for performance as this new generation enters the workforce.

In Chapter 4, "Just What Is Important to Millennial Job Candidates: It's Not What We Assumed," Kyra Leigh Sutton strives to increase our understanding of the expectations and perceptions that Millennial (i.e., Gen Y) job seekers have during the recruiting and selection processes. Based on a survey of Gen Y job seekers currently enrolled in college, but seeking employment opportunities, Sutton argues that Gen Y job seekers' reactions to the selection and recruitment process are important in order to facilitate organizational attraction, and to lessen the likelihood of applicant withdrawal during the selection process. Sutton offers a number of recommendations intended to help organizations learn how to attract Gen Y job seekers, and the importance of preparing the organization's current workforce for the entrance of Gen Y job seekers is also discussed.

In Chapter 5, "Giving Voice to Values: Engaging Millennials and Managing Multigenerational Cultures," Jessica McManus Warnell explores the key tenets of the *Giving Voice to Values* (GVV) approach, including values alignment and implementable skills, and its particular promise for organizations seeking to provide developmental support and capitalize upon the gifts and motivations of Millennials. Warnell notes that GVV is a practical program of study that draws on social psychology, cognitive neuroscience and management research to focus less on ethical reasoning and decision-making and more on ethical action. According to Warnell, GVV offers a resource for corporations to acknowledge and cultivate opportunity in the face of challenges arising from managing Millennials. And in doing so, Warnell posits that Millennials can and do act on their values, and organizations can develop mechanisms to foster values-based decision making in a way that supports organizational culture and furthers shared goals.

Millennials and the Traditional Functions of Human Resource Management

In Chapter 6, "Leveraging Web 2.0 Technologies in the Recruitment of Millennial Job Candidates," Jared J. Llorens and Alexandrea Wilson first discuss the characteristics of Millennial job candidates that necessitate more advanced e-recruitment approaches by employers. The authors then highlight the transformation from traditional recruitment methods to e-recruitment methods, and overview common Web 2.0 technologies currently utilized in many employer recruitment efforts. Finally, Llorens and Wilson discuss how employers can leverage these new technologies in their recruitment efforts and provide examples of organizations in the private, public and nonprofit sectors that have effectively incorporated these new technologies into their existing e-recruitment activities.

In Chapter 7, "New Selection Methods for a New Generation," Jeffrey Crenshaw and Kyle Brink argue that despite the challenge that these generational shifts bring, the current shift also presents significant opportunities to modify and improve traditional human resource management processes and leverage these improvements to attract, select, and retain high quality employees. Crenshaw and Brink discuss utilizing technology—specifically video and multimedia technology—in employee selection to find innovative ways to help address the generational shift. The values and skills of the Millennial generation are presented and, using the context of signaling theory, the authors outline how selection systems communicate to candidates for employment information about job attributes and organizational values that candidates then use to make decisions about the organization. Crenshaw and Brink also discuss how technology-based selection systems not only convey information on organizational values that align with values of the Millennial generation, but also help address traditional selection challenges such as improving validity, reducing group differences, enhancing efficiency, and reducing costs. Finally, Crenshaw and Brink offer a case study involving the design and implementation of a video-based employment selection process and a technology-enhanced testing facility.

In Chapter 8, "Considering Generational Differences in Assessing Work Values ... A Unifying Approach," Kenneth P. Yusko and Brian L. Bellenger note that the prevailing stereotypes of generational groups in the workplace suggest there are substantive differences in work styles and values, work ethic, and job performance across the generations. However, Yusko and Bellenger note how empirical research has challenged this notion and indicated that employees of different generations tend to have similar values and desire similar things from their organizations. Further, Yusko and Bellenger note that as organizations attempt to staff positions in the current work environment, overly focusing on any particular generational category may lead to legal difficulties and result in missed hiring opportunities. The authors emphasize the point that one approach to resolving this issue is to evaluate potential employees for job-relevant knowledge, skills, and abilities as well as cultural fit with the organization. Recruiting strategies can then be tailored to target individuals across the generations to identify those candidates best equipped to handle the specific duties of the job.

In Chapter 9, "Employee-Friendly Policies and Development Benefits for Millennials," the underlying premise of the chapter by Jonathan P. West is that employers need to understand the changing demographics of the workforce and to tailor their Human Resource Management (HRM) policies and practices accordingly. According to West, best practices would suggest that savvy employers be aware of the generational mix of their workers and design programs that appeal to and address the needs of this changing workforce. Further, while employee-friendly policies and development benefits are likely favored by all employees, younger workers have special needs and expectations that deserve employer attention if they are to recruit and retain the best of the new entrants into the workplace. In the end, West notes that the challenge of achieving work-life balance and development benefits through employee-friendly policies aimed at new Millennials is crucial to organizational vitality. West argues the points above by first offering a brief description of changing notions of work and family relations, new labor market conditions and the implications of these developments for Millennials. Then insights from psychological contract theory are used to consider ways to improve work-life balance, employer-employee relations and organizational flexibility. With this in mind, West offers five types of employee-friendly (and not-so-friendly) policies and practices, including flexible and alternative work schedules, work-life programs, stress reduction and wellness initiatives, traditional economic benefits, and reverse mentoring. Finally, the discussion and conclusion sections of this chapter explore the implications of the findings for new Millennials and human resource professionals.

In Chapter 10, "Texts, E-mails, and Google Searches: Training in a Multigenerational Workplace," Patrick Deery notes how technology in the workplace has added another layer to the analysis of adult learning styles, and it is such an analysis that necessitates that we look at the effect on the training of all four generations in the workplace. That is, technology has affected all the generations and how they view and participate in training; thus, the key to understanding the effect is to see how technology has impacted adult learning styles. After a brief comparison/contrast of the four generations' attitudes toward work, work relationships, feedback, and training as a topic, Deery assesses technology's impact on delivery options and participants and concludes that technology is blurring the distinction between online and face-to-face delivery and further loosening the control a trainer has on the timing, frequency, and type of delivery method used. With this warning in mind, Deery next defines some adult learner classification patterns or styles and then relates those patterns to the four generations as a means of predicting how each generation learns in the technologically dense workplace. From this analysis Deery offers some advice for training all generations in general and for Millennials in particular.

Best Practices for Managing Human Resources for the Millennial Generation

In Chapter 11, "Best Practices for Managing Generation Y," Susan Eisner presents representative best practices being used by contemporary companies seeking to heighten the presence and contribution of Gen Y (Millennial) workers. Eisner offers 11 best practices, gathered from extensive foundational research and companies designated, for example, by recognized third party sources as best places to launch a career, best for recent college grads to work for, top entry-level employers, and best to work for, along with companies whose current practices were featured in the *New York Times* Sunday Business Section's weekly "Corner Office" series. Eisner recommends the 11 best practices as key for those seeking to optimize the performance of their Gen Y workers.

In Chapter 12, "A New Talent Agenda," Milano Reyna and Rishap Malhotra suggest that *"If you want to see how a tiger hunts, go to the jungle not the zoo."* With this in mind, the chapter is about understanding the workforce through the lens of a global talent practitioner, a millennial researcher and the people who do the work in an ideas company. Through countless dinners, meetings and observations, Reyna and Malhotra uncovered what they believe is common among past, present and future employees. More specifically, they learned that people want responsibility, recognition, learning and joy. And for these authors an important question is, "How do you do it?" Throughout the chapter Reyna and Malhotra offer their answer to this question by sharing some milestones of their own story in creating a new talent agenda that fulfills employees in the now.

In Chapter 13, "Implications of Values of the Millennial Generation on HR Infrastructure," Sheri K. Bias and Donna L. Phillips define and provide further insight on the values for the Millennial generation in terms of categories of immediacy, teaming, and recognition that are mainly influencing behaviors. To illustrate their main points Bias and Phillips use examples from two distinct organizations: (1) the National Aeronautics and Space Administration (NASA), a Federal Government organization, from a broad perspective of activities from NASA at-large as well as specific examples from NASA Langley Research Center, operating in Hampton Roads, Virginia; and (2) Jaderlund Casting, a privately owned organization that provides casting for films and television productions and talent management services; to describe the alignment of the values important to Millennials with human resources infrastructure and practices utilized by these organizations.

In Chapter 14, "Millennial-Centric Strategic HR: Key Practices for Attracting, Developing, and Retaining Millennials," Scott A. Quatro argues that traditional corporate human resources (HR) practices don't reflect an understanding of the uniqueness of the Millennial generation. Quatro suggests that Google is a rare example of a company that "gets it right" with Millennials. According to Quatro, Google begins with understanding the uniqueness of Millennials as global-minded employees leading integrated lives in search of higher order purpose, and then building key strategic HR practices that reflect this understanding. To that end, Quatro outlines the following as key millennial-centric, strategic HR practices (juxtaposed against their traditional corporate HR practice manifestations): Employer Branding versus Job Advertising; Organizational Purpose versus Shareholder Wealth Maximization; Personal and Peer Coaching versus Performance Appraisal; Work-Life Integration versus Work-Life Balance. For illustrative purposes, the story of Google's strategic HR practices is woven into focused discussion of these key areas of contemporary HR practice.

Special Issues and Contexts

In Chapter 15, "Promises of Telecommuting and Preferences of Millennials: Exploring the Nexus," Ajantha S. Dharmasiri, Danielle Beu Ammeter, John E. Baur and M. Ronald Buckley explore the ongoing technological and operational changes in the organizational setting being brought forth due to the Millennial generation's entrance into the workforce. And one such technology that in their view is becoming more common in organizational use is telecommuting. The authors posit that telecommuting allows employees to check in and conduct meetings while working from home or in different locales. Additionally, the authors note that telecommuting offers many benefits to organizations and their employees including reduced costs, eliminating the wasted time of commuting, and reducing the logistical and scheduling issues associated with a decentralized operation. In order to address the reality that telecommuting is not always successful, Dharmasiri, Ammeter, Baur and Buckley propose a model that incorporates organizational and individual capacity for telecommuting and work amenability for telecommuting as the most important predictors of telecommuting success. Further, the chapter provides a detailed study of the unique characteristics of the Millennial generation, the benefits of telecommuting, critical success factors for telecommuting, and the possible repercussions of relying on this technology.

In Chapter 16, "Millennials in the Workforce: Unions and Management Battle for the Soul of a Generation," Marcia A. Beck and Jonathan P. West examine Millennials' attitudes toward and involvement in unions in the context of declining union influence, after first discussing Generation Y demographics and work-related attitudes and orientations. Beck and West then turn to what they refer to as "a battle and a truce." For these authors, the mutually exclusive battle is between unions and employers to appeal to Millennials' interests and values to capture their loyalty and commitment, and they believe that the battle will be fought over the "rules of engagement." Beck and West suggest that both unions and employers understand that engaging Millennials in organizational causes, goals, operations, and reorientations is crucial for the longevity, effectiveness, and influence of their organizations. Several of these engagement strategies are offered and examined in the chapter. According to Beck and West a truce emerges when employers and unions, compelled to work together by employee choice, develop labor-management partnerships based on mutual goals and common commitments. As the adversarial battle between employers and unions in the private and public sectors rages on, the authors portend that a series of truces has emerged under the radar, providing palpable hope that Millennials will be able exercise their talents and realize their goals in an arena where partnership trumps partisanship.

In Chapter 17, "Small Businesses, Value Added, and the Millennials," Jackie A. DiPofi and Margaret Fitch-Hauser focus on the human resource goals of small business owners for an effective and efficient workforce to share their burden of small business operations. Understanding the role of Millennials—an important emerging segment of the employee selection pool—is discussed in that context. Subsegments of microworkers and multitaskers, solitary and social players are hypothesized as range indicators of Millennial behavior characteristics and skills sets. Emerging new media communicators and old school communicators are introduced in the context of the Millennial employee relative to the owner. The hiring environment of the small business and the complexity of transferring activities from owner to employee are also illustrated by DiPofi and Fitch-Hauser. The authors emphasize that incorporating Millennials into the organization and maximizing their value added contribution is critical. DiPofi and Fitch-Hauser offer recommendations built on proven business principles mixed with new technology tools. And, they note that business owners should clearly define value added activities they expect from their employees, and communicate those expectations using the most advanced electronic media common to the Millennial segment. In summary, DiPofi and Fitch-Hauser highlight the importance of successful human resources management as small business owners grow their businesses with Millennial employees.

Concluding Thoughts

In Chapter 18, "Building Bridges between the Millennials and Other Generations," Ronald R. Sims first takes a brief look at the different generations at work in today's organizations. Sims then introduces the concepts of generationalism and generational consciousness, which are offered as critical components necessary for managing and leveraging the positive interactions between generations in the workplace. Sims next offers some solutions (i.e. dialogue, good conversation and conversational learning) available to HRM professionals to develop connections or bridges among Millennials and other generations in their organizations. Sims goes on to discuss the importance of organizational culture, culture shock and valuing to the creation of a work environment where Millennials and others are successful. Before concluding the chapter, Sims takes a look at the importance of assessment and evaluation of how well an organization is doing in their efforts to recruit and retain Millennials (i.e. create generational consciousness and generationalism).

We hope you enjoy this book and find it beneficial as you seek to manage human resources from the Millennial generation.

REFERENCES

Alsop, R. (2008). *The trophy kids grow up: How the millennial generation is shaking up the workplace.* San Francisco, CA: Jossey-Bass/*The Wall Street Journal.*

Burgess, R. (2011, June). Harnessing the power of your intergenerational workforce. *The Alabama CPA Magazine,* 8-9.

Eisner, S. P. (2005). Managing Generation Y. *SAM Advanced Management Journal,* *70*(4), 4-15.

Howe, N., & Strauss, B. (1993). *13th Gen: Abort, retry, ignore, fail?* New York, NY: Vintage Books.

Howe, N., & Strauss, W. (2000). *Millennials rising: The next great generation.* New York, NY: Vintage Books.

Strauss, W., & Howe, N. (1991). *Generations: The history of America's future, 1584-* *2069.* New York, NY: Quill/William Morrow.

Strauss, W., & Howe, N. (1997). *The fourth turning: An American prophecy.* New York, NY: Broadway Books.

Twenge, J. M. (2006). *Generation me: Why today's young Americans are more confident,* *assertive, entitled—and more miserable than ever before.* New York, NY: Free Press.

Twenge, J. M., Campbell, W. K., & Freeman, E. C. (2012, March 5). Generational differences in young adults' life goals, concern for others, and civic orientation, 1966-2009. *Journal of Personality and Social Psychology.* Advance online publication. doi: 10.1037/a0027408

Twenge, J. M., Campbell, S. M., Hoffman, B. J., & Lance, C. E. (2010). Generational differences in work values: Leisure and extrinsic values increasing, social and intrinsic values decreasing. *Journal of Management, 36*(5), 1117-1142.

Williams, S., Beard, J., & Tanner, M. (2011, July-August). Coping with millennials on campus. *BizEd,* 42-49.

PART I

CHARACTERISTICS AND VALUES OF THE MILLENNIAL GENERATION

CHAPTER 2

MILLENNIALS BREAK OUT AS THE ME GENERATION

Their Attitudes, Expectations and Fears

Daniel D. Butler and William I. Sauser, Jr.

INTRODUCTION

Although the first of the Millenials represent the high school graduating class of 2000 (Howe & Strauss, 2000), the trailing edge of this cohort has been called the Me Generation (Eisner, 2005; Twenge, 2006). The Me Generation is composed of people who are now in the later stages of university education and very early stages of their career, born around 1990. These are the children primarily of Gen Y parents. The Me Generation is widely reported to be distinctly different from Generation X, Y, and possibly the leading edge Millennials themselves (Pew Research Center, 2010; Myers, 2010; Twenge, 2006). The Me Generation is the most immediate group of new employees now facing human resource managers.

Technology and global events have changed the manner in which this group communicates and is educated (Li & Bernoff, 2008; Lenhart,

Managing Human Resources for the Millennial Generation, pp. 23–52
Copyright © 2012 by Information Age Publishing
23

2009). Nationally, almost 100% of college students in this cohort own a communications device of some sort ("Survey Finds," 2009). They live in a world where 84% of them have internet access at home, most own a cell phone, and 87% of them text message daily (Roberts, Foehr, & Rideout, 2005). One third of all entering college students have blogs (Pryor, Hurtado, DeAngelo, Black, & Tran, 2010). The Me Generation brought us multitasking. They use electronic media 7.5 hours a day and pack 10.75 hours into exposure to that media by multitasking (Roberts et al., 2005). They text, Facebook, Tweet, Google, download You Tube, Podcast, talk, and watch course lectures on their Droid phones, doing all of this while walking to class with an umbilical cord they call ear buds embedded in their ears. They incorrectly believe they are very efficient at multitasking (Abate, 2008; Gorlick, 2009).

Downing (2006) and Twenge (2006) identified the historical events that shaped Millennials and the Me Generation. They grew up watching the twin towers fall in New York on September 11, 2001. They have lived with an ongoing war between the United States, Iraq, and Afghanistan most of their lives. They watched the financial crisis impact their parents' daily lives and their own standard of living. This group understands that 25% of workers today work for a company they have been employed with for less than 1 year. This group knows that 50% of employees today have been working at their current job for less than 5 years. The Me Generation has been called the "instant generation" that feels entitled. They expect academic grades of As and Bs. They want their professors to communicate with them, and they want everything, *now*.

The Me Generation is of profound importance to human resource managers (Eisner, 2005) as this is the next cohort they will have to manage, immediately. Gorman, Nelson, and Glassman (2004) suggest there are strategic opportunities for firms that will leverage the competencies of this group in their value chain. In order to harness this resource it is necessary to better understand them. What insight might human resource managers learn from the Me Generation to help their firms be more competitive (Twenge, Campbell, Hoffman, & Lance, 2010)? What will they tell us? Finding this out is the purpose of this chapter.

Following a description of the research process, the chapter is broken down into major themes. These represent General Attitudes, Training, Communication and Feedback, The Work Environment and Ethics, Compensation, Use of Social Media, Overall Fears and Concerns the First 6 Months After Leaving University, and Insight. Each theme presents standard quantitative results. These are buttressed by anonymous unedited open-ended responses "in their own words."

RESEARCH PROCESS

Building off the work of Millennial and Me Generation research, focus groups and surveys were executed at a major Southern university. Assessments were made across a variety of issues. These include general attitudes toward life, expectations of the companies that hire them, and use of technology.

Three focus groups were conducted with a total of 45 participants (45% female, 55% male). Subsequently, a sample frame across university majors resulted in 450 representative students to which an electronic survey was administered. The response rate was 82% (369 completed surveys). Questions included items developed from focus groups as well as replicated questions from a recent Pew Research Center (2010) study focusing on older Millennials. To dig deeper, open-ended questions were content analyzed to provide a better understanding of this cohort.

Not surprisingly, many participants noted they responded to the survey using their I-phones and I-Pads. The target cohort for this study was college juniors and seniors; those who will be newly hired by companies in the next several years. The average age was 21.7, ranging from 19 to 28 (with 95% being between 20 and 22 years old). Males comprised 62% of the sample. Respondents represented students from the colleges and schools of agriculture; architecture, design and construction; business; education; engineering; forestry and wildlife science; human science; liberal arts; nursing; and science and mathematics. Throughout the remainder of this chapter, the term GenMe will be used when referring to the respondents in our study.

GENERAL ATTITUDES

We are Different—but are we Really?

Recent empirical studies have challenged the conventional wisdom that drastic generational differences exist at work (Deal, 2007). Our respondents counter that challenge: they believe they *are* different in terms of their general attitudes toward life. The clear majority (88%) believe themselves to be unique and distinct from previous generations (Pew Research Center, 2010; see Figure 2.1). Overall, they echo what the popular press has written about them in terms that they believe distinguishes them from previous cohorts.

In Their Own Words—Generational Differences

The biggest difference about our generation is the quickness we are used to receiving information. People have become impatient because they expect results immediately.

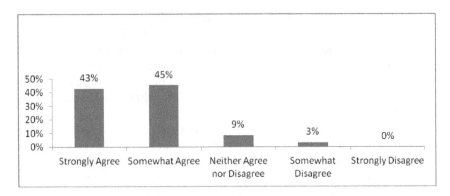

Figure 2.1.   I think of my own age group as unique and distinct from other generations.

My generation grew up during the War on Terrorism. We grew up facing the effects of 9/11 and the ongoing war that resulted after it. For us, there isn't a guarantee that we'll be hired out of college, especially in our personal career field. Our generation has to fight for success the hardest because nothing is guaranteed for us when we graduate.

Our generation is unique and distinct from other generations because of the recession and the economy. We will be the first generation to not exceed our parents' success ... our generation will start out working at a much lower income than our parents.

We have a greater sense of social awareness, in essence, what people want. We are a part of a culture driven by advertisements, social hierarchy, and social media. We are good at staying up to date with social trends, but we tend to be less hard-working, more self-involved, and less apt to invest ourselves in long-term goals.

Our generation really seems to have come full circle. We, generally, have that can-do attitude with a willingness to learn and a desire to succeed. It almost reminds me of the "Greatest Generation." We grew up with war and now are going through tough economic times. So far life hasn't been that American dream where the economy was flourishing and America was free from harm and war. We work very hard just as our forefathers did.

My generation is unique due to the amount of stress put on us by ourselves to excel in everything we do. We understand as a generation, or at least most of us do, that in order to be successful in our world today we have to be the best we can be to live the life we want and sometimes giving our best may not cut it. The opportunities we have, especially in the business world, have decreased dramatically due to the economy level we are at right now.

Not that generations before didn't have a tough time making it in life, believe me I have a tremendous amount of respect for what the generations before mine have done for me. The fact is though the same opportunities that were there for people 25 to 40 years ago just aren't there as much. It's almost a must to be successful in school and even after college the thin line of making the right decisions in life has become much thinner in terms of long term effects because of those decisions.

Our generation is widely adaptable in terms of technological skills/ability to learn new skills quickly. That said, I believe we are disadvantaged by the perception older generations have of us as being cocky, coddled, and lazy. The truth of this assumption is irrelevant (though probable). We are also unique if you consider that we have not been faced with a major war (arguable), and we were raised in an era of unprecedented economic prosperity. A large percentage of our parents are divorced or remarried, compared to older generations who grew up in an era where such things were still heavily frowned upon and widely avoided.

GenMe's Priorities

Management experts know that money is important, yet this group does not see money as their only source of happiness (Martin, 2005). They want a balance of work and life similar to that of leading-edge Millennials (Kirby & Krone, 2002). GenMe has a laundry list of things they hold important in their lives. Table 2.1 compares leading-edge Millennials (Pew Research Center, 2010) to our respondents. Our respondents value almost all priority areas more than leading-edge Millennials. Our respondents want to be good parents (90%), have successful marriages (80%), lead religious lives (55%), own their own home (49%), and help others in need (42%). Interestingly, an articulated access to affordable healthcare has emerged as an area of concern for this group that has been less important to previous generations at this stage of life (53%).

The rise in individualistic traits and positive self-views (cf. Twenge, 2006) suggests that GenMe members might seek jobs that interest them and provide more personal meaning. Overall, this group values intrinsically rewarding work over money (72%; see Figure 2.2). Not surprisingly, when asked in an open-ended question format, "What do you want out of life your first 3 years after graduation?" the number one response was to "find a job" (80%). This was followed by a preferred lifestyle (18%), starting a family (15%), establishing a career (14%), and going to graduate school (14%; see Table 2.2). GenMe is optimistic that they will earn enough for the lifestyle they desire in the future (see Figure 2.3).

Table 2.1.   Life's Priorities

Percent Saying—is one of the most important things in their life

	Millenni-als*	Current Study Me Generation**
Being a good parent	52%	90%
Having a successful marriage	30%	80%
Living a very religious life	15%	55%
Having access to affordable healthcare	NA	53%
Owning your own home	20%	49%
Helping other people who are in need	21%	42%
Being successful in a high-paying career or profession	15%	26%
Having lots of free time to relax or do things you want to do	9%	19%
Becoming famous	1%	1%

*Benchmark data from Pew Research Center (2010) survey.
**Data from present study.

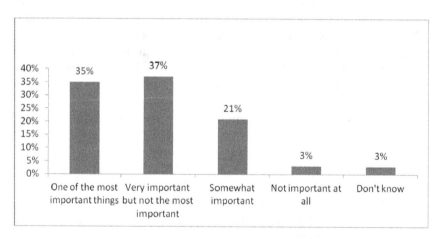

Figure 2.2.   Having a personally rewarding job I enjoy—making less money

In Their Own Words—Attitudes

I want a stable job working with friendly people who I can learn from to prepare me for future career moves. I do not want to work somewhere I will be
obligated to stay for my career.

Table 2.2.   What do you Want out of Life Your First 3 Years After Graduation?

What do you want out of life your first three years after graduation?
(percent indicating)

	Me Generation**
To find a job	80%
To maintain a preferred lifestyle	18%
To start a family	15%
To establish a career	14%
To go to graduate school	14%

**Data from present study.

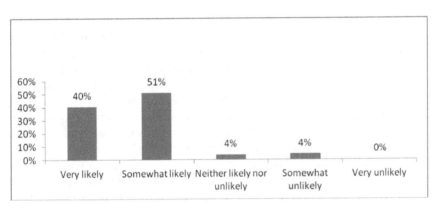

Figure 2.3.   How likely are you to be able to earn enough money in the future to lead the kind of lifestyle you want?

> To be able to support myself, be independent, make enough money to simply be content.

> A job that I enjoy, adventure and excitement, a husband, to experience new things, friends that I love being around, a pay check that takes care of my daily needs.

> A large enough income to support myself so I don't have to live at home. I'd like a job where I can see room to climb in the company.

> We are harder workers than the old generation gives us credit for. Although we enjoy our leisure time, maybe a little too much, we tend to our business and do a great job of it.

TRAINING

Employees need job-specific knowledge and basic skill sets for their occupations including interfacing with equipment and applications created with new technology. Because technology is often used as a means to achieve product diversification and customization, employees must have the ability to listen and communicate with colleagues and customers. Interpersonal skills—such as negotiation and conflict management—and problem-solving skills are important as knowledge workers increasingly work in teams (Noe, 2010). Initial job-specific knowledge and continuing education of all employees is important to remain globally competitive. Almost all GenMe's (94%) expect their job-specific knowledge for their first 3 months on the job to be provided in formal training programs from the companies that hire them (see Figure 2.4). They believe their university is responsible for a strong foundation for this entry level job (56%). Sixty-nine percent believe specific knowledge will come from informal on-the-job training provided by supervisors (accounting for 25%) and coworkers (accounting for the remaining 75%).

Increasingly firms are employing learning platforms based on, and delivered with, technology. These platforms reduce travel costs and provide greater accessibility to training, consistent delivery, the ability to access experts and share learning with others, and the possibility of creating a learning environment with many positive features such as feedback, self-pacing, and practice exercises. While trainer-led classroom instruction remains the most popular way to deliver training, companies report that they plan on delivering a large portion of training through learning technologies such as DVDs, web streaming, intranets, and iPods (Noe, 2010). For all the emphasis on how GenMe is different from their prede-

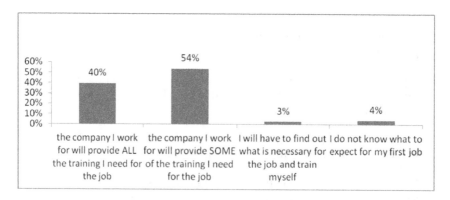

Figure 2.4.   I expect....

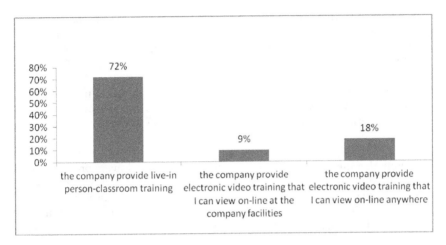

Figure 2.5. I prefer....

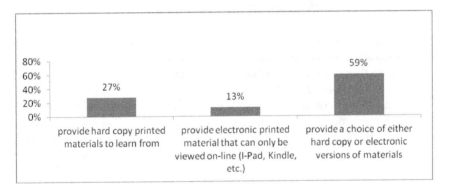

Figure 2.6. I prefer the company....

cessors, including learning styles and uses of technology in their daily lives, 72% prefer their training to be delivered in a live, in-person environment (see Figure 2.5). Almost 60% do not have a preference (either hard copy materials or electronic formats) regarding specific content delivery method (see Figure 2.6).

In Their Own Words—Training

> I want an exciting, stable job that allows me to travel around and an employer that spends a considerable amount of time training and developing me into a solid employee. Good living quarters, steady pay, and a new car.

We are constantly connected through social networks on electronic devices, but, ironically enough, we lack social skills in the real world. We are able to find our way around and have the tools to succeed, but lack the motivation to do so.

We are the first true generation that has been brought up in the world of technology. We know how to work with computers and the internet with ease. So with some extra learning we can far surpass any generation in that regard.

I think that our generation has experienced the first of many progressions toward continuous connectivity and communication. I think we are more socially awkward and isolated due to technology. Our conversations are shorter due to a short attention span. The richness of face-to-face communication will decline due to people spending more time on communicating through technology.

COMMUNICATION AND FEEDBACK

Much has been written about the use of technology and its impact on the communication processes employed by GenMe's. Speculation is that they want everything, now. An important human resource policy issue will entail the method and speed with which supervisors and these newly hired employees communicate with each other. Face-to-face discussion is the preferred mode of two-way communication (54%) when initiated by the newly hired (see Figure 2.7). However, if the contact is to be initiated by the supervisor, 28% of GenMe's expect supervisors to physically come

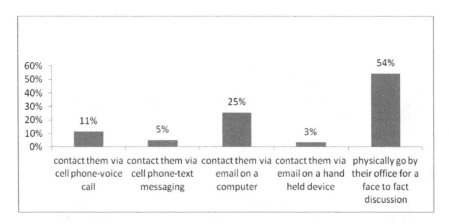

Figure 2.7.   If I have a question for my supervisor, I would prefer to....

to them, to see GenMe's face-to-face. The clear majority (71%) expect some form of electronic communication (see Figure 2.8).

Regarding response speed, when contact is initiated by the supervisor, 35% of GenMe's believe GenMe's should respond immediately, 15% within 15 minutes (see Figure 2.9). When contact is initiated by the employee, the reciprocal level of urgency is reduced such that only 4% of GenMe's believe supervisors should respond immediately to them (see Figure 2.10).

Managerial Concern

This group is tied to their communication devices. Our research confirms these people will be looking for connectivity all the time. It is part of their culture. This suggests multitasking is something that will need to be addressed in training and responsibilities of the employee.

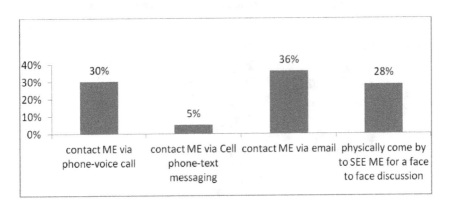

Figure 2.8. I expect my supervisor to....

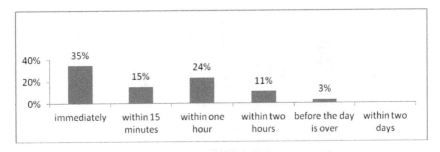

Figure 2.9. When responding to supervisors, I should respond to them....

Performance Feedback

This group's *expectation* of supervisor feedback frequency does not match their *preferences*. Forty-two percent of our survey participants *expect* performance assessment at least every 2 weeks with 8% expecting *daily* feedback (see Figure 2.11). In keeping with their world of immediate response, 60% *prefer* supervisor feedback every 2 weeks *or less* (see Figure 2.12). The good news is that their expectation for actual feedback is less than what they prefer. The bad news is that two-thirds of our respondents expect feedback at least once a month. This issue will most certainly need to be addressed by human resource managers in terms of setting reasonable time frame expectations for performance assessment.

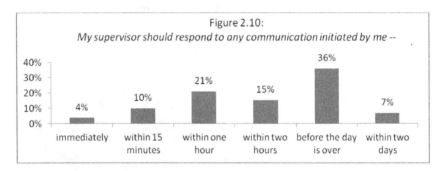

Figure 2.10.   My supervisor should respond to any communication initiated by me....

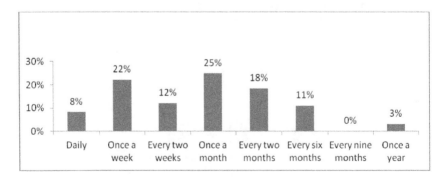

Figure 2.11.   I expect my supervisor will assess my performance/provide feedback....

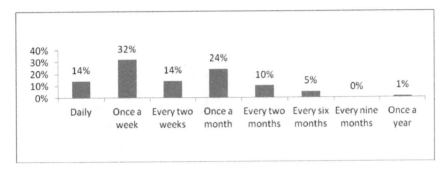

Figure 2.12.   I would prefer feedback from my supervisor....

In Their Own Words: Communication and Feedback

We want what we want, and we want it NOW!

We have a different concept of the work environment. My generation has seen how you can have fun and work at the same time.

We can use technological skills to create a more rapid environment while still being effective. Smartphones have been the most influential invention of our generation as employees can use them for lots of information.

Social media has changed the way we live; we're completely plugged in to the world 24/7.

While technology makes things around us extremely fast moving and easy, our generation is losing people skills tremendously and people are less active.

THE WORK ENVIRONMENT AND ETHICS

Given that GenMe is the primary source of new entrants to the job market today, the recruitment of this generation is a constant theme and a top priority for human resource departments (Erickson 2008; Yeaton, 2008). In addition to recruiting issues, issues of retention will be important for human resource managers. An increasingly important factor impacting both employee recruitment and retention is that of corporate ethics. There has been a consistent association between corporate ethical values and loyalty and commitment to the firm. It is incumbent on human resource managers to signal to this group that their firms maintain high ethical values (Hunt, Wood, & Chonko, 1989). This cohort wants to

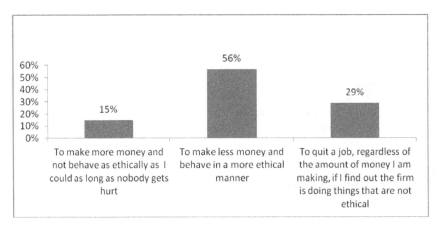

Figure 2.13.   I would prefer....

behave ethically (85%) with almost one-third willing to quit their job if they perceive their firm is behaving unethically (see Figure 2.13). The rise in individualistic traits and positive self-views (cf., Twenge, 2006) suggests that GenMe members will seek jobs that interest them and provide more personal meaning.

Following the Green Movement, members of GenMe also value working for more environmentally conscious companies (53%), and are willing to take less salary to do so (see Figure 2.14). Our surveyed group of GenMe members is altruistic. They care about volunteerism with 85% believing it is important to give back to the community through unpaid service (see Figure 2.15). Human resource managers should take note of this as a recruitment tool.

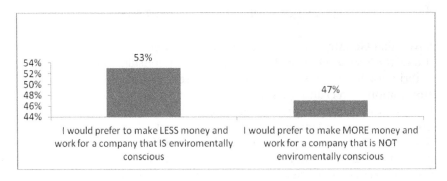

Figure 2.14.   Given the choice....

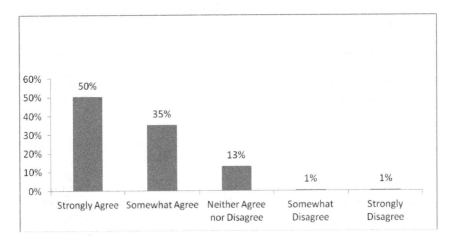

Figure 2.15.   It is important to give back to the community I work in through unpaid community service.

In Their Own Words—The Work Environment:

I don't expect them to be very ethical.

Ethical, probably not … profit is the name of the game nowadays. The only reason companies do ethical things it to make themselves look better. So if we were to be completely honest, most businesses are completely unethical because it truly is the thought that counts.

Not much ethical behavior can be changed by a new employee. It is important that a newly hired person focuses on understanding and working toward the company's overall goals whether ethical or not.

As an entry level person I believe my opinions won't mount up to a hill of beans. Unless I'm working for a very small company I will have little influence.

To treat its employers and customers with respect even if it occasionally means sacrificing some profits.

I would expect my company to operate according to ethical standards, and while I might not be aware of any breaches, I would expect violators to be punished.

I will realistically be able to have only a little ethical effect because my job will most likely not be essential to company processes. I will do all tasks asked of me as long as they do not violate laws or regulations and my own personal code of ethics.

As far as technology goes, my generation is the first one to figure out how easily intellectual property rights can be circumvented on the computer. I suppose that makes our generation unique ethically in that we don't consider "sharing music" to be the same as stealing music, similarly to the rest of the world.

I expect the company to make sure no employees are unfairly treated and I also expect the company to monitor its environmental impact.

I hold myself to high moral standards and I will never compromise myself and what I believe in to "get ahead." I believe in the long run by doing good and leading as an example to your peers you will be much more successful.

I think we expect more from our job and employers at a younger age, but probably don't want to work as hard for what we get. Something distinct about my generation is how easily we can adapt to new technology.

In Their Own Words—Physical Environment:

Our generation is highly involved with the Green movement. Resources are getting more scarce, technology is growing exponentially, and we have a huge government deficit. We have a huge say in whether we'll continue on a downward slope or do something to fix it.

I believe that "going green" is the future. I think that this mindset is something everyone can do since it is saving their own lives.

We may have issues with working extensively, even finding jobs, but we will tend to more aware of protecting and promoting the wellness of our environment.

Loyalty to the Company

One area that directly impacts human resource managers is GenMe's view of loyalty to a company (Deal, 2007; Marston, 2007, 2009). Given the events this cohort has grown up with (i.e., outsourcing, globalization, mergers and acquisitions of U.S. companies, economic uncertainty) they are skeptical of corporate America. Almost 90% understand, as an employee, they are just a pawn on someone else's chess board (see Figure 2.16). They believe companies do not care about them as individuals. So it is not surprising that GenMe's will put their personal goals above the companies' they work for (see Figure 2.17).

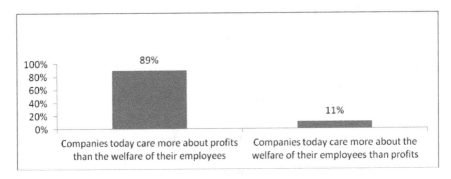

Figure 2.16.   Which statement most closely reflects your opinion?

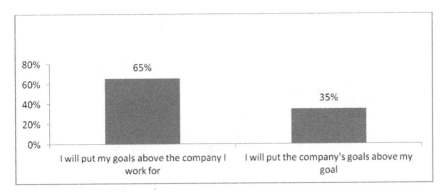

Figure 2.17.   Given the choice....

As is normal for most newly employed university graduates, 75% will use their first job as a stepping stone (see Figure 2.18). They further expect the rapidly changing global economy will require them to retool and change careers (see Figure 2.19). Given the high costs of acquiring new talent, and GenMe's reciprocal attitudes toward company loyalty, human resource managers will need to provide career track training throughout their association with this cohort in order to keep their best talent. This follows the thinking of Kowske, Rasch, and Wiley (2010), who suggest that although attitudes differ across generations (i.e., research results with small effect sizes), Millennials reported similar levels of satisfaction with employer benefits and turnover intentions. Consequently, human resource managers may not need to develop special programs for them, but providing programs that will train and retain them is necessary.

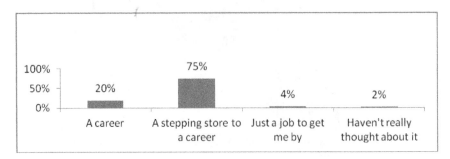

Figure 2.18.   I view my first job out of university as....

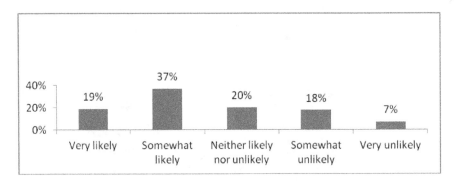

Figure 2.19.   How likely is it that you will switch careers (not jobs) sometime during your working life

In Their Own Words—Work Ethic

We're spoiled, mostly lazy, we don't work enough as a team, we're selfish, we don't respect one another enough, we don't really trust each other.

We have been raised our entire lives on the latest technology and have never had issues with learning how to use it. We have been raised in a time when political correctness reigns supreme, and while that makes us more open to diversity, it also means many of us have been raised spoiled by parents who feel spanking is hitting a child and thus allowing them to get away with a lot more than in ages past.

We like being challenged and learning new things.

We are less verbally social, more technologically savvy, have shorter attention spans, and are better educated.

Our technology level, especially in the ways we communicate, is at an all-time high; information can be accessed quicker and easier. I also believe our generation is forced to have a higher level of creativity to have a great competitive advantage in the workplace.

Technologically advanced and flexible, yet still maintain a high work ethic and discipline.

More tech savvy, in addition to being more "about me."

We rely on technology more than any other generation. We also embrace other genders or different kinds of race that are in the company. We may also be a tad more rebellious than the past.

In many ways we are lazy and depend on people to spoon feed us everything, or just do it for us. We are also more open minded and free thinkers. We have more compassion for others and a longing to change the world. Most are just not prepared or disciplined enough to do so.

Our generation has been exploited by older generations more than any other. We pay into government programs (e.g. social security) and get nothing out of it. Also, because of the economic crisis of 2008, baby boomers who should have retired have stayed in the workforce so there are less jobs available for students who have recently graduated. Basically our generation is unique because all the older generations walk all over us.

COMPENSATION

Expectations of Compensation and Rewards for Efforts

One persistent distinction in work values is between extrinsic and intrinsic values (Porter & Lawler, 1968). Extrinsic work values focus on the consequences or outcomes of work—the tangible rewards external to the individual, such as income, advancement opportunities, and status. In contrast, intrinsic work values include a meaningful job, career growth, and the opportunity to make a difference. Twenge and colleagues (2010) suggest organizational policies directed at increasing or emphasizing the intrinsic value of work (such as highlighting the opportunity to learn new skills or emphasizing the company's commitment to the environment) may not necessarily be more effective at recruiting and retaining Millennial workers than they were with earlier generations. However, it is important for human resource managers to take intrinsic rewards into consideration when recruiting and hiring GenMe's.

Table 2.3 presents the results of a content analysis of an open-ended question relating to the most important issues to GenMe's for their first

Table 2.3 GenMe's Expectations

What compensation, benefits, training or treatment are most important to you for your first year out of university?

Item	Percent Expecting (n = 369)
Health insurance / medical insurance	53%
Livable salary (fair compensation; comparable to co-workers; steady income)	43%
Training programs	35%
Respect (to be treated as an equal; to be treated professionally)	35%
401-K, Retirement plans	11%
Benefits	10%
Vacation time	9%
Positive safe work environment	4%
Work-life balance / flexible working times	4%
Tuition reimbursement	4%
Having a formal mentor	2%
Job security	2%
Patience from supervisor / understanding boss	1%

Note: Total exceeds 100% because multiple responses were allowed.

job out of university: "What compensation, benefits, training or treatment on the job are most important to you for your first year out of university?" The top four most frequently cited responses relate to health insurance (53%), fair compensation (43%), access to training programs (35%), and to be treated with respect (35%). Unexpectedly, the second most important (by frequency of mention) was fair compensation. What jumps out is the importance this cohort places on having *access to health care*. Over half mentioned this specifically. Although access to health care is one of the most important things in their life, who pays for it is viewed differently. Approximately 47% believe companies should provide more than a minimal level of financial support for health care (see Figure 2.20). Although Twenge et al. (2010) suggest training may not be more effective for recruiting and retaining one cohort rather than another, approximately one third of our respondents want to be trained and to have access to continual training on the job.

Generational differences at work affect the perceived fit of employees within the organization. If entering employees hold values that are different from those of the leaders of the company, employees may experi-

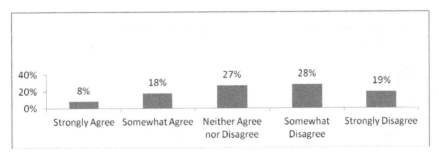

Figure 2.20.   Companies should only provide employees a minimal level of financial support for healthcare.

ence person-organization misfit (Cennamo & Gardner, 2008). Given that GenMe's believe they are different than those in the generations ahead of them, it is not surprising that the third most frequently cited issue is to be treated with respect (as equals and as professionals) as being very important to them. Other expectations include companies providing access to retirement plans of some sort (11%) and a variety of other benefits. However, this group believes they personally should be allowed to set up and manage their own retirement accounts (61%; see Figure 2.21).

In Their Own Words—Treatment On The Job

My generation is focused on individuals, instead of a whole group. People are out to gain power for themselves.

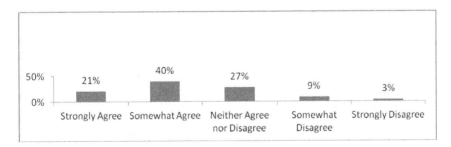

Figure 2.21.   I believe companies should allow employees to set up their own retirement accounts.

I feel we are spoiled and most believe that they are entitled to a good living, job and benefits. This is opposite of our parents' generations who thrived off of hard work.

There's a huge focus on multitasking. I think the older generation sees it as rude (and sometimes it can be), but generally I believe we just try to make the most efficient use of our time given the resources we have. For better or worse, we are ultraconnected to not just our peers but the nation and even world, and that connectivity ultimately leads to a greater capacity for productivity.

USE OF SOCIAL MEDIA

Use of Information Obtained Using Social Media and Technology

The most visible difference between GenMe's and their predecessors is the ease with which they assimilate technology into their everyday lives. Instant access and the processes to acquire information (whether that information is accurate or not) is this generation's strongest talent. Table

Table 2.4.   Use of Technology

GenMe Outpaces Millennials in Technology Usage

	Percent engaged in the behavior	
	Millennials*	*Current Study GenMe's***
Internet Behavior		
Created a social network profile	75%	97%
Used wireless internet away from home	62%	98%
Used Twitter	14%	39%
Cell Phone Behavior		
Used cell to text	88%	97%
Texted in past 24 hours	80%	97%
Median number of texts in past 24 hours	20	75
Read books on line	NA	20%

*Benchmark data from Pew Research Center (2010) survey.
**Data from present study

2.4 compares leading-edge Millennials to GenMe's from the current study. Note the increase in GenMe's employment of technology in every category. The most striking is the median number of text messages sent in the past 24 hours; this has increased from 20 to 75. Interestingly, numerous individuals reported more than 450 text messages sent daily. Thinking this level of messaging was erroneously reported, we queried cell phone providers. This level of text messaging was verified as a reality within this cohort. Note that one in five reads books online (and we predict this will increase dramatically as e-readers (e.g., tablets) become commonplace). This form of digitized delivery of text materials is increasingly being employed in their educational environment on university campuses globally. Human resource managers will find GenMe's to be very accepting of training materials delivered in this format. This will allow companies the ability to easily update and diffuse training materials across this cohort.

The Extent to Which GenMe Is Connected

This group seems constantly to be connected to the internet. Almost all of them (93%) use the internet to obtain information to make their daily decisions (see Figure 2.22). Eighty-seven percent are on the net at least once a day with 74% noting they access it several times a day (see Figure 2.23). A main purpose of that connectivity is to access their social networking site with 60% visiting several times a day (see Figure 2.24). They increasingly use Twitter as a daily source to keep up with topics and sources of interest (25%) (see Figure 2.25). Not surprisingly, this group (62%) believes technology allows them to use their time more efficiently (see Figure 2.26).

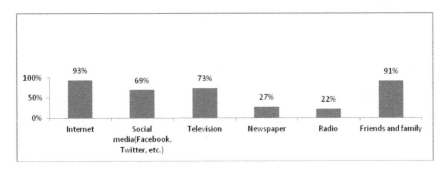

Figure 2.22.   I use _____ to make daily decisions.

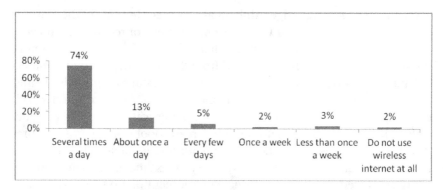

Figure 2.23.   To what extent do you connect to the internet wirelessly?

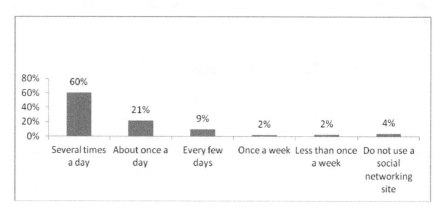

Figure 2.24.   How often do you visit the social networking site you use most often?

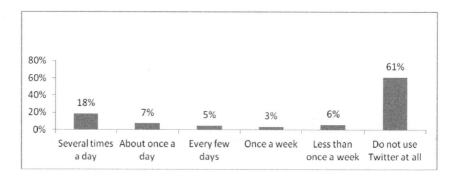

Figure 2.25.   How often do you use Twitter?

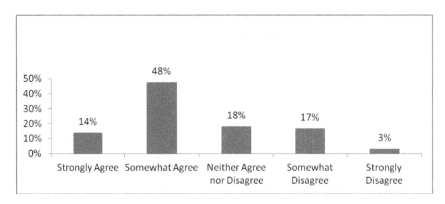

Figure 2.26   New technology allows people to use their time more efficiently.

In Their Own Words—Social Media and Technology

We are completely plugged into technology at all points in time. We practically have seizures without it.

We grew up with technology. When filling out my resume, I almost always forget to write that I know how to use the internet and Microsoft Office because that seems like a given to me!

Our generation has grown up inundated with technology. We've never had to study or work without the Internet, social media, cell phones, etc. like previous generations.

We like to mix business with pleasure.

I personally feel my generation is similar to any previous one. The only difference could be the "new" social media and social networking, and advances in technology. My generation seems more prone to use any form of new technology and it seems to make its way into the workplace.

My generation is ridiculously technology savvy. We are very capable of understanding and using pretty much any device out there.

OVERALL FEARS AND CONCERNS: THE FIRST 6 MONTHS

Content analyzing an open-ended question that asked, "What fears or concerns do you have regarding your first 6 months after leaving university?" we found the majority fear they do not have the knowledge base or are prepared enough to obtain and maintain that first job (see Table

Table 2.5.   What Fears or Concerns do you Have for the First 6 Months After Leaving University?

	Percent of Respondents Noting This is Their Highest Concern
Not Being Prepared or qualified; Not knowing enough to complete my job successfully	24%
Not finding a job; Lack of job availability	19%
Not having a job that I enjoy; stuck in the wrong job	14%
Not Able To Pay Student Loans—make enough at first job to pay bills	8%
Making mistakes on the job, being a failure, not meeting employer's expectation	8%
Getting laid off, fired or downsized after getting the job	7%
Adapting to the world of work; working hours; structured environment	6%
Being overwhelmed—stressed at work	3%
Where to ultimately live—the unknown	3%
Not fitting in with the work culture; being younger than other employees	2%
Unfair supervisor or employer	1%
Job security	1%
Other	4%
Total	100%

2.5). In fact, the fear of not finding a job (19%) is less worrisome than their competency fear (24%). Collectively, the financial aspect of facing the fiscal responsibility of earning a livelihood is GenMe's forthright concern (43%). This is composed of simply finding a job (19%), being paid enough to sustain a living (8%), keeping the job once it is acquired (7%), and not making mistakes on the job leading to failure (8%). Earlier in the chapter we noted that GenMe's seek respect and want to be treated professionally in terms of expectations on the job (35%; see Table 2.3). However, their fear of not fitting in with the work culture is not high but does fall into the top ten concerns of this group. The other major concerns are simply having to adapt to the world of work (i.e., defined working hours, structured environments) (6%) and facing the unknown (3%).

In Their Own Words—Concerns

We are also the generation that does not know what lies in the future … concerning social security, health care, and educational equality.

My generation has to deal with less jobs available in America due to outsourcing. Also all of the technology that came with the internet has distinct advantages and disadvantages.

Not feeling competent or happy in the job or field I have chosen is a major concern.

Being completely overwhelmed.

I am concerned that I will not be adequately qualified to perform the job.

Getting a job that is exactly what I've been studying for my entire college career, and then it turns out that I absolutely hate the job completely and have all the hard work that I put into this career path during college all be wasted.

Not getting paid enough—I don't want to be a billionaire, but I also don't want to have to worry about making ends meet.

I am worried about not being trained properly.

Unemployment, getting fired or laid off, failure.

INSIGHT

These individuals have been called lazy by numerous authors. Although limited in scope our study suggests otherwise. These people are not lazy. Following Levenson (2010), we believe GenMe's do not generally take a privileged view of the world of work. They see their first job out of university as an uphill battle in which they will have to be very competitive to keep the job. They spend countless hours learning on their own time. According to them, they learn differently and they are motivated differently. Based on our personal observations of their in- and out-of classroom activities we concur. They know how to use technology and how to learn to learn with that technology. They have lived through a world lens viewed very differently than people just 5 years their elder. They are motivated, more so than they are given credit for. They are skeptical of companies' motives and fearful of not having competitive skills so they can prosper in the global economy. Just ask them about technology; how to use technology to learn in a world of information they can access and use instantly with a high level of confidence. They strive to be successful and are more fearful of failure given their perceived employment prospects. They want to be welcomed with respect into the employment domain as peers.

The key for human resource managers is to get into their heads, to see the world from their perspective. Based on the survey data analyzed, face-to-face interactions with focus groups, and discussions with numerous administrators and professors—as well as our personal observations—we feel confident in the ability of these people to move the global economy forward. They are connected with their peers, the environment, and the world. They need understanding and programs from human resource managers that will embrace a somewhat different mindset to acculturate them into the company. Given the results of the present study, the Me Generation's uncertainty in their levels of training, knowing what they need to know for their first level of employment, is not unwarranted. The lesson for human resource managers is not only to provide training necessary for entry level workers, but to actively communicate that the necessary knowledge base for employment will be continually provided. Listed below are the main take-aways from our study. This group:

- wants to be trained;
- is used to learning from each other electronically;
- has a different view of ethics in terms of sharing information with each other. If information is exchanged electronically, it is sharing. If it is shared in hard copy or face to face; it is cheating or stealing;
- prefers immediate feedback, and will expect feedback quickly, *very* quickly;
- expects to be in a continual state of flux in terms of their lifetime employment status;
- does *not* expect to receive, nor give, loyalty to the firms they work for. They expect equal pay for equal work and not much more; and
- highly desires access to, and funding of, health care benefits as part of their employment package.

Human resource managers wishing to maximize the use of the talents of the Millennial Generation would do well to pay close attention to these findings.

REFERENCES

Abate, C. (2008). You say multitasking like it's a good thing. *Thought & Action, The NEA Higher Education Journal.* Retrieved from http://www.nea.org/home/30584.htm

Cennamo, L., & Gardner, D. (2008). Generational differences in work values, outcomes and person-organization values fit. *Journal of Managerial Psychology, 23*, 891-906.

Deal, J. J. (2007). *Retiring the generation gap: How employees young and old can find common ground.* San Francisco, CA: Jossey-Bass.

Downing, K. (2006). Next generation: What leaders need to know about the Millennials, *Leadership in Action, 26*(3), 3-6.

Eisner, S. P. (2005). Managing Generation Y. *SAM Advanced Management Journal, 70*(4), 4-15.

Erickson, T. (2008). *Plugged in: Generation Y thriving at work.* Boston, MA: Harvard Business Press.

Gorlick, A. (2009). Media multitaskers pay mental price. *Stanford Report,* August 24. Retrieved from http://news.stanford.edu/news/2009/august24/multitask-research-study-082409.html?view=print

Gorman, P., Nelson, T., & Glassman, A. (2004). The millennial generation: A strategic opportunity. *Organizational Analysis, 12*(3), 255-270.

Howe, N., & Strauss, W. (2000). *Millennials rising: The next great generation.* New York, NY: Vintage.

Hunt, S. D., Wood, V. R., & Chonko, L. B. (1989). Corporate ethical values and organizational commitment in marketing. *Journal of Marketing, 53,* 79-90.

Kirby, E., & Krone, K. (2002). "The policy exists but you can't really use it:" Communication and the structuration of work-family policies. *Journal of Applied Communication Research, 30*(1), 50-77.

Kowske, B. J., Rasch, R., & Wiley, J. (2010). Millennials' (lack of) attitude problem: An empirical examination of generational effects on work attitudes. *Journal of Business Psychology, 25,* 265-279.

Lenhart, A. (2009). Teens and mobile phones over the past five years: Pew Internet looks back. Retrieved from http://www.pewinternet.org/Reports/2009/14--Teens-and-Mobile-Phones-Data-Memo.aspx

Levenson, A. R. (2010). Millennials and the world of work: An economist's perspective. *Journal of Business Psychology, 25,* 257-264.

Li, C., & Bernoff, J. (2008). *Groundswell: Winning in a world transformed by social technologies.* Boston, MA: Harvard Business Press.

Martin, C. A. (2005). From high maintenance to high productivity: What managers need to know about Generation Y. *Industrial and Commercial Training, 37,* 39-44.

Marston, C. (2007). *Motivating the "what's in it for me" workforce.* Hoboken, NJ: Wiley.

Marston, C. (2009). Myths about millennials: Understand the myths to retain millennials. Retrieved from http://humanresources.about.com/od/management-tips/a/millennial_myth_2.htm

Myers, K. K. (2010). Millennials in the workplace: A communication perspective on millennials' organizational relationships and performance. *Journal of Business Psychology, 25,* 225-238.

Noe, R. (2010). *Employee training & development* (5th ed.). New York, NY: McGraw-Hill Higher Education.

Pew Research Center (2010). Millennials: Confident. Connected. Open to change. Pew Social & Demographic Trends, Retrieved from http://www.pewsocial-trends.org/2010/02/24/millennials-confident-connected-open-to-change/

Porter, L. W., & Lawler, E. E. (1968). *Managerial attitudes and performance.* Homewood, IL: Dorsey-Irwin.

Pryor, J. H., Hurtado, S., DeAngelo, L., Black, L. P., & Tran, S. (2010). *The American freshman: National norms for Fall 2009.* Los Angeles, CA: The Higher Education Research Institute at UCLA.

Roberts, D. F., Foehr, U. G., & Rideout, V. (2005), "Generation M2," Media in the lives of 8-18 year-olds. Kaiser Family Foundation. Retrieved from http://www.kff.org/entmedia/upload/Generation-M-Media-in-the-Lives-of-8-18-Year-olds-Report.pdf

Survey finds smart phones transforming mobile lifestyles of college students (2009, March 25). Retrieved from http://www.bsu.edu/news/article/0,1370,--61565,00.html

Twenge, J. M. (2006). *Generation me: Why today's young Americans are more confident, assertive, entitled—And more miserable than ever before.* New York, NY: Free Press.

Twenge, J. M., Campbell, S. M., Hoffman, B. J., & Lance, C. E. (2010). Generational differences in work values: Leisure and extrinsic values increasing, social and intrinsic values decreasing. *Journal of Management, 36*(5), 1117-1142.

Yeaton, K. (2008). Recruiting and managing the "why?" generation. *CPA Journal, 78*(4), 68-72.

CHAPTER 3

MILLENNIAL WORK EXPECTATIONS AND ORGANIZATIONAL INCENTIVE SYSTEMS

"Carrots" for the New Millennium

Daniel J. Svyantek, Kristin L. Cullen, and Frances L. H. Svyantek

INTRODUCTION

Millennials have unique career-related expectations. These expectations may be in conflict. For example, Millennials want to have good pay and benefits in a nurturing organizational environment where work/ life issues are in balance (Ng, Schweitzer, & Lyons, 2010). Millennials are popularly thought to want it all and want it now: These individuals see themselves as entitled to rewards which do not match their actual performance. The expectations of the Millennial generation are thought to be unrealistic by members of other generations: These expectations contain a potential disconnect between reward and performance (Ng et al., 2010).

Managing Human Resources for the Millennial Generation, pp. 53–75

The task of motivating the Millennial generation offers new challenges to organizational human resource management functions. The chapter will address these challenges by presenting information on several issues. First, the chapter will review the literature and provide a description of the expectations of the Millennial generation for extrinsic motivation in the workplace. Second, this chapter will briefly address the basics of motivational theories. Third, this chapter will explore the fit between current organizational incentive systems and the expectation for pay, benefits and advancement held by the Millennial generation and the proposals of work motivation theory. Finally, this chapter will propose organizational reward systems that have the greatest match between the expectations of the Millennial generation and the motivating value of these systems and offer organizations suggestions for developing incentive systems which will appeal to, and motivate, the Millennial generation to meet organizational goals for performance as the newest generation enters the workforce.

THE MILLENNIAL GENERATION

The Millennial generation are those individuals born between 1980 and 2000 (Alsop, 2008). Millenials are adaptable, confident, tenacious and independent workers (Luguericio, 2009) willing, if not wanting, to work in teams with high technical skills (e.g., in use of social networking techniques) (Alsop, 2008). The Millennial generation is seen as a valuable asset by many organizations in the changing workplace of today.

However, a "dark side" exists to the utilization of Millennials in the workplace as well. Millennials have been described as narcissistic, entitled, technology-focused, accepting of diversity and more focused on social responsibility and environmental initiatives than are older generations (Ng et al., 2010). They expect to receive good pay and benefits with rapid advancement *while* maintaining work-life balance and working in a nurturing environment. Millennials are popularly thought to want it all and want it now (Luguericio, 2009). Older works may find them presumptuous and see the Millenials as lacking the necessary social and psychological skills to live in world that threatens their sense of entitlement (Alsop, 2008). Millennials are seen as ill-prepared for working in the world of business. The Millennial worker is often believed to be different from other workers and difficult to work with in an organizational setting.

A description of these individuals has developed in the workplace. This description includes both positive and negative characteristics. These positive and negative characteristics often reflect "two sides of the same coin" in that these characteristics can be strengths or weaknesses for the

Millennial generation. For the purpose of understanding work motivation processes, we propose that these characteristics may be classified into five general categories of attitudes related to themselves which will impact Millennial behavior in the workplace. Each of these categories may have differential positive or negative effects in the workplace. These categories include: (1) high expectations; (2) rewards; (3) feedback; (4) standards; and (5) "teamness." We will look at each of these in this section of the chapter.

HIGH EXPECTATIONS

Millenials have high expectations ... but these expectations are not always realistic. The Millennial generation has a very high sense of entitlement (Alsop, 2008). This leads to a belief they have the right to high pay while maintaining work-life balance (including the ability to perform community service). These individuals see themselves as entitled to rewards which do not match their actual performance (Luguericio, 2009). The Millennial generation has, in effect, developed artificially high self-esteem based on the rearing practices they have been exposed to in the home, at school, and, in some cases, their early work experience. The parents of Millennials are the "helicopter" parents (Alsop, 2008). Millennials have lived in a largely accommodating and affirming world. This may lead them to have inflated estimates of their own performance and levels of self-esteem which are both higher than warranted and unrealistic. Therefore, Millennials will never admit their shortcomings (Luguericio, 2009). Rather, Millennials tend to interpret problems as other people's issues because they know the problem can never be their own fault. Hulett (2006) notes Millennials are optimistic about their performance but this leads to big expectations for their careers and rewards. The Millennials have become accustomed to being told they are great and having others intervene on their behalf. Failure, and learning how to react to failure, has never been a process which has been clearly made evident to these individuals. Their experiences have led to an artificially high sense of self-esteem and entitlement in this generation. The expectations of the Millennial generation are thought to be unrealistic by members of other generations.

REWARDS

Give me rewards ... no matter how I do. The high expectations of Millennials contain a potential disconnect between reward and performance

(Ng et al., 2010). People with normal levels of self-esteem have been shown to (1) overestimate their own good qualities; (2) overestimate their personal control of events; and (3) be unrealistically optimistic (Taylor & Brown, 1988). Normal self-esteem develops when there is a match between performance and environmental feedback (Baumeister, 1997). A potent source of feedback is the rewards received for one's performance. Millennial life histories have not established a clear contingency between performance and rewards for them. These are the individuals who are used to receiving a trophy or ribbon no matter what level of performance they have reached. Kohn (1999) has addressed such a reinforcement strategy in child rearing and has shown that such an approach has, at best, only a short-term effect. It is more likely that such an approach will ultimately fail and may even do harm to the future abilities of those receiving such rewards. There is some evidence of this for Millennials. For example, Hulett (2006), proposes that Millennials are motivated by short-term rewards but seem to be poor at making long-term plans to realize hopes.

FEEDBACK

I need lots of feedback ... but make sure it is positive. Millennials may need a great deal more structure and supervision because of their inexperience on the task *and* because they do not have the interpersonal skills which other generations have mastered (Luguericio, 2009). Millennial workers want to measure their productivity but there is a belief, among older workers, that their definition of "getting the job done" is incomplete and possibly incorrect (Luguericio, 2009). However, the Millennial worker is used to receiving a great deal of positive feedback from parents and teachers. They expect to continue receiving this type of support on the job. Older workers may be seen as a substitute for "adoring parents" by the millennial worker (Sujansky, 2009). The Millennials want feedback, especially praise, on a regular basis from their supervisors (Alsop, 2008). This regular feedback is necessary to keep them engaged and motivated. This means that Millennials seem to require much feedback about their performance and demand individualized management by supervisors (Sujansky & Ferri-Reed, 2010). This feedback may need to be fairly regular and will go well beyond that given in the typical annual performance review (Alsop, 2008). In addition, Millennials expect mentoring and coaching at a high degree as well. Millennials, however, are also sensitive to criticism (Simons, 2009). Millennials, therefore, require careful handling when receiving feedback stating their performance is not up to standard (Alsop, 2008). Criticism may lead to tears and resignations.

This reaction to feedback is probably related to the high sense of self-esteem and high expectations held by Millennials described earlier in this section. Normal self-esteem levels are based on realistic feedback about one's performance from the environment (Baumeister, 1997). These propensities are exaggerated in those with artificially high self-esteem. When feedback on performance does not match the expectations for the feedback, those with artificially high self-esteem feel ego threats. These ego threats may lead to aggressive behaviors against others in the situation (Baumeister, 1997). These aggressive behaviors have the potential to go beyond leaving the situation noted by Alsop (2008) to counterproductive behaviors.

STANDARDS

Standards are nice … and I will follow them because they are there! The Millennial generation thrives on explicit directions and a well-structured situation: They are the "checklist" generation (Alsop, 2008). This means that Millennials do well in very concrete situations in which performance is routinized. They may, however, do less well in more ambiguous situations. Ambiguity, like failure, must be experienced to provide strategies for dealing with unclear priorities. Given the upbringing of the Millennial generation, such ambiguous situations have not been experienced and they have not learned well on how to deal with them. This may make them risk-averse, and afraid of making mistakes, in organizational situations without clear criteria for success.

"TEAMNESS"

There is no "I" in team … but then I cannot spell that well. Millennials are capable of hard work but often have a personal, not organizational definition of success (Hulett, 2006). Millennials still, however, can be, and believe themselves to be, team players. One reason for their propensity to work in teams is that the team provides a means to deal with ambiguity (Alsop, 2008). They have learned to rely on the consensus of the group to provide solutions to ambiguous situations.

We have identified five general categories of attitudes and beliefs about themselves held by Millennials. These are beliefs about (1) high expectations; (2) rewards; (3) feedback; (4) standards; and (5) "teamness." We will return to discussing these characteristics again after a brief review of motivation theories.

WORK MOTIVATION THEORIES

The value of understanding motivation is because it allows us to answer the question of "Why do people do what they do?" (Jex & Britt, 2008). This question is particularly important in the workplace. If we can answer this question, then we can (1) understand work behaviors related to organizational goals; (2) predict these same behaviors; and (3) to structure the work environment to encourage behaviors which relate these goals (Jex & Britt, 2008).

Understanding the motivations of employees, then, is critical to the creation of a work environment in which those employees can meet organizational efficiency and effectiveness goals. Motivation determines the *form, direction, intensity,* and *duration* of behavior in social settings such as the workplace (Pinder, 1998). Form refers to the question of what behaviors an individual chooses to engage in at work. Direction refers to the way that individuals structure behavior to meet a goal they have set for themselves. Intensity defines the amount of effort put into necessary goal-directed behavior. Duration refers to the time that an individual will spend on a task. Duration is particularly relevant for understanding individual persistence in goal-directed behaviors in the face of obstacles to the accomplishment of these goals.

Motivational theories have taken many forms: There are communalities among these forms which have led to several general classes of motivational theories. We will be concerned with how the proposals of three general classes of motivational theory interact with the characteristics of the Millennial generation. These are (1) need theories; (2) cognitive theories; and (3) behavioral approaches to motivation.

Need theories propose that humans have universal needs which motivate goal-directed behaviors (cf., Maslow's hierarchy of needs [Maslow, 1943; Maslow, 1954] and Aldefer's [1972] ERG theory). These universal needs are assumed to motivate behavior in a hierarchical fashion in which, as a lower level need is satisfied, behavior becomes motivated by higher level needs. The needs to be satisfied range from needs which are satisfied by extrinsic rewards (e.g., food and pay) to needs which are satisfied by more intrinsically defined rewards (e.g., esteem and self-actualization).

Cognitive theories emphasize the cognitive evaluation of a situation, and the behavior to be performed, by an individual residing in that situation. We are interested in three primary cognitive theories of motivation: expectancy, equity theory and goal-setting theory. In *expectancy theory,* motivation is the function of the individual's perception that effort will lead to performance and of the perceived desirability of outcomes that may result from performance (Vroom, 1964). Three cognitive evaluations are made by the individual in the situation to choose among behaviors to be performed. These are *expectancy, instrumentality* and *valence* (Vroom, 1964). The individual must first calculate the expectancy for a behavior. Expectancy defines the individual's belief that the effort expended in a behavior will lead to a defined level of performance. Instrumentality defines the individual's belief that a defined level of performance will lead to a defined level of outcome (reward). Valence refers to the value placed on that outcome by the individual in the situation. These three components act multiplicatively as individuals rationally evaluate the various course of action available to them. *Equity theory* is concerned with social comparisons (Adams, 1963, 1965). Individuals, in situations, examine the degree to which the inputs they provide for behavior in a situation (e.g., effort) are balanced by the outcomes they receive. This is done by calculating an input/outcome ratio for themselves and for others in the situation. If these ratios are equivalent, then their behavior is in balance with others. However, unequal ratios produce tension within a person that can be alleviated through cognitive distortion of their inputs or outputs; changing the comparison target; leaving the situation; and/or actively changing their inputs (e.g., working harder or working less hard). *Goal-setting theory* is concerned with the direction and persistence of behavior in the setting. Goals direct attention and action (choice), mobilize energy expenditure (effort), over a long period of time (persistence), and motivate an individual to develop strategies for goal obtainment (Locke, Shaw, Saari, & Latham, 1981). Goal-setting theories propose that goals differ in (1) goal difficulty; (2) goal acceptance; (3) goal specificity; and (4) that feedback on performance is necessary for motivated performance. Goal difficulty is the general finding that more difficult goals are more motivating than easier goals are for the individual (Locke & Latham, 1990). Goal acceptance, however, interacts with goal difficulty. Goal acceptance is related to the degree to which the individual believes that a particular goal is attainable (Latham & Locke, 1991). Acceptance of goals is possible for both participatively set goals and goals that are assigned. Goal specificity refers to the proposal that specific goals are better than general goals as motivating forces (Locke & Latham, 1990). Feedback provides individuals with the information to make sure that their behavior is consistent with goal attainment (Locke & Latham, 1990).

Behavioral approaches to motivation utilize the principles of learning theory (primarily operant conditioning) to motivate behavior. Therefore, the emphasis is on the antecedents of behavior; the behavior itself; and the consequences experienced after a behavior is expressed by an individual. These theories emphasize the relative influences of reinforcement and punishment; reinforcement schedules; and feedback on behavior (cf., Luthans & Kreitner, 1985). Reinforcement theories propose that human behavior can be shaped/altered by manipulating the reinforcement procedures outlined in operant learning theory. These methods assume that an employee's desire for the rewards of positive feedback and recognition will motivate performance at an appropriate level in anticipation of such rewards. The key here is to have a clear contingency relationship between an observable behavior and the consequences of that behavior.

Finally, there is some evidence that different forms of rewards may affect motivated behavior in organizations. Individual motivation is likely important to consider when explaining individual variations in organizational behaviors (e.g., Coyle-Shapiro, Kessler, & Purcell, 2004; Rioux & Penner, 2001; Van Knippenberg, 2000). The motives underlying organizational performance have been widely researched (e.g., to earn a salary and benefits). Self-determination theory posits that motives for engaging in a behavior may be intrinsic or extrinsic (Deci & Ryan, 1985; Ryan & Deci, 2000). Intrinsic motivation is described as engaging in work primarily for its own sake, while extrinsic motivation occurs in response to something apart from the work itself, such as reward, recognition, or requirement (Amabile, Hill, Hennessey, & Tighe, 1994). We shall also investigate the relationship between an individual's orientation toward rewards and how this may affect the behavior of the Millennial generation.

MILLENNIAL ATTITUDES AND MOTIVATION THEORIES

We have identified five general categories of attitudes and beliefs about themselves held by Millennials. These are beliefs about (1) high expectations; (2) reward; (3) feedback; (4) standards; and (5) "teamness." We propose that the first three categories will have a major impact on the way motivational theories may be used to understand Millennial work behavior. In effect, these beliefs moderate the predictions and, therefore, the value of the traditional motivational theories for understanding the work behavior of the Millennial generation.

Need Theories and Millennial Attitudes Toward Rewards

Need theories propose that humans have universal needs which motivate goal-directed behaviors to achieve extrinsic rewards (e.g., food and pay) and intrinsically defined rewards (e.g., esteem and self-actualization). The common premise for such theories of motivation is that individuals will seek to achieve both sets of needs in the workplace. However, in our discussion of the high expectations of the Millennials, there is support for the proposal that the Millennial generation will primarily seek extrinsic rewards in the workplace and probably seek intrinsic rewards outside the workplace (e.g., in community service). Millennials tend to be oriented toward extrinsic rewards at work. There is some support for this proposal as noted earlier. However, this support is not necessarily limited to the Millennial generation as a generational phenomenon solely (Deal, Stawiski, Grave, Gentry, Ruderman, & Weber, in press). Deal and colleagues (in press) have shown that lower level managerial workers are more motivated by extrinsic motivators than intrinsic. As managers climb the career ladder, more intrinsic motivation is seen. Therefore, while it may be true that Millennials are more motivated by extrinsic rewards, this finding is confounded with age and career success. More research may be required to track the Millennials and see if the prediction that their work behavior is primarily motivated by external rewards changes with time. However, given this prediction, need theories will probably provide little insight into understanding the Millennial generation's behavior in the workplace.

Cognitive Theories and Millennial Expectations and Reward and Feedback Beliefs

Cognitive theories emphasize the cognitive evaluation of a situation, and the behavior to be performed, by an individual residing in that situation. The beliefs that Millennials bring to the workplace regarding their expectations for a career; their expectations for how they will be rewarded; and their expectations for the feedback they should receive make traditional cognitive theories less helpful for the organization.

Expectancy Theory

Expectancy theories see motivation as the function of the individual's perception that effort will lead to performance and of perceived desirability of outcomes that may result from performance (Vroom, 1964). The three cognitive evaluations (*expectancy, instrumentality* and *valence*) are presumed to be valid and representative of the real world (Vroom, 1964). Millennial calculations of the expectancy component, however, given their life histories, will not be consistent with the presumed calculations of other generations. The Millennials begin with an overestimate of their ability. They believe that their effort should lead to high performance. Moreover, any perceived error in these calculations will be most likely hypothesized (by the Millennials), at least initially, to be the fault of the rater of their performance, not themselves. Responses may moderate as the Millennial receives more consistent feedback about his/her performance and alters his or her own perception of ability. However, this means the learning curve of performance feedback from the environment will be extended for Millennials in the workplace.

Their initial overestimate of the expectancy of their behavior must be brought into line with reality before calculations of instrumentality and valence may add predictive value in this theory. For example, Millennials' instrumentality calculations may be rejected by themselves because their presumed performance level is not perceived as leading to a defined level of outcome. This, however, is not due to a miscalculation of the instrumentality. Rather, this miscalculation is due to the initial expectancy calculations which were invalid. This lack of instrumentality, in turn, can affect the valence of the outcome by the individual in the situation. Since these three components act multiplicatively, Millennial calculations may be widely different than those of other generations.

Equity Theory

Equity theory is concerned with social comparisons (Adams, 1963, 1965). Individuals, in situations, examine the degree to which the inputs they provide for behavior in a situation (e.g., effort) are balanced by the outcomes they receive. This is done by calculating an input/outcome ratio for themselves and for others in the situation. If these ratios are equivalent, then their behavior is in balance with others. It is likely that Millennial calculations of their inputs will be exaggerated. This means that their equity ratio will be out of balance. This imbalance will lead to perceptions of inequity in extrinsic rewards. These perceptions of inequitable rewards are likely to occur because of the high value placed on their performance by Millennials. This inequity perception may create major problems for the organization.

The notion of equity is a critical component that guides most compensation planning. Both Adams (1963, 1965) and Jaques (1961, 2002) recognize the importance of fairness and perceived equality in influencing human behavior, particularly behavior at work. Adams' (1963, 1965) equity theory has more recently been included in theories on organizational justice and is referred to as *distributive* justice (Colquitt, Conlon, Wesson, Porter, & Ng, 2001; Greenberg, 1987). Distributive justice refers to employee perceptions of fairness when allocating rewards or compensation within the organization (Colquitt et al., 2001). Distributive justice is most frequently discussed in the compensation literature regarding employee satisfaction with the amount of compensation that they receive (Folger & Konovsky, 1989). In addition to distributive justice, employees also judge the fairness of the organization's system or process for allocating rewards and compensation, which is referred to as *procedural* justice (Alexander & Ruderman, 1987; Colquitt et al., 2001; Thibaut & Walker,

1975). Justice has implications for understanding how equity theories provide insight into the Millennial generation.

For example, a Millennial may see inequity in compensation across levels of the organization. Given their sense of self-esteem, they may perceive their inputs as valuable as that of another individual who is their supervisor. Compensation differences will, therefore, be seen as inequitable. Researchers have investigated how perceived inequity disparity in pay might affect employee perceptions of justice (Cowherd & Levine, 1992; Wilhelm, 1993; Zajac & Westphal, 1995). Cowherd and Levine (1992) investigated employee perceptions of pay equity between different levels of the organization and found that employee perceptions of procedural and distributive justice were higher in more egalitarian pay systems. Also, Cowherd and Levine (1992) found that employees' perceptions of justice were significantly positively related to their work output (measured in terms of product quality). Additionally, Pfeffer and Langton (1993) investigated wage inequity within an academic setting and found that the greater the disparity, the lower the faculty's satisfaction, research productivity and willingness to collaborate. A separate study by Pfeffer and Davis-Blake (1992) found that interclass pay inequity was also significantly related to turnover intentions. Thus, perceived violations of either distributive or procedural justice may affect work quality, which could potentially affect organizational performance. Although there is relatively limited empirical evidence of the relationship between interclass pay inequity and justice perceptions, other justice research has found that perceptions of distributive justice are related to employee pay satisfaction (Folger & Konovsky, 1989), job satisfaction, satisfaction with the organization (Tremblay, Sire, & Balkin, 2000), and turnover intentions (Summers & Hendrix, 1991). Additional research has found that organizational commitment (Folger & Konovsky, 1989) and benefits satisfaction are most strongly related to procedural justice (Tremblay, Sire, & Balkin, 2000). Compensation committees should be particularly concerned about the possible consequences of employee perceptions of injustice regarding executive compensation. Research on the consequences of justice violations shows that perceptions of injustice are strongly related to effort reduction, retaliation, skepticism, and sabotage, which could result in decreased organizational effectiveness (Skarlicki & Folger, 1997).

The most likely effect of such perceptions of inequity among Millennials is that they will leave the situation and not change their effort or behavior. However, given the description of ego threat and its relationships to aggressive behavior noted earlier, the counterproductive behaviors outlined by Skarlicki and Folger (1997) are possible reactions of Millennials to perceptions of inequity.

Goal-Setting. Goals direct attention and action (choice), mobilize energy expenditure (effort), over a long period of time (persistence), and motivate an individual to develop strategies for goal obtainment (Locke et al., 1981). However, as noted earlier, one prime characteristic of Millennials is that they prefer short-term goals with constant feedback. This is not necessarily the situation described by traditional goal-setting theory: Such programs may be based on reviewing goals on an annual basis. In effect, managerial time necessary to continually review goals and provide the desired feedback to each Millennial worker may outweigh the value of using goals with Millennials. In addition, goal-setting theory proposes that accurate feedback provides individuals with the information to make sure that their behavior is consistent with goal attainment (Locke & Latham, 1990). Accurate feedback may be resisted by Millennials and seen as criticism. Therefore, goal-setting as a process will have special requirements for use with Millennials.

Behavior Theory. Behavioral approaches to motivation utilize the principles of learning theory (primarily operant conditioning) to motivate behavior. Reinforcement theories propose that human behavior can be shaped/altered by manipulating the reinforcement procedures outlined in operant learning theory. The key here is to have a clear contingency relationship between an observable behavior and the consequences of that behavior. The reward history of the Millennial generation is such that these approaches may be problematic for the Millennial as well. Essentially, Millennials have been on reinforcement schedules which are near continuous (i.e., for each response a reward is earned (cf., Kohn, 1999)). Continuous reinforcement schedules require that each behavior be rewarded. This is a problematic situation for the organization because it requires continuous monitoring, by supervisory and managerial personnel, of the Millennials. Moreover, the behavior learned under conditions of continuous reinforcement are not very stable and are prone to disappear if the reward is withheld (cf., Rachlin, 1976). In addition, the individual who has experienced learning under continuous reinforcement often exhibits "emotional" behaviors when the reinforcement is withheld. Therefore, the use of behavioral approaches with Millennials will most likely lead to undesired behaviors in most situations using traditional organizational behavior management approaches.

Summary. The life-history of the Millennial generation creates unique problems for organizational reward systems and work motivation. Millennials' high expectations for career success; for high levels of extrinsic rewards; and for positive feedback make them uniquely unsuited for most workplaces today. Millennials individually expect that each of them will "win" at work. However, this may not be the case in reality. Workplaces are designed to provide accurate feedback and this is not necessarily a good thing when dealing with Millennials. Therefore, the final question remains—"What methods may organizations use to motivate the Millennial generation?" The following section will turn to this question. We will use the other two categories of Millennial attitudes, standards and "teamness" as leverage points in this discussion of how one well-known incentive system, gainsharing, may provide insight into motivating the Millennial generation.

ORGANIZATIONAL REWARD SYSTEMS AND THE MILLENNIAL GENERATION: ONE EXAMPLE

Current conceptualizations of organizational and individual job performance are multifaceted. Therefore, when designing an organization's reward system it is necessary to decide (1) what type of organizational performance criteria are to be used and (2) then what individual performance criteria are going to be used to meet the organizational criteria. The two general classes of organizational performance criteria are organizational efficiency and organizational effectiveness measures (cf., Svyantek, 2006). Organizational efficiency measures seek to improve the performance of the organization on internally focused criteria (e.g., decrease the production costs to produce a widget). Organizational effectiveness measures seek to improve the performance of the organization on externally focused criteria (e.g., to increase the sales of widgets). Gainsharing seeks to improve organizational efficiency. Other reward systems (e.g., profit sharing) seek to improve organizational effectiveness.

Individual job performance may first be defined as tasks which are part of the job descriptions for individuals within an organization. This is commonly defined as task performance. These are the behaviors evaluated in traditional performance appraisal systems. A second class of important organizational behaviors, however, may be described as organizational citizenship behaviors or contextual performance. These extra role behaviors are collectively referred to as *citizenship performance* (Borman, 2004; Borman, Penner, Allen, & Motowidlo, 2001). Citizenship performance is discretionary and may support the organizational, social, and psychological context in which job tasks are performed. We will first deal with individual task performance as our primary focus. However, we return later to citizenship performance and Millennials during our discussion of the impact of gainsharing on task performance.

Given the expectations of the Millennials for pay and benefits, it is likely that specific forms of organizational incentive systems will differentially affect the performance of Millennials in the workplace. For example, gainsharing and profitsharing incentive systems have been analyzed for their respective effects on motivating employees to attain different organizational goals (Svyantek, 2006). These two incentive systems were shown to create unique expectations for pay and unique linkages between pay and performance. We propose that organizations seeking to motivate Millennials should consider following a gainsharing model to developing reward systems. This approach seems uniquely suited to using the Millennials' attitudes toward standards and teams to leverage change in their artificially created expectations for their careers, rewards, and feedback.

Gainsharing

Gainsharing (GS) is a pay-for-performance system used by organizations to reward workers for increased performance at the group-, unit-, or organization-level (Rynes, Gerhart, & Parks, 2005). The ultimate goal of this plan is to both improve specific aspects of organizational productivity and improve employee attitudes relating to justice, collaboration and teamwork by incorporating the concept of *common fate*. Common fate is integral to the management of performance at the group, unit, organizational level (Werther, Ruch, & McClure, 1986). The performance of an organization is seen as a direct function of the combined efforts of all its members. The margin of success for an organization, then, comes from replacing a potentially adversarial and negative relationship between management and employees with cooperation and collaboration. Gainsharing rewards employees for increases in efficiency on some important organizational criteria (e.g., decreasing wastefulness and/or increasing productivity (Lawler, 1981). The typical GS plan is designed, using one of a number of formula variants, to be implemented within one facility (e.g., one factory). Higher levels of performance are achieved through the involvement and participation of employees in some form of suggestion system (Lawler, 1981; Lawler, 1988; Masternak, 1997). The two components, monetary reward for improved efficiency and the use of participative management, are the defining components of a GS plan. GS uses criteria which are focused on the internal efficiency of the organizational unit in which the plan is being implemented. For example, a GS plan may determine the historical labor cost to produce one "widget" in the plant. This cost is $5.00/widget. Employees receive a bonus for lowering the cost of production of that "widget." If the employees, through their suggestions and changes in work behavior, lower the labor cost to produce to $4.50/widget, the employees are rewarded for this decrease in labor cost through the established GS formula. The criteria chosen for use in GS plans should be those which the employees of the organization may directly impact through changes in their behavior, or suggestions made, in the workplace. GS plans will work only in situations where the inputs of employees are actually influential, and also in labor systems as opposed to capital-intense systems (Kim, 1999).

The mechanism by which GS plans increase organizational performance is proposed to be that GS plans (1) establish the belief that rewards are based on improvement in performance on the organizational criteria being measured; (2) establish ways for employees to influence organizational performance as measured by the reward system; (3) provide feedback about organizational performance to employees; and (4) create opportunities for employees to learn how to contribute to organizational performance (Lawler, 1988). GS programs always are implemented in conjunction with some form of participative management (e.g., a suggestion system) (Lawler, 1988). GS plans have been shown to result in labor cost savings of approximately 29% (Lawler, 1988).

Gainsharing and The Millennial Generation

We propose that gainsharing provides a model for developing a reward system which has the potential to motivate Millennials in the workplace. This form of reward system allows two of the characteristics outlined for Millennials (a desire for rules and standards and teamwork) to leverage change in the other three Millennial characteristics (high, unrealistic expectations; lack of contingency in reward—performance linkages; and desire for feedback coupled with an inability to use feedback to correct behavior) which make Millennials such an issue for managing.

First, a GS plan establishes a formula for performance reward. This formula is based on historical data. This formula establishes the standards toward which employees (here specifically the Millennial generation) work to achieve and strive to better. This formula requires collaborative input and consensus from the team members who are developing the formula. This is done in the beginning stages of a GS plan. It is these beginning stages where the leverage for changing the other three Millennial characteristics begins.

Second, once in place, a GS plan provides feedback on performance to the employees working under the plan. Here Millennials are provided information on their performance based on group-developed standards. This should decrease the negative reaction to feedback which shows low performance. The Millennials have collaborated in the development of these standards. This means that the feedback of not reaching the standard is not criticism from another in the environment (e.g., a supervisor). The target of the reaction should be the self or team. Millennials, here, will have the feedback they received controlled by the standards they have established; this feedback will be consistent and constant; and this feedback will come from their own performance. Therefore, a GS plan should aid the Millennial generation in learning to use and react to feedback appropriately.

Third, GS plans establish the belief that rewards are based on improvement in performance on the organizational criteria being measured. Rewards occur for meaningful improvement. However, one aspect of the GS plan which is consistent with the reinforcement history of the Millennials is that rewards are based on equivalent inputs. Those with equivalent inputs received equivalent levels of reward. Therefore, all individuals can be "winners." In addition, this aspect of the plan may provide Millennials with information on how to create equity calculations which are both realistic and useful. These equity calculations are necessary for both task and citizenship performance. We would like to discuss citizenship performance as a special class of performance for the Millennial generation.

Organizational Citizenship and the Millennial Generation

Citizenship performance refers to extra-role behaviors performed by individuals at work (Borman, 2004; Borman et al., 2001). Citizenship performance is discretionary and may support the organizational, social, and psychological context in which job tasks are performed. Borman and Motowidlo (1993) suggested a causal link between citizenship performance and organizational success. This extra-role performance is important to organizations because higher levels of such activities facilitate the meeting of organizational goals and organizational performance (Allen & Rush, 1998) and help to shape the internal environment of the organization (Kristof, 1996; Schneider, Goldstein, & Smith, 1995). Borman and Motowidlo (1993) stated that currently most arguments offered for a link between organizationally important variables and citizenship performance are usually logical rather than empirical. Conceptually, the argument is, if organizational members help each other with work-related problems, orient new employees, volunteer suggestions for improvement, etc., then organizational resources are freed for other uses (Organ, 1988). Therefore, when employees exhibit a high degree of citizenship the organization can get more work from its members at no additional cost to the organization (Organ, 1988). There seem to be two general factors underlying citizenship performance. The first factor can be characterized as citizenship behavior toward individuals (e.g., coworkers in the same work group) while the second factor relates to citizenship behavior benefitting the larger organization (Organ, 1997).

Researchers have begun investigating how best to predict which employees will engage in consistently high levels of citizenship performance (Borman et al., 2001). Human resource professionals also attempt to identify and select individuals who are likely to engage in these extrarole behaviors (Borman & Motowidlo, 1993). The characteristics described for Millennials earlier provide some interesting predictions about the level, and type, of citizenship performance that will be exhibited by the Millennial generation.

These predictions are based on our discussion of motivation orientation. Due to the discretionary nature of citizenship performance, motivation is likely important to consider when explaining individual variations in these behaviors (e.g., Coyle-Shapiro, Kessler, & Purcell, 2004; Rioux & Penner, 2001; Van Knippenberg, 2000). Motives for task performance have been widely researched (e.g., to earn a salary and benefits), but motives for citizenship performance are less clear. Self-determination theory posits that motives for engaging in a behavior may be intrinsic or extrinsic (Deci & Ryan, 1985; Ryan & Deci, 2000). Intrinsic motivation is described as engaging in work primarily for its own sake, while extrinsic motivation occurs in response to something apart from the work itself, such as reward, recognition, or requirement (Amabile, Hill, Hennessey, & Tighe, 1994). There is not a direct link between reward and citizenship performance; however, individuals may engage in organizational citizenship behaviors for both intrinsic and extrinsic reasons (e.g., impression management; Rioux & Penner, 2001).

One interesting prediction is that those individuals with extrinsic reward orientations will exhibit different patterns of citizenship performance than those with intrinsic reward orientations. Those with extrinsic reward orientations will most likely not perform citizenship behavior directed toward the organization: They will see no benefit toward this type of behavior since they receive no reward for doing such behaviors. One of the characteristics of Millennials noted earlier is that they have an extrinsic reward orientation. Therefore, it may be predicted that the citizenship performance will be lower than other generational groups *at least* for behaviors benefitting the organization that the Millenials perceive are not rewarded by their organizations.

However, it may be that citizenship behaviors directed toward the members of one's own work group will be performed. This form of citizenship behavior is likely to be seen in Millennials: Millennials will perform citizenship behaviors directed at their peers because they have learned to work in teams and probably will have acquired such behaviors while growing up. The actual mechanism supporting this form of citizenship behavior may be either extrinsic or intrinsic reward motivation but it is likely, at a minimum, that the Millennials will have learned the value of reciprocity in the team settings of which they have been part.

There is some additional support for this proposal that different patterns of citizenship performance will be seen in the workplace based on the relationship between performance and rewards. Different patterns of results for the effects of organizational predictors on the measures of citizenship performance directed toward other employees (e.g., the peer group) and toward the organization have been shown (Goodman & Svyantek, 1999).

Goodman and Svyantek (1999) assessed the influence of perceived organizational climate on citizenship performance. They measured perceptions of actual and ideal climates for several climate dimensions. Several of these dimensions have direct implications for the Millennial generation. These dimensions are (1) reward (perceptions of the perceived fairness of the reward system); (2) standards (perception of perceived performance standards); and (3) support (perceptions of the helpfulness of managers and others in the group). These three dimensions were chosen here because they reflect three of the defined characteristics of the Millennials described earlier in this chapter.

An interesting finding occurred for citizenship performance directed at others and at the organization. For citizenship behaviors directed at others, perceptions of the ideal climate to work in in terms of Reward, Standards, and Support predicted exhibited citizenship behaviors more strongly than perceptions of these same dimensions for the actual organization. Citizenship behaviors directed at the organization, however, were more predicted by the perceptions of the actual practices of the organization on these three dimensions than by perceptions of the ideal organization.

Therefore, as noted earlier, citizenship performance directed at others may be expected from Millennials. However, we predict that citizenship performance directed at the organization will be less in Millennials *unless* they perceive they are being treated fairly. However, given their unrealistic expectations, their perception of fair treatment may not match reality. It appears that citizenship performance is not as free as originally proposed by Organ (1988).

The question of how to motivate citizenship performance has implications for organizations in the future. As noted above, citizenship performance is not part of employees' work contracts. Rather, employees' citizenship performance probably derives from a match between their expectations and how they perceive their work environment. Since the Millennial is likely to have unrealistic expectations, organizations must develop means for supporting citizenship performance directed at the organization.

Organizations concerned with citizenship performance must be prepared to reward employees for exhibiting citizenship performance. Organizations must remember the old saying, "You get what you pay for." Organizations, in the future, will need to create some mechanism for rewarding employees exhibiting high levels of citizenship performance. Organizations which do not have such reward systems will face a decline in citizenship performance concomitant with the decline in task performance.

Here, as for task performance, we propose that the GS plan uses the Millennial characteristics of rules and standards and teamwork to change their response to feedback and their ideas of reward contingencies and to move them into a more appropriate view of their role as organizational citizens. This moves the Millennial generation toward having more realistic expectations for their careers in organizations. GS plans provide opportunities for employees to learn how to contribute to organizational performance (Lawler, 1988). The GS model also provides a way to provide Millennial generations with the information necessary to become good organizational citizens by showing how doing good for the organization can lead to improved extrinsic rewards for those performing such behaviors.

CONCLUSION

This chapter has provided a description of the expectations of the Millennial generation for extrinsic motivation in the workplace; addressed the basics of motivational theories; and explored the fit between those motivational theories and the expectation for pay, benefits and advancement held by the Millennial generation. Finally, we proposed gainsharing as a model organizational reward system with the potential to appeal to, and motivate, the Millennial generation to meet organizational goals for performance as the newest generation enters the workforce by using the basic characteristics of the Millennial generation as levers for change.

Earlier authors have emphasized developing new methods for human resource management tasks which directly accommodate the Millennials' needs. Hulett (2006), for example, suggests that organizations provide frequent encouraging feedback and that organizations should make the job fun. Southerland and Hoover (2007) propose that Millennials need to be treated specially (e.g., constant positive feedback). Fallon (2009) advocates that, to keep Millennials happy and motivated, organizations should give them regular feedback; show them the "big picture" of the organization; and build enjoyment into the workplace for them. Sujansky and Ferri-Reed (2010) note that Millennials are used to positive feedback.

Feedback should be encouraging, specific, and concrete. Organizations should create a fun and challenging atmosphere for Millennials including social events at the workplace (e.g., Friday afternoon "happy hour").

As noted earlier, these authors seek to accommodate the Millennial generations' special needs. This, in effect, continues the coddling of the Millennial generation.

The real issue is how to move the Millennials from coddling to competency. We believe that organizational reward systems should provide a mechanism for the Millennials to learn to become good organizational citizens. This mechanism should provide extrinsic rewards for doing appropriate levels of performance. We believe that the use of a gainsharing model as an organizational reward system provides a way to not just accommodate the Millennial generation. This approach seems uniquely suited to using the Millennials' attitudes toward standards and teams to leverage change in their artificially created expectations for their careers, rewards, and feedback and to allow Millennials to become the good organizational citizens necessary in work organizations.

REFERENCES

Adams, J. S. (1963). Toward an understanding of inequity. *Journal of Abnormal and Social Psychology, 67,* 422-436.

Adams, J. S. (1965). Inequity in social exchange. In L. Berkowitz (Ed.), *Advances in experimental psychology* (Vol. 2, pp. 267-299). San Diego, CA: Academic Press.

Alderfer, C. P. (1972). *Existence, relatedness, and growth: Human needs in organizational settings.* New York, NY: Free Press.

Alexander, S., & Ruderman, M. (1987). The role of procedural and distributive justice in organizational behavior. *Social Justice Research, 1,* 177-198.

Allen, T. D., & Rush, M. C. (1998). The effects of organizational citizenship behavior on performance judgments: A field study and a laboratory experiment. *Journal of Applied Psychology, 83,* 247-260.

Alsop, R. (2008). *The trophy kids grow up: How the millennial generation is shaking up the workplace.* San Francisco, CA: Jossey-Bass.

Amabile, T. M., Hill, K. G., Hennessey, B. A., & Tighe, E. M. (1994). The work preference inventory: Assessing intrinsic and extrinsic motivational orientations. *Journal of Personality and Social Psychology, 66,* 950-967.

Baumeister, R. F. (1997). *Evil: Inside human violence and cruelty.* New York, NY: W. H. Freeman.

Borman, W. C. (2004). The concept of organizational citizenship. *Current Directions in Psychological Science, 13,* 238-241.

Borman, W. C., & Motowidlo, S. J. (1993). Expanding the criterion domain to include elements of contextual performance. In N. Schmitt, W. C. Borman, & Associates (Eds.), *Personnel selection in organizations* (pp. 71-98). San Francisco, CA: Jossey-Bass.

Borman, W. C., Penner, L. A., Allen, T. D., & Motowidlo, S. J. (2001). Personality predictors of citizenship performance. *International Journal of Selection and Assessment, 9,* 52-69.

Colquitt, J. A., Conlon, D. E., Wesson, M. J., Porter, C. O. L. H., & Ng, K. Y. (2001). Justice at the millennium: A meta-analytic review of 25 years of organizational justice research. *Journal of Applied Psychology, 86,* 425-445.

Cowherd, D. M., & Levine, D. I. (1992). Product quality and pay equity between lower-level employees and top management: An investigation of distributive justice theory. *Administrative Science Quarterly, 37,* 302-320.

Coyle-Shapiro, J. A-M., Kessler, I., & Purcell, J. (2004). Exploring organizationally directed citizenship behavior: Reciprocity or "it's my job?" *Journal of Management Studies, 41,* 85-106.

Deal, J. J., Stawiski, S., Graves, L., Gentry, W., Ruderman, M., & Weber, T. (in press) Perceptions of authority and leadership: A cross-national, cross-generational investigation. In E. Ng, S. Lyons and L. Schweitzer (Eds.) *Managing the new workforce: International perspectives on the millennial generation.* Northampton, MA: Edward Elgar.

Deci, E. L., & Ryan, R. M. (1985). *Intrinsic motivation and self-determination in human behavior.* New York, NY: Plenum.

Fallon, T. (2009, May). Retain and motivate the next generation. *SuperVision, 70(5),* 5-7. Retrieved from ABI/INFORM Complete. (Document ID: 1690888941)

Folger, R., & Konovsky, M. A. (1989). Effects of procedural and distributive justice on reactions to pay raise decisions. *Academy of Management Journal, 32,* 115-130.

Goodman, S. A., & Svyantek, D. J. (1999). Person-organization fit and contextual performance: Do shared values matter? *Journal of Vocational Behavior, 55,* 254-275.

Greenberg, J. (1987). A taxonomy of organizational justice theories. *Academy of Management Review, 12,* 9-22.

Hulett, K. J. (2006, November). They are here to replace us: Recruiting and retaining millennials. *Journal of Financial Planning: Solutions, 17.* Retrieved from ABI/INFORM Complete. (Document ID: 1170464111).

Jaques, E. (1961). *Equitable payment.* New York, NY: John Wiley and Sons.

Jaques, E. (2002). *Social power and the CEO: Leadership and trust in a sustainable free enterprise system.* Westport, CT: Quorum Books.

Jex, S. M., & Britt, T. W. (2008). *Organizational psychology: A scientist-practitioner approach* (2nd ed.). Hoboken, NJ: John Wiley & Sons.

Kim, D. O. (1999). Determinants of the survival of gainsharing programs. *Industrial and Labor Relations Review, 55(1),* 21-42.

Kohn, A. (1999). *Punished by rewards: The trouble with gold stars, incentive plans, As, praise and other bribes.* Boston, MA: Houghton Mifflin.

Kristof, A. L. (1996). Person-organization fit: An integrative review of its conceptualization, measurement, and implications. *Personnel Psychology, 49,* 1-49.

Latham, G. P., & Locke, E. A. (1991). Self-regulation through goal-setting. *Organizational Behavior and Human Decision Processes, 50,* 212-247.

Lawler, E. E. (1981). *Pay and organization development*. Reading, MA: Addison-Wesley.

Lawler, E. E. (1988). Gainsharing theory and research: Findings and future directions. *Research in organizational change and development, 2,* 323-344.

Locke, E. A., & Latham, G. P. (1990). *A theory of goal setting and task performance.* Englewood Cliffs, NJ: Prentice Hall.

Locke, E. A., Shaw, K. M., Saari, L. M., & Latham, G. P. (1981). Goal setting and task performance: 1960-1980. *Psychological Bulletin, 90,* 125-152.

Luguericio, M. (2009, May). From the Gen C'ers and millenials: Are You "Boomers" listening: Read that again. Are you really listening?" *Insurance Advocate, 30-33.*

Luthans, F., & Kreiter, R. (1985). *Organizational behavior modification and beyond: An operant and social learning approach* (2nd ed.). Glenview, IL: Scott, Foresman.

Maslow, A. H. (1943). A theory of human motivation. *Psychological Review, 50,* 370-396.

Maslow, A. H. (1954). *Motivation and personality.* New York, NY: Harper.

Masternak, R. (1997). How to make gainsharing successful: The collective experience of 17 facilities. *Compensation and Benefits Review, 29,* 43-52.

Ng, E. S., Schweitzer, L., & Lyons, S. T. (2010). New generation, great expectations: A field study of the millenial generation. *Journal of Business and Psychology, 25,* 281-292.

Organ, D. W. (1988). *Organizational citizenship behavior: The good soldier syndrome.* Lexington, MA: Lexington Books.

Organ, D. W. (1997). Organizational citizenship behavior: It's construct clean-up time. *Human Performance, 10,* 85-97.

Pfeffer, J., & Davis-Blake, A. (1992). Salary dispersion, location in the salary distribution, and turnover among college administrators. *Industrial and Labor Relations Review, 45,* 753-763.

Pfeffer, J., & Langton, N. (1993). The effect of wage dispersion on satisfaction, productivity, and working collaboratively: Evidence from college and university faculty. *Administrative Science Quarterly, 38,* 382-407.

Pinder, C. C. (1998). *Work motivation in organizational behavior.* Upper Saddle River, NJ: Prentice-Hall.

Rachlin, H. (1976). *Behavior and learning.* San Francisco, CA: W. H. Freeman.

Rioux, S. M., & Penner, L. A. (2001). The causes of organizational citizenship behavior: A motivational analysis. *Journal of Applied Psychology, 86,* 1306-1314.

Ryan, R. M., & Deci, E. L. (2000). Self-determination theory and the facilitation of intrinsic motivation, social development, and well-being. *American Psychologist, 55,* 68-78.

Rynes, S. L., Gerhart, B., & Parks, L. (2005). Personnel psychology: Performance evaluation and pay for performance. *Annual Review of Psychology, 56,* 571-600.

Schneider, B., Goldstein, H. W., & Smith, D. B. (1995). The ASA framework: An update. *Personnel Psychology, 48,* 747-773.

Simons, A. (2009, May). Changing workplace demographics: T + B + Y+ X = opportunity. *CPA Practice Management Forum,* 15-16, 23.

Skarlicki, D. P., & Folger, R. (1997). Retaliation in the workplace: The roles of distributive, procedural, and interactional justice. *Journal of Applied Psychology, 82,* 434-443.

Southerland, T., & Hoover, G. (2007, Summer). The millennials: Who are these students staring back at you in the classroom? *Accounting Education, 35,* 5-6.

Sujansky, J. (2009, October). Spoiled, impatient, & entitled: Why you need strong millennials in your workplace. *SuperVision, 70(10),* 8-10.   Retrieved from ABI/INFORM Complete. (Document ID: 1867675921).

Sujansky, J., & Ferri-Reed, J. (2010, April). Motivate your millennial employees. *SuperVision, 71(4),* 13-15.   Retrieved from ABI/INFORM Complete. (Document ID: 2002247061)

Summers, T. P., & Hendrix, W. H. (1991). Modeling the role of pay equity perceptions: A field study. *Journal of Occupational Psychology, 64,* 145-157.

Svyantek, D. J. (2006). Gainsharing/profitsharing. In S. Rogelberg (Ed.), *The encyclopedia of industrial and organizational psychology* (pp. 261-263). Thousand Oaks, CA: SAGE.

Taylor, S. E., & Brown, J. D. (1988). Illusion and well-being: A social psychological perspective on mental health. *Psychological Bulletin, 103,* 193-210.

Thibaut, J., & Walker, L. (1975). *Procedural justice: A psychological analysis.* Hillsdale, NJ: Erlbaum.

Tremblay, M., Sire, B., & Balkin, D. B. (2000). The role of organizational justice in pay and employee benefit satisfaction, and its effects on work attitudes. *Group & Organization Management, 25,* 269-290.

Van Knippenberg, D. (2000). Work motivation and performance: A social identity perspective. *Applied Psychology: An International Review, 49,* 357-371.

Vroom, V. H. (1964). *Work motivation.* New York, NY: John Wiley & Sons.

Werther, W. B., Ruch, W. A. & McClure, L. (1986). *Productivity through people.* St. Paul, MN: West.

Wilhelm, P. G. (1993). Application of distributive justice theory to the CEO pay problem: Recommendations for reform. *Journal of Business Ethics, 12,* 469-482.

Zajac, E. J., & Westphal, J. D. (1995). Accounting for the explanations of CEO compensation: Substance and symbolism. *Administrative Science Quarterly, 40,* 283-308.

CHAPTER 4

JUST WHAT IS IMPORTANT TO MILLENNIAL JOB CANDIDATES

It's Not What We Assumed

Kyra Leigh Sutton

INTRODUCTION

The purpose of this chapter is to provide an understanding of the expectations and perceptions that Generation Y (i.e., Gen Y) job seekers have during the recruiting and selection processes. In a survey of Gen Y job seekers currently enrolled in college, but seeking employment opportunities, the study found that: (a) Gen Y job seekers have clear expectations of how they should be treated during the recruitment process, (b) in contrast to prevailing notions, they *do not* desire to connect with recruiters through social media outlets (e.g., Facebook, LinkedIn, Twitter), (c) Gen Y job seekers have definitive ideas about the characteristics that companies should consider about candidates during the interview process (e.g., an applicant's personality, sense of humor, level of maturity), (d) the elements of a "cool" work environment are, surprisingly not technologically driven, rather they are related to working in a workplace where they per-

Managing Human Resources for the Millennial Generation, pp. 77–115
Copyright © 2012 by Information Age Publishing
All rights of reproduction in any form reserved.

ceive they are respected and work environments that are stress free, and (e) while some survey respondents perceived their age and subsequent lack of experience to be a disadvantage, most perceived their age as an advantage during the recruitment process. This chapter argues that Gen Y job seekers' reactions to the selection and recruitment process are important in order to facilitate organizational attraction, and to lessen the likelihood of applicant withdrawal during the selection process. Recommendations are made to help organizations learn how to attract Gen Y job seekers, and the importance of preparing the organization's current workforce for the entrance of Gen Y job seekers is discussed.

Members of the Gen Y generation are defined as those individuals born (roughly) between the years of 1980-2000, and the first "class" of Millennial college graduates entered the workforce in approximately 2004 (Hershatter & Epstein, 2010). During numerous interactions with students of the Millennial generation, I find that they are thoughtful regarding their recruitment experiences. Specifically, students often express disappointment regarding their interactions with prospective employers. That is, the students do not only consider the actual job offer, but they also give consideration to their overall experience and interaction with the company representative(s) during the recruitment and selection process. Most of the disappointment stems from the fact that students feel their expectations were not met during this process. Examples might include, "I don't think they really liked me," "The company didn't show any interest in me", or "They didn't take me seriously." Further, research indicates that members of the Millennial generation desire to make social connections, including connections at work (e.g., McCrindle, 2010).

As a result, there needs to be a better understanding of the expectations that members of the Millennial generation have during the recruitment/selection process. Of note, a lot of the sparse literature that is published about Gen Y characteristics includes many contradictory ideas of what's important to Gen Y job seekers (e.g., Deal, Altman, & Rogelberg, 2010). A clearer understanding of their expectations will assist organizations in targeting and attracting workers of the Millennial generation. Consistent with this notion, several articles have called for research that explores how organizations can incorporate generational characteristics into their recruitment/selection strategies (e.g., Brazeel, 2009; Elmore, 2009; Smith, 2009). Since little is known about the expectations and perceptions that Gen Y job seekers have during the recruitment process, the present study, which was designed to address this deficiency, surveyed Gen Y job seekers that are presently enrolled in college, but seeking employment opportunities. The survey focused on the following aspects of recruitment: (a) discrepancies between what the Gen Y job seekers value as important during the recruitment process, and what actually occurs during the recruitment process, (b) the extent to which Gen Y job seekers seek to connect with recruiters over social media, (c) Gen Y job seekers' perceptions of the (job seeker) attributes that should be considered during the recruitment process, (d) identifying what attracts Gen Y job seekers to "cool" work environments, and (e) Gen Y job seekers' perceptions of age during the recruitment and selection process.

RELEVANT LITERATURE

Despite the importance of studying the recruitment experience(s) of Gen Y job seekers, limited research has been conducted in this area (e.g., Broadbridge, Maxwell, & Ogden, 2007). That is, very few studies have examined recruiter and/or applicant reactions during the recruitment process. Instead, the majority of research (e.g., Deal, Altman, & Rogelberg, 2010), including studies published in the popular press (e.g., Robert Half International's Generation Y study), focus mainly on identifying and studying the working behavior and patterns of Gen Y workers, once they are hired. For example, in a recent book written by Johnson & Johnson (2010), there were several suggestions given on the management of, and retention of Gen Y employees. Examples included employers should create opportunities for Gen Y workers to bond, avoid the enforcement of unnecessary rules, make sure your company uses updated technology, interact with them often, provide feedback often, and acknowledge their accomplishments (Johnson & Johnson, 2010). While all of these suggestions are relevant and viable, they will only work to the extent that organizations are successful in attracting Gen Y job seekers during the preemployment phase. Specifically, while there may be a general consensus, which may or may not be accurate, about the factors that facilitate the retention of Gen Y workers (e.g., salary, benefits, opportunities for career growth/advancement, company's location), there is less known about the preemployment experiences, expectations, and feelings of Gen Y job seekers. It is important to identify and understand these preemployment experiences of Gen Y job seekers because previous research suggests that prehire factors such as how a candidate is treated by a recruiter, will influence organizational attraction which consequently impacts the job seeker's acceptance intentions, and ultimate job choice (e.g., Harold & Ployhart, 2008). Further, to the extent that Gen Y job seekers have a good experience during the recruitment and selection process, this significantly *decreases* the likelihood that a candidate will withdraw from the selection process (e.g., Anderson, Salgado, & Hulsheger, 2010).

Although there has been limited research conducted specifically on the preemployment experiences of Gen Y job seekers, there has been a small, but notable body of research conducted on the applicant's perspective and reactions during the selection/preemployment processes (i.e., how job seekers view the employee selection process) (e.g., Anderson et al., 2010; Morgeson & Ryan, 2009; Ryan & Ployhart, 2000). For a more detailed summary of the *history* of applicant reaction research, see Ryan & Ployhart (2000). These studies were useful in identifying several of the items that were used to build the survey included in this study. Examples include Jacking & De Lange (2009) who explored the expectations held by recruiters and accounting students. The authors operationalized expectations in terms of technical and generic skills: specifically they asked employers to identify the most important graduate skills in their potential employees, and they also asked the students to describe the skills that they perceived were important to acquire during their undergraduate studies. Drawing from the findings of both the recruiter interviews and the surveys completed by students, the study found that specific skills (e.g., technical skills) were perceived by both students and recruiters to be important, as it relates to students being "work ready" (i.e., trained and prepared to meet the requirements of a specific profession) (Jacking & De Lange, 2009). Derous, Born, & Witte (2004) developed a scale to assess the experiences of job interview candidates during the preemployment process; specifically they were interested in general reactions toward the selection process, rather than applicant reactions to specific selection tools. The scale, "selection treatment beliefs," was originally developed as a 46 item scale during which 6 preemployment objectives were assessed: transparency (i.e., insight into the selection process), objectivity (i.e., equal opportunities for all candidates), feedback (i.e., feedback provided on the applicant's performance during the selection/recruitment process), job information (e.g., work conditions, task requirements, future career opportunities, organizational culture), participation (i.e., applicants want to exert control over their own behavior during the selection and recruitment process), and humane treatment (i.e., applicants want to be treated in a warm and respectful way during the recruitment/selection process). In addition, Schreurs, Derous, Proost, Notelaers, & De Witte (2008) developed a secondary measure of selection expectations; where in this study a comparison was made between selection expectations (of applicants) and various organizational outcomes (e.g., organizational attractiveness, job pursuit intentions, organizational prestige) (Schreurs et al., 2008). The authors found that (applicant) selection expectations were correlated with general organizational attractiveness, job pursuit intentions, organizational prestige, and person-organization fit.

Posner (1981) investigated differences in the perceptions held by recruiters, students, and faculty, relevant to important applicant and job characteristics. Some of the differences investigated included personality, sense of humor, and maturity. Posner (1981) found that the importance attached to job applicant characteristics was significantly different between students (i.e., applicants) and recruiters. Specifically, the recruiters viewed maturity and sense of humor as important relevant to applicants, and the students rated those factors as less important (Posner, 1981). Also, students perceived personal recommendations as important, while recruiters perceived personal recommendations as less important (Posner, 1981).

Many of the preemployment applicant reaction studies conducted were driven by one of two needs: (a) leading researchers that study recruitment have called for better research on applicant reactions (Ryan & Ployhart, 2000), and (b) justice researchers have suggested examining the preemployment applicant perspective through a social justice lens (Ryan & Ployhart, 2000). More recently a change in workplace demographics including the influx of Gen Y job seekers requires organizations to understand the experiences of the most recent entrants, specifically related to how they view the preemployment process. That is, previous research suggests that the preemployment stage involves two parties, including the organizations that seek employees, and the applicants that select where they will apply and ultimately work (Ryan & Ployhart, 2000). As such, this study seeks to identify and better understand the expectations, perceptions, and experiences of Gen Y job seekers. Drawing from previous research, it appears the following is true as it relates to the preemployment/selection experience. Schmitt and Gillliand (1992) found situational characteristics (e.g., test type, attitude of company representative) greatly influence procedural justice perceptions (i.e., how decisions are made) during the selection process. As a result, it may be helpful for organizations to provide explanations relevant to various assessment tools that are utilized during the preemployment stage (Morgeson & Ryan, 2009). We also know that job seekers like to be informed on why they were accepted or rejected (e.g., Ployhart & Maynard, 1999). This speaks to the idea that perceptions of fairness and transparency of selection decisions is highly valued.

OBJECTIVES OF THE STUDY

This study seeks to understand the recruitment experiences of Gen Y job seekers by addressing the following questions:

Research Question 1: Are there any discrepancies between what the Gen Y job seekers value as important during the recruitment process, and what actually occurs during the recruitment process?

Research Question 2: Do Gen Y job seekers perceive it's important to connect with recruiters/companies via social media outlets, during the recruitment and selection process?

Research Question 3: What attributes do the Gen Y job seekers perceive should be considered about their generation during the recruitment and selection process?

Research Question 4: What are the characteristics of a company that Gen Y job seekers would consider a "cool" work environment?

Research Question 5: Do they perceive that their age and lack of work experience is an advantage or disadvantage during the recruitment process?

METHOD

Participants and Procedures

Data was collected at a southern university during the Fall Semester of 2011, and there were a total of 397 students invited to participate in the survey. These classes were targeted because most of the students enrolled in the courses were preparing to graduate within 3-12 months, and several of the students were currently seeking postgraduation employment opportunities. In order to participate in the survey, the following criteria had to be met. First, the students had to be over the age of 18. In addition, they had to have completed at least the first round of the interview process (e.g., initial phone interview, initial in-person interview) with the organization within the last year. Next, the students had to be currently enrolled in the university in which the study was conducted. Finally, they had to be born between 1980-2000, which is the approximate birth years used to designate and identify members of the Millennial generation (e.g., Hershatter & Epstein, 2010).

Of the 397 students invited to participate in the study, 233 completed the survey, which indicates a response rate of 59%. Incentives were provided to the students that completed the survey. First, each of the participants was entered into a drawing for one of four prizes, each valued at $25.00. Next, 194 of the participants were offered extra credit from their instructors if they completed the survey.

The survey was administered over 8 weeks, and the students were initially made aware of their opportunity to participate in the study during an announcement made in class. After the initial announcement was made in class, the students were sent an e-mail, which included the link to the survey. During the initial announcement, the students were made aware of the criteria to participate in the study, and the basic premise of the study. Finally, the students were sent two reminders over e-mail encouraging them to complete the survey. The survey took approximately 25-30 minutes to complete, and there were a total of 52 questions on the survey. (The full set of results from the study is not reported in this chapter.) The respondents were informed that results would be used for research purposes only, and data were analyzed with identifying information removed.

Of the 233 participants that completed the survey, 132 of the participants were female (57% of the sample) and the remaining 101 participants were male (43% of the sample). Eighty-eight and four-tenths percent of the sample self-identified as White ($n = 199$), 7.6% self-identified as African American ($n = 17$), 1.8% self-identified as Asian ($n = 4$), 1.8% self-identified as Latino (i.e., Mexican, Mexican American, Chicano, Puerto Rican, Cuban, Cuban American, or some other Spanish, Hispanic, or Latino group) ($n = 4$), and 1 participant self-identified as Native American. The remaining 8 participants did not self-identify their race(s). The mean age was 21.4 years.

There were a variety of majors represented among the participants including: Management ($n = 72$), Business Administration ($n = 38$), Public Relations ($n = 31$), Accounting ($n = 18$), Building Science ($n = 12$), Engineering/Architectural Design ($n = 12$), Finance ($n = 11$), Marketing ($n = 10$), Education ($n = 7$), Hotel and Restaurant Management ($n = 6$), Health Services Administration ($n = 3$), and Other ($n = 13$). While the majority of the students were seniors ($n = 137$), the remaining students self-identified as sophomores ($n = 4$), juniors ($n = 45$), fifth year and beyond ($n = 46$), and there was one transfer student. Finally, the participants were asked to identify their postgraduation plans. The majority of the sample indicated their goal of working in Corporate America ($n = 126$). The remaining participants identified the following postgraduation plans: Attend graduate school ($n = 64$), "Start My Own Company" ($n = 31$), Work for a nonprofit organization ($n = 15$), Work for the State/Federal Government ($n = 15$), Work for a family-owned business ($n = 14$), Work in a university setting ($n = 12$), Work in healthcare ($n = 10$), Attend law school ($n = 10$), Enlist in the military ($n = 5$), Participate in missionary work ($n = 4$), Attend seminary school ($n = 3$), and Other ($n = 10$). The participants were asked to indicate their work status, and just under half of the sample worked at least 1-40 hours per week ($n = 108$). Of those currently employed, they worked an average of 23 hours per week.

MEASURES

Each participant voluntarily completed a survey that included a series of 52 questions about their recruitment experiences. The first *15 questions* of the survey were designed to collect demographic information about each survey participant (e.g., "what is your major"), and they were asked to enter their school e-mail address. The remaining *37 questions* were intended to assess the participant's reaction to various aspects of the recruitment process.

First, 24 items were intended to assess applicant reactions to the recruitment and selection process. Specifically, the 24 items were drawn from the Social Process Questionnaire on Selection-Importance (SPQS-I) and Social Process Questionnaire on Selection-Expectations (SPQS-E) scales developed by Derous, Born, & DeWitte (2004) in order to assess Gen Y applicant reaction to the recruitment and selection process. The Derous and colleagues (2004) scales tap 6 specific applicant reactions including: transparency (e.g., "In general I think it's important that recruiters make clear to candidates how information is gathered about them"), objectivity (e.g., "In general I think it is important that candidates can complain about the selection procedure toward appropriate persons"), feedback (e.g., "In general I think it's important that candidates receive feedback on test results from the recruiter who tested them"), job information (e.g., "In general, I think it's important that candidates are informed about the working conditions (e.g., wage, benefits, work schedule") during the selection process"), participation (e.g., "In general I think it's important that candidates are informed about the professional background of the recruiter (e.g., function, role, position in the organization), and humane treatment (e.g., "In general I think it's important recruiters reduce candidates' stress level during the selection procedure"). The 24 questions drawn from the Derous and colleagues (2004) scale were measured in two ways within this study. First, the respondents responded to each of the 24 items by rating the importance the statement on a 5-point Likert scale, where $1 = $ *very unimportant* to $5 = $ *very important*. For example, the respondents were asked the rate the importance of the following statement, "In general I think it's important that recruiters/ selectors make it clear why particular questions are asked during the selection process." Next, the respondents were asked to rate whether or not they experienced each of the 24 items. For example, "In general I think it's important that recruiters/selectors make it clear why particular questions are asked during the selection process," and "Was this explained to you by the recruiter?" The participant was prompted to answer "Yes," "No," or "N/A" related to his or her experience with a specific item. The purpose of asking the respondents whether they'd experienced each of the 24 items was to identify any discrepancies between the items that the respondents identified as important, and the extent to which they actually experienced those things they deemed important.

The next six items were specifically designed for this study, and the purpose of the questions was to understand the extent to which the participants deemed it important for recruiters to utilize social media to interact with Gen Y job seekers during the recruitment/selection process. Specifically, the participants were asked to identify whether the recruiter used each of the following social media tools: Facebook, LinkedIn, Twitter, personal blogs, YouTube, and interactive games/technology. There were four questions asked about the Gen Y job seeker's interest in connecting with prospective employers through online social networks (i.e., Facebook, LinkedIn, Twitter, and personal blogs). Previous research suggests that people enjoy connecting with prospective employers via online social networks because it allows them to display a significant amount of information about themselves for the purposes of obtaining employment (e.g., Piskorski, 2011). Finally, there was a single item specifically designed for this study that was used to assess the extent to which the participants perceived the recruiter was familiar with the university at which the study was conducted (i.e., "In general I think it's important that the recruiters are familiar with life at _____. That is, what the university stands for, what's popular at the university, etc.").

The social media questions were measured in two ways within this study. First, the students responded to each of the 6 items by rating the importance the statement on a 5-point Likert scale, where 1 = *very unimportant* to 5 = *very important*. For example, the respondents were asked to rate the importance of the following statement, "In general I think it's important that the recruiters try to build a relationship with me, by sending me a LinkedIn request." Next, the respondents were asked to identify whether the recruiter used each of the social media tools to reach out to them. For example, the full question stem read: "In general I think it's important that the recruiters try to build a relationship with me, by sending me a LinkedIn request", and "Did this happen?" The participant was prompted to select one of the following responses for this item: "No, this did not happen," "Yes. I received a LinkedIn request," or "Yes, but I decided not to accept their LinkedIn request." The purpose of asking the respondents whether the recruiter extended social media opportunities was to identify any discrepancies between the importance of each of the social media tools, and whether the recruiter utilized the specific social media tool.

The next six items were developed specifically for this study. Each of the items was open-ended, and they were included to allow the survey participants to share their recruitment experiences. The six open-ended questions were:

- If you think about some of the places that you would really like to work, describe why you like that environment, and why you think that environment is "cool?"
- What's important to you during the recruitment/selection process, that is, when you are interviewing for a position? What causes you to have a BAD experience?
- What's important to you during the recruitment/selection process, that is, when you are interviewing for a position? Do you set any specific goals? Do you want to be treated in a certain way? What causes you to have a GOOD experience?
- Do you perceive being a younger worker to be an advantage or disadvantage during the recruitment/selection process? Please explain why you chose advantage or disadvantage.
- Suppose you had a choice to work for an employer, or open your own business. Which would you prefer to do at this stage in your career? Please explain your choice of WHY you would prefer to work for an employer or open your own business.
- Do you have any additional comments or concerns that you want to express about your recruitment experiences?

The final question on the survey was intended to determine the attributes that companies should consider about Gen Y job seekers during the recruitment and selection process. In total, the participants were given a list of 19 attributes commonly considered during the recruitment and selection process (e.g., comfort with technology, personal appearance) and they were prompted to identify up to 10 attributes that should be considered about job seekers. Several of the attributes included in this question were drawn from the Posner (1981) study, while others were specifically written for this study.

RESULTS—RESEARCH QUESTION 1

The purpose of Research Question 1 was to determine if there is a gap between what Gen Y job seekers perceive as important during the recruitment process and what actually occurs during the recruitment process. In order to address this question, it is important to first identify what's important to the Gen Y job seekers during the recruitment process. The means of the 24 items that assessed applicant reactions were determined for the purpose of identifying the factors of the recruitment/selection process that are most important to Gen Y job seekers. Item means can be found in Table 4.1.

The results above are based on a 5-point Likert scale, where 4 and 5 are important and very important, respectively. A rating of 3 indicates that the statement is neither important, nor unimportant. The results included in Table 4.1 indicate the items that Gen Y job seekers identified as most important. The three most important aspects of the recruitment process included being treated in a courteous and polite manner by recruiters, being informed about their working conditions (e.g., wage, benefits, schedule), and being given the chance to present their strongest attributes during the recruitment and selection process. Related to research question 1, an additional purpose was to understand if there are discrepancies between what Gen Y job seekers identify as important, and what actually occurs during the recruitment process. In Table 4.2 an analysis is presented in which the means of the most important aspects of the recruitment process are compared to whether or not this practice is occurring.

The results presented in Table 4.2 indicate the items that are most important for Gen Y job seekers. It was found that there was generally *little discrepancy* between what they perceive is important and what actually occurs during the recruitment process. The exceptions to this statement include at least *five* aspects of the recruitment process. That is, more than half of the sample (56%) reported that they were not made aware of HOW information during the recruitment/selection process would be collected about them. Next, 37% of the sample was not informed about career perspectives within a prospective organization. In addition, nearly 1/4 of the sample reported that they did not feel they had a chance to show their strengths and potential contributions during the recruitment and selection process, nor did they perceive they had a chance to prove themselves during the recruitment and selection process (22% of the sample indicated this). Finally, approximately 21% of the sample indicated that they were not informed about the performance criteria that would be used to evaluate them; this was not explained during their recruitment and selection process.

There were two additional factors that Gen Y job seekers reported often did not occur. Specifically, while the Gen Y job seekers did not report this as being important (the mean was 3.2 on a 5 point scale), more than 70% of the respondents ($n = 162$) indicated that recruiters did not

Table 4.1. Means and Standard Deviations for Gen Y Applicant Reactions

Items	M	SD
• I expect the recruiters to behave in a courteous manner.	4.4	.84
• In general I think it's important that, I am informed about the working conditions (e.g., wage, benefits, work schedule) during the recruitment/selection process.	4.4	.93
• In general I think it's important that, recruiters/selectors treat me politely.	4.4	.88
• In general I think it's important that, all candidates receive equal opportunities to present their STRONGEST assets during the selection procedure.	4.2	.89
• In general I think it's important that, I get ample opportunity to prove myself during the recruitment/selection.	4.2	.90
• In general I think it's important that, recruiters received appropriate training to interview/test me during the recruitment process.	4.2	.96
• In general I think it's important that, I am informed about the performance criteria (i.e., how my performance will be evaluated) for the position to which I apply.	4.2	.89
• In general I think it's important that I am informed about the organization culture/products/services during the recruitment/selection process.	4.1	.90
• In general I think it's important that, questions/tests respect my privacy.	4.1	.93
• In general, I think it's important that, recruiters/company inform me honestly about my test performance, even if I didn't do well on the test(s) during the recruitment/selection process.	4.0	.96
• In general I think it's important that, I have the opportunity to withdraw from the selection procedure if I choose to withdraw.	4.0	.88
• In general I think it's important that I am informed about career perspectives within the organization during the selection process.	4.0	.96
• In general I think it's important that, recruiters/selectors make it clear to me HOW information is gathered about me (e.g., any web searches conducted, contact people I've listed as references).	4.0	1.04

Item	Mean	SD
• I expect the recruiters/company representatives to make me feel comfortable during the interview process.	4.0	.98
• In general I think it's important that, I am informed about the professional background of the recruiter/company representative (e.g., function, role, position in the organization) during the recruitment and selection process.	3.8	1.03
• In general I think it's important that, I receive feedback about test results (e.g., personality tests, cognitive ability tests) regardless of the outcome (e.g., whether they proceed to the next selection phase or not).	3.8	1.05
• In general I think it's important that, recruiters/selectors make clear to me WHAT kinds of information will be collected about the job seekers (e.g., interests, organizational membership).	3.8	.97
• In general I think it's important that, recruiters put me at ease upon my arrival to the interview.	3.7	1.05
• In general I think it's important that, recruiters reduce my stress level during the recruitment/selection procedure (e.g., interviews).	3.6	1.06
• In general I think it's important that, recruiters/selectors make it clear why particular questions are asked during the selection process.	3.6	.91
• In general I think it's important that the recruiters are familiar with "life at _____ university." That is, what the university stands for; what's popular at the university, etc.	3.6	1.07
• In general I think it's important that, recruiters/selectors make it clear why particular testing tools are used (e.g., personality tests, values assessments).	3.6	.92
• In general I think it's important that, I can complain about the selection procedure towards appropriate persons.	3.2	1.06
• In general I think it's important that, recruiters/selectors inform me about the number of persons applying for the same vacancy.	3.2	1.02

$N = 233$

Table 4.2. Reported Occurrences of Gen Y Recruitment Experiences

Items	Yes (This occurred)	No (This did not occur)	N/A
• I expect the recruiters to behave in a courteous manner.	212 (91%)	22 (9%)	
• In general I think it's important that, I am informed about the working conditions (e.g., wage, benefits, work schedule) during the recruitment/selection process.	203 (87%)	31 (13%)	
• In general I think it's important that, recruiters/selectors treat me politely.	216 (92%)	18 (8%)	
• In general I think it's important that, all candidates receive equal opportunities to present their STRONGEST assets during the selection procedure.	184 (78.5%)	50 (21.5%)	
• In general I think it's important that, I get ample opportunity to prove myself during the recruitment/selection.	182 (78%)	52 (22%)	
• In general I think it's important that, recruiters received appropriate training to interview/test me during the recruitment process.	198 (85%)	36 (15%)	
• In general I think it's important that, I am informed about the performance criteria (i.e., how my performance will be evaluated) for the position to which I apply.	186 (79%)	48 (21%)	
• In general I think it's important that I am informed about the organization culture/products/ services during the recruitment/selection process.	196 (84%)	38 (16%)	
• In general I think it's important that, questions/tests respect my privacy.	197 (84%)	37 (16%)	
• In general, I think it's important that, recruiters/company inform me honestly about my test performance, even if I didn't do well on the test(s) during the recruitment/selection process.	68 (29%)	41 (18%)	125 (53%)
• In general I think it's important that, I have the opportunity to withdraw from the selection procedure if I choose to withdraw.	57 (24%)	18 (8%)	159 (68%)
• In general I think it's important that I am informed about career perspectives within the organization during the selection process.	157 (63%)	77 (37%)	
• In general I think it's important that, recruiters/selectors make it clear to me HOW information is gathered about me (e.g., any web searches conducted, contact people I've listed as references).	104 (44%)	130 (56%)	
• I expect the recruiters/company representatives to make me feel comfortable during the interview process.	157 (67%)	19 (8%)	58 (25%)

$n = 233$

inform them of the number of people that applied for the same vacancy. Also, 64% of the respondents ($n = 149$) reported that it was not explained to them WHY certain selection devices (e.g., personality tests) were utilized. Also, 53% of the respondents ($n = 123$) stated that it was not explained WHY certain questions were asked during the selection process, and 44% of the respondents ($n = 103$) reported that they were not told about the kind of information that will be collected about the job seekers (e.g., interests, organizational membership) during the recruitment and selection process.

Finally, given the importance that Gen Y job seekers indicated about their experiences with recruiters, there was an open-ended question included on the survey that asked the participants to give specific examples of what they expect from recruiters during the interview process (i.e., above and beyond the recruiter being courteous and friendly). Specific insight is articulated through the quotes shared by a few of the survey respondents:

> I often find myself judging a potential job based on the people that I meet during the recruitment process. If recruiters/interviewers/employers make me feel welcome and wanted, then I tend to gravitate more toward that position. If *I don't feel comfortable* with recruiters, interviewers/employers or don't feel like I would fit in well, I start to reconsider my application.

> It is important that I don't *feel like the interviewer is talking down to me* or not giving me a fair chance. I would have a bad experience if I felt uncomfortable and like I was not being considered fairly.

> A bad experience from an interview would be a result of the interviewers being *unprepared, uninterested and unconcerned about me and my abilities* that I can bring to the company.

> I think it's bad when interviewers aren't prepared with *questions related to the job.*

> I had a bad experience with an awful and mean interviewer! She was mean to me and *downplayed my accomplishments* and made herself superior to me.

> I don't like it when they ask *absurd questions* like if you were a fruit, what fruit would you be?

> Things that are important to me are that the recruiter is polite, yet *brief.* The recruitment session *doesn't need to be 3 hours long, which has happened to me before.* A bad experience is one where the recruiter is either very rude, or cannot focus on the task at hand.

> What's important is that the company clearly gets across what it's trying to achieve in the long term and that I'm compatible with the company in

terms of personality, environment and goals. A bad interview experience is when the interviewer drills the candidate with questions, and *not allowing for any back and forth conversation.*

I think it's important that I get respect, as one adult to another, and that I am provided enough time to really be heard. I tend to be on the shy side so anyone who is *too stern or demanding looking,* like they are so important and they know it, will instantly turn me off.

The things that are important to me is that the recruiter not only is informative about the organization and the job the interview is for but that they also seem *interested and happy about their job and the organization.*

The recruiter should be *polite and share some information about their background* to make me feel more comfortable and welcome. They should also share fun experiences/activities they do at the school. Recruiters that are rude and don't share much about themselves or the school would create a bad experience.

It is important for me to get to know my recruiter and why they are looking to recruit. Do they just need a person to work, or are they interested in what I can bring to the company. *I want the company to want me for what I have to offer, not just because they need a warm body.* When it seems like the process is just a production line and not individualized, this disappoints me and turns the experience into a negative one.

It's important for my interviewer to have a *smile on their face* and to get to know me on a personal level in addition to their usual questions. A bad experience might occur if the interviewer makes me feel uncomfortable and acts like they are judging every word I am saying.

I like when the interviewer seems to actually be *interested in your responses and curious about your background* as opposed to interviewers who just read questions from a sheet and constantly write the whole time. I also like to have a good feel for where I stand at the end of the interview.

The recruiter should make me feel comfortable and welcomed into the company. They should share a *little of their background* with me to try to create a bond between us. They should be respectful, kind, and *well trained about the position they are looking to fill.* For a bad experience, when the recruiter doesn't make much eye contact, doesn't share any personal information, isn't well trained, and is somewhat rude."

RESULTS—RESEARCH QUESTION 2

The items intended to measure Research Question 2 included items related to the respondents' perceptions of the organization/recruiters connecting with them through social media outlets during the recruitment and selection process (e.g., Facebook, Twitter, LinkedIn). These questions were designed specifically for this study, and each survey participant was asked to address two questions, per social media outlet (a) In general I think it's important that the recruiter tries to build a relationship with me by using _____ (e.g., Facebook, LinkedIn), and (b) Did this happen? Further, if the survey respondent indicated that establishing this connection wasn't important, he or she was asked to explain why it wasn't important. The items were measured on a 5-point Likert scale, where the anchors included 1 = *not very important* and 5 = *very important*. The results from this question are reported in Table 4.3.

The results reported in Table 4.3 suggest that establishing a connection with the recruiter(s) through a social media outlet isn't perceived as very important to Gen Y job seekers. As indicated by the means, where a mean of 2 is not very important, and a mean of 3 is neither important nor unimportant, the averaged mean for any of the social media outlets did not exceed 2.7. In addition, fewer than 10% of the participants actually connected with the recruiter(s) through social media sites (e.g., Facebook, LinkedIn). Below, are examples of statements regarding *why* Gen Y job seekers are not interested in connecting with employers through various social media outlets:

> I want to keep my *personal life separated from work as much* as possible. Additionally, the truth is that if recruiters send you a FB request it's not to try and build a relationship with you, it's to essentially run an additional background check of sorts.

> I feel like Facebook is more of a way to connect with friends. *Until I am actually employed by someone, I wouldn't want a recruiter to contact me like that.*

> I wouldn't want the employer to receive any *premisconceptions*.

> Honestly, the *social networking sites* give the recruiters an opportunity to see some of the answers to questions that *they aren't allowed to ask in an interview.*

> Normally, a *Twitter account is not relevant* to someone's work ethic or work quality.

These findings go against the prevailing notion that the best way to communicate with Gen Y job seekers is through social media (e.g., Hershatter & Epstein, 2010). However, most of the studies that consider the advantages of connecting with Gen Yers through social media included a sample of Gen Y job seekers that were already employed by the organization. Therefore, organizations may have to consider other nonsocial

Table 4.3. Building a Connection Through Social Media

Item	Importance Rating, Mean	Importance Rating, SD	Did This Happen, Yes	Did This Happen, No
• In general I think it's important that, the recruiters try to build a relationship with me, by sending me a *Facebook* friend request.	M = 2.1	SD (1.02)	38	195
• In general I think it's important that, the recruiters try to build a relationship with me, by sending me a *LinkedIn* request.	M = 2.7	SD (1.16)	19	214
• In general I think it's important that, the recruiters try to build a relationship with me, by following me on *Twitter*.	M = 1.9	SD (1.02)	14	219
• In general I think it's important that, the recruiters try to build a relationship with me, by visiting my *blog page* (if it's included on my resume).	M = 2.4	SD (1.17)	9	224

media outlets to use during the preemployment phase in order to communicate with the Gen Y job seekers, and establish a social media connection with the Gen Yers after they are employed.

RESULTS—RESEARCH QUESTION 3

Research Question 3 was developed in order to assess the personal attributes/professional characteristics that Gen Y job seekers perceive organizations should consider. In part this question was included in the study because anecdotal evidence suggests that Gen Y job seekers are not coming to interviews dressed in professional attire. The notion here is perhaps Gen Y job seekers are not coming to interviews in professional attire because they do not perceive this as being important. Below, a list appears in which the personal attributes/professional characteristics are ranked-ordered from the most important to the least important attributes that Gen Y job seekers perceive organizations should consider during the recruitment and selection process. The results appear in Table 4.4.

As indicated in Table 4.4, the two most important characteristics that Gen Y job seekers perceive companies should consider about them during the recruitment and selection process are their ability to communicate effectively, and the candidate's personality. Further, more than 50% of the sample indicated that organizations should consider the additional, following factors: (1) personal appearance, (2) maturity, (3) future potential, (4) comfort with technology, (5) interest in company, and (6) previous/current work experience. Therefore, it does appear that Gen Y job seekers consider personal appearance, including appropriate attire to be important.

In comparison, the factors that Gen Y job seekers perceive are less important include faculty recommendations, whether they appear to be in good health/fit, and whether they've had an experience, including going to school or working overseas. Related to being in good health/fit, research suggests the following: (a) Gen Yers have much higher rates of obesity and less overall fitness, (b) there has been a social shift in what is perceived as being overweight where heavier people today are perceived as less overweight than they were a year ago, and (c) as a result of the aforementioned phenomena, there is less social pressure to exert the effort to maintain an ideal/healthy body weight (Deal et al., 2010). Given this finding, it may not be as surprising that Gen Y job seekers do not consider this as important of an attribute that employers should consider about them during the recruitment process.

Table 4.4. Characteristics That Should be Considered About Gen Y Job Seekers

Characteristic(s)	Percentage of Respondents That Indicated This Should Count
• *Ability to communicate*—i.e., organizations should consider how job candidates communicate	87.1
• *Personality*—i.e., organizations should consider the job candidate's personality	85.8
• *Personal Appearance*—organizations should consider how candidates dress	64.8
• *Maturity*—the organization should consider if the job candidate is mature	63.5
• *Future Potential*—i.e., organizations should consider whether job candidates are promotable	61.8
• *Comfort with Technology*—the organization should consider if the job candidate is technologically savvy (e.g., Skype job interview)	60.9
• *Interest in the Company*—the organization should consider if the job candidate has genuine interest in the company	60.7
• *Previous or Current Work Experience*—the organization should consider if the job candidate has relevant work history	52.8
• *Interview Preparedness*—i.e., coming to the interview well prepared	43.8
• *Interview Timeliness*—the organization should consider whether the job candidate comes to all interviews on time, including phone interviews	43.8
• *Grades/GPA*—organizations should consider grades and/or GPA	39.1
• *Knowledge of the Company*—the organization should consider if the job candidate has knowledge of the company—e.g., knowledge of company history, mission statement, company products and/or services, profits, revenue, recent press releases	36.5
• *Sense of Humor*—the organization should consider if the job candidate has a good sense of humor	36.1
• *Personal recommendations*—organizations should consider a letter of recommendation written by a personal friend, family member or other personal reference about a job candidate	31.9

96

- *Extra-curricular activities*—organizations should consider participation in extra-curricular activities such as community service, athletics, various organizations, fraternities and sororities   27.5

- *Faculty recommendations*—organizations should consider a letter of recommendation written by a faculty member about a job candidate   24.9

- *Good Health*—organizations should consider if the job candidate appears to be in good health/fit   24.9

- *Study Abroad*—(i.e., if the job applicant has participated in study abroad, worked overseas, volunteered overseas, or traveled overseas)   8.2

RESULTS—RESEARCH QUESTION 4

The purpose of research question 4, which was measured by an open-ended question, was to identify the factors of a work environment that Gen Y job seekers perceive to be "cool;" in other words this open-ended question wanted to discover what attracts Gen Y job seekers to organizations. A content analysis was performed on this question, and there were two major themes that emerged from the analysis, and one minor theme. The two major themes revolved around working in a *friendly environment*, where fellow coworkers are nice, approachable, helpful, and fun to work with. The second major theme spoke to Gen Y job seekers' desire to work in environments that are *stress free, unintimidating, and relaxed*. It appears Gen Y job seekers perceive that environments that lend themselves to stress, also result in lower productivity. In comparison, environments that are less structured, more relaxed, and stress-free result in higher productivity. Finally, although this was not mentioned with the same frequency as good coworkers and stress free environments, some of the survey respondents did mention *specific perks* that they would enjoy at their places of work. Some of the perks included things such as snacks, or a break room, while some described the more physical elements of the work environment (e.g., sitting near a window, not sitting in an office). Consistent with these themes, illustrative comments have been included to further explain each of the attributes that attract Gen Y job seekers to organizations.

Major Theme 1: Good Employees—Friendly Environments, The People Make The Place

An environment is "cool" if there is camaraderie among the employees; social events outside of the office that connect the employees on another level help create a more relaxed environment to work in. When this happens, people are more productive.

I love to work in a friendly, team oriented environment where people care about one another.

(The) Employees respect a younger workforce.

Friendly. The people know how to talk to me.

I would like to work in an environment that is fast paced and where there is a lot of interaction with my fellow employees. I would also like to work in a place that has great communication among its employees and one where everyone is open to working together.

I would like to work in an environment where the coworkers have good relationships with each other and you can have fun while still maintaining professionalism.

I love any environment that has a comfortable "homey" feeling, a place where you don't mind spending so much time.

I was the new guy and everyone else I was working with had been there at least 10 years and they made me feel welcomed and always helped me when I needed help.

An environment that allows me to be flexible throughout the week and with well trained and polite coworkers.

The relationships with my fellow coworkers. If the working environment is laid back and friendly.

I like an environment where people are friendly and not very judging. I like when customers are viewed in a positive light and management allows people to be "who they are."

I would like an environment where employees are able to talk to their superiors about different ideas they have, and are able to contribute to the company. I think it's essential for the environment to be one that fosters creativity and makes the employees comfortable.

I like an environment where the staff all get along and can joke together. I think it's "cool" when a group of employees can support each other and work together no matter the circumstances.

The environment is friendly, everyone gets along, you can be yourself, and we all have a common goal.

Environments that I find appealing are full of friendly, encouraging, well-mannered people. Work environments where fellow employees and managers are welcoming and polite make any kind of work more enjoyable.

Young, engaging culture that is inviting to recent grads.

Major Theme 2: Laid Back Environment, A Desire for Stress-Free Work Environment

Calm environment with minimal stress but very strong work instructions being provided.

Not formally structured.

I think it is important for a work environment to be welcoming, and not scary.

Low key, less stress and a friendly environment. Makes me want to perform at my highest level.

I would like to work in environments that are warm and inviting and laid back. I work best in environments where my stress levels aren't high.

The environment is casual and you are encouraged to bring your personality to the workplace, but the environment remains professional.

I like an environment that is somewhat relaxed and everyone is not so hard pressed for a deadline, however, you are still able to get all your work done in a timely manner.

There would be a good work relationship between coworkers and a laid back style office and humor.

Just enough pressure to make me work hard but not so much that it is a stressful environment.

The environment is not tense, but also not laid back where nothing gets accomplished. Coming into work should be something that I look forward to. I shouldn't have to worry about who I am going to get yelled at by that day.

Everyone would be detailed in what they expected in an unhostile environment.

I would like to work in an environment that is much more laid back or casual than a typical stuffy corporate cubicle workplace. I like open workplaces that encourage conversation and collaboration. Providing an inviting workplace makes your employees want to be there more often, and ultimately be more productive and happier.

It is laid back. People are nice and try to build a relationship with me. It is about getting the work completed in a timely fashion, but bosses and coworkers don't come across as abrasive.

I'd like something laid back and easy going, yet down to business. No need for excess and stress.

Everyone had the same laid back personality and we could make jokes. It was a "low stress" environment.

In an environment where everyone is laid back, I would think that was "cool" because you would be able to interact with your fellow employees and employers on a more personal level which is always nice.

Semirelaxed atmosphere. I don't like seeing employees on edge all the time. But I also need to see a certain level of discipline in the employees. If I want to work there, regardless of the job, I want to be able to relate to and get along with the people I work with.

Minor Theme: Perks Desired at Work

I would like to work in an *open room* because it's welcoming.

There is a *break room and kitchen area*—preferably with free drinks and water. It's a fun colorful environment.

I like having my own desk with a *window* to see outside. It's important for me to be able to see plants outside so I don't feel like work is more like a trap.

I traveled to Ventura to visit my aunt one summer. One of her best friends works in a high position at Patagonia's headquarters. She gave my aunt and me a tour of the headquarters, and the work environment was incredible. They could *dress comfortably* (but neatly) in whatever they wished. Lunch breaks could be spent working out or *playing outside* and the company actually encouraged it. The company also fed their employees *two meals* a day from *an all-natural, organic kitchen* featuring vegan chefs.

I would like an environment that has *break rooms and a casual dress code*.

RESULTS—RESEARCH QUESTION 5

The purpose of the last open-ended question that will be discussed in this chapter is to understand whether the Gen Y job seekers surveyed in this study perceived their age (and lack of work experience) to be an advantage or a disadvantage during the job search process. Of the 233 respondents, 126 respondents (54%) stated that their age/lack of work experience was an advantage. For the respondents that stated that their age was an advantage, the reasons they perceived it was advantage was related to one of eight themes. Specifically, age was perceived as an advantage because: (1) they have technical expertise, (2) they are career driven, (3) they have more opportunity for career growth, (4) they have innovative ideas, (5) they can work more flexible schedules, (6) they have a willingness to work for lower salaries, (7) they are trainable, and (8) they are less likely to turnover. Table 4.5 presents the reasons that Gen Y job seekers perceive their age as an advantage, by theme. In addition, a set of illustrative comments appear after Table 4.5, which provide more specific descriptions of the reasons that Gen Y job seekers perceive their age as an advantage during the recruitment and selection process.

Theme 1: My Age is an Advantage During the Recruitment/Selection Process

Technical Expertise

In some ways we have an advantage because we are more adept with technology.

More up to date on technology.

I believe being younger is an advantage because I'm more up to date with technology and the new strategies the companies are running today.

I perceive it to be an advantage. With technological innovation ever increasing, the youngest generation oftentimes has the upper hand when it comes to this factor.

I think that it is an advantage because of the schooling I have received and because I feel like I would be better with technology than most older potential employees.

Table 4.5.   Reasons That Gen Y Job Seekers Perceive Their age is an Advantage During the Recruitment/Selection Process

Reason	Percentage of Respondents That Stated This Reason
Technical expertise	31
Innovative ideas	27
Trainable/willingness to learn	17
Career growth, potential	10
Flexible schedules	6
Willingness to work for lower salary	5
Will stay with the organization for a longer period of time/less likely to turnover	4

Being a younger worker I think has become an advantage because of technology and how fast it is someone younger can grasp it.

An advantage because my generation is more tech savvy than the older generations. Technology is getting more important each year.

I think it is an advantage because the Gen Y generation knows more about technology. I know I am able to pick up new technology skills quicker than the baby boomer generation.

Innovative Ideas

Advantage. Young people bring new ideas and can advance up in a company rather quickly. Plus younger people have taken over our generation.

An advantage because I have new ideas and the most recent education.

I see it as an advantage because with my age comes fresh new ideas and I would think it would be easier for me to adjust to a new work environment.

Trainable/Willingness to Learn

Advantage, more willingness to learn.

Advantage, because they can be easily trained and eager to learn.

Younger workers are more energetic and more open to learning new things.

Advantage because I'm ready to learn.

An advantage because I have fresh, new ideas in my career and am willing to learn!

Career Growth Opportunities

I believe it is an advantage, because younger individuals have more room for growth.

I consider being young as an advantage. Younger people tend to be more outgoing and interested in furthering their career.

Advantage. I have the opportunity to move up.

Flexible Schedules

The job I worked at required long hours and a lot of "out of office" time. Since I am younger and have a flexible schedule, I think this was to my advantage.

Advantage. We might have more energy where we could work longer hours, or do more intense work.

Willingness to Work for Lower Salaries

Advantage. I think that today recruiters don't want to pay as much as they did in the past. Recent grads with no experience can start at a lower salary and are essentially a "clean slate" to be molded.

Advantage, because employers think they can pay you less so you're more hirable.

Advantage. Companies know they can offer low salary numbers and still get you.

Less Likely to Turnover

I think that is an advantage. If you are younger, you more than likely have intentions of staying/being able to work with the company for a longer period of time. You are probably more physically capable if you are younger, and may be more appreciative of the job since you may not have ever held a real full time job before.

Advantage, because I have more time to spend with the company. (Less likely to turnover)

In comparison, 77 respondents (33%) stated that their age was a disadvantage. The four key themes that evolved from the content analysis related to *why* Gen Y job seekers perceive their age to be a disadvantage included: (1) less work experience, (2) they perceive their opinions and/or suggestions are not taken seriously, (3) they are perceived as overly confidant, or (4) there is a general lack of respect for younger workers in some work environments. Of the four themes that resulted in the content analysis, most Gen Y job seekers perceived a lack of work experience as the most important reason, that their age is a disadvantage during the recruitment and selection process. Finally, 30 respondents (13%) indicated that age could be *both* an advantage and a disadvantage (approx. 1/3 of the sample, or $n = 77$). Below, several illustrative comments are presented, which give further insight into why the Gen Y job seekers perceive their age and lack of work experience to be an advantage or a disadvantage.

Theme 2: My Age is a Disadvantage During the Recruitment/Selection Process

My age is a Disadvantage due to Less Work Experience

I think it is a disadvantage simply because being a younger worker usually means less experience, and having experience is generally what gets a person hired.

Older people have more experience.

Being a young worker could make things more difficult if they are looking for someone with more experience.

It is a disadvantage because there aren't a ton of jobs out there in this economy and I feel like companies would probably rather hire people with experience during this time.

As a disadvantage, I don't have the usual three or more years' experience.

I think it can be a disadvantage because many recruiters may think that younger workers do not have as much work experience and they may look for someone older who has worked a little bit more and longer.

I feel like being a younger worker is a disadvantage in the current economy due to older, more experienced workers who may be willing to work at lower level positions for less money.

I believe that it is a disadvantage. I think that there are a lot of people looking for jobs. I think that companies want people with experience and when I have just graduated from college I do not have the same amount of experience as an older worker who has been in the business longer, and I think that people look down on that.

Disadvantage because I am competing against so many experienced, unemployed applicants in the present economy.

My Age is a Disadvantage Because my Opinions/Suggestions are not Taken Seriously

Disadvantage. People treat me like I don't know what I'm talking about because I'm young, even though I am qualified for the job.

Disadvantage. Older people don't take us seriously.

Disadvantage because sometimes I feel like older people do not take you seriously. You do not have the life experiences they do. And sometimes they think hiring a younger worker will cause them to have to train you more and answer more questions causing them more work.

My Age is a Disadvantage Because I am Perceived as Overly Confident

Disadvantage. Looked as cocky. (Perceived as overly confident)

My age is a disadvantage because there is a lack of respect for younger workers

Disadvantage, they think that they can just push you around. (Lack of respect for younger workers)

Disadvantage, you get looked down on. (Lack of respect for younger workers)

LIMITATIONS AND FUTURE RESEARCH

One of the limitations of this study is that the survey participants were not surveyed throughout the entire recruitment and selection process. Therefore, it is impossible to conclude how the perceptions that Gen Y job seekers have of various aspects of the preemployment process (e.g., whether the recruiter was nice) impacts their decision to join the organization. Future research can address this by gathering data incrementally throughout the recruitment process. Moreover, specific hypotheses can be tested which would allow the researcher to study various recruitment outcomes (e.g., organizational attraction, job choice intentions). Another limitation includes the survey results were exclusive to the perspective of job seekers. Future research should include a matched sample design, where the recruiters/organizational representatives and the Gen Y job seekers are asked to respond to the same set of items. Also, given the exploratory nature of this study, there were no outcome measures included in the study. Some of the outcome measures typically included in applicant reaction studies include organizational attractiveness, job pursuit intentions, intentions toward the organization, attitude toward the company, (job) acceptance intention, withdrawal, job acceptance (e.g., Ryan & Ployhart, 2000). Future studies could explore relationships between several of the factors included in this study (e.g., perception of fair treatment by the recruiter) and any of the aforementioned outcome variables.

Further, related to Research Question 3, where the respondents were asked to identify the most important set of attributes that should be considered about Gen Y job seekers, it would have been helpful to rate the importance of each attribute. That is, the respondents were asked to indicate up to 10 attributes that should be considered. While this may be meaningful, it doesn't allow the respondent to indicate the relative importance of each attribute. For example, while personality and ability to communicate may both be important to a given applicant, there is no way to determine which of those two attributes is considered by the applicant as most important in terms of what an organization should value. Finally, related to the Research Question 2, connecting with job seekers via social media, it would have been informative to understand why it's desirable for the small set of respondents that value connecting with recruiters and organizations through various social media outlets.

IMPLICATIONS

While a commonly held notion among employers may have been that Gen Y workers enjoy work spaces with various technological options, there is a lot of value put on the type of *people* with whom Gen Y job seekers will work. As a result, it is important to ensure that recruiters are trained to interview candidates, and it's also important for the management team to create a supportive work environment for new employees. This may be achieved through organizing gatherings for employees to attend, during which new employees are introduced to various coworkers. Moreover, it will be important for management to identify the expected contributions they expect new employees to make to the work team, as this will encourage the existing employees to be more open and welcoming toward the Gen Y employees that join their organization. Below, there is a brief description of more specific implications for each of the research questions included in the study.

Research Question 1—Implications

The Gen Y job seekers included in this sample generally experienced little discrepancy between their expectations of what should occur during the recruitment and selection process, and what actually did occur. However, organizations could address a few of the discrepancies that occurred in the following matter:

- Organizations should make it transparent to candidates *how* information is gathered about them during the recruitment and selection process. While organizations have to notify candidates that a credit and/or background check is being conducted, there is no other official notification required. To the extent that organizations are transparent, and make it known to job seekers *how* information is gathered (e.g., when references will be called, what information will be asked of the references, what data is collected over social media outlets, what information is verified through a college registrar office), perceptions of procedural justice will be higher, and candidates will be more attracted to the organization, and more likely to accept a job offer.

- Organizations should provide meaningful descriptions of the career and development opportunities that exist, contingent on the employee's performance. Some of the specific details that could be shared during the recruitment and selection process include a description of a how a career development plan is initiated and maintained, and the organization could provide several success stories of employees that have been promoted internally as result of superior performance. In order to attract Gen Y job seekers, it would be helpful to provide specific examples of Gen Y employees that have experienced success within a given organization.

- Aside from asking about strengths and weaknesses during the interview process, organizations could allow interview candidates to share a portfolio of their work. This portfolio could be shared in-person or via e-mail. The portfolio would allow each applicant to demonstrate their strengths, describe potential contributions, and prove themselves worthy of consideration during the recruitment and selection process. The portfolio might include the following contents: (a) demonstrations of work completed while enrolled in college, (b) writing samples, (c) graded assignments, which include feedback from instructors, (d) and additional expressions of the candidate including books read, blogs created, organizations started while in school, academic accomplishments, and summary of volunteer work. By allowing Gen Y job seekers to share a portfolio of their work, the candidates are allowed ample opportunity to demonstrate their strengths. Further, organizations are able to gather more information that will allow them to assess the extent to which there is a strong person-job and person-organization fit across the job seekers.

- Organizations should clearly explain both the performance criteria and how the performance criteria will be evaluated. Anecdotal evidence suggests that the performance of Gen Y employees increases significantly to the extent that they have clear expectations of what they are expected to achieve and how they will be evaluated. Related to the recruitment and selection process, perceptions of procedural justice (and subsequently organizational attraction) should increase to the extent that Gen Y job seekers understand both the performance criteria and how their performance will be evaluated.

Research Question 2—Implications

Although the Gen Y job seekers are very active on multiple social media sites, this does not appear to be a method they enjoy using to interact with prospective employers. Relative to this sample, this lack of desire to connect with prospective employers also included LinkedIn, a top social media tool used by many organizations. One of the concerns that Gen Y job seekers may have relative to social media tools is they are not aware of the type of information that is gathered about them over social media. As indicated by the following comment, "Honestly, the social networking sites give the recruiters an opportunity to see some of the answers to questions that they aren't allowed to ask in an interview," it appears that overall it is unclear to some Gen Y job seekers what employers hope to accomplish by connecting with them. Therefore, to the extent that organizations are more transparent about their intentions and the type of information they will review, should they connect with candidates over social media, this should result in higher procedural justice perceptions. In addition, an organization could use a very strategic approach in connecting with job seekers over social media during the recruitment and selection process. As an example, an organization could encourage someone from the organization that has a shared affiliation with the candidate to reach out to them over social media; perhaps an alumnus of the university that is currently employed at the organization could reach out to the job seeker. Alternatively, an organization could create a group (LinkedIn, Twitter) or a page (Facebook) where they encourage Gen Y job seekers to join their group, or visit their page. For example, Deloitte has a Facebook page, "Your Future at Deloitte (U.S.)," which includes a variety of information including conferences at which Deloitte will be recruiting, examples of current employees and the contributions they've made during their time at Deloitte (e.g., tax professionals), and awards that Deloitte has received (e.g., recognized as a top ten employer for working women).

Research Question 3—Implications

Research Question 3 was written in a way that does not warrant any specific recommendations, as the questions asked the survey respondents to identify the attributes that should be considered about Gen Y job seekers during the recruitment and selection process. However, there is at least one important conclusion that can be drawn from the responses that appear in Table 4.3. That is, it is likely that the attributes that the respondents identified as important are consistent with what the respondents perceive as their strengths. Therefore, despite having relatively less work experience (given that all members of the sample are currently enrolled in college), they do perceive they will contribute specific attributes to a company, and consequently these attributes should be considered. Utilizing a cut-off score of 50%, where at least 50% of the sample indicated that this attribute should be considered, the following attributes were identified: ability to communicate, personality, personal appearance, maturity, future potential, and comfort with technology. Consistent with anecdotal evidence, it is not surprising that Gen Y job seekers think that organizations should consider their comfort with technology. Many Gen Y job seekers consider this as one of their most significant strengths. Finally, the attributes that the Gen Y job seekers think organizations should consider are likely consistent with the training and experiences they've gained during their time in college (e.g., communication skills, personality).

Research Question 4—Implications

The purpose of asking the survey respondents this question was to assist organizations in understanding what Gen Y job seekers perceive to be indicative of a "cool" work environment, and subsequently what will attract them to the organization. This question has generated a lot of articles that have appeared in both the popular press and academic outlets. Examples of factors thought to attract Gen Y job seekers to organizations include flexible hours (e.g., positive work-life balance, ability to spend time with family), opportunities for promotion, personalized career development planning, recognition and rewards, and a welcoming environment (e.g., good rapport with bosses and coworkers, relationships with decision-makers) (see Lowe, Levitt, & Wilson, 2008). Consistent with previous findings, the survey respondents in this study emphasized the importance of working in a friendly work environment, where they can openly express their ideas and suggestions, and they want to avoid working in a stressful work environment, and environments with a lot of stringent rules. The good news for employers is, the preferences mentioned by the Gen Y job seekers in this sample are relatively easy and inexpensive to address. That is, in comparison to attracting Gen Y job seekers with the most recent technology, or attracting them with higher salaries, or providing tuition reimbursement, these job seekers desire to work in a welcoming environment. Organizations can achieve this by training and preparing their current workforce for the entrance of Gen Y employees. This training might be managed in two parts, where the initial training is for current employees. The purpose of this initial training is to help the current employees understand the role of the new Gen Y employees, the skills that they bring to the organization, and the expected contribution of Gen Y employees. The second training may occur once the Gen Y employees join the organization, and the purpose of this training would be to help all members of the workforce understand the value of working in teams, and gather ideas about how teams may be utilized to achieve a specific department or organizational objective. In addition, an introduction of all employees could be done, where each employee's profile is shared with all the employees with whom they are likely to interact, and the profile includes information related to strengths, skills, areas of expertise, and the like. Typically that information is only available to management and/or human resource staff that must make personnel decisions. However, providing this information to a wider audience will allow the employees to better understand how various people within the organization with whom they have to work, partner, or interact are valuable to the overall performance of the organization and within a specific unit. Finally, another initiative an organization could try would be to match mentors with those Gen Y employees that desire this match. A mentor would be responsible for ensuring that the employees are assigned meaningful work, but they would also provide guidance to a Gen Y employee who perceived she or he was not working in a friendly environment, or was mistreated by a fellow employee. It is sometimes easier for employees to voice their concerns related to how they are being treated in a work environment to someone who is not directly responsible for evaluating their performance.

Research Question 5—Implications

Research Question 5 was not written with the intention of providing recommendations. Rather it was written to give Gen Y job seekers an opportunity to share their feelings about whether their age (and subsequent lack of experience) is an advantage, or not, during the time they were on the job market. In short, just over half the respondents perceived their age to be an advantage, and almost all respondents acknowledged that they have relatively less work experience. From an organization's viewpoint, the perspective that the respondents held relative to age are favorable, as this suggests that the Gen Y job seekers are relatively confident in the contribution they can make to an organization, albeit their age. They have a strong desire to learn, and they are prepared to share their technical expertise with a new employer. In short, if given a chance, Gen Y job seekers appear to be a safe bet for employers to make, and one that will result in hiring among a workforce that is ready to work hard, wants to make a contribution, and desires to learn. However, as stated previously, it will be important for organizations to train their current workforce about the value that Gen Y workers add to their organization, and it will be important for organizations to ensure that the Gen Y workers feel psychologically safe within their new work environment.

CONCLUSION

The purpose of the study described in this chapter was to survey Gen Y job seekers in order to gain a clearer understanding of the expectations of the recruitment process. Specifically, this study focused on the preemployment phase that is likely to begin during on-campus interviews, at a career fair, or over the phone. The aim of this study was to inform organizations that seek to attract Gen Y workers about what is important during the preemployment phase. Based on this notion, the following *four* conclusions were drawn as evidenced by the empirical and qualitative results and implications discussed previously.

In order to maintain high procedural justice perceptions, organizations must treat candidates fairly by informing them about *how* information is gathered during the preemployment phase. As an example, many of the Gen Y candidates desire to know more about how information is gathered: will the organization conduct a web search, will they conduct a search on Facebook, will they call personal and professional references, and the like. In addition, the candidates also want to know *how* the information gathered will be used by the companies during the preemployment phase. As an example, if the company views the applicant's Facebook page, how will any pictures or comments viewed on their Facebook page impact decisions that an organization makes during the preemployment phase? This is *very* unclear to the average Gen Y job seeker, and uncertainly lends itself to Gen Y job seekers being less attracted to the organization. Also, Gen Y job seekers want to know *WHY* certain selection devices (e.g., personality tests) were utilized. Secondly, companies can sustain the Gen Y job seeker's interest during the preemployment phase by being transparent; where transparency is also related to (procedural and distributive) justice perceptions. Specifically, Gen Y job seekers want to know more about the organization's career opportunities that would be available to them and they desire to know the performance criteria that will be used to evaluate their position. In addition to being treated fairly, the applicants also value being informed about their working conditions (e.g., wage, benefits, schedule), and being given the chance to present their strongest attributes during the recruitment and selection process. In sum, in order to attract Gen Y applicants, the findings in this study suggest that these job seekers prefer companies that are transparent and will treat them fairly.

The most popular choice for postgraduation plans was seeking opportunities in corporate America, despite the fact that not all people in this sample were enrolled in the College of Business. While Gen Y is often perceived as an innovative generation that seeks to start their own businesses, many of the students in this sample preferred to gain work experience in a more structured environment before stretching out and starting their own business.

Despite prevailing notions and the ever-growing population of companies that seek to attract Gen Y job seekers over various social media platforms (e.g., Twitter, Facebook), the Gen Y job seekers represented in this sample don't desire to build a connection with organizations within a social media domain; at least not immediately. Rather, the Gen Y job seekers represented in the sample prefer that companies advertise over social media (e.g., job openings, information about the company culture, videos of current employees) but they *do not want* the company to extend an invitation to connect during the preemployment phase. Rather, the Gen Y job seekers articulated a desire to connect with an organization within a social media domain *after* they have been hired by the organization. However, this is not to suggest that establishing a "connection" with the Gen Y job seekers is not important. In fact they do want to establish a connection with the organization during the preemployment phase, but they prefer to do this during face-to-face interactions; which do not include Skype interviews! The Gen Y job seekers in this sample are especially sensitive to how they are treated during face-to-face interactions. For example, they want to interact with company representatives (e.g., a member of the human resource team, hiring managers, recent alumni) that appear to be genuinely interested in them. The also desire to interact with company representatives that actively listen, and ones that "care about what they have to say during the interviews." They want to be able to express their views, and share with the company who they are and what they value. They don't want to be hired just for the organization to fill an open position, rather they want the organization to hire them due to their unique personality, and to the extent that their individuality will be celebrated within the organization. Also, their perception of whether an organization cares about them is essential. Thus, rather than companies spending money on furthering their social media presence, organizations are better served by: (1) assigning organizational representatives that are relatable to Gen Y job seekers to their recruitment teams, (2) assigning organizational representatives that are passionate about their job and the organization to their recruitment teams, and (3) making sure that the organizational representative that is responsible for the initial interview is well informed and can thoroughly explain *how* the entire recruitment and selection process works at the company (e.g., information gathered, timeliness of decisions, selection criteria). Finally, organizations should also make sure that organizational representatives are familiar with the university's culture, traditions, and values, as that is likely something they can use to establish an initial connection with Gen Y job seekers.

The survey respondents were asked to identify the characteristics that they deemed organizations should consider across Gen Y job seekers. The most popular choices included: ability to communicate, applicant personality, personal appearance, maturity, future potential, comfort with technology, and interest in the company. The characteristics that the Gen Y job seekers value as important for organizations to consider likely also translate into what they perceive as their strengths during the preemployment process. Consequently, organizations should understand the strengths that this group of job seekers perceives they offer the organization, and communicate those strengths with current job holders, especially those job holders that are not members of the Millennial generation. Expressing the strengths of the Gen Y job seekers will likely ease the transition and inclusion of Gen Y employees into a workforce and help non-Gen Yers understand the immediate contribution that these newly hired employees can make. Finally, if company representatives acknowledge the strengths Gen Y job seekers bring to the organization, this may help to offset the insecurities that some Gen Y job seekers have, given that most have less work experience. In conclusion, while organizations can implement several types of retention programs, all of this work is in vain if companies do not initially attract Gen Y job seekers during the preemployment phase.

REFERENCES

Anderson, N., Salgado, J. F., & Hulsheger, U. (2010). Applicant reactions in selection: Comprehensive meta-analysis into reaction generalization versus situational specificity. *International Journal of Selection and Assessment, 18*(3), 291-304.

Brazeel, S. (2009). Recruitment practices and generational characteristics. *Offshore, 69*(12), 2-2.

Broadbridge, A., Maxwell, G., & Ogden, S. (2007). Students' views of retail employment—key findings from generation Ys. *International Journal of Retail & Distribution Management, 35*(12), 982-992.

Deal, J. D., Altman, D. G., & Rogelberg, S. G. (2010). Millennials at work: What we know and what we need to do (if anything). *Journal of Business Psychology, 25,* 191-199.

Derous, E., Born, M., & De Witte, K. (2004). How applicants want and expect to be treated: Applicants' selection treatment beliefs and the development of the social process questionnaires on selection. *International Journal of Selection and Assessment, 12,* 99-119.

Elmore, L. (2009). Generation gaps. *Women in Business, 62*(2), 8-11.

Harold, C. M., & Ployhart, R. E. (2008). What do applicants want? Examining changes in attribute judgments over time. *Journal of Occupational and Organizational Psychology, 81,* 191-218.

Hershatter, A., & Epstein, M. (2010). Millennials and the world of work: An organizational and management perspective. *Journal of Business Psychology, 25,* 211-223.

Jackling, B., & De Lange, P. (2009). Do accounting graduates' skills meet the expectations of employers? A matter of convergence or divergence. *Accounting Education: An International Journal, 18*(4), 369-385.

Johnson, M., & Johnson, L. (2010). *Generation Inc.: From boomers to linksters-managing the friction between generations at work.* New York, NY: American Management Association.

Lowe, D., Levitt, K. J., & Wilson, T. (2008). Solutions for retaining generation y employees in the workplace. *Business Renaissance Quarterly, 3*(3), 43-57.

McCrindle, M. (2010). Management: Generation Y at work—Part 2: A snapshot of emerging leaders. *Keeping Good Companies, 62*(9), 566-569.

Morgeson, F. P., & Ryan, A. M. (2009). Reacting to applicant perspectives research: What's next? *International Journal of Selection and Assessment, 17*(4), 431-437.

Piskorski, M. (2011). Social strategies that work. *Harvard Business Review, 89*(11), 116-122.

Ployhart, R. E., & Maynard, D. C. (1999, April). *Broadening the scope of applicant reactions research: An exploratory investigation of the effects of job characteristics and level of competition.* Unpublished paper presented at 14th annual SIOP meeting, Atlanta, Ga.

Posner, B. (1981). Comparing recruiter, student, and faculty perceptions of important applicant and job characteristics. *Personnel Psychology, 34,* 329-339.

Ryan, A. M., & Ployhart, R. E. (2000). Applicants' perceptions of selection procedures and decisions: A critical review and agenda for the future. *Journal of Management, 26*(3), 565-606.

Schmitt, N., & Gilliland, W. (1992). Beyond differential prediction: Fairness in selection. In D. M. Saunders (ed.), *New approaches to employee management: Fairness in employee selection* (Vol. I, pp. 21-46). Greenwich, CT: JAI Press.

Schreurs, B., Derous, E., Proost, K., Notelaers, G., & De Witte, K. (2008). Applicant selection expectations: Validating a multidimensional measure in the military. *International Journal of Selection and Assessment, 16*(2), *170*-176.

Smith, K. (2009). Gaining the edge: Connecting with millennials. *Air Force Journal of Logistics, 33,* 2-60.

CHAPTER 5

GIVING VOICE TO VALUES

Engaging Millennials and Managing Multigenerational Cultures

Jessica McManus Warnell

INTRODUCTION

Engaging Millennials toward effective organizations involves acknowledging their capacities, inclinations, strengths and challenges. A useful approach for those who educate, recruit, hire and manage Millennials develops these capacities and prompts effective leadership at all levels of the organization. *Giving Voice to Values* is a program of research, dialogue and curriculum focused on developing values-based decision making, action and leadership for current and emerging professionals. Through skill-building curriculum and publications, *Giving Voice to Values* (GVV) identifies and explores the many ways that professionals can voice and implement their values in the face of countervailing pressures—and can share this capacity with their organizations. This chapter describes the GVV curriculum, designed and directed by Mary C. Gentile, as a resource for corporations and other organizations as they engage Millennials and manage multigenerational cultures.[1]

Managing Human Resources for the Millennial Generation, pp. 117–137
Copyright © 2012 by Information Age Publishing
117

Business students and emerging professionals, and those who manage them, are operating within a dichotomy. In the context of the seemingly never-ending parade of business scandals, business has been routinely criticized as a scourge, with b-schools churning out "economic vandals" (*The Economist*) and business leaders plundering society's spoils. The alternate message is that business is a salvation—the source of a new generation of leaders with the acumen and passion to employ the strengths of the business paradigm—scale, innovation and strategy, among others—to solve the world's most pressing problems. This paradox is reflected in the challenge and promise of capitalizing on the energy and commitment of Millennials.

This opportunity exists in the context of a multigenerational organizational culture facing urgent societal challenges. Organizations are necessarily prompted by sustainability concerns, response to financial challenges, and increasing market and societal demand toward a triple bottom line approach to management—a systematic approach that pursues financial, social and environmental goals in a changing, global context. Research indicates that young people studying business often possess a strong commitment to prosocial enterprise, intending to work for organizations with missions that align with their values—including social engagement, sustainability, and other ethical concerns. At the same time, managers are said to struggle with engaging these young professionals in a manner that channels that interest into productive and measurable change within a diverse professional context.

Additionally, today's globalized organizations demand actionable skills for ethical decision making. A common lament from recruiters and managers of these young professionals is the gap between a solid grasp of theoretical foundations and the skills to move toward decision making and implementation. Educating and managing young people in a manner that bridges the gap between intention and action is key. *Giving Voice to Values* (GVV) is a practical program of study that draws on social psychology, cognitive neuroscience and management research to focus less on ethical reasoning and decision making and more on ethical action. GVV offers a resource for corporations to acknowledge and cultivate opportunity in the face of challenges arising from managing Millennials. Millennials can and do act on their values, and organizations can develop mechanisms to foster values-based decision making in a way that supports organizational culture and furthers shared goals. This chapter explores the key tenets of the GVV approach, including values alignment and implementable skills, and its particular promise for organizations seeking to provide developmental support and capitalize upon the gifts and motivations of Millennials.

MILLENNIALS AND MULTIGENERATIONAL CULTURES

Much emerging research explores characteristics of Millennials in the professions, including sources in this volume; a general consensus emerges around several key features and differences across generational cohorts (Hershatter & Epstein, 2010; Kowske, Rasch & Wiley, 2010; Meriac, Woehr, & Banister, 2010; Myers & Sadaghiani, 2010; Ng, Schweitzer, & Lyons, 2010; Smola & Sutton, 2002; Walker, 2009). Though we must acknowledge that generalizations have limitations, it remains critical for managers and professionals to consider trends in Millennial experiences and capacities. Several key characteristics include technological fluency and facility with social media, proclivity to multitask, and teamwork capacities. Millennials prefer training and mentorship to reflect sustained and personal attention—they explicitly favor regular and open communication with those who supervise them. In addition, they value meaningful and fulfilling work (Lancaster & Stillman, 2002; Yang & Guy, 2006) and reflect increasing awareness of social and environmental sustainability issues. Thus, Millennials present a paradox of challenges and opportunities—not unlike the complex perception and role of business in society, noted above.

Interestingly, empirical studies indicate that although broad generational differences can be observed between Millennials and other age groups, specific characteristics of cohorts may differ by institution (Stewart & Bernhardt, 2010). Managers are encouraged to interpret this data as it applies to their own companies. This finding prompts a consideration of how these differences are experienced and addressed. Thus, if institution or context matters, so do pedagogy and training, or the approaches we use to confront these differences—context and content of these approaches can impact results. How these differences are acknowledged, explored and translated into actionable employment skills can be enhanced through strategic approaches. *Giving Voice to Values* is one such approach. By incorporating key tenets of the GVV approach, managers and other professionals can identify tangible strategies to enhance Millennial engagement and effectively manage multigenerational cultures.

EXPLORING CONTEXT

Before exploring the specific characteristics of Millennials and their relevance to components of the GVV approach, we must briefly acknowledge a primary mechanism through which these emerging leaders develop—business schools. College-age students and young professionals face societal and market demands for effective, implementable and ethical decision-making skills. Educators acknowledge the need for actionable strategies and a progression from "knowing" to "doing"—thus, we fail if we teach students how to discern the "right" thing to do, but then leave them at the postdecision moment unequipped to do it. Opportunities exist around developing skills necessary for translating *intention* to *application and behavior* in the business context. This progression from knowledge to action is key.

Application and problem-solving proficiency and fluency in sustainability solutions are key skills also demanded by the market (U.N. Global Compact/Accenture Chief Executive Officer (CEO) Study, 2010). In the wake of the corporate scandals of the last 2 decades and growing awareness of environmental and social challenges, managers increasingly respond to enhanced calls for responsible and sustainable business. Not surprisingly, legislation arises to fill the void between ethical intention and action, and companies rush to create a culture of internal resolution in response to increasing incentives for whistleblowing and other external demands for accountability. Business is ripe for values-based leaders who can generate measurable results along the triple bottom line. The need for ethical, implementable skills exists; one strategy to address these concerns is to capitalize on the strengths of Millennials and channel their characteristics in a way that meets individual and organizational goals.

Millennials' educational experiences increasingly prime them for explicit integration of values considerations. The number of business schools with substantive content in ethics and sustainability topics continues to rise (Aspen Institute, 2011). Research suggests students completing business courses with such content display considerably increased aptitude to articulate and understand concepts of ethics and leadership with integrity, and are ripe for learning that prompts application and actionable skills (Allen, Bacdayan, Kowalski & Roy, 2005; Hooker, 2004; McManus Warnell, 2010). This curricular attention prompts the progression toward attention to these issues after leaving school, in the context of professional life.

GIVING VOICE TO VALUES FOR ORGANIZATIONAL DEVELOPMENT WITH MILLENNIALS

Most of us, regardless of generational cohort, would like to integrate who we are, and that which we value, with what we do. However, research and experience demonstrate that values conflicts are inherent in our careers— the things we want to accomplish and the way we want to live seem in conflict with expectations of clients, peers, bosses and our organizations (Gentile, 2010). *Giving Voice to Values* recognizes these challenges and helps individuals learn to acknowledge, clarify, speak and act on their values in the face of those conflicts. This leadership development curriculum is appropriate for use with experienced professionals, emerging leaders, new hires and graduate- and undergraduate-level students.[2] Dean Carolyn Woo of the Mendoza College of Business has aptly described the approach as "postdecision making;" that is, once we have identified what we want to do, how do we act on it in a given context? It is not about deciding the right thing to do or what position one is going to take. Rather it is about how one raises these issues effectively, what he or she needs to do and say in order to be heard, and how to correct an existing course of action when necessary. Exploring the key tenets of the GVV approach in the context of the characteristics of Millennials illustrates its promise for organizational development.[3]

CAPACITIES AND OPPORTUNITIES

Research indicates Millennials display technological and social media fluency, proclivity to multitask, teamwork capacities and a preference for sustained and personal attention through training and mentorship, as well as explicit desire for meaningful work and increased awareness of social and environmental sustainability issues. The first several characteristics reflect capacities and inclinations, and the others, preferences for integration of values (personal, societal) into professional life. How can managers develop these capacities toward effective organizations? A foundational concept, and one that resonates with Millennials, is acknowledging *choice*—what we do in the workplace and how we elect to respond to professional challenges, specifically those with a values dimension. Enhancing the capacities of employees to voice values and exercise discernment allows Millennials, and the generational cohorts with whom they work, to contribute effectively.

Toward this end, the GVV program explores case studies and "scripts"—through individual and role-playing exercises, participants practice ethical decision making and action. GVV explores why individuals choose to act, or not. This approach acknowledges research indicating that a shared characteristic of those who act with moral courage in the face of confounding circumstances—garnered from situations as perilous as those faced by rescuers providing safety to those under Nazi threat during WWII—is prescripting, or anticipating values challenges and sharing, out loud, how to confront these challenges (Gentile, 2008). Determining mechanisms for practicing choice and developing our voice is the domain of business schools, and should be that of management as well.

Here we can consider Millennials' desire for training and development, and regular and open feedback from their superiors. This desire for information exchange extends to matters typically reserved for more senior employees (Myers & Sadaghiani, 2010), which, of course, has interesting implications for multigenerational cultures. The GVV approach emphasizes developing one's skills and voice, acknowledging research that demonstrates exchange of diverse ideas and analyses lead to enhanced creativity, opportunities, risk management strategies, and other benefits (Gentile, 2010). This proclivity toward and comfort with dialogue —open, encouraged, two-way and ongoing—sets the stage for organizational cultures that encourage flexing our voices.

To provide further clarity, we can also consider another Millennial phenomenon—we've all heard the disparaging sighs of frustration toward "helicopter parents" (as we simultaneously help our young ones complete their college applications with verve and polish). Millennials were raised in a culture of attention like no generation before. Those experiences of early and consistent intervention and feedback, with their corollary—the self-esteem-building focus where every child gets a trophy, for showing up and giving his or her best—can prove challenging as these young people enter a world rife with competition and little hand holding. It is not surprising that these experiences translate into specific desires in the workplace. Millennials expect not only frequent communication with supervisors, but that the communication be more positive and more affirming than has been the case with other generational cohorts (Myers & Sadaghiani, 2010). Myers and Sadaghiani (2010) and others posit that this need for affirmation develops from childhood experiences of the constant flow of supportive messages from parents, teachers and coaches. We can perhaps understand, then, when young professionals may be struggling to reconcile the messages from their youth—*Reach for the stars! You can be whatever you want to be (and you'll be great at it)!*—with the current economic challenges and a business community that doesn't always seem to respond to this approach.

Rather than lament them, let us channel these tendencies toward shared goals. Even at entry- and low-level positions, Millennials feel a need to be "kept in the loop" of information and expect that supervisors will freely share information such as strategic plans even during the formulation stage by senior management (Myers & Sadaghiani, 2010). These tendencies have strong roots, thus,

> as teens, [millennials] became comfortable expressing their thoughts and opinions to adults, expecting credibility despite their young age and lack of experiences.... They have also been encouraged by their parents to challenge authority, and to assert themselves, asking for preferential treatment

when they believe they can get it. (Myers & Sadaghiani, 2010, p. 229)

Managers would do well to emphasize that increased engagement must be associated with increased responsibility. Modeling and providing opportunities for exercising this responsibility is critical for managers. Investing Millennials with more and broader responsibilities may foster feelings of involvement, which in turn fosters organizational attachment (Myers & Sadaghiani, 2010).

Among other suggested strategies for enhancing Millennials' appreciation for deeper work relationships and respect for experience, an advantage most directly related to the GVV approach acknowledges that "increased organizational openness also might provide additional and important opportunities for frank communication and problem solving between Millennial workers and their supervisors" (Myers & Sadaghiani, 2010, p. 230). Data indicate consistent communication, regular feedback and other types of engagement between employee and supervisor lead to enhanced outcomes. Thus, encouraging and developing voice at work through the GVV approach—effective, constructive engagement around values and perspectives—can channel these characteristics. Additionally, "as a result of this perceived intense socialization from parents, millennials place a high value on and expect personal achievement" (Myers & Sadaghiani, 2010, p. 234). Capitalizing on this value toward organizational goals is a useful approach, perhaps through efforts such as peer recognition of goal achievement and other means to incentivize performance toward shared goals. Acknowledging the role of institution-building in leadership development is another channel for this proclivity.

Research indicates (and anecdotal evidence supports) that parents are also increasingly involved during job recruitment (Myers & Sadaghiani, 2010). Additionally, "millennials are eager to develop close relationships with their supervisors whom many consider to be their workplace parents, according to the popular literature" (Myers & Sadaghiani, 2010, p. 234). This level of alignment may prove an asset for integrating values discussions firmly within professional decision making. Recent research by Beer, Eisenstat, Foote, Fredberg, and Norrgren (2011) and colleagues identifies key characteristics of high-performing CEOs include skills in integrating multiple disciplines into systemic approaches to building better performing organizations, and explicit integration of personal values and principles into their leadership—clear evidence of the role of identifying purpose, broadly and thoughtfully defined, as a critical skill. Beer and colleagues (2011) present data from top companies around the world on leaders' roles in building institutions that do "well" (financially) and "good" (prosocial contribution). A key component of the GVV approach is learning from successful examples—professionals who have successfully acted on their values—and identifying practical steps toward doing so ourselves. This notion of "high-ambition" leaders, those who define their purpose as creating both economic and social value, echoes the GVV model of leadership development.

Additionally, and also consistent with the GVV approach, high-performing CEOs are open to learning through reflection and feedback. My own students indicate a struggle to reconcile the messages of their parents, and their business education—a prosocial conception of business, and business practitioners—with the seemingly never ending scandals and purely profit-driven, as opposed to purpose-driven, companies. Beer and colleagues' work (2011) goes on to call for high-ambition leaders to become intimately involved with business education through leadership development activities. Speaker series, project-based internships and other curricular experiences, and hands-on case-study approaches in collaboration with business executives are several important approaches. Encouraging reflection and open communication on building better businesses, in collaboration with leaders and with peers, is a key tenet of the GVV approach. A fundamental value of the GVV approach is the action focus—clearly aligned with Millennials' goals for impact and engagement. The act of expressing our intent, practicing our scripts and our strategies in front of peers and with aspirational and exemplary leaders, and collaborative action resonate with Millennials' penchant for collective activity and team response to professional challenges.

Millennials' response to unprecedented (in their lifetime) economic hardship more widely experienced during the economic recession also prompts interesting considerations. Research has indicated that some characteristics of Millennials may work in their favor, and to the benefit of their employers, during poor economic conditions. "Management experts note that, while money is important, Millennials do not see money as their only source of happiness. Like Generation X workers, they feel rewarded by work arrangements that offer more flexibility and new technology ... [and] expect to become involved in projects that have a major impact on the organization, soon after their organizational entry" (Myers & Sadaghiani, 2010, p. 233). Acknowledging this dynamic may allow managers to encourage it in their own organizations and may assist with meaningful contribution by Millennials.

Finally, as Gentile (2010) notes, impacting our organizations by effectively voicing our values requires acknowledging that there are many different ways to "speak." There are numerous ways to express our values and some may work better than others in particular circumstances. We ourselves may be more skilled at, comfortable with, or more likely to use one approach over another; as such, our ability to see a way to use that particular approach can be the most important determining factor as to whether we speak. Some organizational contexts or conditions, and some types of leaders, will have a strong impact on our own and others' likelihood of expressing values. There are things we can do to make it more likely that we will voice our values and that we will do so effectively – specifically, practice and coaching (Gentile, 2010).

Meister and Willyerd (2010) discuss mentoring Millennials; one of several tactics explored by these Harvard researchers is group mentoring. They found that manager-led or peer-to-peer mentoring at top companies, including such approaches as online platforms, leads to decreased training costs and enhanced communication. Additionally, "improving your company's ability to give employees honest, timely and useful coaching won't benefit just your 20-something workers." In a survey of the importance of eight managerial skills, respondents

> in all generations placed a high premium on having a manager who "will give straight feedback." And yet when we asked 300 heads of human resource to rate their managers' competence in the same eight skills, giving feedback was ranked dead last. Clearly, that's a critical gap companies need to bridge. (p. 72)

George and Baker (2011) interviewed 125 leaders to explore development of alignment around mission and values and empowering leaders at all levels of the organization. Their research supports the assertion that self-awareness is a precursor to emotional intelligence, a critical leadership component, and that self-awareness requires real-world experiences, reflection and processing one's experiences, and group interactions that allow sharing experiences and receiving feedback. This "missing link" in leadership can be cultivated with the GVV self-assessment, alignment and peer coaching components.

A final point on developing voice merits special attention for managing Millennials. Research acknowledges Millennials' penchant for "sharing" their work through "work narration" on blogs, social media networks, and other technologies (McAffee, 2010). Millennials talk publicly about their work, their progress, the resources they are using, and the challenges that arise. For better (and occasionally worse), this narration becomes part of the organization's digital record.

> As this happens, two broad benefits materialize. First, people who narrate their work become helpful to the rest of the organization because the digital trail they leave makes others more efficient. Second, by airing their questions and challenges work narrators open themselves up to good ideas and helpfulness from others, and so become more efficient themselves. (p. 24)

Channeling this form of voice toward organizational development, and building on Millennials' comfort and fluency with technological voice, may prompt innovative approaches to voicing values within the organization.

Engaging Millennials with interactive feedback acknowledges and develops voice. A natural extension of this engagement includes values dialogue. Voicing our values and our commitment—saying out loud who we are, who we want to be, who we are trying to be—is critical. Building on the discoveries of our self-assessment and alignment, we can formulate an effective, actionable voice.

PURPOSE, SELF-KNOWLEDGE AND ALIGNMENT

Emerging professionals can engage in meaningful, fulfilling work, and their organizations can function with enhanced capacity for leveraging employee strengths into organizational effectiveness. Identifying and actualizing purpose, and translating values into effective decision making and action, are key components of the *Giving Voice to Values* curriculum. The idea of aligning purpose, values and leadership is not new (see George, 2011, among others); what GVV contributes is a practical, integrated, skills-based approach that can be used by professionals at all levels —we know the *why*, and GVV provides the *how*.

Giving Voice to Values explores those values that most people would agree have an ethical dimension to them—beyond qualities such as "innovation" and "creativity" or other important characteristics (Gentile, 2010). When addressing values conflicts in the workplace, several characteristics provide a helpful and manageable foundation to which we can appeal. These characteristics—sometimes called virtues, hypernorms, and core values—include widely shared values identified succinctly by Kidder (2005) as honesty, respect, responsibility, fairness and compassion. Through self-assessments, discussion of conflicts and exploration of relevant research, managers and their employees can consider reframing self-image and perceptions of the business context by recognizing some *values* that they and others in their business experience might share. Meister and Willyerd (2010) polled 2,200 professionals across diverse industries about their values and goals for work—a key characteristic identified was "strong values"—this expressed willingness to engage around values in the workplace provides a platform for leadership development.

Other studies also note this link. Thus, Beer and colleagues (2011) noted that in contrast to most companies that begin determining strategy and direction by looking at markets and competition, "high-ambition" CEOs looked within the organization, and themselves, to determine "who" the company was to identify the most powerful intersection between their capabilities and purpose, and the passions of their people, with market opportunity—a clear alignment with notions of purpose. Beer and colleagues (2011) go on to note, "These CEOs spent a great deal of time crystallizing their values and purpose and how strategy could be defined in a way that integrated strategy with values." Success involves first "forging strategic identity" (Beer et al., 2011)—another way to articulate purpose. Other findings related to characteristics of high-ambition leaders include the need for personal interaction with employees and transparent communication (Beer et al., 2011). Millennials are poised to appreciate and respond to this approach.

Specific GVV exercises prompt this journey toward putting values into action. Recognizing the fact that we are all capable of speaking and acting on our values, as well as the fact that we have not always done so, is both empowering and enlightening (Gentile, 2010). A foundational GVV exercise, "A Tale of Two Stories," invites participants to consider two personal experiences—a time when they acted in a manner consistent with their values, and one when they did not. This exercise has proven popular and effective in professional education and prompts meaningful engagement with other components of the approach. The intention is not to conclude that those who spoke up were necessarily better, more courageous, or more competent. Rather, the exercise prompts us to reflect on the subject of choice—we have all exercised choice, so we know we have it. This acknowledgment is fundamental to the GVV approach. Recognizing choice prompts self-reflection and self-knowledge, along with situational analysis. The essential first step in developing tools to voice values is recognizing we can—and do—act on our values, and that we sometimes choose not to do so. This preempts a dangerous tendency to define ourselves as either ethical or as always unethical—we are neither cast as unethical for all time, nor as relieved from the necessity to challenge ourselves and remain vigilant (Gentile, 2010). Voicing values can become a muscle and a habit. It can become part of our self-definition.

Clearly some characteristics of Millennials can prove challenging for managers. How can we most effectively translate their capacities and preferences into positive impact? An approach with much promise involves responding to Millennials' search for meaning at work, and commitment to social and environmental sustainability concerns. Exploring meaning at work leads us to consider purpose—a key component of the GVV approach.

Defining professional *purpose* explicitly and broadly allows us to see values conflicts as an expected part of doing business, with costs and benefits that are similar to any other business challenge (Gentile, 2010). Millennials' expressed goal of aligning purpose with professional life is translatable to a multigenerational culture—this proclivity can be leveraged within multigenerational work cultures toward sustainable competitive advantage in today's business context:

> For example, if we think of our purpose as doing well, pleasing our bosses, making a good living (or even a great living), then when we face values conflicts in the workplace, we will see our degrees of freedom narrowed by the desire to please those very individuals who may be presenting us with the values conflict. They are the ones who give us performance reviews and raises, or with whom we need to cooperate in order to accomplish our goals, or to whom we need to make the sale to meet a quota. We may feel we have little choice but to do what they ask. Of course, the pursuit of any goal—even a narrowly defined goal—can still be guided and disciplined by a set of commitments and rules. Even if we define our purpose narrowly as "doing well financially," we can still choose to be guided by a set of values and principles that determine how we feel comfortable and justified in doing so, but they may feel more like constraints within which we must operate rather than goals to which we aspire. If, however, we think of our purpose in a broader sense as building and being part of a company that is a respected corporate citizen—for example, providing valuable products or services to consumers, creating good jobs in a healthy work environment, building a firm that investors can trust to report honestly on its performance—then we will see that we have a broader span of operation when we confront values conflicts. We will have a wider set of positive principles and goals to which we can refer and by which we can guide our behavior. (Gentile, 2008, p. 14)

This prosocial conception of purpose aligns clearly with goals of Millennials. Additionally, it is not, of course, the exclusive domain of emerging professionals. Framing professional purpose broadly and explicitly allows all of us to take steps toward building and preserving organizations of which we can be proud.

As Gentile (2010) notes, this broader definition of purpose does not mean that values conflicts are simple; rather, it may complicate matters because it requires us to see choices where we may have previously deferred to the "authority" of our superiors in the organization. However, this broader definition allows us to dignify and recognize efficacy our organizational role at any level—we can see ourselves as part of something valuable, from entry level employee to CEO. As George and Baker (2011) recognize, this approach is reflected in increasing attention to collaborative organizations with flat structures rather than hierarchical. This is the emerging model of the era, and one that resonates with the strengths and capacities of Millennials—companies must develop a broad array of leaders, and not simply a select few. Here we can also consider research noted above (Myers & Sadaghiani, 2010), indicating Millennials' desire to contribute, comfort with interaction with those in authority positions, and desire to be taken seriously as contributing members of the group.

A natural progression of the exploration of purpose includes examining *self-knowledge, self-image* and values *alignment*. Self-awareness is a precursor to values identification and ultimately ethical judgment. GVV exercises prompt participants to explore purpose, including personal and professional goals, and to self-assess comfort with risk, preferred communication styles, understandings of loyalty and self-image. The information they uncover allows them to readily frame levers that enable ethical action in a way that is consistent with who they are. Gentile (2008) notes,

> most of us tend to be susceptible to self-justifying biases or finding ways to view our decisions as positively motivated, even when we would be critical of someone else who made the same choices. By actively considering our personal values profile and crafting a "self-story" that aligns our values, behaviors and self-image with the kind of person who can make the hard choices and act on their values, we are anticipating those choices and prescribing our interpretation. (p. 17)

Creating opportunities to engage in this self-reflection, alignment and prescripting, or practicing out loud with peers, can be the domain of organizations that value a proactive, strength-building approach to professional development.

Millennials indicate the following among their top five characteristics they want in a boss: help with navigating their career paths, straight feedback, mentoring and coaching, and formal professional development (supervisor comfort with flexible schedules rounds out the list) (Meister & Willyerd, 2010). An organization that will develop employees' skills and one with "strong values" were among those characteristics they want in their company. GVV directs these inclinations into effective skill development. At this point some of us may be reflecting a response echoed in Meister and Willyerd (2010): "'Oh, they want total fulfillment?' managers maybe thinking. 'Is *that* all?'" The authors go on, however, to frame this as a strength:

> Yes, Millennials have high expectations of their employers—but they also set high standards for themselves. They've been working on their résumés practically since they were toddlers, because there are so many of them and so few (relatively speaking) spots at top schools and top companies. They're used to overachieving academically and to making strong personal commitments to community service. *Keep them engaged, and they will be happy to overachieve for you.*" (p. 70, emphasis added)

Again here we can consider the critical role of business education. Sims and Felton (2006) note of business education,

> It is vital that students integrate learning and living. The learning process has two core goals. One is to learn the content of a particular subject matter like business ethics. The other is to learn one's own strengths and weaknesses as a learner. When the process works well, students finish their ethics learning experience with not only new intellectual insights but also new understandings of their own learning style. It has been our experience that this understanding of learning strengths and weaknesses helps in the application of what has been learned to real-world situations and provides a framework for continued learning. In this instance, learning is no longer a special activity reserved for the classroom; it becomes an integral and explicit part of the work world business students will encounter upon graduation. (p. 304)

Clearly this approach resonates with Millennials and their role in organizations. It echoes effective business education, specifically, education that prompts discernment of values and their role in the professions. Among the characteristics identified by Sims and Felton (2006) as fundamental to creating an effective learning environment for business ethics is that

> the learning environment should be experience based. The learning begins with and is based on the experiences of the students and their encounters with life. Class discussions do not move from theory to application. To the contrary, the class is inductive. The discussions move from experience to the formulation of generalizations and concepts about appropriate behavior. (p. 303)

Rooting leadership development in the learner's experiences and sense of self is critical to developing capacities to build on those foundations. Moving toward exercising choice and action from that foundation requires voice. Thus, the GVV approach next addresses the transition from decision making to strategy and implementation.

NORMALITY

Framing workplace values conflicts as dilemmas that strike us "out of the blue" can have a disabling effect (Gentile, 2010). Observations suggest that many of us do not see ethical dilemmas as a true part of doing business—because the dilemma is perceived as marginal to "business-as-usual," we are much more likely to think in terms of getting through it so that we can return to business. Approaching careers with the expectation that we will face conflicts, and anticipating some of the most common types of conflicts in our industry and functional area, allow us to manage them more effectively. By anticipating or *normalizing* the idea that we will have to take risks to align with our values, we expand our vision of the degree of freedom we have in our decision making. These conflicts become normal and survivable, and we can more easily understand and communicate with those who place us in these challenging situations (Gentile, 2010). The approach prompts perspective-taking, moving away from a villain/victim frame and recognizing our own tendency toward self-justification, and the tendency to view others as entirely wrong, prompts us toward finding common ground (Gentile, 2010). McGlone, Spain and McGlone (2011) cite data from the Cone Millennial Cause Study indicating nearly 80% of Millennials express a desire to work for a company that is concerned with how it contributes to society, and that Millennials have internalized the need for societal contribution to include activities like volunteering for social causes. Additionally, Millennials expect that the philanthropic approach to corporate social responsibility is not enough; companies they work for should *integrate* corporate social responsibility strategically across its core strategy. This echoes the GVV tenet of normality—values considerations should be considered just another management activity like any other.

Millennials already conceptualize business as inherently values laden. Due to their experiences in business schools, and growing up in the context of the post-Enron era and the global financial crisis, they are familiar with the repercussions of a values vacuum. Even if their orientation is a minimal risk-management conception of responsibility, these concepts have been part of their development as young professionals. Translating these sensibilities into professional processes and decision-making capacity is key. A critical aspect of GVV is transitioning from sometimes immobilizing contemplation of "What is the right thing to do?" to "What if you were going to act on your values? What would you say and do?" This frame moves the issue out of lofty notions of "right and wrong" to the practical (Gentile, 2010). This in turn can activate the "hands-on, can do" approach favored by Millennials.

BARRIERS TO ETHICAL ACTION

Millennials and those who manage them can enhance their professional capacity by strengthening resolve toward ethical action. Given often strong notions of self and purpose, why do we fail to act on our values? When we encounter values conflicts in professional life, we often face barriers—*reasons and rationalizations*—that can confound our best attempts to fulfill our own sense of organizational and personal purpose (Gentile, 2010). Research tells us we may act unethically despite noble intentions, that we overestimate our ability to act ethically, and why concepts like ethical fading, through which ethical dimensions are eliminated from a decision, lead good people to unethical behavior (Bazerman & Tenbrunsel, 2011). The GVV collection provides specific and actionable levers for addressing these dynamics. Thus, the GVV approach prompts us to ask, what are the reasons and rationalizations for the behavior we question, and how can we develop persuasive arguments or "scripts" for responding to them? If we want to do what we think is right, we need to know how to communicate powerfully and persuasively in the face of strong countervailing organizational or individual norms, reasons and rationalizations (Gentile, 2010). The approach presents several questions whose answers provide useful information for framing these challenges. As Gentile notes, these questions are not asking us to apply ethical analysis. Rather they are about understanding the reasons and motivations—both rational and emotional, organizational and personal, ethical and perhaps unethical—that guide the behavior and choices of those with whom we want to communicate.

This approach is helpful in prompting us to recognize familiar categories of argument or reasons for the defense of ethically questionable behavior. Similarly, there are useful questions, persuasive arguments, and ways of framing information that can help us respond effectively to these common arguments. Importantly, the very act of "naming" the argument can reduce its power—we have made it discussable and subject to equal, or hopefully stronger, counter arguments. *Choice* becomes possible—the fundamental tenet of the GVV approach (Gentile, 2010).

Research uncovers common categorizations or patterns of dilemmas outlined in more detail in the *Giving Voice to Values* curriculum: truth versus loyalty, individual versus community, short term versus long term, and justice versus mercy (Kidder, 2005). These dichotomies are misrepresentations and can be a form of rationalization. Sometimes values conflicts only appear to be such "right versus right" dilemmas due to the way they are framed, ignoring the "wrong" that may be there. For example, a colleague may appeal to personal loyalty in order to persuade us to go along with an unethical reporting tactic—don't let "the team" down—presenting his appeal as a "truth versus loyalty" dilemma. With preparation, we can see this as the rationalization that it is, and begin to formulate a response. Thus,

> once we recognize that attempts to persuade us to violate our own values are often framed in this way, we might recognize that our colleague is not showing the same loyalty *to* us (by not respecting our personal integrity) that he

or she is asking *from* us.... Loyalty does not mean doing anything our friend would prefer, but rather it is an appeal to what our friend can *legitimately* ask or expect from us, and us from him or her. (Gentile, 2010, p. 177)

One need only revisit the Enron debacle to witness the destruction this misguided appeal can engender. Sims and Brinkmann (2003) note,

Enron's culture [was] a good example of groupthink ... where individuals feel extreme pressure not to express any real strong arguments against any coworkers' actions. Although very individualistic, the culture at Enron was at the same conformist.... Employees were loyal in an ambiguous sense of the term, for example they wanted to be seen as part of the start team and to partake in the benefits that that honor entailed.... Loyalty required ... [that employees] "keep drinking the Enron water." (p. 252)

Familiarizing ourselves with these common categories of values conflicts allows us to clearly consider whether the values at issue—loyalty, truth, mercy, justice, etcetera—are truly relevant to the given dilemma (Gentile, 2010).

We also often encounter common categories of argument or rationalization, which the GVV approach explores in detail. As we recognize these categories of argument, we become more adept at responding to them. For example, the appeal to "expected practice" ("*everyone is doing it*") is often an exaggeration—if the practice were truly accepted, why are there rules, laws or policies against it (Gentile, 2010)? These and other common categories of rationalization are discussed and specific strategies to confront them are provided. Thus we consider categories of argument and rationalization, along with categories of values dilemmas, to help us recognize them, understand the ways of thinking that produce them, and to be practiced in responding to them. They are expected, and they are vulnerable to reasoned response.

These core tenets of *Giving Voice to Values* are explored in more detail in materials available to educators and managers. Critically, the observations and lenses require active practice for them to be useful. Dedicating time to focusing on what we would say and do, and examining the experiences of others who have voiced their values, can build the muscle and instincts to do so. It becomes just one more managerial duty. Values-based decision making is a necessary next iteration of effective leadership. This fluency requires explicit attention and development for its meaningful integration.

A focus on individual integrity as proffered by the GVV curriculum acknowledges the factors, both internal and contextually, that surround ethical decision making. To achieve organizational effectiveness, individual participants—Millennials and their multigenerational coworkers—

must develop ethical fluency in the organizational and societal contexts. Developing moral courage in individuals is the precursor to managing ethical, effective organizations. As GVV author and director Mary C. Gentile (2010) writes, by understanding how we as individuals develop skills to voice our values, we identify the conditions that make it more likely we will do so, and these "enabling" conditions become a checklist for the type of organizational culture and context of the organizations we lead. The roles and responsibilities of individuals within the organization shape the culture and expectations—and policies and processes must be structured to provide incentive for those behaviors that allow for success across the triple bottom line—ethical, environmental, and financial performance. Efforts strengthening moral courage and the capacity for internal ethical decision making are foundational to effective organizations.

These tactics are effective within multigenerational professional cultures and have wide implications for managing Millennials as a subgroup of employees. Even more broadly, as Deal, Altman, and Rogelberg (2010) note,

> The approach that appears to be the most practical and have the greatest potential benefit for the organization as a whole (across all generations) is to treat all employees well. If you provide employees with an interesting job, good compensation, opportunities to learn and advance, colleagues they like to work with, a boss they trust, and leaders who are competent, employees of all generations will respond positively. (p. 196)

We can manage Millennials and enhance management of the organization by aligning work with purpose and enabling voice. As Meister and Willyerd (2010) note,

> All employees want to feel valued, empowered, and engaged at work. This is a fundamental need, not a generational issue. And, though Gen Xers and Millennials openly discuss and even demand more flexibility in their jobs, Boomers and Traditionalists (also known as the "Silent Generation") want it too, even if they are less vocal about it. You can think of the Millennials as pushing for change that all generations want to see happen. "Am I continuing to learn and grow?" is a question that resonates with employees of all ages. The way your organization helps them answer that question may be your competitive advantage in attracting, developing, and keeping tomorrow's talent. (p. 72)

CONCLUSION

Too often, popular media laments the failings of the Millennial generation and management experts resignedly sigh and focus on making do.

What if we change the frame, and leverage their strengths toward a new business paradigm? Millennials are primed for a managerial approach that channels their strengths (and challenges) into effective strategies for action-oriented, values-based contribution and leadership. *Giving Voice to Values* offers a resource for organizations to build on the promise of business by developing individual skills and organizational culture. GVV prompts action, while the false dichotomy of business—a scourge or a salvation—may be immobilizing. The thesis of the *Giving Voice to Values* approach is that "if enough of us felt empowered—and were skillful and practiced enough—to voice and act on our values effectively on those occasions when our bests selves are in the driver's seat, business would be a different place" (Gentile, 2010, p. xxiii). This progression to an action orientation is demanded by the market and recognized by those who educate and train new hires – and is inherently compatible with the strengths and proclivities of Millennials. Those characteristics—including desire for meaningful work, technological fluency and facility with social media, proclivity to multitask, and teamwork capacities—are clearly aligned with key GVV tenets including purpose, voice, peer coaching and a skills-based approach to ethical development, among others. Millennials' explicit values considerations prime them to contribute to values-driven organizations. A vibrant, ethical, innovative business community that capitalizes on its promise—the sector with the flexibility, resources, and reach for impact on the world's most pressing challenges—must start with developing leaders with the skills and capacity for ethical decision making. Let us develop that capacity for all leaders in multigenerational professional cultures.

NOTES

1. The *Giving Voice to Values* curriculum collection is based and supported at Babson College. It was created with The Aspen Institute as Incubator, and, along with Yale School of Management, Founding Partner. It can be found at www.GivingVoiceTo Values.org.
2. Materials available include case studies and teaching notes, foundational readings and exercises and self-assessment instruments. Faculty and professionals can adapt the GVV approach into stand-alone workshops, functional or topical modules within existing courses and activities, dedicated programs of studies, custom peer coaching programs or custom curriculum development and training exercises. *Giving Voice To Values* has been used in over 150 pilots on six continents
3. Descriptions of the GVV curriculum were primarily derived from *Giving Voice to Values: How to Speak Your Mind When You Know What's Right.* (Mary C. Gentile, 2010). New Haven & London: Yale University Press.

ACKNOWLEDGMENT

The author would like to thank Amanda Rahie for research assistance.

REFERENCES

Aspen Institute. (2011). Beyond Grey Pinstripes 2011, The Aspen Institute Center for Business Education. Retrieved from www.beyondgreypinstripes.org

Allen, W., Bacdayan, P., Kowalski, K., & Roy, M. (2005). Examining the impact of ethics training on business student values. *Education + Training, 47*(3), 170-182.

Bazerman, M. H., & Tenbrunsel, A. E. (2011). *Blind spots: Why we fail to do what's right and what to do about it.* Princeton, NJ: Princeton University Press.

Beer, M., Eisenstat, R. A., Foote, N., Fredberg, T., & Norrgren, F. (2011). *Higher-ambition: How great leaders create economic and social value.* Boston, MA: Harvard Business Press.

Deal, J., Altman, D., & Rogelberg, S. (2010). Millennials at work: What we know and what we need to do (if anything). *Journal of Business and Psychology, 25*(2), 191-199.

The Economist "Schumpeter" Column. (2009, September 26). The pedagogy of the privileged. *The Economist.* Retrieved from http://www.economist.com/node/14493183

Gentile, M. C. (2008). Ways of thinking about our values. Retrieved from www.GivingVoiceToValues.org

Gentile, M. C. (2010). *Giving voice to values: How to speak your mind when you know what's right.* New Haven, CT: Yale University Press.

George, B., & Baker, D. (2011). *True north groups: A powerful path to personal and leadership development.* San Francisco, CA: Berrett-Koehler.

Hershatter, A., & Epstein, M. (2010). Millennials and the world of work: An organization and management perspective. *Journal of Business and Psychology, 25*(2), 211-223.

Hooker, J. (2004). The case against bad ethics education: A study in bad arguments. *Journal of Business Ethics Education, 1*(1), 73-86.

Kidder, R. M. (2005). *Moral courage: Taking action when your values are put to the test.* New York, NY: William Morrow, HarperCollins.

Kowske, B., Rasch, R., & Wiley, J. (2010). Millennials' (lack of) attitude problem: An empirical examination of generational effects on work attitudes. *Journal of Business and Psychology, 25*(2), 265-279.

Lancaster, L. C., & Stillman, D. (2002). *When generations collide: Who they are. Why they clash. How to solve the generational puzzle at work.* New York, NY: Collins.

McAfee, A. (2010). How millennials' sharing habits can benefit organizations. *Harvard Business Review, 88.* Retrieved from http://blogs.hbr.org/hbr/mcafee/2010/08/how-millennials-sharing-habits.html

McGlone, T., Spain, J., & McGlone, V. (2011). Corporate social responsibility and the millennials. *Journal of Education for Business, 86*(4), 195-200.

McManus Warnell, J. (2010). An undergraduate business ethics curriculum: Learning and development outcomes. *Journal of Business Ethics Education*, 7, 63-84.

Meister, J., & Willyerd, K. (2010). Mentoring millennials. *Harvard Business Review*, *88*(5), 68-72.

Meriac, J., Woehr, D., & Banister, C. (2010). Generational differences in work ethic: An examination of measurement equivalence across three cohorts. *Journal of Business and Psychology*, *25*(2), 315-324.

Myers, K. E., & Sadaghiani, K. (2010). Millennials in the workplace: A communication perspective on millennials' organizational relationships and performance. *Journal of Business and Psychology*, *25*, 225-238.

Ng, E., Schweitzer, L., & Lyons, S. (2010). New generation, great expectations: A field study of the millennial generation. *Journal of Business and Psychology*, *25*(2), 281-292.

Sims, R. R., & Brinkmann, J. (2003). Enron ethics (or: Culture matters more than codes). *Journal of Business Ethics*, *45*(3), 243-256.

Sims, R. R., & Felton, E. (2006). Designing and delivering business ethics teaching and learning. *Journal of Business Ethics*, *63*(3), 297-312.

Smola, K. W., & Sutton, C. (2002). Generational differences: Revisiting generational work values for the new millennium. *Journal of Organizational Behavior*, *23*(4), 363-382.

Stewart, K., & Bernhardt, P. (2010). Comparing millennials to pre-1987 students and with one another. *North American Journal of Psychology*, *12*(3), 579-602.

United Nations Global Compact. (2010). A new era of sustainability. *United Nations Global Compact-Accenture CEO Study 2010*. Retrieved from http://www.unglobalcompact.org/docs/news_events/8.1/UNGC_Accenture_CEO_Study_2010.pdf

Walker, K. (2009). Excavating the millennial teacher mine. *NASSP Bulletin*, *93*(1), 73-77.

Yang. S. M., & Guy, M. E. (2006). GenXers versus boomers: Work motivators and management implications. *Public Performance & Management Review, 29*, 267-284.

PART II

MILLENNIALS AND THE TRADITIONAL FUNCTIONS OF HUMAN RESOURCE MANAGEMENT

CHAPTER 6

LEVERAGING WEB 2.0 TECHNOLOGIES IN THE RECRUITMENT OF MILLENNIAL JOB CANDIDATES

Jared J. Llorens and Alexandrea Wilson

INTRODUCTION

One of the key challenges for employers in both the public and private sector is the recruitment and selection of talented candidates, and the ability to do so is one of the key components of developing a high performing workforce. While most areas of human resources management have been substantially impacted by new and developing technologies over the past decade, the recruitment function has undergone perhaps the most dramatic transformation due to the emergence of new e-recruitment technologies under the Web 2.0 umbrella and the developing preferences of Millennial job candidates. While just 10 years ago it was considered progressive for employers to maintain informative and highly functional employment websites that allowed candidates to locate and apply for positions online, the growth of e-recruitment technologies and the prevalence of social networking websites such as Facebook and Twitter

Managing Human Resources for the Millennial Generation, pp. 141–157

have drastically transformed the extent to which employers are able to communicate with and attract Millennial candidates.

In an effort to address this topic of growing importance to job candidates, employers and human resources professionals, the first section of this chapter discusses the characteristics of Millennial job candidates that necessitate more advanced e-recruitment approaches by employers. The second section highlights the transformation from traditional recruitment methods to e-recruitment methods, and overviews common Web 2.0 technologies currently utilized in many employer recruitment efforts. Finally, the last section discusses how employers can leverage these new technologies in their recruitment efforts and provides examples of organizations in the private, public and nonprofit sectors that have effectively incorporated these new technologies into their existing e-recruitment activities.

THE CHALLENGE OF ATTRACTING MILLENNIAL JOB CANDIDATES

Over the past few decades, there has been a growing body of academic research and popular media coverage on the role of generational differences in the labor market and how these differences have impacted core human resources management practices (see for example, Myers & Sadaghiani, 2010; Jurkiewicz & Brown, 1998; Twenge, Campbell, Hoffman, & Lance, 2010). While the contemporary labor market includes members of the Silent Generation (ages 65 and older), Baby Boomer Generation (ages 46-64), Generation X (ages 30-45) and the Millennial Generation (ages 18-29), the Millennial generation has received heightened attention in recent years due to their unique characteristics and rapid growth in the overall labor market (Pew, 2010). Other terms used to describe the Millennial generation include Baby Boomer Echo, Generation Y, Digital Natives, Generation Next, Google Generation, and the "Look at Me" Generation (Hirschman, 2006; Meister & Willyerd, 2010; Myers & Sadaghiani, 2010; Pew, 2007). In terms of employment, ongoing research regarding the career expectations and priorities of Millennials has found that, in contrast to members of prior generations, Millennials tend to prioritize individualistic aspects of a job and career advancement, and further, Millennials actively seek out careers that will assist them in the development of new skills and provide mentorship and coaching along the way. For this generation, meaningful and satisfying work is just as important as a meaningful and satisfying life outside of work (Hirschman, 2006; Ng, Schweitzer, & Lyons, 2010; Smola & Sutton, 2002).

Another defining characteristic of the Millennial generation is its degree of technological savvy. While members of preceding generations were introduced to new web-based technologies relatively late in their careers, Millennials are often considered "digital natives" given that they have been exposed to and have utilized many web-based technologies since their childhood (Yeaton, 2008). This early exposure to newer technologies has ultimately shaped both the way in which Millennials communicate and their expectations of the ease and accessibility of information available to them. For example, if the stereotypical Millennial were asked "Who is the founder of Facebook?" she or he would most likely whip out a smart phone, Google the question, and in less than 5 seconds, find that in 2004 Mark Zuckerberg and his friends founded Facebook in their dorm room at Harvard University.

Although their familiarity with technology and expectations regarding information availability can influence many aspects of communicating with Millennials, these characteristics are particularly pertinent to the recruitment function. While it was once the norm for members of the preceding generations to seek employment through more time consuming print-based media or meeting one-on-one with recruiters, Millennials have entered the labor market at a time where such traditional methods are often considered obsolete. For Millennials, their labor market norm is for employers to publicize employment opportunities through web-based media and to provide information that is timely, comprehensive and tailored to them as potential candidates. Further, Millennials don't just want to know the basic duties and characteristics of a particular employment opportunity, they also want to learn about an employer's workplace culture, the experiences of its employees and the reasons why they would be a good fit for a particular organization. In many respects, Web 2.0 technologies are perfectly tailored for this purpose, especially given the familiarity of Millennials with contemporary web-based tools. While traditional recruitment methods were substantially limited with regards to the breath of employment information that could be provided to a potential candidate, tools such as web blogs or video posting can now provide a virtually limitless amount of real-time employment information that can be readily adapted to current labor market trends. Ultimately, those employers with the resources and skills to leverage these new technologies will find themselves at a competitive advantage in the quest to recruit Millennial job candidates.

LEVERAGING E-RECRUITMENT TECHNOLOGIES

Over the past 20 years, the recruitment function has been substantially transformed by the advent of new technologies that have expanded both the manner in which job information is communicated to candidates and the scope of information that can be provided by employers. Prior to the growth of web-based computing, employers were tasked with advertising their job vacancies through a combination of methods which included print-based advertisements, employee referrals and the use of recruiters at job fairs and college campuses. While their goal was to increase the pool of qualified applicants, each method was limited compared to contemporary e-recruitment methods. Advertisements in local newspapers or trade publications reached only those applicants actively seeking employment through these sources, and the use of employee referrals and job fairs were often restricted geographically. The early recruitment efforts of the U.S. federal government serve as a good example of such efforts. Prior to the development of the federal government's USAJobs web portal, vacancy announcements for federal positions were posted on job boards located in federal buildings or distributed at regional job fairs and college campuses (Llorens & Kellough, 2007). In both instances, resulting applicant pools were restricted to those candidates who happened to intersect with the federal government's recruitment efforts, and the amount of information that could be provided by federal recruiters was also limited by what could be communicated by recruiters or placed within a print advertisement.

While recruiters were significantly limited by these traditional recruitment methods, the growth of web access and personal computer processing power has vastly expanded the reach of employer recruitment efforts. Unlike traditional methods, contemporary recruitment efforts have allowed employers to provide large amounts of vacancy information to a limitless number of potential applicants, and they are now able to do so in real time. While earlier efforts were characterized by a focus on specific labor markets, employers can now post vacancies on their institutional web-pages and eligible applicants are able to view those announcements from around the world. Additionally, recent advancements in web-based computing have vastly improved upon early e-recruitment efforts. When employers first began to leverage web-based capabilities, the focus was primarily on posting vacancy information and providing candidates with the opportunity to apply for positions online. However, the growth of Web 2.0 technologies has enabled employers to further advance their recruitment efforts through such tools web-based videos and social networking. As will be discussed in the remaining sections of the chapter, the use of these more advanced techniques promise to play a critical role in the recruitment of Millennial job candidates.

There is also a growing body of research that has highlighted the relationship between e-recruitment practices and organizational attractiveness. For example, researchers have found that the initial job advertisement or recruitment message received by the job seeker plays an significant role in how job seekers view an organization and their intent to pursue employment (Cober, Brown, Blumental, Doverspike, & Levy, 2000; Zusman & Landis, 2002), thus suggesting that it is critical that employers pay attention to the overall recruitment messages they advertise to job seekers and to brand themselves in a way that will attract the desired candidates (Walker, Feild, Giles, & Bernerth, 2008). If, for example, an employer uses social media tools in the recruitment process, then the perceived message to the job seeker might be that the company is open to new technologies, is innovative, and an exciting place to work.

Additionally, job seekers, especially Millennials, may research companies to determine if a particular organization is a good match for their employment interests (Rubaii-Barrett & Wise, 2007). When determining the person-organization fit, the job seeker will evaluate all the information that is available, such as the website, the realistic job previews, mission statements, employee testimonials, and overall image and reputation (Selden & Orenstein, 2011). Candidates may be further influenced by peripheral cues, or pictures and icons that are desirable (Walker et al., 2008) and a company that has a website with links to a Facebook profile, Twitter page and YouTube channel may appear to be a more desirable place to work for Millennials because they are digitally confident and tech savvy (Rubaii-Barrett & Wise, 2007).[1]

WEB 2.0 RECRITING AT A GLANCE

As stated earlier, Web 2.0 technologies are optimal tools for the recruitment of Millennial job candidates. In general, Web 2.0 technologies refer to a large spectrum of popular technologies that have been developed during the last wave of web-based innovation, and the term itself was first coined in 2004 by web visionaries and publishing executives, Tim O'Reilly and John Battelle (Funk, 2009). Web 2.0 technologies are also referred to as a form of participatory or "social" media since many of these technologies are centered upon the interaction between developers and end users, and put more power and control of content into the hands of regular users, not just big site owners. Figure 6.1 helps illustrate the interactive nature of recruiting when using Web 2.0 technologies. More traditional print and electronic recruitment methods provided for limited, one-way communication between employers and candidates with employers being primarily responsible for simply posting information on position vacancies and candidates responsible for submitting their applications in a timely manner. In contrast, Web 2.0 technologies have opened the avenues for communication between candidates and employers and have created recruitment environments where constant communication and

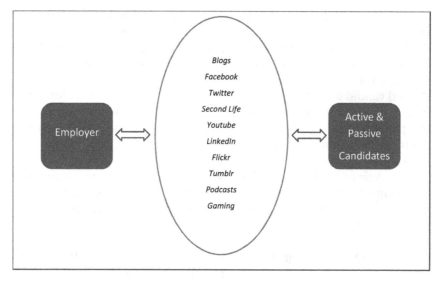

Figure 6.1.   Interactive recruitment in a Web 2.0 environment.

information sharing is not only possible, but expected in many cases. The wide range of existing technologies has also allowed employers to simultaneously utilize multiple avenues for communicating with job candidates.[2]

Additionally, these newer social media technologies can be very helpful in gaining the interest of both active and passive candidates. Active candidates are generally defined as those candidates who are unemployed but actively searching for a job, whereas passive candidates are defined as those candidates who are currently employed but would consider changing jobs if the conditions were optimal. Social media can be particularly useful in recruiting passive candidates because it allows companies to maintain ongoing relationships with potential future candidates that may one day be ready for a career change (Joos, 2008). Jeanne Meister and Karie Willyerd refer to these practices as social recruiting, "a practice that leverages social and professional networks, both online and offline, from both a candidate's perspective and the hiring side, to connect to, communicate with, engage, inform, and attract future talent" (2010, p. 95). According to Meister and Willyerd, the three most popular Web sites among "social recruiters" are LinkedIn (95% usage), Facebook (59% usage), and Twitter (42% usage) (2010). Other popular social networking tools used for recruiting include blogs, video- and photo-sharing, podcasts, wikis, and web-based gaming. While the Web 2.0 landscape is continuously evolving, this section overviews those Web 2.0 technologies beneficial to the recruitment function.

Social Networking Media

As one of the most widely used Web 2.0 technologies, social networking sites such as Facebook, LinkedIn and Twitter, allow both organizations and individuals to create online profiles and develop a virtual network of interested parties. While individuals can use social networking sites recreationally to stay connected with friends and family, employers and job seekers are increasingly utilizing these sites to establish current and future employment relationships. According to Jobvite's 2010 recruiting survey, 83% of respondents (over 600 human resource and recruiting professionals) use or plan to use social networking for recruitment in 2011 (Giehll, 2011). Given their growth over the past decade, social networking sites are extremely popular with Millennials, as well as a growing number of older and younger generations. According to the Pew Research Center, three-quarters of Millennials admitted to having a profile on a social networking site, compared with half of Generation Xers, 30% of Baby Boomers and 6% of the Silent Generation (2010).

There are many social networking sites currently in the marketplace, but, by many measures, the social networking site Facebook is the most popular among social networking users of all age groups. Initially launched as a tool for connecting college students on multiple campuses, Facebook has now grown to over 900 million active users that cover virtually all segments of society, from college students to elderly grandparents (Facebook, 2012). Facebook serves as a sort of generic social networking tool, its ease of use and broad user base have made it a popular networking tool for employers and job candidates. LinkedIn is commonly used for a more professional audience that is interested in networking with other professionals and can be a good tool for recruitment. Creating a LinkedIn profile allows users to create an online resume in order to showcase educational background, work experience, references, special skills and interests.

Another popular social networking site among Millennials is Twitter (Pew, 2010). The site serves as a real-time information network that allows people to connect to the latest information regarding personal interests. Information is shared through "tweets" and each tweet is limited to 140 characters in length (Twitter, 2011). Although publicly launched only 5 years ago, Twitter is quickly becoming one of the more popular social networking tools, and according to Twitter's engineering department, over 350 billion tweets are delivered each day (Olivarez-Giles, 2011). Most recently, Google has launched a social media platform called Google+ (G+). G+ is very similar to other social networking sites; however, it claims to be different by allowing users to connect "on the web more like connecting in the real world." G+ allows users to create "circles," which are private groups of friends, coworkers, family members, or other types of groups that users may affiliate with (Google+, 2011). Although G+ has not been widely leveraged for recruitment purposes to date, its future applicability will be greatly influenced by the extent of its adoption among social media users.

Video- and Photo-Sharing Media

Video- and photo-sharing sites, such as YouTube and Flickr, allow people to publish and share videos and photos easily. These types of sites can give job candidates a realistic view into organizations and the jobs that are available. An example of how a company might use a video-sharing site, such as YouTube, to recruit candidates is "The Green Dot" video created by a Deloitte employee. Deloitte sponsored a contest open to all Deloitte employees to create a 5-minute video to answer the question, "What's your Deloitte?" "The Green Dot" was one of the videos that stood out among the 2,000 video entries. In "The Green Dot" video an employee dressed as a client services "superhero" and used comedy and ingenuity to explain what it meant to work at Deloitte in terms of the values, traditions, and daily work at the firm. The video has been viewed over 37,000 times and is even featured in Deloitte recruiting materials (DeloitteFilm-Fest, 2007; Meister & Willyerd, 2010).

Overall, companies may use photo-sharing sites to highlight office work environments or to show current employees interacting with clients in order to give candidates a visual image of what a potential job will entail. Many companies are also uploading recruitment posters to attract candidates. For example, the New York Fire Department uses Flickr to post a "2011 Firefighter Recruitment Poster" that provides visual images of firefighters helping the community, as well as benefits information, how to apply, as well as an enticing catch phrase: "The work is demanding. The schedules are flexible" (2011, Official New York City Fire Department [FDNY]'s Photostream).

Blogs

One of the older Web 2.0 technologies, a blog is a basic Web publishing system that enables users to create Web pages in the format of a personal diary (Rigby, 2008). The term "blog" is the contraction for the term Web log. Blogs have been around in some form since the 1990s. The Open Diary blog was launched in 1998 followed by Blogger in 1999 (Funk, 2009). Blogs are usually hosted and written by a particular individual and in some cases allow readers to post comments and replies to blog entries. Sometimes "bloggers"—blog authors—only focus on a certain subject, such as food, fashion, politics, etc., whereas other bloggers choose to include and write about a variety of topics (Joos, 2008). Establishing a blog can be relatively easy to set up and can be useful for employers seeking to provide web-based updates on their employment opportunities.

In 2007, Tumblr, a microblogging platform, emerged as "the easiest way to blog." Combining the capabilities of social networking media, video/photo sharing and blogs, Tumblr was launched to make it easier for users to not only post text, but to share photos, links, quotes, music and videos to their tumblelog, a short-form blog (Boutin, 2009; Tumblr, 2011). Like other social media tools, users can follow other users, or choose to make their tumblelog private. Viewing someone's tumblelog can allow for quick and fascinating absorption of information about an individual or company without having to read large amounts of text (Dannen, 2009). Companies are slowly making their way to Tumblr, which could prove to be beneficial for communicating with and building relationships with Tumblr's younger crowd. The Millennial founder of Tumblr, David Karp, emphasizes that Tumblr is less focused on mass broadcasting to an audience but more about communicating with a community (Wortham, 2010).

In terms of recruitment, blogs can be used to announce job openings and exciting new opportunities within organizations, and can also serve the purposes of providing a platform for companies to respond to criticism or praise. The information organizations choose to post to their blog can help convey organizational messages, and can also be constructed to actively engage potential candidates by soliciting questions and providing responses, which can be a great tool for recruiting Millennials because it appeals to their desire for knowledge and communication. However, after establishing a blog it is imperative that employers keep their blog content timely and interesting in order to engage readers (Joos, 2008).

Podcasts

Another Web 2.0 technology that has gained popularity in recent years is the podcast. A podcast is an audio file that is delivered via the Internet to computers or mobile devices. Podcasts are similar to radio shows and include a variety of media sources such as music, entertainment talk shows, tutorials, lectures, and even information about recruiting and hiring (Joos, 2008). There are many free podcasts available to listeners and some are offered for a small fee. Users can also choose to subscribe to a podcast where they will automatically receive the most recently recorded podcast in their media library, for example in iTunes.

The Boston-based law firm, Goulston & Storrs, recorded a series of podcasts on its Web site called the "Goulston & Storrs Recruiting Podcast Series." In these podcasts job candidates were able to hear from current partners and associates in regards to matters such as what it's like to be a lawyer at their firm (Joos, 2008). There is an online company called Jobs in Pods that offers "Jobcasting" services for companies in order to put a "voice" to their available jobs. According to the Pew Research Center nearly one out of five (19%) Internet users in the U.S. say they have downloaded a podcast (2010). Podcasts are expected to gain in popularity in the coming years (Joos, 2008).

Web-Based Gaming

Once thought to be useful solely for recreational purposes, many employers are now expanding their recruitment efforts to leverage web-based gaming technologies. In contrast to more traditional gaming systems that rely upon proprietary hardware that must be purchased by the end user, web-based games provide the ability for end users to actively play a game by solely having access to the internet, and, in some cases, related software. In terms of recruitment, this platform has allowed employers to develop targeted recruitment games that specifically relate to their labor needs, organizational goals and core occupational functions.

In particular, the web-based game Second Life has increasingly been used for recruitment purposes. A virtual community with over 16 million users, Second Life allows recruiters to establish virtual recruiting offices and virtual job fairs. This virtual world works by users creating an avatar, which is an actual or fanciful graphical representation of a person, and then using one's avatar to participate in job fairs or to drop one's resume off at a company's virtual building. The participants on Second Life come from all over the world, with the majority coming from Europe at 61%, Asia at 13 and from North America at 19% (Meister & Willyerd, 2010). This diverse pool of prospective employees allows recruiters to reach out to candidates on a global scale. Having access to candidates from all over the world without having to leave one's office can have great cost saving benefits for companies. Recruiting in Second Life can also help to reach candidates that have digital literacy skills, which has become a highly sought after trait in potential job candidates.

WEB 2.0 IN PRACTICE: EVIDENCE FROM THE PRIVATE, PUBLIC, AND NONPROFIT SECTORS

One of the hallmarks of using Web 2.0 technologies in the recruitment process is the vast range of approaches that have been employed and the ease with which organizations in both the public and private sectors can leverage existing technologies such as social media sites and web-based gaming. Unlike more traditional recruitment methods such as print media and the use of trained recruiters, Web 2.0 technologies can generally be developed with minimal start-up costs and can be easily adapted to existing skills within a workforce and recruitment needs. In many respects, employers are provided with a virtually limitless range of options in terms how they can structure their Web 2.0 recruitment practices, and, to date, there has been relatively little empirical research assessing the most effective practices in the field or highlighting approaches that may be more suitable for distinct employment contexts (Llorens, in press). Despite this shortcoming, however, it can be quite helpful to overview the Web 2.0 recruitment practices of a select group of employers that possess unique employment needs and labor market demands.

The e-recruitment practices of Google provide a great example of a private organization that has fully leveraged Web 2.0 technologies to attract high quality candidates. As one would expect, Google's quest to remain at the forefront of technological innovation necessitates an e-recruitment approach that speaks directly to the needs of Millennial job candidates, and while the organization is ranked highly in terms of desirability by college students (Partnership, 2009), they have also gone to great lengths to demonstrate the benefits of working for Google beyond simply the opportunity to work for an innovative organization. One of the primary ways they have done so is by making available to job seekers an extensive library of approximately 180 web-based videos, posted through YouTube, showing Google employees in their actual work environments and employee testimonials of why they enjoy working for the organization. Video subjects include such topics as what it's like to work in Google's Paris office, environmentally friendly ("green") practices within Google, interning at Google, Google's commitment to work-life balance and, most notably, the massage program available to employees (Google, 2011). On the whole, candidates interested in positions within the organization are provided video-based data on most key aspects of working for the organization, and since Google continuously adds to its YouTube video library, new or developing candidate interests can easily be incorporated into the organization's recruitment efforts.

In contrast to Google's ability to provide generous wage and non-wage benefits, public sector employers have also leveraged some of the same Web 2.0 technologies to promote their job opportunities and the nonpecuniary benefits of public sector employment, namely the opportunity to serve the public interest. Two agencies at the federal level of government that stand out for their efforts include the Internal Revenue Service (IRS) and the U.S. Peace Corps. When one thinks of in-demand employers, the IRS is not likely to be high on that list because of prevailing negative stereotypes of government tax collectors, but, like any organization competing for talented employees, the organization has recognized the need to reach out to a younger generation of candidates in a manner that suits them best. In the area of social networking, the IRS has developed a comprehensive approach to recruitment which includes the use of three tailored Twitter accounts, a Facebook page for answering career oriented questions, a Linkedin account to link recruiters and current employees and, last, a page on the social networking site Govloop.com. [3]

Similar to Google, the IRS also posts web-based videos through YouTube featuring testimonials by current IRS employees, and most interestingly, the agency has also developed a comprehensive web-based gaming approach for attracting younger job candidates. First, the agency maintains the *IRS Careers Island* on Second Life which allows candidates to interact with recruiters in a virtual environment (U.S. Internal Revenue Service, 2011a). Second, the agency has also developed three additional gaming options aimed at potential job applicants. One game functions as a "match style" game which requires players to solve a memory-based puzzle. A second game—*Got a Grip on College?*—targets college students and their financial management practices, and a third game—*Follow the Money*,—a screenshot of which is shown below, allows players to test their analytical and critical thinking skills as a financial crimes investigator (U.S. Internal Revenue Service, 2011b) (see Figure 6.2).

Taken as a whole, it is evident that the IRS has made a strategic commitment to engage a younger generation of job applicants despite the relatively critical perceptions of the agency in the broader U.S. labor market.

Much like the IRS, the Peace Corps has also extensively employed Web 2.0 technologies to promote the benefits of volunteering across the world. Although the pecuniary benefits afforded Peace Corps volunteers are minimal and the working conditions are typically in challenging and harsh environments, the organization employs a wide variety of tools to

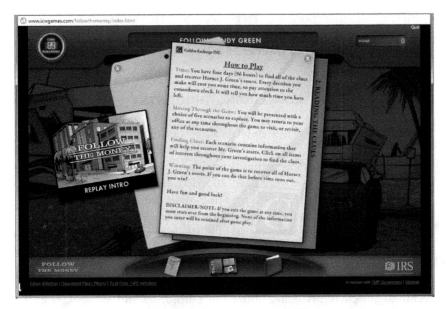

Figure 6.2.   IRS careers—Web-based recruitment game "Show me the money."

attract potential volunteers. In addition to networking with candidates through Facebook and Twitter, the Peace Corps also highlights the experiences of current volunteers through streaming image libraries on the popular sites Flickr and Tumblr. To further educate potential applicants on the working conditions and duties of volunteers, the organization also hosts a web-based game—*Peace Corps Challenge*—on its primary career website. The game places players in a fictional village named Wanzuzu where they are confronted with scenarios such as addressing a contaminated water supply and working with village elders (Peace Corps, 2011).

As previously stated, one of the key characteristics of employing Web 2.0 technologies in the recruitment process is the relatively low cost associated with their use. This characteristic can be considered a major benefit to nonprofit organizations, especially those relying primarily on volunteer service to meet their mission goals. In this regard, the United Way stands out as a nonprofit organization that has fully leveraged these new technologies in reaching out to current and future volunteers. Like the other highlighted organizations, the United Way maintains Facebook, Twitter and YouTube pages, and also maintains an up-to-date blog promoting their volunteer efforts across the country (United Way, 2011). Big Brothers Big Sisters of America has also adopted a similar approach to Web 2.0

recruiting by incorporating Facebook and Twitter into its volunteer recruitment efforts, as well as posting volunteer testimonials on a dedicated YouTube page (Big Brothers Big Sisters of America, 2011).

CONCLUDING THOUGHTS

Overall, while the previously described recruitment efforts represent only a small fraction of the innovative Web 2.0 recruitment practices available to employers, what is clear is that the relatively low start-up costs for initiating web-recruitment efforts have afforded employers across all sectors the opportunity to reach out to Millennial candidates in a way that addresses their predominant communication patterns and their employment needs. Perhaps the one constant in the recruitment of Millennial job candidates is the hyper-pace with which new technologies are ushered into the workplace and leveraged in the quest for talented candidates. While this chapter has sought to describe some of the primary Web 2.0 technologies currently being utilized by employers and job seekers in the private, public and nonprofit sectors, it is inevitable that new technologies are currently being developed, and it is only matter of time before these newer technologies supplant and/or supplement those currently considered mainstream.

For human resources professionals, this environment of rapid technological innovation necessitates a commitment to continuous learning and adaptation, especially as it relates to the recruitment of Millennial job candidates and the younger candidates that will follow them. Although organizations such as Google and the U.S. Internal Revenue Service may be at the forefront of leveraging contemporary Web 2.0 recruitment methods in their quest to attract Millennial candidates, to remain at a competitive advantage will require a continued commitment to seek out and adopt newer technologies. Even as this chapter is being written, technologies related to mobile computing devices (i.e., smart phones and tablet computers) hold the promise to further transform the manner in which employers provide relevant employment information to potential applicants. For example, the market for mobile computing recruitment applications is beginning to rapidly expand with private employers such as PepsiCo and public employers such as the U.S. Office of Personnel Management formally launching mobile career applications for users of Apple's Ipad and Iphone, as well as Android based mobile computing devices (PepsiCo, 2011; U.S. Office of Personnel Management, 2011). Suffice it to say that while these developments may now represent the cutting edge of e-recruitment efforts, newer technologies are inevitably a few years, if not months, away.

NOTES

1. Just as job seekers will research the companies they wish to work for, companies may also research job seekers, especially ones that have applied for a position and who have sent in their resume. Companies might "Googilize" potential candidates by entering their name in a search engine and see what comes up. Individuals with common names, such as Smith or Jones, may not produce any results but individuals with unique names may produce some useful information to help determine if the candidate is a good match for the company, such as their Facebook profile (Lane, 2003, p. 40). Not only is it important for companies to maintain their online image and brand, but job candidates must also be aware of the image they are portraying on the Web as well.

2. In recent years, the U.S. federal government has taken an active role in promoting governmentwide Web 2.0 use as a means of sharing information related to a wide range of topic areas from federal job vacancies to policy initiatives. For a comprehensive description of federal Web 2.0 practices use, see http://www.howto.gov/social-media (U.S. General Services Administration, 2011).

3. Govloop is an independent social networking site that was launched in 2008 as a tool to connect government employees and recruiters across federal, state and local government. Similar to other social networking sites, Govloop users can establish unique web profiles and communicate with fellow members concerning employment opportunities and other characteristics of public sector employment.

REFERENCES

Big Brothers Big Sisters of America. (2011). Volunteer to start something. Retrieved from http://www.bbbs.org/site/c.9iILI3NGKhK6F/b.5962345/k.E123/Volunteer_to_start_something.htm.

Boutin, P. (2009, March 13). Tumblr makes blogging blissfully easy. *The New York Times*. Retrieved from http://gadgetwise.blogs.nytimes.com/2009/03/13/tumblr-makes-blogging-blissfully-easy/

Cober, R. T., Brown, D., Blumental, A., Doverspike, D., & Levy, P. (2000). The quest for the qualified job surfer: It's time the public sector catches the wave. *Public Personnel Management, 29*, 479-495.

Dannen, C. (2009, May). What the hell is Tumblr? And other worthwhile questions. *Fast Company*. Retrieved from http://www.fastcompany.com/blog/chris-dannen/techwatch/what-hell-tumblr-and-other-worthwhile-questions

DeloitteFilmFest (poster). Deloitte Film Festival—The Green Dot [Video]. (2007, September). Retrieved from http://www.youtube.com/watch?v=id0uHBuhXtY.

Facebook. (2012). Key facts. Retrieved from http://newsroom.fb.com/content/default.aspx?NewsAreaId=22

Funk, T. (2009). *Web 2.0 and beyond: Understanding the new online business models, trends, and technologies*. Westport, CT: Praeger.

Gielhll, T. (2011). The use of social networks in recruiting continues to grow. Retrieved from http://www.hci.org/lib/use-social-networks-recruiting-continues-grow

Google. (2011). Life at Google. Retrieved from http://www.youtube.com/lifeatgoogle

Google+. (2011). Retrieved from http://www.google.com/intl/en/+/learnmore/

Hirschman, C. (2006, July). Here they come. *Human Resource Executive Online*. Retrieved from http://www.hreonline.com/HRE/printstory.jsp?storyId=5931825

Joos, J. G. (2008). Social media: New frontiers in hiring and recruiting. *Employment Relations Today*, 51-59.

Jurkiewicz, C. E., & Brown, R. G. (1998). GenXers vs. boomers vs. matures: Generational comparisons of public employee motivation. *Review of Public Personnel Administration, 18*, 18-37.

Lane, F. S. (2003). *The naked employee: How technology is compromising workplace privacy*. New York, NY: AMACOM.

Llorens, J. J. (2011). A model of public sector e-recruitment adoption in a time of hyper technological change. *Review of Public Personnel Administration, 31*(4), 410-423.

Llorens, J. J., & Kellough, E. J. (2007). A revolution in public personnel administration: The growth of web-based recruitment and selection processes in the federal service. *Public Personnel Management, 36*, 207-222.

Meister, J. C., & Willyerd, K. (2010). *The 2020 workplace: How innovative companies attract, develop, and keep tomorrow's employees today*. New York, NY: Harper Collins.

Myers, K. K., & Sadaghiani, K. (2010). Millennials in the workplace: A communication perspective on millennials' organizational relationships and performance. *Journal of Business Psychology, 25*, 225-238.

Ng, E. S. W., Schweitzer, L., & Lyons, S. T. (2010). New generation, great expectation: A field study of the millennial generation. *Journal of Business & Psychology, 25*, 281-292.

Official New York City Fire Department (FDNY)'s Photostream. (2011). *2011 Firefighter recruitment poster* [online image]. Retrieved from http://www.flickr.com/photos/fdnyhome/5950800903

Olivarez-Giles, N. (2011, July 15). Twitter, launched 5 years ago, delivers 350 billion tweets a day. *Los Angeles Times*. Retrieved http://latimesblogs.latimes.com/technology/2011/07/twitter-delivers-350-billion-tweets-a-day.html

Partnership for Public Service & Universum. (2009). Great expectations: What students want in an employer and how federal agencies can deliver it. Retrieved from http://www.ourpublicservice.org/OPS/publications/viewcontentdetails.php?id=131.

Pepsico. (2011). Careers—Mobile Applications. Retrieved from http://www.pepsico.com/Careers/Mobile-Apps.html

Pew Research Center for the People and the Press. (2007). *How young people view their lives, futures and politics: A portrait of "Generation Next."* Retrieved from http://people-press.org/files/legacy-pdf/300.pdf

Pew Research Center for the People and the Press. (2010). *Millennials a portrait of generation next: Confident. Connected. Open to change.* Retrieved from http://pew-socialtrends.org/files/2010/10/millennials-confident-connected-open-to-change.pdf

Rigby, B. (2008). *Mobilizing generation 2.0: A practical guide to using web 2.0 technologies to recruit, organize, and engage youth.* San Francisco, CA: Jossey-Bass.

Rubaii-Barrett, N., & Wise, L. R. (2007, March). From want ads to web sites: What diversity messages are state governments projecting? *Review of Public Administration, 27*(1), 21-38.

Selden, S., & Orenstein, J. (2011). Content, usability, and innovation: An evaluative methodology for government recruiting websites. *Review of Public Personnel Administration, 31*(2), 209-223.

Smola, K. W., & Sutton, C. D. (2002). Generational differences: Revisiting generational work values for the new millennium. *Journal of Organizational Behavior, 23*, 363-382.

Tumblr. (2011). About Tumblr. Retrieved from http://www.tumblr.com/about

Twenge, J. M., Campbell, S. M., Hoffman, B. J., & Lance, C. E. (2010). Generational differences in work values: Leisure and extrinsic values increasing, social and intrinsic values decreasing. *Journal of Management, 36*, 1117-1142.

Twitter. (2011). About Twitter. Retrieved from http://twitter.com/about

U.S. Internal Revenue Service. (2011a). IRS careers island in second life. Retrieved from http://jobs.irs.gov/secondlife.html

U.S. Internal Revenue Service. (2011b). Explore your future: Follow the money. Retrieved from http://www.icwgames.com/followthemoney/index.html

U.S. General Services Administration. (2011). Howto.gov—Social media. Retrieved from http://www.howto.gov/social-media

U.S. Office of Personnel Management. (2011). Mobile assistance on the road to success—the USAJOBS iPhone/iPad app. Retrieved from https://my.usa-jobs.gov/FeaturedArticle/FeaturedArticleContent.aspx?ArticleID=474&ArticleTypeID=1&count=5

U.S. Peace Corps. (2011). Peace corps challenge. Retrieved from http://www.peacecorps.gov/game/

United Way. (2011). Live united. Retrieved from http://liveunited.org/blog/

Walker, H. J., Feild, H. S., Giles, W. F., & Bernerth, J. B. (2008). The interactive effects of job advertisement characteristics and applicant experience on reactions to recruitment messages. *Journal of Occupational and Organizational Psychology, 81*, 619-638.

Wortham, J. (2010, August 1). Media companies try getting social with Tumblr. *The New York Times.* Retrieved from http://www.nytimes.com/2010/08/02/technology/02tumblr.html

Yeaton, K. (2008). Recruiting and managing the "Why?" generation: Gen Y. *The CPA Journal, 78*, 68-72.

Zusman, R. R., & Landis, R. S. (2002). Applicant preferences for web-based versus traditional job postings. *Computers in Human Behavior, 18*, 285-296.

CHAPTER 7

NEW SELECTION METHODS FOR A NEW GENERATION

Jeffrey Crenshaw and Kyle Brink

INTRODUCTION

Although organizations experience subtle changes in the relevant labor market and workforce over time, every few decades organizations are faced with a more significant shift as one generation begins to retire and a new generation enters the workforce. Organizations and businesses are currently facing this type of transition as members of the Millennial Generation (i.e., "Millennials") are rapidly replacing many retiring Baby Boomers. With any such change, organizations, and particularly human resources departments, are faced with a number of challenges, including identifying the values of the members of the incoming generation, leveraging those values to attract individuals to the organization, and selecting those individuals most likely to succeed on the job.

Despite the challenge that these generational shifts bring, the current shift also presents significant opportunities to modify and improve traditional human resource management processes and leverage these improvements to attract, select, and retain high quality employees. This chapter discusses utilizing technology, specifically video and multimedia technology, in employee selection to find innovative ways to help address

Managing Human Resources for the Millennial Generation, pp. 159–181
Copyright © 2012 by Information Age Publishing
159

the generational shift. The values and skills of the Millennial Generation are presented and, using the context of signaling theory, we outline how selection systems communicate to candidates for employment information about job attributes and organizational values that candidates then use to make decisions about the organization (Rynes, Bretz, & Gerhart, 1991). In addition, the chapter outlines how technology-based selection systems not only convey information on organizational values that align with values of the Millennial Generation, but also help address traditional selection challenges such as improving validity, reducing group differences, enhancing efficiency, and reducing costs. Finally, a case study involving the design and implementation of a video-based employment selection process and a technology-enhanced testing facility is presented.

THE MILLENNIAL GENERATION

A generation is defined as a group or cohort that shares a range of birth years and, as a result of similar age, experience the same historical events or sociocultural experiences at similar critical development stages (Kupperschmidt, 2000; Smola & Sutton, 2002). These shared experiences and events work to collectively shape the preferences, feelings, and values of the cohort, ultimately influencing major life decisions regarding issues such as work, family, and politics, among others. It is generally accepted that there are five living generations: "The Greatest Generation" (those born before 1925), "The Silent Generation" (those born between 1928 and 1945), The Baby Boomers (born from 1946 through 1964), "Generation X" (born from 1965 to 1980), and "The Millennial Generation" (born between 1980 and 1995) (Pew Research Center, 2010).

As mentioned, generational groups share many common attitudes, values and preferences that develop in the context of social, historical, and economic events of a defined time period. As each new generation comes of age, its members are often defined, labeled and, at times, stereotyped based on differences in generational norms, behaviors, or even pop culture. The key for human resource professionals it to weed through stereotypical labels to identify any true differences between generations, particularly as new generations enter the workforce, and find ways to attract and select the best and brightest. So, to understand differences between the approximately 75 million members of the Millennial generation and those of previous generations, it is necessary to consider the events and times in which they grew up and the impact on their skills and values.

Millennials get their label from the fact that they are the first generation to come of age in the new millennium. Their development has corresponded with a number of social and economical shifts, as well as significant historical events. Millennials are said to have been raised at the most child-centric time in our history (Thielfoldt & Scheef, 2004). This purported focus on the child during developmental years has led to Millennials being characterized or portrayed as self-confident and well adjusted (CBS News, 2008). Millennials are also the most racially diverse generation in American history (PBS NewsHour, 2010) and are characterized as *celebrating* diversity, moving beyond their Generation X predecessors who were characterized as *tolerating* diversity (Thielfoldt & Scheef, 2004). Additionally, significant sociocultural events such as the terrorist attacks of 9/11 have also impacted this generation during a crucial period of socialization. Reports have indicated that this event has led Millennials to evaluate life priorities and pursue careers that allow them to make their personal lives a top priority (Corporate Leadership Council, 2005). Members of the Millennial Generation have also experienced salient political shifts, as well as military wars and the consequences of those wars (Noble & Schewe, 2003). Additionally, in recent years, large portions of Millennials have started to enter the workforce or are attempting to enter the workforce during a period of severe recession, which has dampened their optimism about their opportunities in the labor market and expectations of work-life balance (De Hauw & De Vos, 2010).

Although the aforementioned events and factors have helped to shape the Millennial Generation and separate it from previous generations, none have been more significant than the increased pervasiveness and accessibility of information technology. Major technological advances generally impact the work and home life of all people; however, such developments often go hand in hand with generational shifts or changes (Pew Research Center, 2010). Unlike Generation X before them, Millennials were not introduced to "modern" technology as much as they were born into a time that has been marked by an information technology revolution. Individuals within this generation have experienced little, if any of their lives without significant exposure to continual developments in technology, including personal computers and laptops, mobile phones, digital video, and the internet. Millennials have been described as "history's first 'always connected' generation" (Pew Research Center, 2010, p. 1) and the "wired generation" (Hanman, 2005). As a result, where Generation X is characterized as *using* technology, the Millennial Generation is described as *assuming* technology (Thielfoldt & Scheef, 2004).

Recent research by the Pew Research Center (2010) took an in-depth look at the values, attitudes, and behaviors of the Millennial Generation and found that not only do Millennials embrace technology, but that they view it as the defining characteristic of their generation that differentiates them from their predecessors. Millennials are described as being:

Steeped in digital technology and social media, they treat their multitasking hand-held gadgets almost like a body part—for better and worse. More than eight-in-ten say they sleep with a cell phone glowing by the bed, poised to disgorge texts, phone calls, e-mails, songs, news, videos, games and wake-up jingles. (Pew Research Center, 2010, p. 1)

Not surprisingly, Millennials' use of technology outpaces previous generations in all areas identified in the survey, including internet use, social networking, wireless connectivity, online videos, cell phone use, and texting (Pew Research Center, 2010). Where many members of previous generations may see value in technological advances, many also see challenges and downsides to keeping up with a fast changing and evolving field. A significant portion of Millennials, on the other hand, have a level of familiarity with technology that has led them to value it as an integral part of their lives. They are comfortable with evolving technology and they expect technology to advance and to be used in new and innovative ways.

With the increasing number of Baby Boomers reaching retirement age, organizations are approaching a crisis as they seek to attract, hire, and retain Millennials to fill the gap (Ng, Schweitzer, & Lyons, 2010). The manner in which organizations handle this transition has major implications for a number of organizational issues, including the success or failure of human resources initiatives (Jurkiewicz, 2000; Smola & Sutton, 2010). Thus, part of the challenge facing human resource professionals is identifying and leveraging the values of the incoming generation. Smola and Sutton (2002) define values as "what people believe to be fundamentally right or wrong" (p. 365); however, as they consider values in the context of work and generational differences they cite Dose's (1997) definition of work values: "Work values are the evaluative standards relating to work or the work environment by which individuals discern what is 'right' or assess the importance of preferences" (p. 366). Understanding and responding to generational differences in work values, as defined, can enhance work and organizational effectiveness (Egri & Ralston, 2004).

As previously outlined, there are a number of reports of different values of the Millennial Generation, many of which are unsubstantiated by research or insufficient to meet the definition of a work value as previously defined. Despite the lack of clear data on some attributed values, one primary area that has been clearly established as core to the identity of Millennials, and one of their primary values, is technology. It is within the framework of technology and employee selection that there are significant opportunities for organizations to connect with Millennials and transition smoothly through this generational shift.

EMPLOYEE SELECTION AND THE MILLENNIAL GENERATION

Although recent years have experienced a recession and higher unemployment rates, there is still a significant need for organizations to plan for aggressive recruitment and selection of effective workers. As Millennials are entering the workforce, Baby Boomers are reaching retirement age at a significantly increasing rate. Because the number of Baby Boomers far exceeds the number of Millennials, many business reports have asserted that the future labor supply will not meet employer demand, resulting in a labor shortage (Levine, 2008). Though the extent of any shortage is difficult to predict, organizations that fail to adapt and plan for a tightening labor market could face a staffing crisis (Ng, Schweitzer, & Lyons, 2010). In such times, employee selection methods and processes become even more critical as the need to accurately predict job performance and attract high performing employees is paramount.

Multimedia/Video-Based Selection Tests as Hiring Instruments

When devising a hiring process the ideal selection procedure would be highly predictive of job performance, would maximize diversity by resulting in low or no differences in test performance between protected groups, would be efficient and cost effective to administer, and would be well received by candidates. Despite extensive research on traditional selection measures, no single selection procedure has been able to consistently meet all of these goals. Traditionally, many individually-administered selection procedures (e.g., structured interviews, job simulations, and work samples) have resulted in comparably high levels of validity and lower group differences than their group-administered, paper and pencil counterparts (e.g., cognitive ability tests, job knowledge tests). Notwithstanding these positive outcomes, individually-administered selection processes are used less frequently than group-administered tests because they are typically more expensive and time consuming for organizations to administer. However, as Millennials are beginning to enter the workforce, organizations have an opportunity to capitalize on the increased value they place on technology and their enhanced skill sets in the application of technology to improve employee selection procedures.

A particularly fruitful area for improvement in personnel selection processes is multimedia and video technology. Technological advances have enhanced the ease of use and increased the accessibility of tools, equipment, and software designed for editing, producing, recording, and delivering digital videos. In this age of rapid technological innovation, a number of organizations have begun to reduce the administrative draw-backs of individually-administered selection measures by utilizing video-based test administration and assessment processes. Administrative costs can be greatly reduced to the extent that selection processes can be administered via a video monitor in lieu of live test administrators. Multimedia technology allows for greater administrative efficiency by increasing the number of candidates that can be tested at the same time (limited, of course, by the amount of video presentation and recording equipment available) and reducing human resource costs associated with the administration of selection instruments, such as structured interviews, by greatly reducing the number of individuals needed to staff the test.

In addition to improving the efficiency of administration, video technology can also be used to more efficiently and cost-effectively evaluate candidate performance. Candidates' verbal and nonverbal responses to video-presented test stimuli can be video recorded for assessment outside of the administration process. Armed with little more than a laptop computer (depending upon the mode of recording) evaluators can view candidates' recorded responses *after* the administration and make appropriate ratings. This approach eliminates time that evaluators would traditionally spend administering the process, instead allowing them to focus time and effort solely on the evaluation of the quality of the candidates' responses. The sophistication of the recording and playback equipment is a significant driver of the time and cost efficiencies that can be achieved in the assessment process.

The use of video and multimedia technology in selection has not only resulted in positive outcomes for administrative issues, but also other key factors such as validity, group differences, and applicant reactions. The extent to which video is used in a selection administration can vary greatly. For example, video used in its most basic form could simply provide test questions in text on a video monitor while a narrator presents the questions orally; however, substantially more benefit would be expected by incorporating a greater degree of video-based information in the process. Callinan and Robertson (2000) state that "Video and computer-based situational testing offers the potential for creating more realistic simulations of work contexts than afforded by written tests, but with more practical convenience than live simulations" (p. 254). More advanced use of video, for example, could include incorporating video vignettes or scenarios into a structured interview to enhance the content of questions. Incorporating multimedia technology in this manner increases the fidelity of selection exercises in terms of the stimuli presented to candidates and helps depict more realistic and more detailed behavioral incidents (Weekley & Jones, 1997). Lievens and Sackett (2006) stated that increased fidelity resulting from the inclusion of video can enhance point-to-point correspondence to the criterion. Supporting this assertion, Lievens and Sackett (2006) and Christian, Edwards, and Bradley (2010) found that video-based situational judgment tests (SJTs) had a stronger relationship to job performance criteria than did paper-and-pencil SJTs.

In addition to enhancing validity, increasing the fidelity of selection processes has the potential for significant benefits to diversity. By increasing fidelity, reducing ambiguity, and lowering the amount of reading required for the test researchers expect reductions in race-based group differences. Chapman and Webster (2003) also argue that "by removing or reducing the human element from the selection procedure, and introducing a standardized, impartial, technology solution many hope that adverse impact can be significantly reduced or eliminated and more valid decisions made" (p. 114). A number of research studies have provided support for these assertions, finding that incorporating video significantly reduced group differences and adverse impact (Chan & Schmitt, 1997; Pulakos & Schmitt, 1996). Such outcomes align very well with the increased value Millennials' place on diversity.

Several additional studies have also demonstrated positive applicant reactions to multimedia based selection processes. As mentioned, video increases the fidelity of the test and Burke (1993) found that "applicants favor procedures with a strong relationship to job content, particularly when administered in nonpaper-and-pencil formats, such as work samples or simulations" (p. 245). Lievans & Sackett (2006) found higher levels of user acceptance of high fidelity SJTs than SJTs with lower levels of fidelity. Richman-Hirsch, Olson-Buchanon, and Drasgow (2000) investigated the impact of multimedia technology on perceptions of the Conflict Resolution Skills Assessment and found that compared to computerized and paper-and-pencil versions the multimedia version: yielded more positive reactions, was perceived as being more valid, provided more relevant information about the job, and was found it to be more enjoyable.

In addition to these significant advantages, Van Iddekinge, Raymark, and Roth (2003) outline a number of other benefits of incorporating video into selection processes. First, video administration can increase the fairness and standardization of the testing process by eliminating any variance across administrators and ensuring that all candidates receive the exact same information. Secondly, they state that using recorded responses for evaluation can help maximize the number of candidates who can be evaluated by an interviewer (or interview panel), which can improve the validity and reliability of the interview. Because different raters have different rating tendencies, minimizing the number of interview raters reduces the number of different rater tendencies introduced into the evaluation process, which should subsequently further improve reliability and validity.

Multimedia/Video-Based Selection Tests as Recruiting and Signaling Instruments

Research has primarily focused on employee selection from the perspective of the organization and the process of predicting the best candidate(s) for employment. However, Anderson (2001) aptly points out that, "While it is nonsensical to claim that selection techniques do not act as predictors, it is equally nonsensical to claim that is all that they do" (p. 84). A singular focus on a selection measure's role in identifying potentially successful employees can lead to other important aspects of a selection process, such as serving as a mechanism for communicating organizational values and preentry socialization, to be grossly underutilized. Although it is of paramount importance to ensure that your selection system accurately identifies those individuals most likely to succeed on the job, organizations that ignore what their selection devices communicate to applicants run the potential of missing significant opportunities to leverage their ability to attract quality employees, particularly Millennials.

Signaling theory is a communication-based theory in which "signals" are used to reduce information asymmetry between two parties (Spence, 2002). The basic premise of the theory is that decisions are made based on information at hand and that individuals (or organizations) can strategically send signals to increase information available for making decisions. Conelly and colleagues (2011) describe three primary elements to signaling theory: the signaler, the signal, and the receiver. The signaler is the entity that is attempting to provide information about its attributes, values, or information believed to be important; the signal is the mechanism for communicating the information; and the receiver is an "outsider" who lacks information about the organization in question, but who would like to receive the information (Connelly et al., 2010). As signaling theory is focused on information that the signaler generally wishes to convey, the signal is almost always designed to communicate positive information that the receiver values (Connelly et al., 2010).

Signaling theory is often used to demonstrate how applicant attraction to an organization can be influenced by information, or signals, about an organization's characteristics or values revealed during recruitment or selection activities (Celani & Singh, 2011; Rynes, 1991). Thus, the manner in which applicants are recruited and the manner in which their ability to perform the job is assessed can be critical in an applicant's decision making processes regarding whether he or she desires to work for the given organization. During a recruitment and hiring process an organization can send two types of information: instrumental attributes and symbolic meanings (Lievens & Highhouse, 2003). Instrumental attributes refers to factual information about the organization, such as pay, work hours and promotional opportunities, that can be conveyed more directly (Celani & Singh, 2011). Symbolic meanings, on the other hand, refer to more subjective organizational attributes, such as the organization's value of diversity and level of innovation that applicants infer from less direct communication through signals picked up during the recruitment and selection process (Celani & Singh, 2011). Lievens and Highhouse (2003) found that both instrumental attributes and symbolic meanings predict organizational attractiveness.

Despite the ability of an organization to attempt to attract applicants through signaling information in recruiting and selection processes, it is insufficient to simply communicate *any* information about the organization. Celani and Singh (2011), using research by Highhouse, Thornbury, and Little (2005), suggest that the signaling process depends upon the signals sent *and* upon the inferences drawn by the applicants receiving those signals. Celanie and Singh (2011) state:

> the greater the extent to which applicants believe that being a member of the recruiting organization is relevant to their social identity, the more likely they are to infer a greater number of positive inferences about the organization from its recruiting activities and thus have a more positive view of that organization ... stronger organizational identification by applicants will provide more of a positive impact on applicant attraction to the recruiting organization via outcomes such as job pursuit intentions, job-organization attraction, and job acceptance intentions. Increased applicant attraction to the recruiting organization will also positively impact the quantity and quality of the organization's applicant pool. (p. 225).

Not only does an applicant's identification with the organization have the potential to impact hiring decisions, but posthire organizational identification can also positively impact organizational tenure and job involvement (Riketta, 2005).

A number of positive applicant reactions to video-based selection tests have been discussed; however, such innovative approaches can signal something even greater to Millennials. Given the strong identification that Millennials have with technological innovation, incorporating technology into the selection process can signal to Millennials that the hiring organization has similar values. It can also signal to the Millennial Generation that the organization values the skills they bring to the workforce. Finally, creating selection tests that heavily incorporate video content can give an organization an opportunity to indirectly signal other values. For example, if an organization values diversity and wants to ensure that is conveyed to candidates for employment, video scenarios incorporated into the testing process can include diverse groups of people playing the roles of employees in various work-related situations to which the candidates must respond. Thus, video gives organizations greater ability to communicate their mission, goals, and values while also enhancing their selection decisions.

A NEXT GENERATION SELECTION PROCESS—A CASE STUDY

It was from the multifunctional perspective of employee selection outlined above that the Personnel Board of Jefferson County (henceforth referred to as the "Personnel Board") approached overhauling its selection practices. Presented in this section is a case study involving the Personnel Board's design and implementation of a "new generation" technology-enhanced testing center and selection processes.

The Organization

The Personnel Board serves as a human resources agency responsible for administering the civil service system for municipalities and government agencies located in Jefferson County, Alabama. Established in 1935 by Alabama state statute, the Personnel Board serves municipalities located within Jefferson County (currently 18 in total) and five countywide governmental entities (e.g., Jefferson County Department of Health, Emergency Management Agency, et al.) for a total of 23 "jurisdictions." The Personnel Board civil service (or merit) system is comprised of roughly 9,000 employees within approximately 700 different job classes. Despite providing services to the aforementioned jurisdictions, the Personnel Board is an independent agency and is not a part of any political, county, or municipal organization within the system (Crenshaw & McCullough, 2010). Instead, the Personnel Board is governed by a 3-member Board and reports to a Citizens' Supervisory Commission comprised of community leaders, including heads of local colleges, universities, and civic groups. The services provided by the Personnel Board include (Crenshaw & McCullough, 2010):

- developing, managing, and administering a job classification system and compensation structure for its member jurisdictions;

- maintaining and managing employee civil service records for all employees within the Personnel Board system;
- conducting needs analysis and developing and delivering employee training programs;
- developing, distributing, and maintaining performance appraisal instruments;
- facilitating employee relations functions to include providing consultation and advice regarding employee rights and responsibilities; and
- facilitating the hiring of qualified individuals to fill vacancies within the system by recruiting and testing candidates for employment, and referring names of the most qualified candidates based on test performance.

Despite these functions and services being part of the Personnel Board operations for decades, not all were performed to needed standards and, in 2002, the Personnel Board was faced with a significant organizational crisis. Two decades earlier, in 1981, the Personnel Board entered into a federal consent decree due to discriminatory selection practices. After more than 20 years of struggling to make the changes necessary to comply with the requirements of its decree, in 2002 the U.S. District Court for the Northern Division of Alabama found the Personnel Board in contempt of the consent decree (Crenshaw & McCullough, 2010). Based on an evaluation of the progress made in complying with the decree, the federal court determined that the Personnel Board was ill-equipped in terms of staff and infrastructure to meet its obligation to administer the civil service system for its member jurisdictions, particularly the employee selection processes, in a fair and nondiscriminatory manner (McCullough & Sims, 2007). As a result of this conclusion, the federal court appointed a Receiver to assume control over most of the Personnel Board's functions (Crenshaw & McCullough, 2010).

It was under those circumstances that the Personnel Board of Jefferson County found itself in late 2002. The Personnel Board had to find a way to ensure that it could administer selection systems for its member jurisdictions in a valid and legally defensible manner, and in a manner that complied with all aspects of its consent decree. In addition to these significant challenges, the Personnel Board also faced the issue of a severely tarnished image in the minds of its member jurisdictions and the general public, particularly the potential labor force from which it hoped to attract top-notch, high quality talent to fill government positions within the system. Thus, in late 2002, the Personnel Board launched an intensive business reengineering initiative that included revamping its selection processes (McCullough & Sims, 2007).

A Revamped Selection Process

As the Personnel Board began its strategic planning process, the organization's goals were not only to administer highly valid tests, but also to administer tests that maximized the diversity of the system's workforce, that could be implemented in a cost-effective manner, and that allowed the organization to become a model agency in the minds of its relevant stakeholders and, specifically, potential candidates for employment. Officials within the Personnel Board knew that taking a traditional approach to its selection system would leave the organization facing a number of significant issues. Simply utilizing traditional paper and pencil tests to administer to individuals for employment into its system may have achieved one or two of the Personnel Board's goals, but certainly not all.

A thorough review of research findings indicated that high-fidelity selection measures (e.g., structured interviews, work samples, and job simulations) are among the most valid predictors of job performance and result in substantially lower group differences than traditional paper-and-pencil tests. Consequently, the Personal Board believed that favoring high-fidelity measures over traditional paper-and-pencil measures could minimize historical barriers to employment access. So, to maximize the validity and diversity resulting from its selection processes, the Personnel Board sought to implement large scale high fidelity measures that, as outlined earlier, can best accomplish both of these objectives. However, when considering a shift in the manner in which the Personnel Board approached employment testing, substantial practical limitations, including time-consuming and costly administrations for large applicant pools, were apparent.

The new millennium ushered in a period of rapid technological innovation that presented a number of opportunities for a variety of human resources initiatives. Strategic planning discussions at the Personnel Board heavily involved the potential for technology to serve as a key facilitator of organizational change and help meet all of the desired goals of the revamped selection process. At that time, a number of organizations were beginning to explore the potential for video in selection. "Video is the Next Wave" was the title of an article in the January, 2004, edition of *The Industrial-Organizational Psychologist* that described video as the "next 'must-have' tool" (Weiss, 2004) and Van Iddekinge and colleagues (2003) indicated that using video in selection interviews was a growing trend. It was in this context that the Personnel Board considered video technology as a means of reducing the administrative time and costs typically associated with the aforementioned individualized selection methods.

There were immense benefits to leveraging the technological advances and the growing accessibility of video software and equipment, as well as the growing video production and editing skill set of Millennials who were just beginning to enter the workforce. Video and audio technology could be used to present test stimuli, such as interview questions, to candidates in lieu of live administrators. In addition, video and audio recording equipment allow candidates' oral and behavioral responses to test stimuli to be recorded for later evaluation or assessment. The Personnel Board believed these two important functions of video technology could eliminate the need for extensive human resources during the administration of a structured interview or job simulation to a large candidate pool, one of the drivers of the increased cost and time typically associated with such selection instruments.

Finally, strategic planning discussions also focused on the impact of the implementation of technology-driven selection processes on the Personnel Board's image. Such an aggressive and bold approach to employee selection, and the marked difference from past practices, would allow the Personnel Board to signal to all relevant stakeholders, including parties to the consent decree, its member jurisdictions, and potential candidates for employment, that this was a new and improved Personnel Board. The implementation of such processes would be designed to signal that the Personnel Board system is an innovative and exciting place to work that is committed to fair and valid selection procedures and dedicated to building a diverse workforce. Additionally, such changes would signal to the younger generation entering the workforce that the Personnel Board values technology and the skills that Millennials bring to the table; hopefully leading to a substantial interest in employment within the Personnel Board system from a new group of highly skilled individuals.

After thoroughly vetting the potential benefits of designing a process for incorporating video technology into high fidelity selection measures, the Personnel Board decided that, where feasible, multimedia playing devices would be used to present test stimuli for candidates and video and audio recording equipment would be used to record candidates' responses to the test stimuli. Multimedia playing devices (e.g., laptops) would then be used after the test administration for trained assessors to playback, observe, and rate candidates' responses. This process translated in its most basic form would be a video-enhanced structured interview. In this situation, job-related interview questions and evaluation criteria would be developed through professionally and legally appropriate means. The interview questions would then be translated into a video recording. This may be as simple as the question being presented in text form on a video monitor with a narrator orally reading the question or more complex with video vignettes included to provide additional context and fidelity to the question. Once recorded, the video would be duplicated a designated number of times so that multiple interviews could be conducted simultaneously with multiple candidates in different rooms or locations. When it is time to start the interview, the candidate would observe a video monitor that would present the question, along with a designated response time. Once the question is presented, the candidate would respond verbally while his or her response is recorded using a video camera and microphone. After answering all questions, the candidate's video recorded responses would be stored for later assessment and another candidate would be escorted to the interview room to go through an identical process. After the interview is administered to all candidates, the recorded candidate response videos would be viewed by trained assessors and appropriate ratings would be made. Essentially the same process would be used regardless of the exact nature of the video-based test being administered. Once the process was generally defined and understood, the Personnel Board turned attention to the type of equipment and facilities needed to allow for this type of process to be administered efficiently and effectively. The result was the development of a technology-enhanced testing facility.

The Technology-Enhanced Testing Facility

In order to administer the multimedia, high-fidelity selection measures outlined, the Personnel Board needed a facility equipped with the necessary equipment and devices to present and record video, a sufficient number of rooms to test multiple candidates simultaneously, a physical layout conducive to processing large numbers of candidates quickly and efficiently, and a centralized control center that allowed for observing candidates and controlling video and audio equipment remotely. A technology-enhanced testing facility was developed through extensive commitment by management and staff at the Personnel Board, as well as significant input from external experts in architecture and video and software engineering.

The development of the facility involved gathering substantial amounts of test administration data (e.g., projected number of candidates to be processed in a given test day, estimated length [in time] of tests to be administered, number of administrative staff needed, etc.), conducting extensive research on various aspects of video technology, thoroughly reviewing and vetting the test administration process, and conducting numerous meetings that involved planning, projecting costs and evaluating proposed ideas. Once a general sense of the needs and layout was established, the Personnel Board then worked to anticipate any potential problems. Many discussions were held to cover issues such as cost, logistics, practicality and feasibility of what was desired, and system reliability and security, among others, before final equipment specifications and technical drawings were finalized.

From these processes, a test administration facility was designed within the existing footprint of the building in which the Personnel Board was located and, over the course of a year, the test administration facility was built. The facility consists of 19 individual testing rooms, four group-level examination rooms for group-based exercises or test preparation, a check-in/orientation room to greet and hold groups of applicants prior to their examinations, a processing room to serve as a test administration hub, and a central control room from which the entire facility can be observed and all video-based equipment controlled. All rooms, except the processing room, are equipped with video and audio presentation and recording capabilities through flat panel LCD monitors and ceiling mounted 360-degree motorized pivot video cameras and multidirectional microphones. The control room contains five DVD players that allow for five different sets of test stimuli to be pushed to the testing rooms simultaneously, two touch panel control monitors for operating the video playing and recording equipment in each room, 48 digital video recorder encoders and storage units (a primary and secondary for each test room to prevent information loss due to equipment failure), and two network storage devices for long-term digital video storage. Figure 7.1 contains a blueprint of the physical layout of the facility. Photographs of select rooms from the technology-enhanced testing facility are presented in Figure 7.2.

The Administration and Assessment Process

The technology-enhanced testing facility is used to administer high-fidelity video-based tests to large groups of candidates for many jobs within the Personnel Board system. Candidates for a given job are invited to arrive at the check-in room at a scheduled test time. In this room, candidates sign in and observe video-based realistic job previews or receive other helpful information about the job or test while they wait to begin the testing process. In the typical process, candidates are taken in groups of 18 to a group-based examination/exercise room where they are provided information via video presented on flat screen LCD monitors that is fed from the control room. Then, depending on the nature of the given test, candidates are allowed a designated amount of time to prepare for subsequent test components or are oriented to the testing process. After

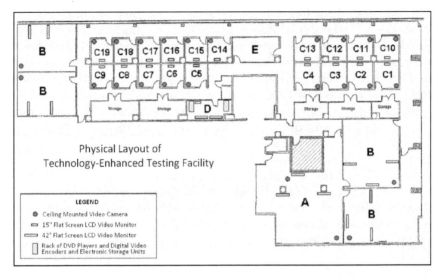

Note: Room A is the check-in/group orientation room, rooms denoted by a B are group-level examination/prep rooms, rooms denoted with a C are individual examination rooms, room D is the central control room, and room E is the processing room

Figure 7.1.   Physical layout of the technology-enhanced testing facility.

the conclusion of the time in the group exercise room, all 18 candidates are then escorted to individual testing rooms equipped with audio and video presentation and recording equipment (the 19th room is used as a back-up in case of equipment failure). Video test stimuli (e.g., interview questions or job simulations) are simultaneously fed from the control room to specified individual testing rooms. Candidates observe the test stimuli and typically respond verbally to prompts from the test video. Each candidate's verbal and nonverbal responses are fed to the control room where they are recorded to digital video files and stored on network storage devices. Once each group of 18 completes a phase of the examination process, the room is backfilled with the next group of 18 candidates until all candidates have completed the test.

Once the test administration is complete, the Personnel Board has each candidate's examination responses recorded to an individual digital video file stored on network storage device. At a date shortly after the test administration is complete, the Personnel Board conducts a process where candidate videos are observed and the candidates' responses evaluated or assessed. For this assessment process, the Personnel Board recruits subject

Note: Top-left is an individual testing room; top-right is the hallway outside of the individual test rooms; bottom left is a group level test room; bottom right is the central control room.

Figure 7.2.   Photographs of technology-enhanced testing facility.

matter experts (i.e., assessors) from across the country, thoroughly trains the assessors on how to make valid and accurate ratings, and thoroughly reviews the test questions and rating criteria with the assessors. Once the assessors are fully trained, they are placed in appropriate panels and instructed to access designated candidate files using a computer connected to the network drive containing the video files, observe the candidate's responses, and make appropriate ratings. While most of these assessment processes are conducted within the individual testing rooms in the testing facility, the storage of video files on the Personnel Board network has opened up additional remote assessment opportunities. With the increased accessibility videoconferencing software and/or websites, the Personnel Board is exploring the feasibility of conducting remote assessment processes whereby assessors are trained via webinar and then set up in assessor panels via videoconferencing. In such instances, assessors will be able to remote access candidate video files through a secure virtual private network connection. Such advances can result in even greater reduction in costs due to the elimination of expenses associated with assessor travel and lodging that occurs with on site assessment.

The Results

As with any major initiative, the implementation of this "next generation" testing facility required extensive planning and hard work to accomplish, but the results experienced by the Personnel Board as a result of its implementation have been extremely positive. Overall, the facility utilizes cutting-edge technology and improves on traditional employment testing through the development of better tests with greater levels of fidelity, increased test standardization and fairness, greater administrative efficiency and reduced costs associated with administering and assessing high-fidelity selection tests, reduced test performance differences for protected groups, and a significantly improved image of the Personnel Board.

Better Tests

The video-based testing approach adopted by the Personnel Board allows the test developer flexibility in the presentation of test stimuli that many other types of tests do not. Commonly used tests, such as multiple-choice job knowledge tests or traditional structured interviews for example, can measure various types of knowledge and/or abilities necessary for successful job performance; however, adding video to these types of tests creates greater levels of richness and realism that can lead to more accurate assessments of candidates' proficiency levels. Not only does increased fidelity have the potential to lead to more accurate assessments, it also leads to increased job-relatedness and greater levels of content validity.

Greater Standardization

Another advantage of the approach taken by the Personnel Board to employment testing over other individualized assessments (e.g., traditional face-to-face structured interviews) is that it is the apex of standardization (i.e., consistency in treatment of candidates). Using video to provide instruction and test stimuli ensures that every candidate experiences the exact same administration. For example, using video-based structured interviews not only allows video stimuli to provide greater contextual information, but also improves standardization by ensuring that the context (or question) is presented in the exact same manner to all candidates and that the scenario being portrayed is consistent across all candidates. The results of this standardization are increased fairness of the process, reduction in the potential biases that can be associated with face-to-face interactions, and reduced litigation over inconsistent treatment.

Greater Efficiency and Lower Costs

With the appropriate equipment, using video to administer high-fidelity examinations reduces the human resources necessary to present test stimuli, increases the number of candidates that can complete a process in a given period, and reduces the number of individuals needed for assessment of candidate performance. These administrative improvements substantially increase the feasibility of using high-fidelity tests for large applicant pools. In its first year of use, the Personnel Board experienced over a 50% increase in the number of high-fidelity tests administered compared to the preceding year and in 2010 the Personnel Board processed over 8,000 candidates through high-fidelity tests using the technology-enhanced testing facility. To understand the scale of testing that can occur using the facility, the Personnel Board has administered video-based structured interviews to over 400 candidates in a single day.

Reduced Demographic Test Performance Differences

The video based testing approach used by the Personal Board results in substantially lowered race-based group differences than traditional paper-based measures, therefore creating fairer access to employment opportunities. A meta-analysis using data from over 30 video-based structured interviews administered by the Personnel Board revealed mean score group differences between Blacks and Whites of approximately .29 standard deviations (Crenshaw, 2006). This difference is consistent with past research on high-fidelity measures, and is substantially lower than the 1.0 standard deviation difference typically found with many paper-based measures.

Improved Organizational Image

As previously discussed, one of the goals of the overhaul to the selection process was to rebrand the Personnel Board and repair its tarnished image in the eyes of its stakeholders and potential applicants. Since the implementation of this new generation testing process and facility, the Personnel Board has been featured in *IPMA-HR News*, been the basis for a number of presentations made at professional conferences, and won the International Personnel Assessment Council's 2008 Innovation in Assessment Award.

In addition to the positive attention garnered from the human resources community, the Personnel Board has seen nearly a 50% increase in the number of applications received 2006 compared to 2010. Although there are a number of external factors that would likely help explain a substantial portion of this increase (e.g., the strength of the economy, the unemployment rate), this increase is still noteworthy. Although it is impossible to tell the amount of increase, if any, that is due to greater candidate attraction to the organization as a result of its revamped selection procedures, it is likely safe to conclude that the revised process is not negatively impacting candidate attraction.

Legal Compliance

Of the positive results experienced by the Personnel Board as a result of the revamped selection process and test facility, one of the most important has been legal compliance. Using this process, the Personnel Board was able to achieve undisputed release of selection procedures for all remaining Personal Board job classes (over 30 in total) from the federal consent decree, successfully meet all other requirements of its consent decree, and end decades of federal oversight and court supervision. Such progress closed the book on a tortured legal history of the Personnel Board and allowed the system to move forward with a fresh and innovative start.

SUMMARY

Although generational shifts in the workforce can present challenges, this chapter set out to illustrate that these shifts can also present great opportunities for organizations to evaluate and improve traditional human resource management processes. Not only do new generations bring different values and attitudes, but they also bring new skill sets and new perspectives on many work-related issues. The Millennial Generation is fostering an increased focus on technology and the ways in which it can aid traditional business practices. By focusing on the opportunities to leverage technology, specifically video and multimedia technology, in personnel selection we sought to illustrate the significant benefits that can be achieved when such workforce shifts are embraced. Utilizing video and multimedia technology in selection has demonstrated the ability to improve many historically troubling issues in selection, to include maximizing both validity and diversity, reducing administrative costs, and enhancing candidate perceptions. It also holds the potential to allow organizations to provide applicants with greater insight into organizational values in an effort to attract the best of the incoming workforce. The presentation of the case study sought to emphasize the potential of multimedia technology in employee selection, provide insight into the processes for accomplishing this type of initiative, and exemplify the types of positive outcomes that can be achieved when an organization embraces new opportunities to enhance human resource practices.

REFERENCES

Anderson N. (2001). Towards a theory of socialization impact. Selection as pre-entry socialization. *International Journal of Selection & Assessment, 9*, 84-91.

Burke, M. J. (1993). Computerized psychological testing, impacts on measuring predictor constructs and future job behavior. In N. Schmitt & W. C. Borman (Eds.), *Personnel selection in organizations* (pp. 203-239). San Francisco, CA: Jossey-Bass.

Callinan, M., & Robertson I. T. (2000). Work sample testing. *International Journal of Selection and Assessment, 8*, 248-260.

CBS News. (2008). The Millennials are coming. *CBS News*. Retrieved from http://www.cbsnews.com/stories/2007/11/08/60minutes/ main3475200.shtml

Celani, A., & Singh, P. (2011). Signaling theory and applicant attraction outcomes. *Personnel Review, 40*, 222-238.

Chan, D., & Schmitt, N. (1997). Video-based versus paper-and-pencil method of assessment in situational judgment tests: Subgroup differences in test performance and face validity perceptions. *Journal of Applied Psychology, 82*, 471-485.

Chapman, D. S., & Webster, J. (2003). The use of technologies in the recruiting, screening, and selection processes for job candidates. *International Journal of Selection & Assessment. 11*, 113-120.

Christian, M. S., Edwards, B. E., & Bradley, J. C. (2010). Situational judgment tests: Constructs assessed and a meta-analysis of their criterion-related validities. *Personnel Psychology, 63*, 83-117.

Connelly, B. L., Certo, S. T., Ireland, R. D., & Reutzel, C. R. (2011). Signaling theory: A review and assessment. *Journal of Management, 37*, 39-67.

Corporate Leadership Council. (2005). *HR considerations for engaging Generation Y employees*. Washington, DC: Corporate Executive Board.

Crenshaw, J. L. (2006). The use of video and audio technology in structured interviews: Effects on psychometric properties, group differences, and candidate perceptions. *Dissertation Abstracts International, Section B: The Sciences and Engineering, 69*(1-B), 723.

Crenshaw, J. L., & McCullough, R. (2010). Managing change in a job classification system. In R. R. Sims (Ed.), *Change (transformation) in government organizations* (pp. 119-135). Charlotte, NC: Information Age.

De Hauw, S., & De Vos, A. (2010). Millennials' career perspective and psychological contract expectations. *Journal of Business and Psychology, 25*, 293-302.

Dose J. (1997). Work values: An integrative framework and illustrative application to organizational socialization. *Journal of Occupational and Organizational Psychology, 70*, 219-241.

Egri, C. P., & Ralston, D. A. (2004). Generation cohorts and personal values: A comparison of China and the U.S. *Organization Science, 15*, 210-220.

Hanman, N. (2005). Growing up with the wired generation. *The Guardian.* Retrieved from http://www.guardian.co.uk/technology/2005/nov/10/newmedia.media

Highhouse, S., Thornbury, E. E., & Little, I. S. (2005). Social-identity functions of attraction to organizations. *Organizational Behavior and Human Decision Processes, 103,* 134-146.

Jurkiewicz, C. L. (2000). Generation X and the public employee. *Public Personnel Management, 29*(1), 55-74.

Kupperschmidt, B. (2000). Multigeneration employees: Strategies for effective management. *Health Care Manager, 19,* 65-76.

Levine, L. (2008). Retiring baby-boomers = A labor shortage? *United States Senate Special Committee on Aging.* Retrieved from http://aging.senate.gov/crs/pension36.pdf

Lievens, F., & Highhouse, S. (2003). The relation of instrumental and symbolic attributes to a company's attractiveness as an employer, *Personnel Psychology, 56,* 75-102.

Lievens F., & Sackett P. R. (2006). Video-based vs. written situational judgment tests: A comparison in terms of predictive validity. *Journal of Applied Psychology, 91,* 1181-1188.

McCullough, R., & Sims, R. R. (2007). A look at contemporary human resource management information systems. In R. R. Sims (Ed.), *Human resource management: Contemporary issues, challenges and opportunities* (pp. 537-571). Charlotte, NC: Information Age.

Ng, E. S. W., Schweitzer, L., & Lyons, S. T. (2010). New generation, great expectations: A field study of the millennial generation. *Journal of Business and Psychology, 25,* 281-292.

Noble, S. M., & Schewe, C. D. (2003). Cohort segmentation: An exploration of its validity. *Journal of Business Research, 56,* 979-987.

PBS NewsHour. (2010). Millennials: A new generation takes center stage. *PBS.* Retrieved from http://www.pbs.org/newshour/extra/ features/us/jan-june10/millennials_02-26.html

Pew Research Center. (2010). Millennials: A portrait of generation next. *Pew Research Center.* Retrieved from http://pewresearch.org/ millennials/

Pulakos, E, & Schmitt, N. (1996). An evaluation of two strategies for reducing adverse impact and their effects on criterion-related validity. *Human Performance, 9,* 241-258.

Richman-Hirsch, W. L., Olson-Buchanon, J. B., & Drasgow, F. (2000). Examining the impact of administration medium on examinee perceptions and attitudes. *Journal of Applied Psychology, 85,* 880-887.

Riketta, M. (2005). Organizational identification; A meta-analysis. *Journal of Vocational Behavior, 66,* 358-384.

Rynes, S. L. (1991), Recruitment, job choice, and posthire consequences. In M. D. Dunnette (Ed.), *Handbook of industrial and organizational psychology* (2nd ed. pp. 399-444). Palo Alto, CA: Consulting Psychologists Press.

Rynes, S. L., Bretz, R. D. J., & Gerhart, B. (1991). The importance of recruitment in job choice: A different way of looking. *Personnel Psychology, 44,* 487-521.

Smola, K. W., & Sutton, C. D. (2002). Generational differences: Revisiting generational work values for the new millennium. *Journal of Organizational Behavior, 23*, 363-382.

Spence, M. (2002). Signaling in retrospect and the informational structure of markets. *American Economic Review, 92*, 434-459.

Thielfoldt, D., & Scheef, D. (2004). Generation X and the Millennials: What you need to know about mentoring new generations. *Law Practice Today—American Bar Association.* Retrieved from http://www.abanet.org/lpm/lpt/articles/mgt08044.html

Van Iddekinge, C. H., Raymark, P. H., & Roth, P. L. (2003, April). *Live versus videotaped structured interviews: Are they comparable?* Paper presented at the 20th annual Society for Industrial and Organizational Psychology Conference, Chicago, IL.

Weekley, J. A., & Jones, C. (1997). Video-based situational testing. *Personnel Psychology, 50*, 25-49.

Weiss, R. J. (2004). Leading edge: Video is the next wave. *The Industrial-Organizational Psychologist, 41*, 101-107.

CHAPTER 8

CONSIDERING GENERATIONAL DIFFERENCES IN ASSESSING WORK VALUES ... A UNIFYING APPROACH

Kenneth P. Yusko and Brian L. Bellenger

INTRODUCTION

Published works on generational differences often include a list of the values commonly associated with particular generations (for example, see Brazeel, 2009; Crampton & Hodge, 2006; Jenkins, 2008; Karp, Fuller, & Sirias, 2002; Lancaster & Stillman, 2002; Lockwood, Cepero, & Williams, 2009; Zemke, Raines, & Filipczak, 2000). Traditionalists are seen as loyal, detail-oriented (Lockwood et al., 2009) and risk-averse (Jenkins, 2008). Baby Boomers are process-oriented (Zemke, 2000) and competitive (Lancaster & Stillman, 2002). Generation Xers are independent (Zemke et al., 2000) and results-oriented (Crampton & Hodge, 2006). Millennials are tech-savvy (Brazeel, 2009; Lockwood et al., 2009) and socially responsible (Lockwood et al., 2009). Potential differences in generational values, particularly work values, present interesting possibilities for improving the quality of an organization's staffing choices.

Managing Human Resources for the Millennial Generation, pp. 183–200
Copyright © 2012 by Information Age Publishing
All rights of reproduction in any form reserved.

To make the best hiring decisions, a firm must correctly assess how well a candidate fits the culture it is trying to promote (Bowen, Ledford, & Nathan, 1991). Traditional staffing systems focus on finding candidates who have the competencies necessary to succeed on the job. These conventional selection methods try to evaluate a candidate's knowledge, skills, and abilities. However, such techniques often fail to systematically take into account the work values, interests, and goals that define a firm's culture, such as embracing change, work ethic, and team orientation.[1]

Selecting employees who share these work values is critical. This is because identifying candidates who are a good fit increases the chance that the candidate will support and reinforce the organization's values, priorities, and "way of doing business" such as working long hours as necessary, taking a courageous or ethical stance even when there is an easy way out, or constantly seeking opportunities to innovate and improve the organization's products and services.

Beyond simply getting the most competent employees, maximizing candidate/organization fit provides a host of other benefits. For example, new employees tend to more readily adjust to their new jobs and surroundings and can more quickly get up to speed and begin to contribute. Employees who are a good fit are likely to be more committed to the firm and exhibit good attitudes, modeling effective "organizational citizenship behaviors" such as going the extra mile by staying late when needed, or, when possible, covering for a coworker who is overwhelmed with another set of tasks. Employees who fit in well are likely to be more satisfied with the firm and their jobs, enhance firm morale, have better attendance, and contribute to lower unwanted turnover rates (Corporate Leadership Council, 2006).

A central question in generational research is whether certain work values are reliably and differentially distributed across particular generational categories. If so (legal issues around age discrimination aside, for the moment), organizations that prize certain values could conceivably shape their recruiting and hiring practices to maximize the likelihood of identifying employees who possess these key values. Examples of work values that, according to many authors, might be found more often within one generational category than another include the following:

Traditionalists

- loyalty to the organization (Jenkins, 2008; Lockwood et al., 2009; Tolbize, 2008);
- detail-orientation (Lockwood et al., 2009; Zemke et al., 2000);
- team-orientation (Jenkins, 2008; Tolbize, 2008);

- risk aversion (Jenkins, 2008; Tolbize, 2008); and
- formality (Tolbize, 2008).

Baby Boomers

- process-orientation (vs. results-focused) (Tolbize, 2008; Zemke et al., 2000);
- embracing change (Zemke et al., 2000);
- team-orientation (Lockwood et al., 2009);
- competitiveness (Brazeel, 2009; Lancaster & Stillman, 2002); and
- learning-orientation (Lancaster & Stillman, 2002).

Generation Xers

- independence (Zemke et al., 2000);
- limited loyalty to the organization (Bova & Kroth, 2001);
- results orientation (vs. focus on process) (Crampton & Hodge, 2006; Lockwood et al., 2009);
- informality (Lancaster & Stillman, 2002; Lockwood et al., 2009);
- embracing change (Lockwood et al., 2009; Zemke et al., 2000); and
- individual and team orientation (Karp, Fuller, & Sirias, 2002).

Generation Yers/Millennials

- team orientation (Lancaster & Stillman, 2002; Lockwood et al., 2009; Zemke et al., 2000);
- embrace change (Sujansky & Ferri-Reed, 2009);
- learning orientation (Lancaster & Stillman, 2002);
- results orientation (vs. focus on process) (Crampton & Hodge, 2006); and
- comfort with technology (Brazeel, 2009; Lockwood et al., 2009).

However, before we can begin to consider shaping our staffing systems to capitalize on such potential differences, we have to ensure these differences really exist. The prevailing belief, certainly in the popular press, has been that generational differences are real and HR systems should be developed and adjusted, accordingly (DeMeuse & Miodzik, 2010; Renn, 2008). However, evidence is mounting that this may not be the case (see

Deal, 2007; De Meuse & Miodzik, 2010; Giancola, 2006; Macky, Gardner, & Forsyth, 2008; Reeves & Oh, 2008).

There are multiple reasons to be cautious about leaning too heavily on the common generational difference—work value scheme to tailor an organization's recruiting and hiring practices. The first and most important is that the validity of the generational difference construct with respect to work values has, thus far, received limited empirical support (Jurkiewicz & Brown, 1998; Macky, Gardner, & Forsyth, 2008). According to Reeves and Oh (2008), there is a lack of consensus across researchers about whether generational differences exist. These researchers conclude that "generational differences are weak as a researchable variable in a manner similar to learning styles" (p. 302) and maintain that the generational difference literature includes little rigorous scientific support. Similarly, Giancola (2006) found the weight of the research evidence "lends credence to the notion that the generational approach may be more popular culture than social science" (p. 33). Parry and Urwin (2011) agree, noting that although the concept of generational differences has a strong basis in theory, the empirical evidence is mixed, at best, and many studies fail to find the predicted differences. Finally, Deal (2007) concluded that the concept of generational differences was largely a myth, finding few differences across generations and noting that people are more similar than different across the categories. "When you hold the stereotypes up to the light, they don't cast much of a shadow," Deal (2007b, p. 11) cautions.

It should be noted that methodological problems have challenged generational differences research (Macky, Gardner, & Forsyth, 2008; Parry & Urwin, 2010). In particular, the frequent use of a cross-sectional survey approach has entangled potential true generational differences with other variables, such as age (Deal, 2007; Parry & Urwin, 2010). According to Reeves and Oh (2008):

> the bottom line on generational differences is that ... researchers should treat this variable as failing to meet the rigor of definition and measurement required for robust individual difference variables. The gross generalizations based on weak survey research and the speculations of profit-oriented consultants should be treated with extreme caution, in a research and development context. (p. 302)

Even allowing for the possibility of generational differences existing, a key concern is the size of the effect. In studies where differences are found, the effect size tends to be relatively small (Macky, Gardner, & Forsyth, 2008). Related to this is an issue central to any cross group research —that of the degree of within-group variation. In generational differences research, studies have found significant within-group variation relative to across-group variation (Deal, 2007). Thus, validity issues aside, the potential utility of the generational construct is a concern.

Another potential concern with crafting staffing systems with respect to generational differences is legal issues relating to age. The Age Discrimination in Employment Act (1967, as amended in 1986 and 1991) specifically prohibits discrimination in hiring against individuals at least 40 years of age in the United States. Thus staffing practices favoring, say, Millennials at the expense of the older generations would face legal scrutiny and bear the burden of demonstrating job-relatedness. This would also obviously make it unacceptable for a hiring manager, who prefers to hire Millennials because of their perceived technological savvy or flair for innovation, to exclude other generational groups from receiving appropriate consideration.

Finally, in addition to legal issues, scarcity of candidate talent considerations would make it unduly restrictive to overly favor a particular generational group. That is, given the large degree of individual within-group generational variation, looking too closely at one group, and excluding others from consideration, would result in the organization overlooking too many candidates with the appropriate qualities—something very few organizations can afford to do.

ASSESSING WORK VALUES ACROSSS ALL GENERATIONS

Thus, given concerns such as those outlined above, researchers such as Deal (2007) and Renn (2008) advise organizations to spend less time focusing on generational labels and more time on the variables and characteristics they are interested in promoting, such as particular work values, across the entire set of generational categories. That said, what are the options for organizations to recruit and assess candidates with a particular set of work values (potentially reflecting the "best" aspects of each of the generational groups as identified in the popular press)?

Tools that reliably enable an organization to find candidates who match its culture on values such as the above have only recently emerged.[2] Because relatively few firms currently possess such technology, this area presents an excellent opportunity to secure a competitive edge in identifying top talent that will really mesh with the organization.

Step 1: Assess the Organization's Culture

Before attempting to decide which candidates would be a good match, we must first take the pulse of the organization's culture. That is, the climate and culture of the firm must be systematically analyzed. Both qualitative (e.g., interview) and quantitative (e.g., survey) methods exist for conducting culture audits. Both approaches aim to derive a profile on a number of key culture dimensions (distributed across generations), such as those discussed above. For example, the following set of work values and interests, related to the key generational values discussed thus far, may be useful in helping to diagnose a firm's culture (see O'Reilley, Chatman, & Caldwell, 1991):

- innovation;
- collaboration/competition;
- focus on results vs. process;
- risk seeking vs. risk aversion;
- social and environmental responsibility; and
- independence vs. team orientation.

Note that these are only categories or cultural dimension labels. To be useful, the dimensions must be well-defined and/or contain detailed examples.

Step 2: Obtain Candidate Cultural Profiles

After assessing the organization's culture, one must measure, at a behavioral level, the extent to which a candidate's preferences and work values match the culture of the firm. A candidate's work values, interests, and goals are best measured by personal work values assessment instruments. These tools are multi-item surveys that yield a value profile for each candidate. The questions are designed to measure personal attributes that relate to the cultural elements presented above.

One example is the Organizational Culture Profile designed by Siena Consulting, different forms of which can be used both to profile a candidate's work values as well as characterize an organization's culture. The following are examples from the 63 item Organizational Culture Profile (© 2009 Siena Consulting, all rights reserved) that map on to the generational work values of interest discussed at the beginning of the chapter.

Sample Organizational Culture Profile
Work Value-Culture Match Items

1. I prefer a work environment with

    (a) Team-based work assignments

    (b) Individual work assignments

2. I prefer a work environment that is

    (a) More structured
    (b) Less structured

3. I prefer a work environment that is

    (a) Formal
    (b) Informal

4. I prefer a work environment that is

    (a) Cooperative
    (b) Competitive

5. I prefer a work environment where I can

    (a) Express my individuality
    (b) Fit in with the group

6. I prefer a work environment where

    (a) There are standard procedures to follow
    (b) There are few rules and regulations

7. I prefer a work environment where we

    (a) Embrace change
    (b) Respect precedent

8. I prefer a work environment that is

    (a) Big picture oriented
    (b) Detail oriented

9. I prefer a work environment that

    (a) Uses tried-and-true solutions
    (b) Experiments with new ideas

10. I prefer a work environment where

    (a) Results are rewarded
    (b) Effort is rewarded

11. I prefer a work environment where

(a) My supervisor is involved in my day-to-day work
(b) My supervisor leaves me alone to do my work

12. I prefer a work environment with

   (a) High job security
   (b) Opportunities for quick advancement

13. I prefer a work environment that has lots of

   (a) Structure
   (b) Flexibility

14. I prefer a work environment that is

   (a) Goal oriented
   (b) Process oriented

15. I prefer a work environment where I am rewarded for

   (a) Working hard
   (b) Results

16. I prefer a work environment that is focused on

   (a) Innovation
   (b) Implementation

17. I prefer a work environment that has

   (a) Ambiguity
   (b) Cut and dry answers

18. I prefer a work environment where I receive

   (a) Constant feedback about how I am doing
   (b) Intermittent feedback about how I am doing

19. I prefer I work environment that

   (a) Values loyalty
   (b) Values performance

20. I prefer a work environment where

   (a) My role is well-defined
   (b) My role is what I make of it

Candidates can manifest differences on the above cultural values in two key ways. First, on any given item two candidates may endorse different options. For example, one candidate may prefer to work in teams while another prefers working alone; one candidate may prefer to work in a highly unstructured environment while another seeks out structured situations and clear guidelines; one candidate may prefer the informality of a dot com office while another enjoys the relative formality of a Wall Street firm, etc.

Second, even if candidates agree on the same options for any number of items, they may differ on the centrality or importance of any given item. That is some items (or sets of items that form the culture dimension) may be critical and others merely "nice to have."

In the same way, organizations will differ on how intensely each item or dimension defines their climates and cultures. For example, everyone may agree that diversity, job security, a strong work ethic, and innovation are valuable cultural attributes. However, organizations vary immensely on the relative importance they place on these, and other, characteristics of their culture. A culture audit is aimed at specifying the degree of criticality of each item in defining the firm's culture and yields a list of those characteristics most (and least) central to the organization's culture. As a side benefit, in addition to using the audit to hire the people who best fit with the firm, a culture profile can also be used to periodically change or adjust the organization's culture to fit its changing needs and the needs of its employees.

An important consideration when conducting a culture audit is taking into account the idea of *"profile"* versus *"level"* (*see* Bowen, Ledford, & Nathan, 1991; O'Reilly, Chatman, & Caldwell, 1991). Profiles illustrate how well the firm and candidate match in terms of their relative rankings on cultural factors. That is, a profile reveals the cultural characteristics that are most and least important to the organization and the candidate. For example, when considering the importance of compensation, both the firm and the candidate might agree that compensation is relatively unimportant (as long as it is reasonable) versus other factors such as the opportunity to perform interesting work and do a great deal of socially responsible pro bono work of one's choice. That would indicate a good profile match.

Level is important in an absolute sense. Considering the above example, although the organization and the candidate agree that compensation is relatively unimportant (as long as it is reasonable), perhaps the candidate's idea of a low but reasonable salary is many thousands of dollars more than the organization's conception. This would be a levels difference.

In terms of socially responsible pro bono work, although both the candidate and organization value it highly, perhaps the firm's idea of providing good pro bono opportunities is to specify what type of work can be done and to make a lot of firm resources available to support as much work as the employee wants to do. The candidate, on the other hand, wants to choose his or her own type of pro bono initiatives, have organizational resources to support them, and have the work count as much as work servicing clients. Although both parties see pro bono work as a priority, there may be a clear difference in absolute value. Thus, there is a profile match but a difference in levels. In order to maximize fit, both profile and level factors must match.

In addition to the culture profile fit method discussed above personality inventories can also be used to measure certain personal attributes relevant for determining fit. These instruments often contain hundreds of items that measure diverse aspects of personality (e.g., need for achievement). Some are very well established and based on a great deal of research. However, many are off-the-shelf products that were not designed for cultural fit applications. As a result, key cultural attributes may not be measured. Furthermore, many of these personality tests require interpretation by a trained interpreter. Assuming the organization wants to invest the time and resources, information provided by these established personality measures can be very rich and informative.

Selection techniques that usually focus on competencies, such as simulations and structured interviews, can also be adapted to measure some culturally relevant candidate attributes. For example, if teamwork is a major cultural theme of the organization, simulations can be designed to focus on team-related issues including joint problem solving and interpersonal conflict. These assessment exercises might be conducted in contexts such as project-team meetings that focus on collaboration and communication. Similarly, structured interviews might be designed to tap culturally relevant elements such as work ethic, orientation to rules, and risk taking.

Although simulations and interviews can provide a great deal of useful culturally-relevant information, their main purpose is to assess competencies important for the job. These techniques cannot simultaneously and comprehensively measure both competencies and culturally relevant attributes. In addition, personal work value assessment instruments are likely to be more efficient in providing information relating to organizational culture. For this reason, data derived from simulations and structured interviews are better used as a supplementary rather than primary source of culture-related information.

Legal Requirements[3]

Some people may also question the legality of making hiring decisions based on fit. In fact, the legal requirements for using a candidate-firm fit process are identical to competency, or knowledge, skill, and ability-based approaches. First, selection procedures resulting in no adverse impact on protected groups are not illegal. As discussed, culture match tools often promote demographic diversity and result in lower levels of adverse impact than other selection tools (such as cognitive ability tests). Second, if the hiring system does result in adverse impact, the selection process must be shown to be related to job performance. The organizational audit and candidate matching methods presented above help to ensure that the procedure is job-related. This would be in sharp contrast to selecting individuals possessing the presumed desired work values based on their membership in a particular generational group.

Capitalizing on Recruiting Channels

The challenges of staffing an organization in a manner that promotes diversity, meets legal requirements, and supports the cultural and operational goals of the organization are significant. As the Baby Boomer generation begins to retire, the workforce is shrinking such that older workers are needed to remain on the job in order to stimulate economic growth (Feyrer, 2007). Rapid advances in technology may suggest that Millennials (perceived as more "tech savvy") are ideal candidates for jobs, but research suggests that job performance differences between younger and older workers are either nonexistent or nonsignificant (Prenda & Stahl, 2001). How then do organizations make appropriate hiring decisions?

Preliminary Screening Tools

In order to begin targeted recruiting and preliminary screening of job candidates, organizations must first determine the preferred outcome. Using cultural and/or personality measures to determine an applicant's fit to the job and the organization, as described above, is certainly appropriate and viable for selecting candidates. However, jobs also have requisite knowledge, skills and abilities (KSAs) necessary for successful performance of the duties and tasks making up the job. As organizations conduct organizational culture assessments, they should also conduct job reviews in order to identify cultural and job factors that could serve as the basis for screening.

Many organizations, particularly in the public sector, rely on minimum qualifications to serve as initial screens of applicants (Schwartz, 1977). Traditionally, minimum qualifications have focused on specific education requirements for entry-level jobs (e.g., bachelor's degree in marketing) and additional work experience for jobs beyond the entry-level (e.g., 3 years of experience in a public relations or marketing firm). Recent studies have demonstrated that qualifications based on a thorough job analysis and validated through linkage to the KSAs required for the job have proven to better promote diversity and correlate better with performance on subsequent selection tools than traditional minimum qualifications (Buster, Roth, & Bobko, 2005; Lange, 2005). So, in addition to cultural fit questions such as those outlined earlier in this chapter, employers might ask job applicants questions such as:

- Have you completed college-level coursework in the field of marketing?

and/or

- Do you have work experience developing and managing a marketing plan/program for an organization or product?

By developing a comprehensive screening tool that addresses task and duty oriented factors and cultural fit factors organizations can create a profile of their ideal candidate. Using this type of screen removes factors such as age/generation (as well as other protected characteristics such as race and gender) from the selection process. As long as these instruments can be shown to be job related, or if they do not adversely impact a protected class (ideally meeting both standards), they can be used to make selections.

Recruiting Strategies

Being "selective" in the assessment phase doesn't have much impact if the recruiting process fails to identify a large, deep pool of talent from which to identify the best candidates. Similar to a general approach to assessment, which focuses on key work values across all generational categories, a recruiting strategy should be multifaceted. That is, we should go beyond just focusing on, say, social networking channels to identify and recruit candidates typically associated with social media, such as Millennials.

The recruitment process, which is a key factor in determining an organization's success, consists of three phases: generating applicants, maintaining applicant interest in the organization, and influencing job choice (Barber, 1998). A comprehensive recruitment strategy, aimed at surfacing the ideal candidate, must leverage numerous tools in all three phases in order to be successful.

Phase I: Generating Applicants

The initial phase of a recruiting process involves attracting applicants to the organization through the dissemination of organizational and job information to a broad spectrum of the workforce (Barber, 1998). Traditional means of generating interest included placing advertisements in newspapers and professional publications, using radio and television to promote job vacancies, and for some higher level jobs, conducting "cold calls" of potential candidates for jobs. Additionally, organizations often send recruiters to job fairs at colleges, universities, and technical schools to promote the job opportunities offered by the organization. In recent years, web sites have become a mainstay in the recruiting process, allowing easy access to organizational information as well as a means by which job seekers can submit applications for jobs at all levels (Chapman & Webster, 2003; Kehoe, Dickter, Russell, & Sacco, 2005).

With the advent of social media tools such as LinkedIn, Facebook, MySpace, and Twitter, organizations have additional means by which to attract applicants and communicate job-relevant information. Such tools are more likely to be accessed and used by Millennials (although not exclusively so), providing the same job information as traditional recruiting means while also communicating information about the technological prowess of the organization. Some studies of recruitment have framed this initial phase of the process in a person-organization fit model, such that applicants seek to determine how well their personal values and expectations fit with the initial impressions of the organization (Turban, Lau, Ngo, Chow, & Si, 2001). By using a comprehensive recruiting model that incorporates both traditional and technologically innovative tools to attract applicants, organizations not only reach a broader spectrum of job seekers, but they also communicate a richer, more detailed image of the organization as being both conventional and forward thinking.

Phase II: Maintaining Applicant Interest in the Organization

Once an organization has generated a large applicant pool for a job, by promoting the job and the organization through a wide variety of media, the organization is then charged with the task of screening those applicants to narrow the pool, while simultaneously maintaining the applicants' interest in the organization (Barber, 1998). Each generation represented in the applicant pool may have different aspects of the organization that they find attractive. For older generations, factors such as health and retirement benefits or organizational stability may be more appealing, while Millennials may be more concerned with work flexibility, telecommuting, access to technology, or rewards for innovation. Organizations may consider tailoring messages to applicants that highlight those factors that would be most appealing, or at least make access to information regarding all of these factors readily available to applicants. Ultimately, in this phase of the recruitment process, organizations must take the broad applicant pool, and using tools such as application reviews, evaluations of cultural fit, and/or assessments of critical KSAs, make decisions regarding which applicants are best suited for employment within the organization.

An emerging concern with the use of social media in this phase of the recruiting process is that employers are beginning to require applicants to provide full access to their Facebook and other accounts as a means of checking backgrounds for inappropriate behavior and relationships. The *Wall Street Journal* reported in March, 2012 (Favate, 2012) that the legality of such actions is being questioned, and the American Civil Liberties Union is calling the action on the part of organizations an invasion of privacy. While some public safety organizations may be justified in seeking such information on applicants for law enforcement jobs, it may be perceived as unfair or irrelevant to individuals seeking jobs in fields such as engineering or marketing. As organizations attempt to narrow their applicant pool to identify top job candidates, they should balance the need to make sound selections with the desire to attract, rather than repel, such candidates.

Phase III: Influencing Job Choice

The final phase of a comprehensive recruiting program is to match job applicants to specific positions within the organization (Barber, 1998). After screening applicants using the various tools described in this chapter, it falls to the organization to determine which job finalists are best suited for vacancies within the organization. It is also critical to ensure that these applicants are satisfied with the choice(s) offered them in terms of employment.

Here again, generational differences may become factors in the staffing process. Positions that are team oriented, for example, may be more appealing to Generation X members than Millennials, while jobs that are more autonomous may be highly attractive to Millennials. With the aging and decline of the workforce, creating positions and working conditions that are favorable to employees of all working generations will be increasingly important. Factors that may seem fairly minor, such as dress codes, may have a profound impact on attraction to the organization. Leveraging technology to attract bright and motivated employees will certainly become increasingly important, but capitalizing on the wisdom and experience of more seasoned workers will also be critical to long-term success.

CONCLUSIONS

Generational differences in motivation, job performance, and commitment appear to lack support in the social science lexicon, although the prevailing perception among organizations and workers is that such differences exist. Without rigorous research to undergird these perceptions, organizations are faced with the challenge of staffing vacancies in a manner that uses the strengths of each generation to meet their needs and goals. Legally defensible systems must be in place to hire individuals in a manner that is nondiscriminatory and valid, and, in the context of this chapter, that specifically avoid age-based decision making. Using assessments that collectively evaluate applicants' work values, cultural fit, and job-relevant KSAs will likely produce a broad spectrum of qualified job candidates.

Broad and inclusive recruiting strategies will increasingly be the norm for organizations seeking to capitalize on the unique skill sets and work values of all generations. There is nothing wrong with including social networking options in the organization's recruiting strategy. In fact, sites such as Facebook, Twitter, LinkedIn, etc. have a great deal of promise for expanding the organization's reach. It is just that organizations should be as inclusive as possible in covering all recruiting options to ensure maximal coverage across the generations. Thus, instead of focusing too narrowly on exploring the recruiting potential of Facebook, the organization should be sure to also pursue other avenues of recruiting, such as networking with veteran's associations, working with AARP to identify seniors interested in returning to the workforce, visiting university campuses that cater to adults returning to school, etc. This will ensure that valued employees of all generations have access to employment opportunities in the organization.

NOTES

1.   Several sections in this chapter are drawn from Yusko, K. P., Goldstein, H. W., & Fabrizio, S. B. (2009). *The management of human capital: Essential practices for law offices.* Eagan, MN: Thomson Reuters/West.

2. Many ideas presented in this chapter are elaborated on in the following works, including Cable and Parsons (2001); Cable and Judge (1997); Ashkanasy, Broadfoot, and Falkus (2000); Bowen, Ledford, and Nathan (1991); O'Reilley, Chatman, and Caldwell (1991); Adkins, Russell, and Werbel (1994).

3. See Bowen, Ledford, and Nathan (1991).

REFERENCES

Adkins, C. L., Russell, C. J., & Werbel, J. D. (1994). Judgments of fit in the selection process: The role of work value congruence. *Personnel Psychology, 47*(3), 605-623.

Ashkanasy, N. M., Broadfoot, L. E. & Falkus, S. (2000). Questionnaire measures of organizational culture and climate. In N. M. Ashkanasy, C. P. Wilderom, & M. F. Peterson (Eds.), *Handbook of organizational culture and climate* (pp. 131-146). Thousand Oaks, CA: SAGE.

Barber, A. E. (1998). *Recruiting employees: Individual and organizational perspectives.* Thousand Oaks, CA: SAGE.

Bova, B., & Kroth, M. (2001). Workplace learning and Generation X. *Journal of Workplace Learning, 13,* 57-65.

Bowen, D. E., Ledford, G. E., & Nathan, B. R. (1991). Hiring for the organization, not the job. *The Academy of Management Executive, 5*(4), 35-51.

Brazeel, S. (2009). Recruitment practices generational characteristics. *Oil and Gas Journal, 107*(45), S2.

Buster, M. A., Roth P. L., & Bobko, P. (2005). A process for content validation of education and experience-based minimum qualifications: An approach resulting in federal court approval. *Personnel Psychology, 58,* 771-799.

Cable, D. M. & Judge, T. A. (1997). Interviewers perceptions of person-organization fit and organizational selection decisions. *Journal of Applied Psychology, 82*(4), 546-561

Cable, D. M., & Parsons, C. K. (2001). Socialization tactics and person—organizational fit, *Personnel Psychology, 54*(1), 1-24

Chapman, D. S., & Webster, J. (2003). The use of technologies in the recruiting, screening, and selection processes for job candidates. *International Journal of Selection and Assessment, 11,* 113-120.

Crampton, S. M., & Hodge, J. W. (2006). The supervisor and generational differences. *Proceedings of the Academy of Organizational Culture, Communications, and Conflict, 11,* 19-22.

Corporate Leadership Council. (2006). *HR's role in mergers and acquisitions: Tools and mandates for the chief human resources officer.* Arlington, VA: Author.

Deal, J. J. (2007). *Retiring the generation gap: How employees young and old can find common ground.* Hoboken, NJ: John Wiley.

De Meuse, K. P., & Miodzik, K. J. (2010). A second look at generational differences in the workforce: Implications for HR and talent management. *People and Strategy, 33*(2), 50-58.

Favate, S. (2012, March). Can job applicants be asked for Facebook passwords? Retrieved from http://blogs.wsj.com/law/2012/03/21/can-job-applicants-be-asked-for-facebook-passwords/?mod=google_news_blog

Feyrer, J. (2007). Demographics and productivity. *Review of Economics and Statistics, 89,* 100-109.

Giancola, F. (2006). The generation gap: More myth than reality. *Human Resource Planning, 29*(4), 32-37.

Jenkins, J. (2008). Strategies for managing talent in a multigenerational workforce. *Employment Relations Today, Winter, 34*(4), 19-26.

Jurkiewicz, C. E., & Brown, R. G. (1998). Genxers vs. boomers vs. matures: Generational comparisons of public employee motivation. *Review of Public Personnel Administration, 18,* 18-37.

Karp, H., Fuller, C., & Sirias, D. (2002). *Bridging the boomer xer-gap. Creating authentic teams for high performance at work.* Palo Alto, CA: Davies-Black.

Kehoe, J., Dickter, D., Russell, D., & Sacco, J. (2005). eSelection. In H. Gueutal & D. Stone (Eds.), *The brave new world of eHR* (pp. 54-103). San Francisco, CA: Jossey-Bass.

Lancaster, L. C., & Stillman, D. (2002). *When generations collide: Who they are, why they clash. How to solve the generational puzzle at work.* New York, NY: Harper Collins.

Lange, S. L. (2005). Content validity of minimum qualifications: Does it reduce adverse impact? (Doctoral dissertation). *Available from ProQuest Dissertations and Theses database* (UMI No. 3194493).

Lockwood, N. R., Cepero, F. R., & Williams, S. (2009). The multigenerational workforce: Opportunity for competitive success. *SHRM Research Quarterly, First Quarter,* 1-9.

Macky, K., Gardner, D., & Forsyth, S. (2008). Generational differences at work: Introduction and overview. *Journal of Managerial Psychology, 23*(8), 857-861.

O'Reilley, C. A., Chatman, J., & Caldwell, D. F. (1991). People and organizational culture: A profile comparison approach to assessing person-organization fit. *Academy of Management Journal, 34*(3), 487-516.

Parry, E., & Urwin, P. (2011). Generational differences in work values: A review of theory and evidence. *International Journal of Management Reviews, 13*(1), 79-96.

Prenda, K. M., & Stahl, S. M. (2001). The truth about older workers. *Business and Health, 19,* 30-35.

Reeves, T. C., & Oh, E. (2008). Generational differences. In J. Spector, M. Merrill, J. Van Merrienboer, & M. Driscoll (Eds.), *Handbook of research on educational communications and technology* (pp. 295-303). New York, NY: Erlbaum.

Renn, M. (2008). Debunking generational differences. *Leadership in Action, 28*(1), 23.

Sujansky, J., & Ferri-Reed, J. (2009). *Keeping the millennials: Why companies are losing billions in turnover to this generation- and what to do about it.* Hoboken, NJ: John Wiley & Sons.

Schwartz, D. J. (1977). Job sampling approach to merit system examining. *Personnel Psychology, 30,* 175-185.

Tolbize, A. (2008). *Generational differences in the workplace*. Minneapolis, MN: Research and Training Center on Community Living, University of Minnesota.

Turban, D. B., Lau, C., Ngo, H., Chow, I., & Si, S. X. (2001). Organizational attractiveness of firms in the People's Republic of China: A person–organization fit perspective. *Journal of Applied Psychology, 86*, 194-206.

Zemke, R., Raines, C., & Filipczak, B. (2000). *Generations at work: Managing the clash of veterans, boomers, xers, and nexters in your workplace*. New York NY: AMACOM.

CHAPTER 9

EMPLOYEE-FRIENDLY POLICIES AND DEVELOPMENT BENEFITS FOR MILLENNIALS

Jonathan P. West

INTRODUCTION

Work-life balance is a top career priority for many younger workers. Career demands often conflict with personal pressures, and juggling the two poses problems in both settings. Some employers, responding to employee expectations, especially among younger Millennials, have introduced employee-friendly policies to reduce home-work conflict and to help people achieve a better balance between work and nonwork life. Career development needs of younger workers also deserve special attention. Many employers have adopted employee-friendly policies and development programs that are tailored to the specific concerns of Millennial workers.

This chapter focuses on employee expectations and preferences regarding work-life issues. For instance, flextime might be a boon to some, enabling them to care for young children, telecommuting and compressed workweek could provide additional desired flexibility, and some combination of part-time or temporary employment might be preferred

Managing Human Resources for the Millennial Generation, pp. 201–228
Copyright © 2012 by Information Age Publishing

by younger workers, enabling them to better resolve competing work and personal demands. Given their age, those in Generation Y [the Millennials] are likely to be concerned about child care, adoption assistance, parental and military leave, domestic partnership coverage, and wellness programs. They are also interested in traditional economic benefits. This chapter unpackages these various policy and program alternatives as they relate to the unique needs of younger workers.

Younger workers like to receive constant feedback about their performance and to be clear regarding what is expected of them. They are likely to prefer a work environment that establishes psychological contracts which clearly spell out performance expectations and obligations. These unwritten understandings with employers help to clarify mutual needs, goals, and procedures (Berman, Bowman, West, & Van Wart, 2010). Mentoring programs can be a further boon to inexperienced younger employees who can profit from periodic dialogue and coaching from senior managers (Bowman, West, & Beck, 2010); senior managers can benefit from such mentoring relationships with younger workers as well. Generation Y employees are also anxious to have continuous learning opportunities and access to development programs (Marston, 2007; McDonald & Hite, 2008). Millennials want their good work to be recognized. They are likely to favor work settings where fast track advancement is possible.

The premise of the chapter is that employers need to understand the changing demographics of the workforce and to tailor their human resource management (HRM) policies and practices accordingly. Best practices would suggest that savvy employers be aware of the generational mix of their workers and design programs that appeal to and address the needs of this changing workforce. While employee-friendly policies and development benefits are likely favored by all employees, younger workers have special needs and expectations that deserve employer attention if they are to recruit and retain the best of the new entrants into the workplace. The challenge of achieving work-life balance and development benefits through employee-friendly policies aimed at new Millennials is crucial to organizational vitality.

The discussion begins with a brief description of changing notions of work and family relations, new labor market conditions and the implications of these developments for Millennials. The insights from psychological contract theory are then used to consider ways to improve work-life balance, employer-employee relations and organizational flexibility. With this in mind, five types of employee-friendly (and not-so-friendly) policies and practices are discussed, including flexible and alternative work schedules, work-life programs, stress reduction and wellness initiatives, traditional economic benefits, and reverse mentoring. Finally, the discussion and conclusion explore the implications of the findings for new Millennials and human resource professionals.

BACKGROUND AND DEVELOPMENTS

The modern workplace has confronted staggering changes both demographically and in employee career expectations that require organizations to design appropriate responses. Work-family policies have become increasingly salient with the influx of women into the workforce and more recently have broadened into work-life initiatives. The notion of work and family as separate domains, each with its own pressures and competing demands but operating as distinct and different spheres, has given way to what Barnett (1999) refers to as an "overlapping spheres" model. This more contemporary characterization recognizes that work and life overlap and employers need to design policies and practices that respond to these developments (Cayer & Roach, 2008; Ezra & Deckman, 1996; Saltzstein, Ting, & Saltzstein, 2001). Figure 9.1 depicts this transition from separate to overlapping spheres between work and life outside of work. The policy response, where it has occurred, has been to institute employee-friendly policies that seek to establish work-life balance and flexible schedules.

As the work situation and attitudes have changed, many workers have experienced a new psychological contract (Hilltrip, 1995; McDonald & Hite, 2008). The psychological contract goes beyond the formal contract of employment and refers to an individual's belief regarding the terms and conditions of an exchange relationship with another party (Rousseau, 1989). It encompasses the perceptions of the employer and employee regarding what each owes to the other (Berman & West, 2003; Rousseau, 1995); contracts are specific to a time and to a person. Psychological contracts include promises new employees are willing to make and inducements they expect to receive in turn (Anderson & Thomas, 1996; De Vos, De Stobbeleir, & Meganck, 2009). Perceived organizational support, a related but different concept, refers to an individual's perception concerning the extent to which an employer values an employee's contribution and cares about his or her well-being (Eisenberger, Huntington, Hutchison, & Sowa, 1986).

As the psychological contract has changed and employers have responded with new policies reflecting the move to the "overlapping spheres" model, employees may perceive these developments as forms of organizational support and respond in turn with renewed commitment and engagement at work. Conversely, perceived lack of organizational support (a breach of the psychological contract), can lead to detrimental

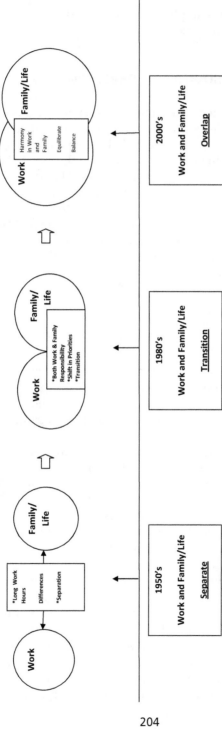

Note: The visual flow chart model shows how over time we have undergone a transition of work and family/life being separate to now being overlapping.

Figure 9.1.   Transition in work-life relations 1950 to the present.

results in areas such as job satisfaction, commitment, and job performance (Rigotti, 2009; Zhao Wayne, Glibkowski, & Bravo, 2007). Millennials, in particular, will likely respond favorably to organizational policies that improve work-life balance, enhance autonomy, and add organizational flexibility, whereas withdrawal of such policies will be perceived negatively. Before discussing these organizational initiatives, the challenges that members of Generation Y are facing as they try to join the workforce will be considered.

Job Insecurity and Changing Psychological Contract

Prior to the labor market changes in recent years, many employees expected to have a job for life and organizations would provide various appealing benefits to reinforce this expectation and to secure employee loyalty and commitment. Traditionally there was an implicit social contract where one could reasonably expect that there was a reciprocal relationship between hard work and job security. In today's labor market, younger workers can no longer rely on these assumptions given recent changes in work organization (downsizing, contracting) that emphasize increased flexibility and reduced job security. The short-term orientation of the "just-in-time" labor model has altered the psychological contract. Employees today are viewed by some employers as expendable, as noted by Adams and Balfour (2010): "The notion that organizations should care for their employees, or make long-term commitments to them, is seen as an anachronism" (p. 774). As a consequence, Millennials have reduced their expectations regarding job security, but still highly value it (Dries, Pepermans, & De Kerpel, 2008; Kowske, Rasch, & Wiley, 2010). They recognize that in today's workplace lifetime employment is rare (Tomlinson, 2007). As a result, they are more prone to have a "work to live" attitude than a "live to work" attitude (Hamidullah, 2012). What issues does this raise in the current and future work and nonwork lives of Millennials?

The "postjob-security" era has had many consequences for Millennials seeking to enter the job market. In some cases they have extended the time line of their career by spending time in graduate school; some have entered "short-term" careers (manual and nonmanual work) or "careerless" tracks resulting in less skilled work (see Lee, 2011). Uncertainty in the labor market has made the pathways to work uncertain, complex and risky, leading to job insecurity among those in Generation Y. This insecurity is reflected in the results of a 2011 national survey of Millennials showing nearly half of respondents were *very concerned* about both the U.S. financial situation and their own financial situation (nearly a third were *moderately concerned* about both) (iOMe Challenge, 2011). Nonetheless, despite this uncertainty, some young workers appreciate the added flexibility found in nonpermanent contracts and willingly choose such options, while others may agree to a fixed term or temporary contact, but prefer a permanent one. Millennials are especially hard hit by these trends: In the 25 European Union countries, 31% of workers under age 30 were on fixed-term contracts, more than double the proportion of employees of all ages employed on such contracts (Eurostat, 2007).

The increased use of contingent workers, in part, is linked to employers' need for flexibility and employees' desires for variable work schedules and employment options. The hiring of "temps" has become common in business and government. Temporary employment does allow workers to meet family responsibilities, complete schooling, develop new skills, or seek full-time work. It provides employers a source of skills for a specified time period, makes it possible to expand and contract the workforce as budgets rise and fall, and helps to control labor costs by shifting such costs from fixed to variable expenses.

Research by Smithson and Lewis (2000) used focus groups and individual interviews of young workers in the United Kingdom to examine issues of job insecurity. Many of those surveyed were unhappy with the loss of the idea of "a job for life," but they recognized the new realities accompanying the increase of nonstandard forms of employment. Their notions of job security had to be adjusted to shorter time horizons (often a fixed number of years) and limited benefits (sometimes paid leave). Their adaptation often put a priority on training to make themselves more marketable to employers, substituting skill development for traditional notions of job security. They distinguished between short-term job insecurity, deemed acceptable, and longer term insecurity (unacceptable) because the longer term posed obstacles to home ownership and starting a family (limited maternity rights, paternity leave). As psychological contract theory suggests, this lack of long-term job security can lead to limited loyalty and organizational commitment to organizations when employees feel their expectations are not met and their hard work is not rewarded. These consequences depend, in part, on the type of contract in question. Smithson and Lewis distinguish between two types of "transactional contracts" that have emerged in recent years: first, the short-term commitment contract where workers are motivated and committed to short-term projects rather than to employers; second, the balanced-lives contract where one gives up long-term security and suboptimal conditions in exchange for flexibility and reasonable hours that enable better work-life balance.

The transition from full-time permanent workers to a contingent workforce is likely to continue, but it disproportionally impacts younger workers, and HR professionals should carefully weigh gains in flexibility against potential losses in effectiveness before initiating new workplace initiatives. Now attention will shift to other efforts to provide work-life balance and organizational flexibility.

FLEXIBLE AND ALTERNATIVE WORK SCHEDULES

Flexible policies and practices can help reduce work-life conflict.[1] Substantial portions of the workforce support practices like flextime and telecommuting. Employees are interested in the range of alternatives available to them in the workplace that might minimize problems at home. Employers are interested in successfully completing the work. They have to weigh the costs and benefits of flexible arrangements prior to offering such options to large numbers of workers. This section briefly considers two alternative work arrangements: flex options and telecommuting,

Flex Options

Increased workforce diversity has prompted work schedule variations. Flextime allows different starting and quitting times but specifies the number of hours required within a particular period. Instituting flex options is one way for employers to respond to Millennials' concerns about developing a healthy work-life balance. Flextime is typically limited to full-time, permanent workers and to organizations with 50 or more employees; in these instances approximately 50% of workers are eligible for flextime (Galinsky, Bond, & Hill, 2004; Stockwell, 2006). In general, women are more likely than men to use flextime and parents are more likely than childless couples to use it (Galinsky et al., 2004). About 27 million full-time wage and salary workers (27.5%) had flexible schedules in 2004, down from 29 million in 2001 (Bureau of Labor Statistics, 2005).

Only about one in 10 workers is actually enrolled in a formal, employer-sponsored flextime program. Flexible schedules in the private sector are most prevalent in financial activities (37.7%), professional and business services (37.6%), and information (34.9%). Flexible schedules in the public sector are more prevalent in federal (28.8%) and state government (28.4%) than in local government (13.7%). In the public sector formal flextime programs are more prevalent than in private industry: more than half of public service workers with flexible schedules have a formal program. Three out of four federal employees with flextime participated in a formal program, whereas only about one out of three private sector workers with flextime participated in such a program.

The compressed workweek is another flex option capable of easing work-family conflict that Millennials seek to avoid. Under such arrangements the number of hours worked per week is condensed into fewer days. For example, employees work a set 160-hour schedule per month but do it in fewer than 20 workdays by working more than 8 hours a day and fewer than 5 days a week. Such scheduling allows employers to extend hours of operation and enables workers to shrink commuting costs and expand leisure time. Compressed workweeks, however, may introduce problems of employer supervision and employee fatigue. In 2008, Utah was the first state to implement a mandatory 4-day workweek for most state employees (Copeland, 2008; West, Condrey, & Rush, 2010), but Utah is now returning to a 5-day workweek (Kerrigan, 2011). Results from Condrey, West and Ledvinka's (2010) national survey of large cities indicated that there is both an upside and a downside to the 4-day workweek and the authors suggest that jurisdictions considering making the switch should do so cautiously. Flextime is more likely to be offered by organizations than compressed workweek options. It is generally estimated that 50% of employees are eligible for flextime (Galinsky et al., 2004; Stockwell, 2006).

Flextime can take various forms: core hours (required presence at work), band of flexible hours (typically at the end or beginning of the day), variable lunch hours, sliding schedule (variation in the start or stop times daily, weekly, or monthly), and bank time (variable length of workday; hours from long days can be banked for short days later on). Some employees are consciously downshifting (living simpler lives to escape the obsession with materialism and reduce work-related stress), and/or seeking part- or reduced-scheduling, which can be a boon to employers who can save money by not paying or prorating benefit costs for part-time workers (Galinsky et al., 2004; Reich, 2001). Job sharing where two or more employees share one job is another flex option that might appeal to some young workers. Career exit and reentry options are an additional flex strategy that can help employees who, by choice or necessity, leave the workforce for a while, but subsequently want to resume employment.

Clearly, the greatest flexibility, and the greatest appeal to Millennials, is present when a combination of options is available. Implementation problems can occur when employees are expected to work as a team, when unions or supervisors object to flextime, and when laws (e.g., maximum hours and overtime requirements) create complications. Telecommuting is another flex option that is consistent with the values of many Generation Y workers.

Telecommuting

Teleworkers are people who work away from the traditional work site (e.g., at home, at satellite locations, or on the road). Telework is a way for employers to save expenses and increase productivity and for employees to enjoy flexibility, savings, and reduced stress. Telework is also likely to be an attractive work option for Millennials who seek autonomy, work-life balance, and opportunities to use their computer competencies. Young workers may be attracted to ecological and environmental benefits linked to teleworking as well, such as reduced gas consumption, less pollution, and decreased traffic congestion (Nicholas, 2007). A survey of 730 business students drawn from a sample of 250 U.S. universities found that over half of the respondents had an interest in telecommuting when they graduated (Lomo-David & Griffin, 2001).

It is estimated that 45% of the U.S. workforce is employed in a job that is compatible with at least part-time telework (or workshifting) (Lister & Harnish, 2011). Three fourths of the existing teleworkers work in the private sector, down from 81% in 2005, due in part to increased telework among state and federal employees (Heathfield, 2011). More than 8 in 10 of *Fortune's* "100 Best Companies to Work For" allow employees to telecommute at least 20% of the time (About.com, 2010). In 2008, although 62% of the 1.9 million strong federal workforce were eligible to telework, less than 6% of full-time federal workers took advantage of the opportunity at least one day a week (Partnership for Public Service, 2010). Indeed, only 44 of 78 agencies had actually integrated telework into their formal operations planning. What explains the underutilization of telework? A combination of factors, including managerial worries about limited productivity, inaccessibility of teleworkers, access to classified information in nonsecure settings, uncertainty about who provides equipment, lack of accountability, limited face-to-face contact, and potential for abuse (Partnership for Public Service, 2010). Despite these concerns, several agencies have experienced success.

Recent federal legislation (P.L. 106–346) requires each executive agency to implement a policy whereby eligible employees can participate in telecommuting to the maximum extent possible without impeding employee performance. A goal of 150,000 federal employees teleworking by 2011 was set in 2010 by President Obama. A goal of 600,000 federal civil servants teleworking by 2014 was set by the Partnership for Public Service (2010). President Obama also signed the Telework Enhancement Act of 2010. This act, among other things, requires the head of each federal agency to: adopt a telework policy clarifying employee eligibility to telecommute, identify employees eligible to telework, and notify them of their eligibility.

While many private firms offer the telecommuting option (Lister & Karnish, 2011), it was used by only 2% of employees in 2007 (International Public Management Association for Human Resources HR Center, 2007). Telecommuting programs can result in increased productivity, flexibility, economy, and satisfaction. They enable employees to work and take care of family needs, have flexible work hours, have control over their time schedule, and work during hours when their productivity is greatest (Yap & Ting, 1990), all potentially conducive to greater satisfaction. With more flexible spatial and temporal boundaries, workers could work at home, in the car, at the local coffee house; the times they choose to work—1:00 A.M. or P.M.—are up to them. As Susan Eisner (2005) notes, such flexible work conditions are likely to appeal to Millenials: "Gen Y is likely to equate job satisfaction with a positive work climate, flexibility, and the opportunity to learn and grow more than any prior generation" (p. 8).

Impediments include loss of management control, inadequate technology, insufficient policy guidance, resistance by stakeholders, concerns about customer complaints, inadequate office coverage, problems scheduling meetings, and lack of funds. Telecommuters may feel left out of important office communications, experience isolation, and miss affiliation with coworkers. However, the wide use of cell phones and text messaging, instant messaging, social media, chat rooms, blogging, and e-mail by young workers is likely to compensate for fewer face-to-face interactions (Smith, 2005/2006). Further, virtual collaboration need not impede team project performance. One potential sticky point for Millennials considering telecommuting: they generally prefer supportive supervision and structure at work (Society for Human Resource Management, 2009), which may be lacking in a telework setting.

WORK-LIFE PROGRAMS

It is important for employees to be aware of what work-life conflicts might exist and how they can be resolved. The issues for employers are what programs, if any, to offer and how to implement them. This section briefly examines these questions from both perspectives. Employees with dependent children are concerned about their work-family responsibilities. They are interested in the support and benefits that might be provided by the organization to reduce conflicts. Employers need to decide the best way to respond to work-family conflicts and whether such responses require organization-sponsored services or reconfiguration of benefit packages.

Four programs address these dual employee and employer concerns: child care, parental and military leave, adoption assistance, and domestic partners coverage. These program types, plus those discussed subsequently, illustrate that one activity (e.g., childcare service) represents a small part of a much broader approach to "holistically" managing employee-responsive policies. Each of these initiatives is relevant to Millennials and they will be discussed in turn below.

Child Care

Here a key question is: What to do about dependent children while parents are working? The issue touches most people, especially Millennials, in one way or another. Consider these facts: (1) about three quarters of all mothers have joined the workforce (Cayer & Roach, 2008), many as members of the Millennial generation; (2) younger employees are more concerned with family and work-life issues than the two preceding generations (Bond, Galinsky, Kim, & Brownfield, 2005); (3) recent surveys report that only 14% of men and 10% of women think a full-time job for a woman with a young child is an "ideal situation," with 44% of the public saying a part-time job is ideal for the mother of a young child, and 38% saying the "ideal" is for such a mother not to work outside the home (Pew Research Center, 2009); and (4) of the 20.2 million children under 5 years of age in the United States, more than half of children under six (14.3 million) need child care because both parents work outside the home (U.S. Census, 2010, 2006). Most parents at one time or another have encountered problems with childcare arrangements that conflicted with work. Tardiness, stress, fatigue, energy level, absenteeism, and productivity are all affected. Even if employees arrive on time and work productively throughout the day, parents may be subject to the 3:00 syndrome—attention to work-related tasks wanes as they begin thinking about children ready to leave school and return home. One way employers can minimize these disruptions and distractions is by providing childcare benefits.

Employers can make available various types of benefits to working parents. Ten percent of private and government employers provide childcare on or off work premises (Bureau of Labor Statistics, 2010). A far larger proportion offers financial aid for off-site child care, and many more provide information and referral services. Paradoxically, a majority of federal agencies offers on-site, near-site, or referral services for child care; however, a very small proportion of eligible employees actually use these services. By contrast, only 7% of private employers in a 2002 survey provided direct-cost child care on or near site. The same survey found that 45% of employers provided dependent-care assistance plans, and a third offered resources and referral services for child care (Bond et al., 2005). President George W. Bush signed a law (P.L. 197–67) in 2001 authorizing the use of appropriated funds by executive agencies to provide childcare services for federal civilian employees. However, countries like Sweden go further: eligible parents caring for ill children up to age 12 (and sometimes up to age 16) are entitled to 120 benefit days per year (Todd, 2004). Adoption assistance is another way organizations can show support for younger employees.

Adoption Assistance

Adoption-related benefits range from time off to reimbursement of expenses following adoption of a child. Workers who give birth to a child usually enjoy paid leave and medical coverage; such benefits may or may not be available to those adopting a child. Costs can be significant, ranging from zero to $40,000 (for, e.g., medical costs, legal fees, travel expenses, etc.; Adoption.com, n.d.). Employers are becoming aware that adoptive parents need assistance too. They need to consider three issues: eligibility, leave time, and reimbursement. Eligibility considerations are length of employment, the child's age, and whether to cover step- or foster-care children. Leave-related considerations are the length of time available for unpaid leave; whether sick leave, annual leave, or personal leave can be used; and whether those taking leave are guaranteed job reinstatement. Reimbursement issues concern the coverage of legal or medical expenses.

A survey of 1,020 employers by Hewitt Associates found that nearly one third (32%) offered adoption benefits ("Overview of Employer-Provide Adoption Benefits," n.d.), a substantial increase over a 10-year period. Among the corporations offering adoption benefit programs are Dow Chemicals USA, Wendy's International, and Campbell Soups. The city of Philadelphia is a government pioneer in offering such coverage. The state of Washington provides 5 weeks of partially paid leave for the adoption of a child (Reddick & Coggburn, 2008). It is not unusual in the private sector to reimburse up to $10,000 for adoption expenses (Adoptive Families, 2008).

The justification for employers to provide such benefits is tied to equity: if parents giving birth are entitled to benefits, why not adoptive parents? Two other reasons are important: cost factors (adoption benefits are low cost because few use them) and stakeholder loyalty (support for adoptive parents can increase loyalty, morale, and retention). Similar equity, cost, and loyalty issues surround questions of lifestyle–friendly policies such as domestic partner benefits.

Lifestyle-Friendly Policies

A third of the workforce has children age 18 or younger and single or childless employees may resent the emphasis given to child-centered benefits (Hoyman & Duer, 2004). The value of policies designed for their married coworkers with children may be questioned by these single or childless employees (Kim & Wiggins, 2011; Wells, 2007). When employers expect them to "take up the slack" for their absent coworkers who are given "special help" in dealing with spousal or child-related problems, single or childless employees may feel overburdened or shortchanged. If single or childless workers receive fewer benefits, subsidized benefits for which they are ineligible, and are expected to assume more responsibilities than others, friction will likely result. In seeking to achieve work and life balance, it is important for employers to design "lifestyle-friendly" policies that are inclusive, flexible, and offer choices to workers (Kirkpatrick, 1997; Lynem, 2001), all signal concerns of Generation Y. Domestic partnership coverage demonstrates that an organization is "lifestyle friendly."

Domestic partnership coverage refers to benefits such as health insurance and sick or bereavement leave that may be made available to a person designated as a domestic partner of an employee. Less-encompassing (and less expensive) policies might involve little more than public recognition of cohabiting couples; more-encompassing plans include dental and vision benefits, employee assistance programs, and posttermination benefits for domestic partners. In recent years, the need for such coverage has increased because of changes in the American family and workforce, the importance of benefits as a key component in an employee's total compensation package, and efforts to avoid discrimination against gays, lesbians and transgender groups. According to the 2010 census, 7.5 million opposite-sex unmarried couples are living together, while 620 thousand same sex couples were living together. From 2003 to 2007, there was a 61% increase in the number of employers offering health insurance to same-sex domestic partners (Human Rights Campaign Foundation, 2003, 2007).

As of 2007, benefits to domestic partners of employees were provided in 13 states, 145 city and county governments, and 303 colleges and universities (Cayer & Roach, 2008; Human Rights Campaign Fund, 2007). New York City provides benefits for domestic partners of employees, and San Francisco goes even farther, requiring private organizations that contract with the city to provide such benefits. In response to such initiatives, the House of Representatives denied federal housing dollars to cities that require organizations doing business with them to provide same-sex domestic partner benefits to the organization's employees. Granting domestic partner coverage is contentious in the private and nonprofit sector as well: it pleases some stakeholders and angers others. Additional obstacles to domestic partner benefits are rising costs of healthcare benefits and reluctance by insurance companies to cover unknown risks. As workforce diversity continues, pressures for such benefits will mount. At the same time, younger workers will push for more flexible leave policies.

Parental and Military Leave

In addition to traditional leave policies (e.g., sick leave, vacation, holidays, and bereavement) is the emergence of family leave. The Family and Medical Leave Act of 1993 provides eligible workers with up to 12 weeks, during any 12-month period, of *unpaid* leave for childbirth or adoption; for caregiving to a child, elderly parent, or spouse with a serious health problem; or for a personal illness. Six in ten members in the U.S. labor force, including public and private sector employees, work for employers covered by the Family and Medical Leave Act (American Association of University Women, 2007). Also, the Federal Employees Family Friendly Leave Act of 1994 provides sick leave time for federal government workers to care for family members. Thus, it is not surprising that parental leave policies are among the most prevalent of the four items discussed in this section. It is estimated that more than 50 million Americans, many of whom are Millennials, have taken advantage of the program since 1993 (AAUW, 2007).

The United States remains behind many other nations in its leave policies. In Scandanavian countries, for example, public supports for parental leave are much greater for those on permanent employment contract: In Sweden, paid parental leave (full salary for 360 days) for 450 days (standard rate after 360 days) is available up until the child is 8 years old, and 280 supplemental days per child for the second and additional children is provided (Lewis, Smithson, & Brannen, 1999).

Federal and state laws in the United States protect those who serve in the military. Discrimination against those in the military or the reserves is prohibited by provisions in the Uniformed Services Employment and Reemployment Rights Act of 1994. Negative job actions against employees because they are in the armed forces or reserves are prohibited. Furthermore, any people who leave their job to serve in the armed forces must be reinstated when they are released so long as certain conditions are met (e.g., advance notice, time limitations, honorable release). Additional protections are found in most state laws prohibiting discrimination against those in the state's militia or National Guard (NOLO, 2003).

Each of the four work-family/life programs discussed in this section is likely to appeal to younger workers. Potential gains in loyalty and productivity may warrant investments in these areas. Health and wellness programs, covered in the next section, are likely to provide similar returns on human capital investments.

STRESS REDUCTION AND WELLNESS PROGRAMS

A recent article in the *New England Journal of Medicine* was titled, "Employers as Health Coach," highlighting the employee-friendly activities of organizations in the area of health promotion (Oakie, 2007). One way for employers to improve employees' perceptions' of organizational support is to offer initiatives such as stress reduction, wellness programs, and employee assistance programs. Providing such programs reinforces the employer side of the psychological contract by offering benefits to employees that employers hope will bring a return to the organization in the form of improved employee performance, commitment, and satisfaction. As is the case with traditional economic benefits, withdrawing or reducing these programs can be viewed as reneging on promises to employees.

Stress reduction and wellness programs promote healthy lifestyles and reduce the likelihood of serious illness. Employee assistance programs can be helpful in addressing health-related problems when they appear. While a certain amount of stress can improve job performance, too much "negative stress" can impede it. Optimal stress levels advance employee wellbeing while minimizing the likelihood of chronic mental or physical problems. Preventing, detecting, and managing negative stress is challenging, but it can benefit both employees and employers. Obesity and related pathologies (diabetes, heart disease, orthopedic disorders, psychological wellbeing) among Millennials are higher and overall fitness lower in comparison to Boomers or Generation Xers at the same age (Putnam & Pulcher, 2007; Wang, Beydoun, Liang, Caballero, & Kunanyika, 2008). This could result in increases in illness-related absenteeism, higher health costs, and reduced productivity (Deal, Altman, & Rogelberg, 2010). Stress reduction, wellness initiatives, and employee assistance programs are among the ways managers might address this issue. Such initiatives are consistent with the soft HRM "caring" approach as well as the bottom-line oriented hard HRM perspective (see the following section on traditional economic benefits for an elaboration of this distinction in HRM viewpoints).

Stress Reduction

Human resource managers can do their part in helping to reduce stress by ensuring that recruitment efforts promote a good person-environment fit, matching the right person with the right job, and using realistic job previews to reduce the gap between job expectations and reality. Once hired, HR managers can ensure that young employees receive appropriate assessment, feedback, and coaching for career development and that they have access to worker support systems to foster workplace attachments. Where necessary, intervention counseling could be provided to assist those experiencing especially stressful situations. HR professionals could track indicators of stress, offer training in behavioral self-control skills, and introduce problem solving techniques and time management strategies to reduce stress.

The psychological contract typically involves each party accepting the obligation of reciprocity. Managers, for their part, can work to reduce employee stress by clarifying objectives and communicating them to employees, establishing performance targets that are challenging but realistic, and making sure tasks are well defined and responsibilities are clear. Establishing good two-way communication, avoiding work overload or underload, and decreasing role conflict and ambiguity can help to reduce stress. Some important stressors that may impede employee performance can be removed by following a consistent management style and treating all employees fairly. Employees can also do their part to reduce stress and improve performance by identifying sources of stress, mentally rehearsing stressful situations, reviewing their priorities and lifestyle, and accepting situations they cannot control. Scheduling time realistically, exploring ways to reduce caregiving and work conflicts, taking advantage of support networks, exercising regularly, and spending time each day in a relaxing activity are additional ways to minimize negative stress. Each party in the employment relationship—manager and employee—can contribute to stress reduction and performance improvement.

Wellness Programs

Similarly, wellness programs can be useful in promoting healthy behavior and altering unhealthy personal habits and lifestyles. Employers can offer a host of services that are health promoting, including health assessment, risk appraisal, screening (blood pressure, etc.), nutrition education, and counseling, among others. Increasingly employers are providing exercise equipment or helping defray costs of health club membership for employees. Programming can focus on weight control, smoking cessation, or general health awareness. Research results pleasing to the eye of hard HRM enthusiasts show the potential payoff to the organization from wellness initiatives in the form of improved morale, commitment, recruitment, retention, and productivity. Soft HRM supporters will view these investments as money well spent to further cultivate stable, trusting relations with employees. Millennials, like other employees, will likely appreciate the availability of such services as an indication of organizational support and investment in their well being. Indeed, there are some initiatives customized to the tech-savvy Millennials, such as using a cyber wellness approach to address physical and psychological well being by relying on the internet to focus on education, risk behavior, and lifestyle modifications of those in the college community (Putnam & Pulcher, 2007).

When employee personal problems become severe enough to impede their performance, despite the best efforts of managers and HR professionals to address them, the employee assistance program (EAP) can be a helpful resource. EAPs typically offer help with problems such as alcohol abuse, personal debt, domestic abuse, and so forth. EAPs often provide counseling and referral for employees and their families, employ clinically qualified staff, educate employees regarding covered services in the health benefit package, and assist in the training of employees, managers, and supervisors. They typically conduct reference checks of service providers to insure quality referrals. Health-conscious Millennials will want to take advantage of the health promotion options that the organization offers. While work-life balance is a high priority to today's young workers, traditional economic benefits continue to be important as well.

TRADITIONAL ECONOMIC BENEFITS

Pensions and Health Care

Traditional benefit programs such as pensions and health care provisions are especially costly and have become targets for cost-cutting with the downturn in the economy (West & Condrey, 2011). Such targeting is not surprising given that benefits comprise a large part of employee compensation, often upwards of 40%. While pension and health benefits might not be a first-order priority for young and healthy Millennials, recent developments should capture their attention. In the pension area, employers have sought savings by shifting, wherever possible, from defined-benefit pension plans—with preset life-time payments guaranteed—to defined-contribution plans (e.g., 401 (k) accounts, with the accompanying risks of a volatile stock market). Employers have also been altering their plans in the health care area and employees have been absorbing the cost of higher premiums, copays and deductibles (Hacker, 2006, p. 139).

Lucero and Allen (1994) employ psychological contract theory to high-light the diverging views of employers and employees regarding benefits and the implications when benefits are cut. From the employers' perspective, they are offering benefits that address employees' current and future needs and expect reciprocity from employees in the form of their contributions as organization members. From the perspective of employees, their contributions based on this arrangement are contingent on employers' honoring promises to meet their needs by providing current and future benefits. Employees may view recent actions by employers as a breach of the psychological contract when efforts to control labor costs result in withdrawal of benefits or cost-shifting to employees. The perception that employers have failed to uphold their side of the bargain can have adverse consequences for employee morale and organizational commitment.

A related development, of special relevance to Millennials, is the emergence in many organizations of a "two-tier labor force" (core and peripheral) which is linked to "load-shedding" as a cost-saving strategy. Under this arrangement, part-time, temporary or sometimes newly hired employees are provided inferior benefits compared to those offered to current first-tier employees. This development clearly impacts younger workers, as previously noted, because they are disproportionately found in these less secure contingent jobs. How do HR managers react to cost cuts in pension and health care programs?

Competing HR Perspectives

There are two competing perspectives about human resource management briefly alluded to previously—one hard, the other soft—that can be related to the way pension and health care reforms are pursued. First, with regard to pensions, hard HRM (utilitarian-instrumental) views employees primarily as costs to be contained or reduced and resources to be used for maximum return. By contrast, the soft HRM (developmental-humanistic) approach regards employees as assets worthy of investment and a resource of competitive advantage. As West and Bowman (2008) observe, from the soft HRM view, "reneging on promised pensions (or severely cutting them) is theft, robbing employees of their investment; the principle of "fidelity of purpose" is crucial in building enduring, trustworthy relationships with workers. The obligation to pay for "human depreciation" has been likened to the responsibility to pay replacement cost for worn out equipment" (p. 38). From this perspective, the breach of the psychological contract should be avoided wherever possible. With regard to health care benefits, the soft HRM approach "seeks coverage that expresses "caring" by addressing employee needs, respecting individual rights and promoting healthy lifestyles" (p. 36).

By contrast, the hard HRM perspective on pensions, according to West and Bowman, is that "pensions are viewed as a voluntary and expensive obligation of management. Stewardship of stockholder and taxpayer resources requires prudent decision making, especially in an era of rising costs, competitive pressures and an unpredictable future. If the benefits of pensions (e.g., employee loyalty, recruitment and retention edge) do not outweigh the costs, then the reality of doing business requires moving away from paternalistic policies of the past and insisting that employees assume more personal responsibility for their financial future" (p. 39). Where such a view prevails, breaching the psychological contract would be considered necessary. Similarly, regarding health care benefits, hard strategies "look to the bottom line and managerial prerogatives, supporting health benefits as long as they promote business objectives and conserve resources. Proponents of this approach advance shareholder value theory and focus on the expense of obligation to the workforce" (p. 36).

In today's economic environment, West and Bowman conclude that the language used to support health and pension policies is often linked to the soft approach, but the reality of what is offered is more in sync with the hard HRM perspective. This is consistent with Hilltrip's (1995) observation regarding the changing psychological contract in the current era of greater uncertainty, reduced benefits, and increased workloads. While some HR policies are employee-friendly, others are less so. Millennials have been part of this workforce for a decade or more; many more will be entering in the near future and will need to be prepared for this new and evolving relationship between the employee and the employing organization. One way of assisting and developing young employees in this ever-changing environment is through mentoring, the final focus of this analysis.

REVERSE MENTORING FOR DEVELOPMENT

Today's multigenerational workforce is a mix of Matures ("Silents"), Baby Boomers, Generation X and Millennials. Older Baby Boomers and younger Millennials comprise the two largest groups, with 78 million and 86+ million workers respectively (U.S. Census, 2010). Given their numbers in the workforce, each vastly outnumbering Generation Xers, they will be the focus of this discussion of reverse mentoring for development.

Traditional mentoring usually pairs older, more experienced workers or managers with mentees who are newly hired, junior, or less experienced. The more senior employee could guide the protégé in ways that help him or her learn the ropes, discover how things are done in the organization, and become aware of accepted behaviors required to succeed. Mentoring provides the opportunity to learn soft skills (how to dress, speak, and act), test new ideas and express frustrations, ease entry into the workforce, and help in adjustment to the organizational culture. It can aid in hard skill acquisition, help to avoid career stagnation, improve retention and increase employee loyalty (Bowman, West, & Beck, 2010; National Mentoring Partnership, 2008; U.S. DOT, 2009). Those in Generation Y highly value mentoring in order to upgrade their skills and remain marketable (DeHauw & DeVos, 2010; Loughlin & Barling, 2001; Sturges, Guest, Conway, & Davey, 2002). The prevalence of formal mentoring in government is mixed: One in five members of the federal Senior Executive Service has received mentoring advice, including more than a third of the Senior Executive Service in the Nuclear Regulatory Commission, but a far lower percentage did so in the Small Business Administration (U.S.Office of Personnel Management, 2008).

Reverse mentoring also pairs new or junior employees with more experienced managers or employees, but here the expectation is for the older employee to learn from their younger counterpart (Hannam & Yordi, 2010; Meister & Willyerd, 2010; Raines, 2002). Millennials, with their technological savvy, would be able to educate Baby Boomers to the work-related benefits linked to effective use of information technology. They might also help older workers develop a deeper appreciation of the benefits of workplace diversity, multiculturalism, work-life balance, and/or gender equity. Companies like General Electric, General Motors, and Procter & Gamble, among others, have implemented reverse mentoring with good results.

When the characteristics and workplace expectations of Baby Boomers and those in Generation Y are examined, the potential advantages of reverse mentoring become more apparent. Baby Boomers (born between 1946 and 1964) are characterized by a strong work ethic, a competitive need for achievement, an expectation of lifetime employment, and a sense of loyalty to the employing organization. They seek personal growth opportunities, vertical advancement in the organization, and workplace flexibility (Albright & Cluff, 2005). Millennials (born between 1977 and 1997), also desire workplace flexibility; they prefer flatter hierarchy, value diversity, seek feedback and recognition, and enjoy working in teams. Whereas Baby Boomers may be threatened by new technology, Millennials understand and embrace it. While Boomers feel that presence on the job is critical and "putting in the time" is an indicator of productivity, Millennials are more impatient and results oriented; they tend to be multitaskers and, by some accounts, possess a sense of entitlement and pursue personal fulfillment at work. Both Boomers and Millennials have liabilities. In some cases Boomers have reached a career plateau where they have few opportunities to advance vertically in the organization or where they perceive their jobs as routine and no longer challenging. Younger workers, while often optimistic by nature, may be anxious or frustrated due to a skill deficit based on their lack of experience, ill equipped to deal with difficult people, and/or unhappy with unchallenging assignments. They prefer explicit guidelines regarding paths to success (Smola & Sutton, 2002).

Reverse mentoring is a way to bridge the experiential divide, cultivate relationships, and provide opportunities for mutual coaching. For mentees it may increase their visibility to work with a senior executive, thereby enhancing their possibilities of enhanced career progression. It exposes seasoned employees to a portion of the workforce with which they may have previously had little or no contact. Each participant gains a window into the world of the other. The senior employee may become aware of the benefits of social media as a way to interact with customers or citizens; the junior employee might glean insights based on the "view from the top" otherwise unavailable to them (Meister & Willyerd, 2010). Recent survey research indicates that more than three-fourths of Millennials say they enjoy working with Boomers, with most preferring to turn to Boomers rather than Gen Xers for mentoring advice (Hewlett, Sherbin, & Sumberg, 2009). Properly executed, a reverse mentoring program could bring developmental dividends in the form of increased organizational engagement and commitment by both parties.

Recent research by Chaudhuri and Ghosh (2011) used social exchange theory, perceived organizational support and leader-member exchange theory to examine reverse mentoring. They posit that initiating reverse mentoring by employers can be seen as a form of organizational support by both Boomers and Millennials if each generation perceives this initiative as an indication that the employer recognizes their particular competencies and seeks to develop or increase their skills. Boomers who may be experiencing diminished job challenges, limited advancement opportunities, ageist stereotypes, or lagging interest in their work, might be pleased that the organization is investing in upgrading their skills through this new mentoring system. They may discover that mentoring by a junior or new employee could help by tutoring them on the latest technological developments (e.g., text messaging, wiki collaboration, social media), thereby opening up possible new opportunities, such as telecommuting. The learning from these junior to senior exchanges could lead to positive outcomes, such as job satisfaction, employee engagement and improved performance.

Millennials may be pleased that the organization recognizes their novel insights and ability to contribute by sharing their values and skills with

(2010); West and Bowman (2008); West, Condrey, and Rush (2010); West & Condrey, 2011.

REFERENCES

American Association of University Women. (2007). *Family friendly workplaces: Expand family and medical leave and paid sick leave.* Washington, DC: Author.

About.com. (2010, January). Work-at-home moms. Retrieved from http://workathomemoms.about.com/b/2010/01/27/tops-for-telecommuting-fortunes-100-be

Adams, G., & Balfour, D. (2010). The prospects for revitalizing ethics in a new governance era. In R. Durant (Ed.), *The Oxford handbook of American bureaucracy* (pp. 766-785). Oxford, England: Oxford University Press.

Adoption.com. (n.d.). Adoption costs. Retrieved from http://costs.adoption.com

Adoptive Families. (2008). Making it work: Top adoption-friendly companies. Retrieved from http://adoptivefamilies.com/ articles.php?aid=832

Albright, W., & Cluff, G. (2005). Ahead of the curve: How Mitre recruits and retains older workers. *Journal of Organizational Excellence, 24,* 53-63.

Anderson, N., & Thomas, H. (1996). Work group socialization. In M. West (Ed.), *Handbook of work groups* (pp. 423-450). Chichester, England: Wiley.

Barnett, R. (1999). A new work-life model for the twenty-first century. *The ANNALS of the American Academy of Political and Social Science, 562,* 143-158.

Berman, E., & West, J. (2003). Psychological contracts in local government: A preliminary survey. *Review of Public Personnel Administration, 23*(4), 267-285.

Berman, E., Bowman, J., West, J., & Van Wart, M. (2010). *Human resource management in public service.* Thousand Oaks, CA: SAGE.

Bond, Galinsky, E., Kim, S., & Brownfield, E. (2005). *National study of employers.* New York, NY: Families and Work Institute.

Bowman, J., West, J., & Beck, M. (2010). *Achieving competencies in public service: The professional edge.* Armonk, NY: M. E. Sharpe.

Bureau of Labor Statistics, U.S. Department of Labor. (2005). *Workers on flexible and shift schedules in May 2004.* Retrieved from http://www.bls.gov/news.release/pdf/flex.pdf

Bureau of Labor Statistics, U.S. Department of Labor. (2010). *National compensation survey.* Washington, DC.

Cayer, J., & Roach, C. (2008). Work-life benefits. In C. Reddick & J. Coggburn (Eds.), *Handbook of employee benefits and administration* (pp. 309-334). New York, NY: Taylor & Francis.

Chaudhuri, S., & Ghosh, R. (2011). Reverse mentoring: A social exchange tool for keeping the boomers engaged and millennials committed. *Human Resource Development Review.* Retrieved from http://hrd.sagepub.com/content/early/2011/08/20/1534484311417562

Copeland (2008, June 30). Most state workers in Utah shifting to 4-day week. *USA Today.* Retrieved from www.usatoday.com/news/naton/2008-06-30-four-day_N.htm

Condrey, S., West, J., & Ledvinka, C. (2010). Making the switch: Implementing the 4-day workweek in America's largest cities. In R. Sims (Ed.), *Change (transformation) in government organizations* (pp. 137-158). Charlotte, NC: Information Age.

Deal, J., Altman, D., & Rogelberg, S. (2010). Millennials at work: What we know and what we need to do (if anything). *Journal of Business Psychology, 25,* 191-199.

DeHauw, S., & DeVos, A. (2010). Millennials' career perspective and psychological contract expectations: Does the recession lead to lowered expectations? *Journal of Business Psychology, 25,* 293-302.

DeVos, A., De Stobbeleir, K., & Meganck, A. (2009). The relationship between career-related antecedents and graduates' anticipatory psychological contracts. *Journal of Business and Psychology, 24*(3), 289-298.

Dries, N., Pepermans, R., & De Kerpel, E. (2008). Exploring four generations' beliefs about career. Is satisfied the new successful? *Journal of Managerial Psychology, 23*(8), 907-928.

Eisenberger, R., Huntington, R., Hutchison, S., & Sowa, D. (1986). Perceived organizational support. *Journal of Applied Psychology, 75*(1), 51-59.

Eisner, S. (2005). Managing generation Y. *S.A.M. Advanced Management Journal, 70*(4), 4-15.

Eurostat. (2007). *Statistics in focus: Population and social conditions.* Luxembourg City, Luxembourg: EU Labour Force Survey, European Commission.

Ezra, M., & Deckman, M. (1996). Balancing work and family responsibilities: Flextime and child care in the federal government. *Public Administration Review, 56*(2), 174-197.

Galinsky, E., Bond, J. T., & Hill, E. J. (2004). *Workplace flexibility: What is it? Who has it? Who want it? Does it make a difference?* New York, NY: Families and Work Institute.

Hacker, J. (2006). *The great risk shift.* New York, NY: Oxford University Press.

Hamidullah, M. (2012). Generational differences and the public sector workforce, In N. Riccucci (Ed.), *Public personnel management: Current concerns, future challenges* (pp. 28-38). Boston, MA: Pearson.

Hannam, S., & Yordi, B. (2011). *Engaging a multi-generational workforce: Practical advice for government managers.* Washington, DC: IBM Center for the Business of Government.

Heathfield. (2011). Reasons why teleworking belongs in your future. Retrieved from http://humanresurces.about.com/od/workschedules/a/teleworking .thm?nl=1

Hewitt Associates. (n.d.). Overview of employer-provided adoption benefits. Retrieved from http://library.adoption.com/articles/overview-of-employer-provided-adoption-benefits.html

Hewlett, S., Sherbin, L., & Sumberg, K. (2009). How gen Y and boomers will reshape your agenda. *Harvard Business Review, 87*(7/8), 71-76.

Hilltrip, M. (1995). The changing psychological contract: The human resource challenge of the 1990s. *European Management Journal, 13*(3), 286-294.

Hoyman, M., & Duer, H. (2004). A typology of workplace policies: Worker friendly vs. family friendly? *Review of Public Personnel Administration, 24*(2), 113-32.

Human Rights Campaign Foundation. (2003/2007). Retrieved from http://www.hrc.org/content/contentgroups/publications1/state.of.the.family/SoTF.pdf

iOMe Challenge. (2011). *Millennials genuinely concerned about their financial future.* Depere, WI: Author.

International Public Management Association for Human Resources HR Center. (2007). *Personnel practices: Telecommuting policies.* Alexandria, VA: Author.

Kerrigan, H. (2011, July). Utah's demise of the four-day workweek. Retrieved from www.governing.com

Kim, J., & Wiggins, M. E. (2011). Family-friendly human resource policy: Is it still working in the public sector? *Public Administration Review, 71*(5), 728-729.

Kirkpatrick (1997, April). Child-free employees see another side of equation. *Wall Street Journal Interactive Edition.* Retrieved from http://lexisnexis.com/

Kowske, B, Rasch, R., & Wiley, J. (2010). Millennials' (lack of) attitude problem: An empirical examination of generational effects on work attitudes. *Journal of Business Psychology, 25,* 265-279.

Lee, J. (2011, August 31). Generation limbo: Waiting it out. *New York Times.* Retrieved from http://www.nytimes.com/2011/09/01/fashion/recent-college-graduates-wait-for-their-real-ca

Lewis, S., Smithson, J., & Brannen, J. (1999). Young Europeans' orientations to families and work. *The ANNALS of the American Academy of Political and Social Science, 562,* 83-97.

Lister, K., & Harnish, T. (2011). *The state of telework in the U.S.* Retrieved from http://www.workshifting.com/downloads/downloads/Telework-Trends-US.pdf

Lomo-David, E., & Griffin, F. (2001). Personality traits of white-collar telecommuters: Perceptions of graduating business students. *Journal of Education for Business, 75*(5), 257-261.

Loughlin, C., & Barling, J. (2001). Young workers' work values, attitudes and behaviors. *Journal of Occupational and Organizational Psychology, 74,* 543-558.

Lucero, M., & Allen, R. (1994). Employee benefits: A growing source of psychological contract. *Human Resource Management. 33*(3), 425-446.

Lynem, J. (2001, May). Family-friendly or single-hostile? Unwed employees feel short changed by policies aimed at helping parents. *San Francisco Chronicle.* Retrieved from http://sfgate.com/cgibin/article.cgi?file=/chronicle/archive/2001/05/13/AW1525`.DTL

Marston, C. (2007). *Motivating the "what's in it for me?" workforce: Managing across generational divide.* Hoboken, NJ: Wiley.

McDonald, K., & Hite, L. (2008). The next generation of career success: Implications for HRD. *Advances in Developing Human Resources, 10,* 86-103.

Meister, J., & Willyerd, K. (2010, May). Mentoring Millennials. *Harvard Business Review, 88*(5), 1-4.

National Mentoring Partnership. (2008). Checklist for mentoring programs. Retrieved from http://www.ed.gov/pubs/YesYuoCan/sect3-checklist.html

Nicholas, A. (2007). Millennial interest in teleworking. (Unpublished Doctoral Dissertation). Available from Touro University International. UMI Number: (3273822).

NOLO. (2003). *Providing military* leave. Retrieved from www.nolo.com/lawcenter/ency/article.cfm/ObjectID/8077364D-A7D1-4E44-8E88F9B97B187DFB/catID/40338C48-92FD-49FA-93CB1BF16195D519

Oakie, S. (2007, October). Employers as health coach. *New England Journal of Medicine, 357,* 1465-1469.

Partnership for Public Service. (2010). *On demand government: Deploying flexibilities to ensure eservice continuity.* Washington, DC: Partnership for Public Service.

Pew Research Center. (2009). *America's changing workforce: Recession turns a graying office grayer.* New York, NY: Author.

Putnam, J., & Pulcher, K. (2007). An e-learning strategy towards a culture of cyber wellness and health for WMSCI 2007. Retrieved from http://www.iiisci.org/journal/cv$/sci/pdfs/s372dt.pdf

Raines, C. (2002). Managing millennials. Retrieved from http://www.generationsatwork.com/articles/millennials.htm

Reddick, C., & Coggburn, J. (Eds.). (2008). *Handbook of employee benefits and administration.* New York, NY: Taylor & Francis.

Reich, R. (2001). *The future of success.* New York, NY: Knopf.

Rigotti, T. (2009). Enough is enough? Threshold models for the relationship between psychological contract breach and job-related attitudes. *European Journal of Work and Organizational Psychology, 18*(4), 442-463.

Rousseau, D. (1989). Psychological and implied contract in organizations. *Employee Responsibilities and Rights Journal, 2*(2), 121-139.

Rousseau, D. (1995). *Promises in action: Psychological contracts in organizations.* Newbury Park, CA: SAGE.

Saltzstein, A., Ting, Y., & Saltzstein, G. (2001). Work-family balance and job satisfaction: The impact of family-friendly policies on attitudes of federal government employees. *Public Administration Review 61*(4), 452-67.

Society for Human Resource Management. (2009). *The multigenerational workforce: Opportunity for competitive success.* Retrieved from http://www.shrm.org/Research/Articles/Articles/Documents/09-0027_RQ_March_2009_FINAL_noad.pdf

Smith, W. S. (2005/2006). Employers and the new generation of employees. *Community College Journal, 76*(3), 27-39.

Smithson, J., & Lewis, S. (2000). Is job insecurity changing the psychological contract? *Personnel Review, 29*(6), 680-702.

Smola, K., & Sutton, C. (2002). Generational differences: Revisiting generational work *values* for the new millennium. *Journal of Organizational Behavior, 23,* 363-382.

Stockwell, M. (2006). Flexible work for strong families. Progressive Policy Institute. Retrieved from http://www.ppionline.org/documents/family_agenda_111506.pdf

Sturges, J., Guest, D., Conway, N., & Davey, K. (2002). A longitudinal study of the relationship between career management and organizational commitment among graduates in the first ten years at work. *Journal of Organizational Behavior, 23,* 731-748.

Todd, S. (2004). Improving work-life balance—what other countries are doing? Labor Program, Human Resources and Skill Development, Canada.

Retrieved from www.hrsdc.gc.ca/en/lp/spila/wlb/pdf/improving-work-life-bal-ance.pdf

Tomlinson, M. (2007). Graduate employability and student attitudes and orientations to the labor market. *Journal of Education and Work, 20(*4), 285-304.

U.S. Bureau of the Census. (2006). *American community survey.* Washington, DC: Author.

U.S. Bureau of the Census. (2010). Retrieved from http://www.crmtrends.com/ConsumerDemographics.htm

U.S. Bureau of the Census. (2011). *American community survey.* Washington, DC: Author.

U.S. Office of Personnel Management. (2008). Senior executive service survey results. Retrieved from http://www.opm.gov/ses/SES_survey_results _complete.pdf

U. S. Department of Transportation. (2009). Departmental Office of Human Resource Management. *DOT mentoring handbook.* Retrieved from www.au.af.mil/au/awc/awcgate/mentor/mentorhb.htm

Wang, Y., Beydoun, M. A., Liang, L., Caballero, B., & Kumanyika, S. K. (2008). Will all Americans become overweight or obese? Estimating the progression and cost of the U.S. obesity epidemic. *Obesity, 16*(10), 2323-2330.

Wells, S. (2007, October). Are you too family friendly? *HR Magazine, 52*(10), 35-39.

West, J. P., & Bowman, J. (2008). Employee benefits: Weighing ethical principles and economic imperatives. *Handbook of employee benefits and administration* (pp. 29–53). Boca Raton, FL: CRC Press.

West, J. P., Condrey, S., & Rush, C. (2010). Implementing the 4-day workweek in our largest cities. *The Public Manager, 39*(3), 68-73.

West, J., & Condrey, S. (2011). Municipal government strategies for controlling personnel costs during the fiscal storm. *Journal of Public Budgeting, Accounting and Financial Management, 23*(3), 423-454.

Yap, C., & Ting, H. (1990). Factors associated with attitudes towards telecommuting. *Information & Management, 19*(4), 227-235.

Zhao, H., Wayne, S., Glibkowski, B., & Bravo, J. (2007). The impact of psychological contract breach on work-related outcomes: A meta-analysis. *Personnel Psychology, 60,* 647-680.

CHAPTER 10

TEXTS, E-MAILS, AND GOOGLE SEARCHES

Training in a Multigenerational Workplace

Patrick Deery

INTRODUCTION

Several years ago, my boss approached me and said that one of the executives in our organization had complained to her about cell phone usage in meetings. Noting that she felt that this was a cultural problem that required training to set things right, the executive went on to cite the story of a cell phone user who had stayed in the meeting to answer a call but had been polite enough to crawl under the table to complete the conversation. I suggested to my boss that training was probably not the answer to this kind of problem, but I did cause signs to be posted outside our training areas asking participants to mute their cells while in training, and we added something about being polite with the use of cell phones to our "Effective Meetings" training.

With the proliferation of, first, smart phones and then electronic tablets, such cautions have become meaningless as participants now text,

Managing Human Resources for the Millennial Generation, pp. 229–247

instant message, e-mail, and network during training. What is one to do to keep attention in the traditional training classroom? I am reminded of the new employee starting out on his first job who insisted on texting throughout the benefits portion of our new employees' orientation. His multitasking prevented him from comprehending his health care, investment opportunities, retirement, and life insurance options to the extent that we had to ask him to put up the phone and pay attention to the benefits person now working with him one-on-one. Then there was the young lady looking for our payroll and benefits office who had the building name and room number and could not understand why Google Maps on her smart phone could not pull up the address.

Have such devices as smart phones and electronic tablets in the hands of Generation X and Millenials, or for that matter any training participant, become so essential to our staying connected that we can not be without them for even a few moments? Are these things blessings or curses? Is it really the technology or is it the technology in the hands of Millennials?

I would like to address those questions in the preceding paragraph by suggesting that we approach this problem of technology in the hands of four generations in the classroom by looking at the issue as adding another layer to our analysis of adult learning styles. That is, it is not the technology that is affecting what goes on as much as it is the technology in the hands of the different generations. It is not just the Millennials who are texting and checking Facebook.

What we need to do in the training and development environment is first address technology's impact and then try to understand how that, in turn, impacts learning styles. That is, technology's rapid growth and pervasiveness are here to stay, so we need to use it to our advantage and then we need to come to grips with how four generations in the classroom adds another element to consider when analyzing our audience. It is not so much accommodating Millennials in the classroom as much as it is giving serious consideration to how this fourth generation adds another dimension to analyzing the audience in adult learning situations.

WHO ARE THE FOUR GENERATIONS

It is probably helpful to start our analysis with a brief description of the four generations currently active in the workplace. I will follow that up with a consideration of their attitudes toward work, teamwork, feedback, and training. Except where specifically noted otherwise, these characterizations are taken from Lynne Lancaster's and David Stillman's *When Generations Collide*, 2002. Traditionalists (also labeled Traditionals, Veterans,

Matures, Seniors, Builders, the Greatest Generation) are generally dedicated, loyal, long-term employees; they currently make up 4.7% of the work force. Baby Boomers (also known as Boomers) are considered optimistic, competitive, and willing to work long hours to achieve success in the workplace; they make up 38.6% of the work force. Members of Generation X (also known as Xers or Busters) are skeptical, resourceful and independent with a work ethic and loyalty personally rather than organizationally defined; they comprise 32.1% of the work force. Millennials (also known as Generation Y, Generation Why, and Echo Boomers) are optimistic, realistic, and techno-savvy; they are about 24.7% of the workforce. (Workforce percentages are Bureau of Labor statistics cited in Catalyst *Quicktakes*, 2011).

Each generation has a different attitude toward work: According to Bernstein (2006), Traditionalists view work as an obligation of adulthood, something necessary to be done to support the family. As long as that pay check is hitting the bank, all is well. They do everything by the rules, concerning themselves with how things are accomplished as well as what gets done. Baby Boomers find in work a source of personal identity and, more importantly, a sense of fulfillment. It is not just the money but also the status and recognition that come with the job. They are willing to work long hours to get the job done; nights and weekends are not a problem. Gen Xers view work as a contract they have to provide results for pay; they want to be told what the desired results are but not how to arrive at those results. Finally, Millennials see work as a means of filling time between weekends that should be fun and for an employer that is socially conscious.

Their work relationships are characterized by differing attitudes toward teamwork and individuality. Traditionalists and Millennials both see themselves as team players, but to the Traditionalist work is accomplished under a clearly defined chain of command while the Millennial prefers a team where everyone counts and has the opportunity to be the team leader. The Boomer and Gen Xer are individuals with the Boomer doing his own work but well within the rules, and the Gen Xer doing what needs to be done in the fastest way possible; rules and traditional methods are easily bypassed for the sake of speed.

Feedback in general is significant for our discussion of training, and here too generational attitudes differ. Traditionalists would just as soon be left alone to work without any indication of how well or how poorly they might be doing, and Baby Boomers are pretty much the same except that they particularly like public praise. Gen Xers and Millennials would like to be kept well informed with the former preferring immediate feedback on how they are doing and the latter seeking immediate and constant feedback. Positive reinforcement in the classroom is essential.

Training and development, according to Birch and Shaw (2010), are also viewed differently by each generation. Traditionalists would just as soon not attend training or partake of it in any way. They believe that one learns from experience; if they are working, they are learning. They prefer being informed through tried-and-true means: newspapers, libraries, company publications. Baby Boomers very much enjoy the social aspects of the training opportunity; they enjoy meeting and greeting fellow employees whom they may not have met previously or seen for a while. Boomers are used to being graded on how well they get along and have no problem listening to and pulling information from lectures; even those presentations that are not dynamic and active. Gen Xers expect to be kept up to date with the latest training; they may not stay with an organization that does provide training; but they will definitely leave if there is no potential for development. Organizations that do not train are stealing from them. They trust online sources more than they do presenters. Millennials expect training and development online and immediately available. Although not experienced, they still want to contribute; they want to learn and have fun doing it. They are not interested in the social aspects of training, unlike the Boomer, since Millennials network outside the classroom.

While these attitudes may seem to underscore marked differences among the generations concerning their willingness to participate in training and development activities, recent studies contradict that finding: Citing a 2011 Rouen Business School study, Ladan Nikravan (2011) points out that "many employers continue to believe that the desire for development varies depending on an employee's age" (p. 37). Nikravan goes on to highlight Southwest Airlines approach to learning which focuses on appealing to adult learning styles rather than consideration of generational differences. According to Southwest's manager of leadership development, they first address different adult learning styles and then "try to … make sure we have components to engage all four generations" (p. 37). Nikravan notes that at Southwest "new development opportunities created may cater to Gen Y, but they are available to, utilized for, and appreciated by all employees" (p. 37). Nikravan also quotes Lynne Lancaster, coauthor of *When Generations Collide*: Commenting on "continuous learning" as opposed to "urgent" or "remedial" learning, Lancaster says that "we all need to be more comfortable learning all the time," and "That can present challenges for the different generations" (Nikravan, 2011, p. 41).

We can draw two lessons from this last point: The learning environment in the workplace of four generations should be one that considers all of the generations. A way to cater to Millennials and still include all generations is to approach the learning environment based on adult learning styles.

HOW LIKELY ARE WE TO CONTINUE TO SEE FOUR GENERATIONS IN THE WORKPLACE?

Because of the differences in the four generations, one might be tempted to ride out the changes that should take place and just wait until the Traditionalists drop out, the Baby Boomers retire, and the Millennials amass enough numbers to take over. That is not going to happen anytime soon.

Traditionalists' numbers in the workplace are gradually coming down, but Baby Boomers are working longer than expected. The Bureau of Labor Statistics reports that 29.1% of people aged 65 to 69 were employed at least part time in 2010 and almost 7% of people aged 75 or older worked in that same year (The Associated Press, 2011). Additionally, the percentage of Americans age 55 and older in the workplace is at an all-time high: 1975-34.6%; 1993-29.4%; 2010-40.2%. Such increases are likely to continue as healthcare costs rise, longer life spans are experienced, long-term care costs and numbers increase, and confidence in the ability to maintain a life style in retirement decreases (The Employee Benefit Research Institute, 2011). We need to be prepared for the four generations for some time to come.

TECHNOLOGY'S IMPACT ON THE 21ST CENTURY DELIVERY OPTIONS AND PARTICIPANTS

With this broad sketch of each generation in mind, let us first consider how technology has impacted training delivery options: Over the last several years, technology has changed the nature of the traditional classroom by forcing trainers and developers to move more and more toward "blended learning" but without the complete surrender of the traditional classroom. That is, technology has caused us to employ multiple training delivery media in one curriculum, to combine classroom instruction with online capabilities thus producing "blended learning" (Mitchell & Russo, 2005). We have not completely abandoned the classroom since trainers and developers report that classroom delivery is the dominant medium, between 41 (Anderson, 2010) and 59% (American Society of Training and Development, 2010) of all delivery methods.

Increasingly, we are seeing the use of videos, CD-ROM, satellite broadcasts, interactive TV, webinars, Ipods, and the list goes on, to supplement what used to take place strictly in the classroom. Additionally, we are seeing the increase of informal learning or learning not part of a structured program; e.g., how often have you "Googled" a term? This is just one example of informal learning.

Let us define some terms that will be helpful to use in talking about technology and delivery methods:

- Synchronous: An instructor/facilitator is simultaneously present and assisting with the learning experience; for example, classroom, webinars, formal on-the-job training;
- Asynchronous: An instructor is not simultaneously present as the learning is taking place; for example, videos, CDs, webinars;
- E-learning: Electronic learning; content and instructional methods delivered via intranet/extranet, audio and video tape, satellite broadcast, interactive TV, CD-ROM, etcetera.;
- Web 2.0 Technologies: An evolving collection of trends and technologies that foster user-generated content, user interactivity, collaboration, and information sharing; for example, wikis, blogs, social networking, podcasts; can be synchronous or asynchronous; and
- Blended learning: A combination of synchronous, asynchronous, and e-learning delivery options.

These are the most common delivery methods:

- Classroom: The traditional method of training delivery done in a specified training area;
- Formal on-the-job training: Structured training delivery at a work site; just-in-time training;
- Synchronous e-learning: An instructor/facilitator is simultaneously present and assisting with the learning experience using electronic delivery means;
- Asynchronous e-learning: An instructor is not simultaneously present as the learning is taking place using electronic delivery methods;
- Instructor-prescribed blended: The instructor structures the learning and uses blended delivery methods;
- Student-prescribed blended: The learner structures the learning and takes advantage of blended delivery methods; and

• Informal learning: Learning is not part of a structured program.

(Technology and delivery definitions are adapted from Mitchell & Russo, 2005.)

Graphically, we could depict the relationship of delivery methods to technology as shown in Figure 10.1.

As we have more and more technology available, that is, as we move into Web 2.0, we begin to see the blurring of the line between the electronic and the face-to-face. The use of mobile devices, by U.S. based organizations, in learning increased from 9% in 2007 to 20% in 2010 (Bersin, 2011). According to a TrainingIndustry, Inc. and Citrix/Online (n.d.) study, the 21st century approach to learning is a collaborative workplace joined together by a texting capability, e-mail, social networking, and online meetings. Learning opportunities are pulled by the learner rather than pushed out by the central training and development department. These "on-demand" sessions are smaller in size and less formal than the traditional classroom approach (How to Promote the Value of Online Training Within Your Organization, pp. 4-5).

If we compared delivery options by the facilitator's degree of control and the participant's access to them, it would look like what is shown in Figure 10.2.

As we move down the available delivery methods, the facilitator loses control of when learning takes place and the participant gains more control of when he or she participates. This graphic will be of some help as we consider the various generations' preferences for access to the delivery method and how the facilitator can meet those expectations.

Synchronous (e.g. webinar, closed circuit broadcast)	Instructor-led, classroom training:
Asynchronous (e.g. CD; Inter-or Intranet; podcast)	On-the-job training:
Electronic	**Face-to-Face**

Figure 10.1.   The relationship of delivery methods to technology.

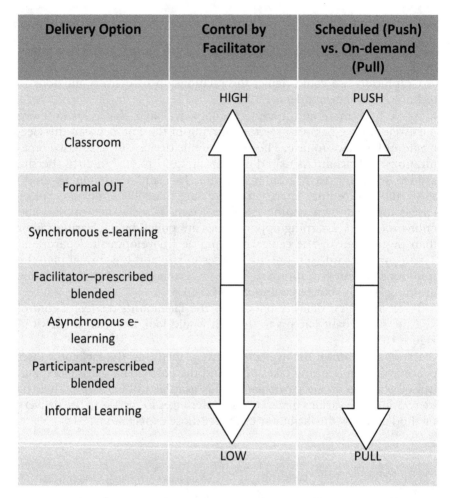

Figure 10.2.   A comparison of delivery options by the facilitator's degree of control and the participant's access to them.

GENERATIONS AND TECHNOLOGY

Now let us consider the relationship generations have with technology: The four generations currently comprising our workforce—Traditionalists, Baby Boomers, Generation X, and Millennials—have differing relationships with technology. Traditionalists view technology as a foreign country to visit occasionally but never to stay for any length of time; they do not speak the language or have any great desire to learn it; they can be characterized as Digital Foreigners. Baby Boomers, on the other hand, are Digital Tourists who speak some of the language, have invested in guide books, and are considering buying the digital player that converts their spoken language into the correct Technospeak. Gen Xers are Digital Immigrants who have moved permanently to Technoslavakia; they are not native speakers, but it is hard to tell them from the natives; when they were very young technology moved into their homes. Finally, Millennials are Digital Natives: They were born in Technoslavakia and have never known a world without the quick connection to all things Internet.

For Millennials, technology provides the opportunity to collaborate with peers and more direct contact with a supervisor; it provides material on demand so that they can learn when they want to; and it can provide distractions. For them multitasking is not a strategy for getting the job done; it is the way that they have always done things. What we need to teach them is how to multitask effectively: Not to accomplish everything at the same rate of speed and get it all done at the pace of mediocrity, but to prioritize effectively and accomplish the important things rapidly (Xavier & Doyle, 2010).

We are facing a collision of technology and attitudes toward training that will result in changes in how we train. If we increase the use of technology, we are not necessarily improving our ability to train because of the way the different generations react to the technology. Thus it is not possible to suggest, in isolation, how we should accommodate Millennials since we will not be developing training for *only* Millennials. We must balance what is to be done about this fourth generation with what it is we are doing with the other three.

LEARNER CLASSIFICATION PATTERNS

The last piece of data that we need before we can draw some specific conclusions about Millennials and training is an understanding of learners in general. There are several tools available to analyze adult learners as learners, in a cosmic sense. Three of the more popular are how adults process information or learning modalities, how they value training and their approach to or how they best like to learn.

First we group learners by "learning modalities" or how adults take in information; that is, we all process information audibly (hearing), visually (seeing), and kinesthetically (doing). By the time we are adults, we have learned to use all three but generally prefer a particular modality. *Auditory learners* prefer to hear information; they are particularly fond of lectures. *Visual learners* like to see or observe information; they like visually stimulating presentations that contain pictures, graphs, and illustrations and take advantage of all types of visuals—slides, videos, models, etcetera; and they prefer to read things themselves. *Kinesthetic learners* prefer hands-on or minds-on activities; they like to interact with the information and prefer to try out the concept or experience the activity, as in engaging in the demonstration or participating in the activity (Mind Works Resources, 2011).

According to Hoyle (1961), we can also classify learners by how they **value learning**; thus we find that learners are goal-, activity-, and learner-oriented. *Goal-oriented learners* want to learn so that they can achieve a specific goal or objective; some clear-cut purpose motivates them to learn; and they want to put learning to an immediate use. They prefer reality based activities, flexible learning schedules, and no unnecessary data. *Activity-oriented learners* are not interested in learning for the knowledge gained in the learning activity—their pursuit of learning has nothing to do with the content or purpose of the learning opportunity; they are interested in the activities provided and the opportunity to socialize. They like learning that is fun, uses group activities, offers tests of what they have learned, and provides recognition for what has been learned. *Learner–oriented learners* seek to learn for the sake of learning; for them learning is a constant, never-ending activity. They like additional learning resources, self-paced and self-directed training, and homework assignments (Hoyle, 1961).

Finally, in a more refined sense learners can be grouped—according to Kolb and colleagues (1984)—by **how they approach the learning process**: *Convergers* look for a single answer and prefer to determine things by themselves by watching someone else; they would prefer to observe the learning activity; they do best in dealing with technical activities and issues rather than social and interpersonal issues. *Divergers,* the opposite of the converger, generate alternative solutions and implications and prefer to jump right into an activity; they are risk-takers and would prefer to dive directly into a learning activity; they are interested in people and are very imaginative. *Assimilators* pull ideas together into an integrated explanation and appreciate being guided in their training efforts; they would prefer to read the training manual thoroughly or receive detailed instruction; like convergers, they prefer to deal with the abstract as opposed to the personal. And *accommodators* adapt to changing circumstances and prefer controlled experimentation such as a simulation; they like new experiences, risk-taking, and activities; they are adaptable (Kolb et al., 1984).

FOUR GENERATIONS IN THE CLASSROOM: SOME HELPFUL MEANS OF PREDICTING HOW THEY LEARN

Bringing all these elements—generational characteristics, the impact of technology on the classroom, and learner classification patterns—

together can provide us a means of responding to the four generations, in general, and, more specifically, the Millennials in the 21st century classroom. The following generalizations about how the four generations process information, value learning, and approach training are intended as general guides of how one might prepare for training the four generations in general and Millennials in particular. These generalizations should not be extended to stereotypes; that is, not all Millennials will respond as predicted by following the guidelines laid out here. The caution is, do not expect all members of any one generation to act the same way. We are, after all, human beings and will act individually.

Process Information A, V, or K? Comparing the characteristics of the four generations, first, to the way that adults process information demonstrates that Traditionalists would seem to learn best by listening and doing or audibly and kinesthetically. Since they trust in the authority of an established chain of command and value experience, Traditionalists will pay a great deal of attention to a credible source facilitating a presentation. They will also tend to credit experience, actually doing something, as one of the best means of learning. Lectures and hands-on experiences are best for this generation.

Baby Boomers prefer to learn audibly and visually: They will listen to a lecture and easily forgive lots of less than valuable information as long as there are a few "nuggets" available. Coming of age as television moved into the living room has created in this generation an increasing reliance on the visual. Generation X process information visually and kinesthetically. They are skeptical and want things demonstrated so that they can see how they work and then test drive them to see if they really work. They have always had television in the home and would, therefore, respond well to visual learning. Millennials process information best visually, even more so than Boomers and Gen Xers. This youngest generation is used to sophisticated visual techniques and highly entertaining means of learning; remember that they grew up on Sesame Street watching Nickelodeon.

Value Learning: As for how they value learning, Traditionalists are goal-oriented based on their dedication and desire to stick to the job at hand; Baby Boomers are activity- and goal-oriented since they enjoy the social aspects of learning and consider training and development as a means to advance in the job; Gen Xers are goal-oriented in that they view training and development as an opportunity to improve job skills for their careers in a particular area; and Millennials are learner- and activity-oriented since they wish to be learning all the time and they enjoy the activities associated with learning.

Approach to Learning: As with processing information and valuing learning, the generations differ in their approach to new learning: Tradi-

Table 10.1.   Learner Assessments

	Learner Classification Patterns		
Generations	*Process Information*	*Value Training*	*Approach Training*
Traditionalists	Audibly & kinesthetically	Goal- oriented	Assimilators
Baby Boomers	Audibly & visually	Activity- and goal-oriented	Accommodators
Generation X	Visually & kinesthetically	Goal-oriented	Convergers
Millennials	Visually	Activity- and learner- oriented	Divergers

tionalists would seem to be assimilators who liked to be guided to a training solution. Baby Boomers seem most comfortable as accommodators who approach new learning as controlled experimentation. Gen Xers appear to be convergers who act on their own after some instruction. And Millennials are divergers who like to jump right in to any activity.

Table 10.1 above summarizes these learner assessments.

ADVICE FOR THE CLASSROOM AND BEYOND

General, Four Generations

Since for at least the foreseeable future, most formal training will be predominantly classroom training, my focus for interpreting the above analysis will be primarily on that mode, but I will also suggest that training and development be moved into web 3.0 technologies; thus demonstrating how and why training and development needs to be "blended learning."

Based on the learner analyses above, here are some things to do with and because of this mix of four generations:

- Keep the classroom as active as possible before, during, and after presentations.
- Establish credibility, cautiously.
- Be prepared to be flexible.
- Build fun in.
- "Get over it" as quickly as possible; park self-consciousness at the door.
- Move the participants around.

- Be more visual than normal.
- Do not overwhelm participants with technology even if you can.
- Begin to move to blended learning that allows for more learning on demand.

By **keeping the classroom active,** I am suggesting that facilitators start the presentation before participants arrive in the classroom and find a means of sustaining activity throughout the presentation; all generations will appreciate this approach since it will help them to begin to connect to the learning. For example, portions of the knowledge needed for the training could be put on line before the participants come to the classroom. Then once they are in the classroom, some device should be used to begin to engage them in the topic. I recommend that you create something that will begin to make connections learner to learner (climate setting), learner to topic (distinguishing old from new learning), learner to personal goals (aligning learner's goals with course outcomes), and learner to outcomes (developing buy-in and an idea of what can be done with the new learning). I find surveys or self-assessments to be useful to begin forging these kinds of connections. For example, in a course on four generations in the classroom, participants could be surveyed at the beginning on what generation they think they are, what generation bugs them the most, and what it is about that generation that bothers them. The classroom activity could have been preceded by online material with workforce figures explaining how we came to have four generations in the workforce. That same survey could be used again at the end of the session to see if the participant has changed his or her mind. From that point, homework assignments could be offered as a voluntary option, or other means could be devised that would help participants to connect after the class is over. I encourage such connections in some classes by having participants create action plans which they exchange with other participants (I use paper airplanes to accomplish the exchange and e-mail addresses as the means of communicating later) with the promise of follow up in a couple of weeks.

Traditionalists will appreciate the guided help in focusing on the topic. Boomers will enjoy the increased socialization of learner to learner and the continued means of connection afterwards. Gen Xers will like the opportunity to go online before class and get an idea of what is coming; they may want to back out of the class if they do not see any value. Millennials want the context that prework provides and the opportunity to work with someone else particularly if they think that creating an action plan is worthwhile.

Facilitators will next want to **establish credibility** but with care. Traditionalists will appreciate having a facilitator who is an expert; Boomers will be impressed by credentials, someone who has made it; but Gen Xers may tend to be skeptical if the facilitator is too glowing with self-praise or too elaborate with the resume but will appreciate having the expert in their presence; and Millennialls regard their parents as very knowledge-able and are willing to accept the authority and expertise of an expert. In instances where the facilitator is not an expert, then it is best to admit that and point out the role as just that: facilitation.

Be **prepared to be flexible**; that is, build in different directions to take with the presentation should it become necessary and plan spontaneity. Facilitators will want optional directions to take the presentation based on the opening connections of learner to topic and goals. This discussion or activity may necessitate that the planned sequence be altered; thus the facilitator should be prepared for these changes. Traditionalists and Boomers will not like the idea of changing but will appreciate the guid-ance given to make the change. Gen Xers and Millennials will appreciate the changes: Xers because the material would better meet their needs and Millennials because the material is special for them.

I have suggested that spontaneity should be planned, which would seem to be contradictory. My intent is to suggest that any really good pre-sentation that appeals to all four generations needs to have a degree of uncertainty to it. Again, Traditionalists and Boomers may be turned off by such actions, but Xers and Millenials will appreciate that the unexpected has been interjected. Such spontaneity or changes in direction should be well signaled. I like to have a game or two ready to play, and if the audi-ence seems to be struggling with comprehension of a particular point, then we can stop and play the game and see if it helps illustrate the point.

A corollary to flexibility is fun: **Fun should be built in** to the presenta-tion. All of the generations but especially Millennials want training to be enjoyable. I recommend games that help to convey the learning; not just games for the sake of games; but games that help advance the learning. There are several versions of *Jeopardy* that can be used to provide reviews of material previously covered; some are quite high-tech but you can cre-ate your own versions without the high-tech accessories.

So far I have suggested lots of activity, flexibility, and fun. Now comes the really hard part: Keeping one's dignity intact while being active, flexi-ble, and funny. Facilitators want to enjoy what they are doing just as much as we want participants to enjoy learning, but all my suggestions so far may seem, to some, an attack on the dignity of the classroom. This is not my intent. With the mixture of generations and especially Millennials, the classroom needs to be a place of fun as well as learning. This approach may seem undignified, so my suggestion to those who feel this way is to **park self-consciousness at the door**. Let go and be natural, relaxed, and enjoy the presentation. Those facilitators who can do so will find an appreciative audience that will also enjoy the presentation.

Move the participants around within the classroom to effectively mix the generations so that they have contact with others outside their own generation. Such tactics as having various stations around the classroom with posters to which participants contribute can provide movement. For longer sessions that use group activities, the groups can be mixed in various nonthreatening ways. Movement and mixing groups is particularly helpful for Millennials since they will desire to lead a group, and giving them that opportunity with the other generations will be helpful to them and the other generations. Traditionalists will not like switching to any great extent but will go along with the authority of the facilitator.

A review of the summary table above under the "Process Information" column shows that all but Traditionalists have some visual tendencies when processing information. Thus there is a need to be **more visual in the classroom**. This tending to the visual should be at the expense of the audible; that is, cut down on the lecture and up the use of videos, pictures, etc. One useful technique is to ask the audience to prepare visuals to represent key points.

Even though some of the previous suggestions might force it and even though you may have the funds to support it, **do not use as much technology as you might be tempted to use**. Do not try to fill the classroom with technology but do encourage participants to bring their own technology. Once you encourage this bring your own technology, allow participants to use the devices to assist learning. For example, ask those with smart phones or tablets to look up definitions or "Google" certain terms. There is no reason why we should not use what technology we have regardless of who paid for it or how it arrived in the classroom or learning environment.

Lastly, begin to gradually work in more and more opportunities for participants to prepare for the classroom with activities outside the classroom; in other words gradually **increase blended learning opportunities**. These will appeal especially to Millennials and Gen Xers but should also be available to the other, older generations. By gradually expanding such things as read-ahead materials and exercises, postcourse offerings, and online training opportunities (short videos, podcasts or self-paced learning programs), on-demand training opportunities will also expand.

Specific, Millennials

In addition to these suggestions, Millennials can be better engaged in training and development by doing the following:

- Provide them opportunities to lead the group.
- Explain both "whys"—the big picture and the significance—to them.
- Ask their opinion.
- Let them use their own technology.
- Research and provide them safe social media.
- Provide on-demand learning opportunities.

Even though they might not be ready, Millennials want to be leaders. While they might lack the political savvy to lead in the organization, there is no reason that they cannot **lead discussion groups**. Be sure to lay out clear parameters for the discussion—time (length), purpose, and ground rules, but let the Millennials have the group leader job. It is a good test tube situation for them to learn in a relatively risk-free environment.

Millennials are often known alternatively as Generation Why for good reason. They like to know both the context of a task, **the big picture why**, and the significance of an action, **the why it has to be done**. Millennials were taught that there is something to be learned in everything that they do, so they want to know how their contribution fits in with everything around them and that their job has a significance to, a contribution to be made to the whole (Murphy, 2011) The big-picture why or context will provide the larger view of a process or procedure and where the Millennial fits into that larger context; the why of significance will help the Millennial to understand why something is being done and underlying concepts which will, in turn, be helpful in trouble-shooting and problem-solving (Kapp, 2011). I do not suggest that Millennials be singled out and told this information but rather that it be included in the introduction to the learning.

Once the context and significance are known, the Millennial will be ready to offer his or her opinion. They should be encouraged to do so, as should all participants. Millennials' parents have encouraged them to engage in discussions and told them that their opinions have value: The training classroom will not be any different, so we should be prepared for and **encourage the offering of opinions**. Questions on the part of the facilitator will be important to draw out these opinions and not seem as if this group is being pampered or, on the other hand, being singled out for unfair treatment. Facilitators should be careful not to overdo this drawing out; it is more likely that the Millennials will not be reluctant to offer their opinion; thus, the facilitator will need to be prepared to temper or qualify opinions.

In fact, I recommend that we not only allow them to express those opinions but that we **encourage the use of their technology to assist us**

in the classroom. Millennials will have their smart phones and tablets with them, so crank up the Wi-Fi and give them assignments to help you with the course material; encourage them to bring their own technology to the classroom. When I see that Millennials have their technology, I ask them to "Google" things such as the definition of terms.

Beyond this use of technology in the classroom, we should also delve into its use outside the classroom: social media sources safe for the Millennial to use should be vetted by the facilitator. That is, we should **explore and locate safe social media** that the Millennial could use on the job. Our role as facilitators and subject-matter experts should not be the limitation of such sources but rather the exploration of such sources as we could recommend to the Millennial and Gen Xers.

Taking this idea a further step, we should be creating an opportunity for on-demand training: Millennials would like to be learning at any and all times. For this reason, we need to move outside the classroom and **provide learning on demand**. Once again, this expanded learning opportunity should not be just for Millennials but for all generations. We should begin now to expand learning beyond the confines of the classroom so that as we gradually see the Baby Boomers leave the work force, the Gen Xers to diminish because their numbers are small and not large enough to completely replace the Boomers, and the Millennials to enter the work force in larger numbers, we should be moving training more and more out of the classroom and into electronic means—either supplied by the organization or the individual.

A FEW CONCLUDING THOUGHTS

Now we have arrived at the same point for Millennials as we have for the other three generations: blended learning that offers greater on-demand, informal learning opportunities. Thus as the Traditionalists drop out of the workplace, we will be better prepared for their replacements, Generation 2020; and still we have four generations in the workplace.

For all generations, here are nine suggestions to improve classroom training: (1) keep the classroom as active as possible; (2) establish credibility, cautiously; (3) be prepared to be flexible; (4) build fun in; (5) park facilitator self-consciousness at the door; (6) move the participants around; (7) be more visual than normal; (8) do not overwhelm participants with technology; and (9) begin to move to blended learning. In effect, I am suggesting that we move what learning purposes we can, particularly knowledge, to an online delivery method; take it out of the classroom.

For Millenials specifically, there are six "take-aways" for the classroom and training in general: (1) provide Millenials opportunities to lead groups; (2) explain both "whys"—the big picture and the significance—to them; (3) ask their opinion; (4) allow them to use their own technology; (5) research and provide them safe social media; and (6) provide on-demand learning opportunities.

Going back to Figure 10. 2 concerning delivery options, we can now suggest that training and development need to move away from the classroom with its control by the facilitator and push-situations and toward informal learning with its participant-prescribed options and pull, on-demand opportunities. As we attempt, increasingly, to blend learning in this fashion, we will be preparing more and more asynchronous e-learning and making it available to our participants. The need for the classroom and employer-assisted, on-the-job training will diminish. The training and development manager will not have disappeared: He or she will be preparing training and development opportunities as they are increasingly demanded by the learner—all learners of all generations, but informal learning directed by the participant will become the dominant delivery mode.

Workplace learning is moving in the direction of social learning, a highly flexible learning environment with learners actively controlling and generating the content using real-time communication (Allen & Naughton, 2011). Millennials will be ready for this new environment as will Generation X. Baby Boomers will be okay with this trend, sighing over its seeming chaos, and Traditionalists will struggle with this totally undisciplined approach, counting the days until they can walk away from the nonsense, but they will nonetheless comply with what they have been asked to do.

REFERENCES

Allen, M., & Naughton, J. (2011, August). Social learning: A call to action for learning professionals. *Training and Development, 65*(8), 50-55.

American Society of Training and Development. (2010). 2010 state of the industry report. Retrieved from http://www.astd.org/ASTD

Anderson, C. (2010, July). The medium is the message. *Chief Learning Officer, 9*(7), 54-56.

The Associated Press. (2011, July 20). Boomers worry about finances, health costs. *Opelika Auburn News, 106*(211), 1A, 6A.

Bernstein, L. E. (2006). *Generations working together: What everybody needs to KNOW and DO!* Dallas, TX: The Walk the Talk Company and Vision Point, pp. 13-19.

Bersin, J. (2011, August). Have learning will travel. *Chief Learning Officer, 10*(8), 14.

Birch, C, & Shaw, H. (2010, February). "Teaching multiple generations," Franklin Covey's *February 2010 Academy: Facilitation Tip Sheet*. Blue Bell, PA: Franklin-Covey.

Catalyst *Quicktakes* (2011), Generations in the workplace in the United States & Canada. Retrieved from http://www.catalyst.org/publication/434/generations-in-the-workplace-in-the-united-states-canada

The Employee Benefit Research Institute (2011, March). Report finds higher percentage of older workers in workforce, *The Alabama Employment Law Letter*. Retrieved from http://www.hrlaws.com/

Hoyle, C. O. (1961). *The inquiring mind*. Madison, WI: The University of Wisconsin Press.

Kapp, K. M. (2011, July). Matching the right design strategy to the right content. *Training and Development, 65*(7), 48-52.

Kolb, D. A., Rubin, I. M., & McIntyre, J. M. (1984). *Organizational psychology: An experiential approach to organizational behavior.* Englewood Cliffs, NJ: Prentice-Hall.

Lancaster, L. C., & Stillman, D. (2002). *When generations collide*. New York, NY: Harper Collins.

MindWorks Resources. (2011). 3 primary learning modalities every person uses. Retrieved from http://www.mindworksresources.com/p-324-3-primary-learning-modalities-every-person-uses.aspx

Mitchell, J., & Russo, C. (Eds.). (2005) *The Infoline dictionary of basic trainer terms*. Alexandria, VA: ASTD Press.

Murphy, M. (2011, July). Managing generation "why?" LeadershipIQ. Retrieved from http://www.leadershipiq.com/print/articles/managing-generation-why

Nikravan, L. (2011, October). The Gen Y workplace. *Chief Learning Officer, 10*(10), 36-41.

TrainingIndustry, Inc. & Citrix/Online. (n.d.). How to promote the value of online training within your organization. Retrieved from http://now.eloqua.com/e/f2.aspx?elqSiteID=607&elqFormName=AssetTrackingForm&Email=?e =deerypd@auburn.edu&assetURL=http://img.en25.com/Web/CitrixOnline/GoToMeeting_TrainingIndustry_OnlineTrainingROI.pdf&SFDC_Campaign _ID=701000000005JtV

Xavier, S., & Doyle, S. (2010, July). Succession across the generations. *Talent Management, 6*(7), 40-42, 56.

PART III

BEST PRACTICES FOR MANAGING HUMAN RESOURCES FOR THE MILLENNIAL GENERATION

CHAPTER 11

BEST PRACTICES FOR MANAGING GENERATION Y

Susan Eisner

INTRODUCTION

Generation Y (Gen Y) has been given several labels, ranging from Millennials and Generation Why to Echo Boomers and Boomlets to Gen Next and Internet Generation. But there is little divergence in the experience employers are having as they seek to manage this newest human resource cohort group. The attributes and expectations of Gen Y are presenting new challenges and opportunities for companies seeking to attain, develop, retain, and obtain high performance from these workers. The saliency of developing successful strategies for doing so is known to employers, given shifting demographics and predicted job requirements that underscore the importance of their having and fully utilizing those of Gen Y (Cal State Fullerton Career Center & Spectrum Knowledge, 2010).

As companies attempt to craft attendant strategies and practices, the need to get it right has additional value due to transparency heightened by technology, which Gen Y tends to frequent. Through Internet searches, the companies identified by third party media as best for Gen Y to work for can be identified, as can the human resource (HR) policies and practices of individual companies. Simultaneously, social media and career

Managing Human Resources for the Millennial Generation, pp. 251–278
Copyright © 2012 by Information Age Publishing
All rights of reproduction in any form reserved.

websites provide access to present and former company employees' descriptions of their work experiences and employers' practices. Similarly, modern technology allows for workforce access, input, collaboration, development, and feedback that can transform traditional performance norms and costs.

Within this context, a range of contemporary practices are reported. These include some companies recasting their workplaces as "campuses" that span traditional work-life barriers by providing a full spectrum of on-site services for employees, some enhancing their culture's "community" through shared nonwork activities ranging from meals to athletic activities and field trips, some designing career paths individualized for employees from point of entry, some delivering ongoing employee development in on-site "universities," some delivering performance incentives ranging from on-the-spot bonuses to earned "points" that can be converted to cash equivalent use, some offering benefit "menus" allowing employees to choose which benefits they receive, some attracting employees including those not actively seeking work through comprehensive corporate culture and career opportunity descriptions linked to the company website's homepage, some adapting nontraditional work scheduling and telecommuting, and some "flattening" their organizations to heighten 360 degree communication, teamwork, and transparency.

The extent of change these practices embody may be especially evident to those of prior generations. To them the notion of an entering employee e-mailing the chief executive officer (CEO) with an idea, receiving a reply, and then being green-lighted to proceed with the project, as has occurred for instance at JC Penney (Hira, 2007), may well seem to be a pipe dream. The impact of these changes, though, is likely to be experienced by all, as research indicates that such contemporary practices may well be becoming the new workplace normal.

As a result, this chapter presents representative best practices being used by contemporary companies seeking to heighten the presence and contribution of Gen Y workers. Companies designated by recognized third party sources as best places to launch a career (Gerdes, 2006, 2007, & 2008), best for recent college grads to work for[1] (Experience.com, 2009, 2010, & 2011), top entry-level employers[2] (Lynch, 2011), and best to work for[3] (*Fortune*, 2010, 2011) were intentionally identified, as were companies whose current practices have been featured in the *New York Times* Sunday Business Section's weekly "Corner Office"[4] series. Relevant best practices used by this foundational cohort group were found through academic and practitioner publications, and in company websites and career sites focused on those practices. Recent studies surveying Gen Y workplace preferences and expectations were then consulted to provide context for identifying workplace practices that align with Gen Y wants and needs. Literature from several recent years was intentionally reviewed both to insure currency and to override potential unrepresentative impact that economic conditions might have on data from any one year. Moreover, studies from several respondent pools and sources were deliberately consulted to avoid skew that might result from situational factors particularly salient to a specific source. From this foundational research, 11 best practices emerge that can be recommended for those seeking to optimize the performance of their Gen Y workers.

WHAT GEN Y SEEKS AT WORK

As effective workplace practices will be compatible with the interests of those they are designed to impact (Piktialis, 2004), relevant recent studies examining Gen Y workplace wants and needs were reviewed. The first of these is a 2007 study by CareerBuilder, conducted by Harris Interactive, titled "Connecting with Generation Y Workers." The study surveyed some 2,500 U.S. hiring managers and HR professionals representing all major industries. As summarized in Table 11.1, the majority of respondents reported that Gen Y expects employers to provide higher pay, flexible work scheduling, promotion within a year, and more vacation or personal time. A sizable minority also reported that Gen Y expects workplace access to state of the art technology, but that was the lowest ranked Gen Y expectation reported. When Gen Y expectations are compared to policy and program adaptations, the reported expectations appear to parallel but to be ahead of the policy and program changes actually made. The

**Table 11.1.   Hiring Managers and HR Professionals
Report Expectations and Changes, 2007**

	% Say Gen Y expects	% Changed policy/program
Higher pay	74	26 (increased salaries/bonuses)
Flexible work schedule	61	57
		18 (more telecommuting options)
Promotion within a year	56	33 (more recognition programs)
More vacation or personal time	50	11 (more vacation time)
Access to state of art technology	37	26
		20 (pay for cell phone/ blackberry)
Ongoing education programs		24

majority of respondents report changes that provide more flexibility in work scheduling, and respondents do report changes that parallel each of Gen Y's expectations. But except for flexible work schedules, policies and programs have been changed to accommodate Gen Y expectations by at most 33% and as few as 11% of respondents. Additionally, a quarter of respondents initiated changes in an attribute they do not report to be a Gen Y expectation, ongoing education programs (CareerBuilder, 2007).

A 2008 study by Robert Half International and Yahoo!hotjobs surveyed more than 1,000 U.S. workers aged 21-28. The findings, "Generation Y: What Millennial Workers Want," are consistent with those of the 2007 CareerBuilder study in concluding that Gen Y prioritizes financial and career advancement aspects of work. This 2008 study, though, is more specific in identifying benefits as a workplace priority for Gen Y workers as they focus on practical need for healthcare, retirement savings, and work-life balance ("Focused on the Future," 2008); three-quarters of respondents feel they will have to work harder than prior generations and save more money for retirement (Robert Half International & Yahoo!hotjobs, 2008).

The Robert Half/Yahoo! study also delineates factors in the work environment important to Gen Y workers. These include a manager they can admire and who will help them develop without micromanaging, continual communication with and feedback from managers, compatible peers, and interesting work. The latter does not necessitate impressive titles and offices for Gen Y. Professional development and advancement is the valued objective as Gen Y workers think they should have to spend no more than 2 years in entry levels, and most expect to stay in whatever position they currently hold for no more than 5 years. Gen Y workers also value an organization that benefits the individual and society at large. They do not, though, want that to be achieved at the cost of their own professional growth and security (2008).

The above findings are consistent with factors respondents report would cause them to leave their current job for another one. Using a scale of 5 most important to 1 least important, they stated factors salient to retention as higher pay (4.63), better perks and benefits (4.44), more opportunity for advancement (4.22), more interesting work (4.14), better work environment (3.99), shorter commute (3.51), and more prestigious job title (3.39) (Robert Half International & Yahoo!hotjobs, 2008).

Table 11.2 summarizes the overall findings of the Robert Half/Yahoo! study. The study used a scale of 10 high to 1 low in ranking the importance that Gen Y workers place on 35 attributes of job, benefits, and work environment (2008).

In 2009, *Harvard Business Review* published results of a study by Hewlett, Sherbin, and Sumberg reporting on workplace preferences of

Table 11.2. Gen Y Workers Report Importance, 2008

Attributes rated 9.00-10.00 (#1-2)	1) Salary 9.05, 2) health care coverage 9.02
Attributes rated 8.00-8.99 (#3-12)	3) Paid vacation 8.82, 4) dental care coverage 8.80, 5-6) career growth/advancement opportunity 8.74, 5-6) working with manager I can respect and learn from 8.74, 7) working with people I enjoy 8.69, 8) having work/life balance 8.63, 9) 401K programs 8.58, 10) company location 8.44, 11) bonuses 8.25, 12) flexible work hours/ telecommuting 8.06
Attributes rated 7.00-7.99 (#13-20)	13) Company leadership 7.95, 14) company reputation/ brand recognition 7.56, 15) short commute 7.55, 16) profit-sharing 7.52, 17) subsidized training/education 7.51, 18) working for socially responsible company 7.42, 19) job title 7.19, 20) nice office space 7.15
Attributes rated 6.00-6.99 (#21-28)	21) In-house training 6.95, 22) working with state of art technology 6.89, 23) tuition reimbursement 6.44, 24) mentoring programs 6.41, 25) housing/relocation aid 6.38, 26) staff diversity 6.07, 27) company philanthropy 6.06, 28) free/subsidized snacks/lunch 6.02
Attributes rated 5.00-5.99 (#29-33)	29) Subsidized transportation 5.73, 30) on-site perks (e.g. dry cleaning/fitness center) 5.59, 31) subsidized gym membership 5.59, 32) matching gifts programs for charitable contributions 5.33, 33) sabbaticals 5.26
Attributes rated 4.00-4.99 (#34-35)	34) On-site childcare 4.92, 35) adoption assistance 4.05

U.S. college graduates by comparing survey responses of Gen Y workers to those given by the largest other generational group present in the workplace, Baby Boomers. The study, "How Gen Y & Baby Boomers Will Reshape Your Agenda," reported Gen Y results consistent with those of the 2007 and 2008 studies described above in finding work flexibility, self-growth, connection to peers and company, and the chance to make a difference important to Gen Y workers. The results of the 2009 study add to the portrait of Gen Y workplace preferences by finding both Gen Y and Baby Boom generations valuing those attributes. In addition, Gen Y responses reported in this study rated several forms of reward to be at least as important to them as financial compensation: valued colleagues, work arrangements that are flexible, opportunity for and ongoing advancement/promotion, acknowledgement by company and/or manager, and chance to have new challenges and experiences (2009).

In 2010, Cal State (California State University) Fullerton Career Center and Spectrum Knowledge released a cross-industry study of workforce preferences in "The Guide to Managing and Developing Young Professionals." The report surveyed and conducted focus groups of more than 2,300 U.S. respondents to identify best practices and recommendations for managing contemporary workers. Like the 2009 *Harvard Business Review* study, this 2010 "The Guide to Managing and Developing Young Professionals" included intergenerational comparisons. As a result, it adds contextual information for those seeking to craft practices most likely to resonate with all workers.

Consistent with the earlier studies that specified Gen Y respondent ranking of financial compensation, the 2010 study found money to be top priority for Gen Y workers both in accepting an offered job and remaining in a job held. The study reported pay to be a "threshold issue" and "first filter" for two-thirds of Gen Y, who will not only consider other attributes of a job offered only if the pay is high enough for them to consider accepting it but who will also leave a job if they are able to receive higher compensation at another. In comparison, 40% or less of Gen Y respondents found position, benefits, work environment, or supervisor more important or equal to pay as a key workplace factor. Work environment was valued more by Gen Y than any other generation's respondents, and all generations report healthcare as the most important benefit to be provided. More than 60% of Gen Y ranked healthcare as the top benefit. They were more disparate in their valuing of other benefits which they ranked, after healthcare, from most to least important as retirement, flexible hours, time off, tuition, ability to work at home, and on-site perks (Cal State Fullerton Career Center & Spectrum Knowledge, 2010).

Table 11.3 summarizes the priorities each generation's respondents placed on 11 workplace attributes, as reported by the Cal State/Spectrum Knowledge 2010 study. The majority of Gen Y respondents top rank opportunity for career advancement; the next ranked priority, flexible work, is cited by almost a majority. Gen Y values eight of the 11 attributes more highly than does either of the other demographic groups. Only importance of challenging and innovative work, importance of a boss open to suggestion and supportive of decisions, and ability to work from home is valued less by Gen Y than by the other demographics group. Five of the 11 attributes are prioritized by at least one-quarter of each of the demographic groups: opportunity for career advancement, flexible work, work environment impact on retention, challenging and innovative work, and constructive feedback. Only one of the attributes was prioritized by at least one-third of each of the demographic groups, challenging and innovative work. These responses suggest that a "menu" of various practices may be an effective workplace strategy, in that all workers are likely to appreciate the importance and availability of the practice to others but also to value the opportunity to choose those most tailored and adaptable to their own evolving interests and needs.

Table 11.3.   Generations of Workers Report Importance, 2010

	Gen Y	Gen X	Boomers+
Opportunities for career advancement	53%	47%	25%
Flexible work hours or schedule	46%	42%	31%
Work environment impact on decision to stay with a company	39%	32%	25%
Challenging and innovative work	38%	42%	47%
Constructive feedback	33%	26.5%	26.5%
Mentoring and training	28%	28%	17%
Work environment impact on decision to accept job offer	25%	20%	18%
Boss with friendly personality and easy to get along with	23%	18%	14%
Ability to develop friends at work	22%	8%	5%
Boss open to my suggestions and supportive of my decisions	19%	25%	30%
Ability to work from home	8%	17%	10%

A 2010 study reported results of a 3-year survey conducted by the Corporate Executive Board in "Gen Y at Work: Not So Different After All." More than 400,000 workers across employed generations were asked about their workplace attitudes. Results of the study were consistent with those described above that found financial compensation to be a priority for Gen Y workers. This 2010 study found it to be the first or second most important job aspect, out of 38 attributes ranked, for respondents of all generations. The study adds to understanding of compensation's impact by distinguishing its saliency to different generations' workers. It reports that Gen X and Baby Boomer workers tend to be concerned with the specific amount they are paid and whether that will be sufficient for their needs. Alternatively, Gen Y workers tend to be concerned with the amount they are paid when compared with their peers, which also underscores the importance of providing them with transparent communication (Kopp, 2010).

WHAT BEST LISTED COMPANIES DO

Given what studies report Gen Y workers expect to find and want at work, a review of overall relevant practices at *Fortune*'s 2011 list of 100 best companies to work for provides useful context within which to formulate optimal practices for managing these workers. That review finds that allowing workers to telecommute or work from home at least one-fifth of the time is the benefit that most of these top-ranked companies provide. Among the top 25 of *Fortune*'s best-ranked companies[5] Cisco has the most tele-commuters and is the only one to rank within the top 10, of the overall 100 best-ranked company list, in percentage of workers who access this benefit; 85% of Cisco's workers do so. Additionally, at least one-quarter of the 100 top-ranked companies offer onsite child-care centers. Among the top 25 of the top-ranked companies, onsite child-care centers are pro-vided at SAS, Google, Alston & Bird, JM Family Enterprises, USAA, Cisco, and Goldman Sachs. Boston Consulting Group (BCG), Recreational Equipment, Dreamworks Animation SKG, Alston & Bird, Robert Baird & Co., Container Store, and DPR Construction offer fully paid sabbaticals. And BCG, Zappos.com, Nugget Market, Whole Foods Market, and Umpqua Market pay 100% of employee health-care premiums. Six of the 10 companies on *Fortune*'s 100 best-ranked companies whose workers feel most encouraged to balance their work and personal lives are among *Fortune*'s 25 best-ranked companies: SAS, REI, Wegmans Food Markets, Camden Property Trust, Edward Jones, and Methodist Hospital System. Table 11.4, below, summarizes these benefits at the 100, and 25, compa-nies top-ranked by *Fortune* (Fortune, 2011).

A specific review of *Fortune*'s 25 top-ranked companies finds them all offering professional training. The majority also offer compressed work weeks (offered by 18), subsidized gym membership (offered by 17), and onsite fitness centers (offered by 15). Twelve of the 25 top-ranked compa-nies offer job sharing programs. The companies among the top-ranked 25 offering each of these is identified in Note 6;[6] the majority of the top-ranked 25 companies offer at least four of these five practices. These five practices are all present at five of the companies: SAS, Dreamworks Ani-mation SKG, Alston & Bird, Methodist Hospital System, and Goldman Sachs. Four of these five practices are present at Wegmans Food Markets, Google, NetApp, Edward Jones, Robert W. Baird, Mercedes-Benz USA, JM Family Enterprises, Cisco, and DPR Construction. None of these five

**Table 11.4.   Benefits at Companies *Fortune*
Lists as Best to Work For, 2011**

	# of top 100	*# of top 25*
Allow workers to telecommute or work at home at least 1/5 of time	82	18
Have onsite childcare	25+	7
Offer fully paid sabbaticals	21	7
Pay 100% of employee health-care premiums	14	5
In top 10 encouraging workers to balance work and personal life	10	6

practices are present at three of the 25 top-ranked companies: Nugget Market, Container Store, and Umpqua Bank (Fortune, 2011).

RECOMMENDED BEST PRACTICES

Generational literature asserts that optimal management practices will be tailored to and consistent with characteristics of generations they seek to impact (Piktialis, 2004). The studies and practices described above are underscored by academic and practitioner research cited below along with specific examples of successful operationalization by companies positively recognized for these practices. They collectively suggest that the following 11 practices for managing Gen Y workers may be optimal.

Create a Contemporary Culture

A culture of community, inclusion, positivism, and respect should resonate well with Gen Y workers. Physical adaptations ranging from lowering walls between workspaces to designing kinetic and fun break rooms to hosting shared events reflective of Gen Y interests can contribute to making work and workplace enjoyable and interactive for these workers (Cal State Fullerton Career Center & Spectrum Knowledge, 2010) as can the casual dress days, employee recognition and rewards programs, and free food and snacks now regularly provided at *Fortune*'s top-ranked companies to work for (Lowe, Levitt, & Wilson, 2008). Moreover, treating Gen Y workers as value-adding colleagues from day one should model a norm of respect that can be expected from them in return (Martin, 2008). This can be furthered by "onboarding" Gen Y entry with personalized manuals, training materials that use Gen Y-friendly media, peer interaction integrated into training, and performance expectations clarified from the start (Cal State Fullerton Career Center & Spectrum Knowledge, 2010).

FactSet Research Systems is a company reflecting this practice. It helps its workers to establish Facebook groups to facilitate their being in contact with each other, and includes a strong social component in its training program. Its trainees, for instance, go bowling together after training sessions end (Flander, 2008). Qualcomm strengthens this acculturation through a New Grad Program providing networking events, off-site gatherings, and team building activities (Experience.com, 2009). Rainmaker Entertainment does so by encouraging all of its workers to develop story ideas based on the company's mascots; the strongest will be produced into animated shorts (Flander, 2008). Starbucks levels the value of its workers by providing health insurance and stock options to part-time as well as full-time workers, and CEO Howard Schultz strives each day to thank those who work there (Bryant, 2010h). Google's publicly available materials express cultural norms that each worker is equally important to its company's success. It says that all feel free both to question its CEO at weekly "TGIF" meetings which all can attend, and to throw a volleyball at a corporate officer on site (Google, n.d.). And Target's online career page has a link to "Fast, Fun and Friendly" through a "Working at Target/Culture" tab. There, Target is described as a "world-class" fast-paced and enjoyable place to work with friendly, empowered, respected and recognized people who as teams bring forward ideas and solutions (http://www.target.com/careers).

Flatten and Wire the Organization

Leveling work processes should further show, validate, and operationalize norms and attributes that align well with Gen Y. In addition to constructing office spaces that ease Gen Y workers' ability to brainstorm and share ideas (Raines, 2002), updating technology to support seamless connectivity between home and work environment and between individual and team should promote the creativity, flexibility (Lowe et al., 2008), project-centered work (Allen, 2004), and accessibility Gen Y workers seek. Recent studies indicate these to be investments well made. A 2006 survey found 90% of workers reporting their office spaces affect their attitudes about work. A study by Pfeffer the following year found companies whose workplaces encourage informal worker interaction outperforming those with cubicle-bound staffs (Lowe et al., 2008).

Yammer is among companies with open door policies. Its CEO, though, not only is accessible to anyone wanting to walk into his office and talk, but also walks around the company to understand what is being worked on and to facilitate employee influence in decision-making through one-on-one questioning, debate, and input (Bryant, 2011d). Iron Mountain has a formal "Open Door" policy allowing any employee to bring something they feel is being handled wrongly to upper management (Bryant, 2010i). Verizon Wireless' website says that all employees can express themselves and listen to anyone else in the company, and that ideas are assessed on merit rather than who or where they come from (http://www.vzwcareers.com). IBM has an online ThinkPlace suggestion box in which any employee can contribute ideas (Gerdes, 2008). And at Rainmaker Entertainment, horizontal connections are fostered through a practice in which individuals, groups, or teams can be nominated and publicly acknowledged by coworkers for strong achievement, teamwork, or leadership (Bryant, 2011a).

At Halleland, which was founded by those who left large companies, offices are all of one size and new hires are urged to send work to higher ups (Hira, 2007). Zappos.com flattens its workplace by having all enter through the same front door, and serving free lunch to all of its employees (Bryant, 2010b). At Watershed Asset Management all employees have the same desks, sit in one open space, and can be heard by each other (Bryant, 2010c). AdMob also has an open office concept, and its CEO moves his own desk to a different place within it every 6 weeks (Bryant, 2010f). Microsoft, on the other hand, provides most employees with traditional offices and doors to reduce noise and support concentration. But it is providing flexible workspace as a means to attract talented Gen Y workers (Lowe et al., 2008). And Accenture's website describes its use of "Collaboration 2.0" technology to foster flexibility by helping workers perform from locations balancing work and life, minimize travel, and stay connected with each other including while on leave (http://www.accenture.com).

An emerging question at some companies appears to be how to address employee usage of Internet and social networking sites for nonwork purposes while at work. As this may reflect generational differences and stereotypes, best practice may be to separate motivational from management aspects when formulating policies regarding such usage. Gen Y workers tend to visit social networking sites and YouTube, instant message and text, and check headlines on Google several times a day. Many say that taking 10 minute "virtual coffee breaks" recharges them and returns them to work refocused. Allowing such "digital breaks" may then be a practice that motivates Gen Y workers and signals a contemporary culture which includes them. If doing so in fact reduces productivity and engagement, it may not be something to ban for all but instead be a localized abuse for management to correct (Wright, 2010).

Trigger High Performance

Gen Y workers want to know that and how they are contributing, and to grow and advance. They do not want to be bored or stay in place. So challenging and meaningful work they can take ownership of in which objectives and expectations are explicit and measurable from the start (Lowe et al., 2008), need and importance are explained ("Tips," 2006), team projects are evaluated as a whole (Raines, 2002), performance reviews are 360 degree (Brusman, 2009), and performance is rewarded with competitive pay and benefits should motivate and facilitate Gen Y achievement. Where possible, performance rewards should be in sync with workers' fundamental needs for money, benefits, and growth. Incidental rewards are not a substitute (Robert Half International & Yahoo!hotjobs, 2008) and are unlikely to retain a Gen Y worker who is offered higher compensation elsewhere. As Gen Y appreciates time as well as money, though, if financial reward is not possible to give, paid time off or various forms of flextime may be an acceptable substitute (Cal State Fullerton Career Center & Spectrum Knowledge, 2010).

PricewaterhouseCoopers is among companies whose practices facilitate performance review and clarity. Its employees can decide to meet with their manager anytime during their first 90 days on the job, rather than at preset monthly intervals, and a third party reviews the first written evaluation to be sure it is understandable (Experience.com, 2009). Yammer strives to create a sense of performance ownership for its employees by defining the role each employee has in the company (Bryant, 2011d). At Atlantic Records, employees are intentionally moved around to fully understand all jobs, how tough they are, how they relate to each other, and to build a level of respect foundational to hard work (Bryant, 2011b). And Enterprise Rent-A-Car's website explicitly states that great performance equals great reward, high performers will be able to impact all core areas of the company, and those performers will be compensated for doing so. It states its employees can "earn a salary that has no ceiling," and "How much can you earn? If you perform, that's up to you" (http://www.erac.com).

Container Store is among companies which recognize that Gen Y workers' first response is to money. It intentionally offers compensations at levels well beyond its industry's average to build a workforce that can outperform others (Bryant, 2010d). Hormel Food's experience demonstrates the positive impact on retention this can also deliver. Its strong compensation and benefits package results in a strong 5-year retention rate of 60% of its workers (Experience.com, 2010).

Some have implemented creative pay practices. When Google profits experienced a recent surge it gave each of its workers $1,000 holiday aftertax cash bonuses, a salary raise of at least 10% effective January 1, 2011, an additional raise based on the worker's annual target bonus, and eligibility for further individually earned "merit increases" (Drell, 2011). It also allows peers to award $175 on-the-spot bonuses; two-thirds of its workers did so in 2010 (*Fortune*, 2011). And when Continental Airlines instituted a plan giving a bonus to all workers or to none, targets which triggered bonus payments were always met (Bryant, 2010a).

Stimulate and Support Innovation

Within this culture and infrastructure, practices that permit a Gen Y worker to find the best way to meet expected results (Lowe et al., 2008) may generate new methods and yield new products. Accomplishing this may be furthered by refocusing performance management on task completion rather than on time spent, providing noncritical assignments with varied tasks that stretch the individual worker and make risk-taking safe, and encouraging competiveness in product and process innovation (Cal State Fullerton Career Center & Spectrum Knowledge, 2010).

Symantec CEO Enrique Salem operationalized a risk-adverse environment by focusing it on winning. He stresses the attendant importance of being willing to make decisions and take chances, and of valuing those who "beg for forgiveness" for something gone wrong rather than those who seek permission for something they would like to try (Bryant, 2011e). Proteus Cofounder and CEO Andrew Thompson fosters this aspect of innovation by encouraging "a bias to action" in which failure is not rewarded but is not punished (Bryant, 2011f).

Enterprise's website publicly describes its performance-based company as entrepreneurial driven by innovation, motivation, and ability (http://www.erac.com). Marriott is a company that stimulates this through in-kind reward. If a team discovers ways to work faster, it can have more flexible work schedules (Flander, 2008). At Whirlpool, employees can fast-track their careers by working on special projects (Gerdes, 2008). At Dreamworks Animation SKG, any employee can suggest an idea for a movie to the executives, and can take its "Life's A Pitch" workshop to learn how to do so (Gerdes, 2006). And at Google, employees are encouraged to spend 1 day each week developing a new idea of their own (Drell, 2011; *Fortune*, 2010).

Lead by Example and Transparency

Those who model expected behavior, speak candidly, drive the organization forward, move toward openness, and engage with and challenge Gen Y workers are likely to have leadership attributes that Gen Y workers gravitate toward ("Dealing With," 2004). Not only should leaders seeking to resonate with Gen Y avoid hype, but only job conditions and commitments that can be attained or met should be promised (Loughlin & Barline, 2001). Moreover, Gen Y's relationship with immediate managers is critical to its level of engagement (Lowe et al., 2008). That manager should be a highly present role model rather than a friend, be honest and fair, communicate regularly and interactively, and provide timely and constructive feedback (Cal State Fullerton Career Center & Spectrum Knowledge, 2010). Gen Y also seeks a company and leaders with clear vision expressing shared values actualized in structures and processes that advance accessibility, collaboration, and contribution; these, not mission statements, are likely to positively impress Gen Y workers (Hira, 2007).

Iron Mountain is among companies whose leadership appears to have these characteristics. Its President and CEO sees business as "going through this transformation where command-and-control leadership is dead," and says leaders must establish constructs in which all know what behavior is desired, and in which managers and their reports are continually providing constructive performance feedback to each other (Bryant, 2010i). JetBlue's CEO feels the visibility to him of those at the top of the company when he was a young manager fast-tracked that understanding for him about company behaviors and goals. This perspective may be the impetus for his practice of "leading from the back of the room" in which he is continually on the lookout for those anywhere in the company who are standouts in guiding and supporting the performance of others (Bryant, 2011g). JetBlue is not alone in recognizing the merit of leader visibility and modeling. GEICO, for instance, has structured formal and competitive Leadership Development programs in which new hires work directly with management (Experience.com, 2009).

Still others are making their presence known through one to one contact. HSN's CEO went through orientation along with all other new employees on her own first day, both to be fully present from the start and to develop a shared perspective more directly (Bryant, 2009b). Macy's CEO makes his presence regularly felt by dropping in unannounced at the stores (Bryant, 2009a). Novartis' CEO connects with his 120,000 employees by regularly blogging to them about what he did the prior week, and replying to every comment made in response. The blog, comments, and responses are public to all employees (Bryant, 2011h). And KPMG LLP's website brands the company as vision-centered. The website not only publicly states its values, but says they are guiding principles upon which company culture and practice are established and used by each worker at every level (http://www.kpmg.com/us/en/joinus/pages/default.aspx).

Create Career Paths and Opportunity to Advance

Gen Y workers want their careers to advance and value companies where routes are available and chances to access them are possible (Cal State Fullerton Career Center & Spectrum Knowledge, 2010). In the absence of that, Gen Y is likely to look for opportunity to advance at another company (Robert Half International & Yahoo!hotjobs, 2008). Customizing job descriptions (Wright, 2010) to reflect aspirations, interests, and skills of the individual Gen Y worker may further this (Martin, 2008), as may communicating position and development opportunities through media they frequent (Cal State Fullerton Career Center & Spectrum Knowledge, 2010).

Reflecting this, many leading companies have created multiple career paths for their workers (Kropp, 2010). A study by Deloitte suggests the efficacy of doing so. It found two-thirds of those who left the company did so to perform work they might have performed at the company but the company made it hard for them to make the transition, with a resulting cost of $150,000 to the company for each employee lost. As a result Deloitte created programs to help its workers determine the career moves they would like to make next; for many that next move might be available within the company (Trunk, 2007). FactSet Research Systems not only allows its workers to make job changes internally but also holds career fairs for those on the job so they know what is available before leaving to find it elsewhere (Flander, 2008). At Progressive Group of Insurance Companies, employees can create and share their career goals and plans on an internal "Career Quest" web site (Experience.com, 2009). And KPMG LLP created a web-based program for those wanting training to help build their careers. More then 9,000 logged onto the program, and 2,500 used it to create career paths for themselves (Gerdes, 2007). KPMG LLP's "Branding U" program is publicly available at the Campus page of its website (http://www.kpmg.com/us/en/joinus/pages/default.aspx).

Target's website has a link titled "Take the First Step to Your Career Path with Target." There, one can click by major to Target workers with that major and see the career path experienced (http://www.target.com/careers). Accenture's website states that each of its employees is assigned to a career counselor who provides career management and support (http://www.accenture.com/us-en/company/overview/awards). Intuit is a company that fosters advancement through a rotational development program. New workers move between finance, marketing, and product development every 6 months giving them a variety of credentials and preparing them for future leadership roles at the company (Millennial Leaders, 2010). At Pepsi Bottling Group, new hires can manage a team within 6 months to a year after training, as compared with 2 to 3 years elsewhere (Gerdes, 2006). Chesapeake Energy gives its new workers responsibility early, filling positions by those best qualified rather than seniority (Flander, 2008). And Philip Morris USA considers employees for a new position when they are ready, rather than when a position is vacant (Gerdes, 2009).

Mentor, Coach, and Train

As Gen Y workers tend to enter the full-time workforce with more education and experience than did those of prior generations, a coaching management style is likely to best fit (Sujansky, 2002). At the same time, Gen Y's helicoptered socialization accustoms it to a "handholding" combined with a respect for elders, interest in accessible management, and habit of being schooled. This helps explain Gen Y's strong desire to be mentored and its call for leadership training (Orell, 2011). Including acculturation to business culture and decision-making in a company's developmental activities is also recommended ("Tips," 2006), as is including reverse mentor programs allowing Gen Y's technical dexterity to be leveraged and recognized in return for the training it is receiving (Raines, 2002).

A PricewaterhouseCoopers Gen Y study indicates the value of providing such programs. The study found 98% of Gen Y workers reporting that strong coaching and mentoring are important to their professional development (Cal State Fullerton Career Center & Spectrum Knowledge, 2010). This is further reflected in *BusinessWeek*'s finding that 21 of the 25 best companies at which to launch a career provide comprehensive training programs to help entering workers develop skills and careers (Gerdes, 2008).

KPMG LLP is among companies that operationalize a prescription to mentor, coach, and train. Every junior staff member is expected to have a mentor, every manager is expected to be a mentor, and those in the middle ranks are expected to mentor and be mentored. A website facilitates the company's mentoring program formally, social activities reinforce it informally (Hira, 2007), and the company invested $100 million dollars on training-related projects in the last year reported (http://www.kpmg.com/us/en/joinus/pages/default.aspx). Time Warner's mentoring program connects people on both ends of their careers through Digital Reverse Mentoring. There, technically astute Gen Y workers mentor senior executives on upcoming technologies and trends (Hewlett et al., 2009). Accenture's Core Analyst School prepares new college graduates with skills they will need on first assignments (Experience.com, 2009), and the company's MyLearning online hub offers 20,000 full spectrum courses globally (http://www.accenture.com). At Deloitte, all new hires are eligible for its Future Leaders Apprentice Program. Its Gen Y workers identify the program and Deloitte's strong mentoring and coaching programs as key reasons they stay or later return to the company (Millennial Leaders, 2010). Hyatt's Corporate Management Trainee Program is another company where such programs are highly valued. The company retains 90% of the Program's participants (Experience.com, 2009). And Boeing's training includes programs for managers. There, managers learn how to deliver criticism along with praise, how to be clear and candid, and how to give ongoing and personalized feedback (Gerdes, 2007).

The attractiveness of mentoring, coaching, and training programs is reflected in their prominence on websites of many companies that are top-ranked for Gen Y employment. PricewaterhouseCoopers, for instance, prominently notes that its learning and education programs have earned its being ranked number one by *Training Magazine* in recent years (http:www.pwc.com/us/en/careers). Ernst & Young's website describes an Emerging Leaders Program in which its company culture is explored and leadership skills are gained in onsite interactive learning sessions. It lists career and professional development programs that include a companywide network, membership in business/civic/professional organizations, orientation and ongoing growth programs, professional certification reimbursement, and bonuses (http://www.ey.com/Careers). And Enterprise Rent-A-Car's website states its workers will work and learn from mentors who began where the new worker is. It says:

> You bring the skills and the passion. We'll make sure you have the tools to succeed. This is where you'll run a business, lead a team, have fun and prepare for just about anything. It all begins in our Management Training Program ... How far can we take you? That depends. How far do you want to go?... Does it work? Absolutely. Nearly all of our managers and corporate executives started out as management trainees—including our Chairman and CEO (http://www.erac.com).

Operationalize Work-Life Balance

The Robert Half/Yahoo study summarized above found nearly three-quarters of its Gen Y respondents concerned about work-life balance. The study says that a company with programs helping Gen Y workers balance career and personal aspects of their lives will receive their retention and loyalty in return. To do this, it suggests that companies rethink traditional career paths and timetables for advancement, and consider flexible work arrangements such as job-sharing, telecommuting, compressed work-weeks, and alternative scheduling (Robert Half International & Yahoo!hotjobs, 2008). Table 11.4, discussed earlier, illustrates the extent to which *Fortune*'s 100 top-ranked employers have implemented programs and practices supporting work-life balance. The great majority of these 100 companies offer telecommuting, at least one-quarter have onsite childcare centers, and almost one quarter offer fully paid sabbaticals. In addition, a majority of *Fortune*'s 25 top-ranked companies offer compressed work weeks (offered by 18), almost a half offer job sharing (offered by 12), and seven offer onsite child care (*Fortune*, 2011).

Cisco is among companies whose programs support work-life balance. Some 85% of its workers telecommute. Along with telecommuting, Mercedes-Benz USA has flexible work schedules and compressed work weeks. Alston & Bird has its own child-care center near its office and contributes to the child-care costs of its lower salaried workers (*Fortune*,

2011). And Verizon Wireless offers its workers a 10% discount on more than 2,000 childcare centers (http://www.vzwcareers.com).

A review of Silicon Valley companies, of varying size, illustrates the extent of such programs at these technology companies which would seem to be designing practices resonant with a Gen Y workforce. In addition to the practices summarized in Table 11.5, below, all of these companies offer unlimited sick days (Drell, 2011).

Deliver Perks

Studies summarized above also indicate that being provided with health insurance is highly important to Gen Y workers. Gen Y's interest in fitness is also reflected in its tendency to go to a gym three to four times a week (Millennial Leaders, 2010). The extensive number and range of "perks" being provided by contemporary companies suggests that establishing linkage between and facilitating health and wellness, widely defined, should have strong appeal to Gen Y workers. The list of companies operationalizing such practices, and the practices they are implementing, almost defies meaningful classification. That it is impossible to craft a truly representative list or a comprehensive list of best practices being implemented in this category underscores the truly stunning state of this aspect of optimal employer-employee exchange.

Table 11.5.   Work-Life Balance Practices in Silicon Valley, 2011

	Paid days off	*Holidays*	*Telecommute*	*Parental leave*	*Childcare*
Google	Year 1-4: 15 Year 4-5: 20 Year 6: 25	12 days		$500, 3 months maternal; and 6 months if work 1 year	Free onsite
Faceboook	21	11 days		4 month, $4000 credit	Reimburse $3000 for child under 5 born after start work
LinkedIn	15 days	13 days	Yes	Yes	
Twitter	Flexible	Flexible		Yes	
Tagged	Unlimited	13 days	Yes	4 month	
Eventbrite	Flexible	Flexible	Yes	Paid maternal	
Gaia online	Flexible	Flexible		Paid maternal	

To many, Google sets the bar for perks. The Great Place to Work Institute Study finds Google the company Gen Y would most like to work for. The many perks Google provides range from medical and dental facilities onsite to free meals at 11 gourmet restaurants, global education program allowing employee leave of absence to further education for up to 5 years and $150,000 reimbursement (Millennial Leaders, 2010), free laundry, onsite climbing wall (*Fortune*, 2011), and pet care referrals. Workers' dogs can come to work, as they can at Tagged who also provides pet insurance. Facebook, Twitter, and Tagged pay 100% of their employees' health insurance, and workers at Eventbrite can see any MD worldwide for a $10 copay fee (Drell, 2011). Table 11.6 shows representative amenities, activities and games at Silicon Valley companies, all of whom also provide their workers with transportation assistance (Drell, 2011).

Microsoft is headquartered in Seattle, but its practices would seem to contend with Silicon Valley's. Microsoft's website describes its onsite Commons with sports field and retail shops ranging from salon and miniday

Table 11.6.   Perks at These Silicon Valley Companies, 2011

Google	Amenities in office include onsite gym, yoga, fitness classes, rock climbing wall, running track, dry cleaning, free laundry machines, subsidized massage, hair cuts, bike repair, car washes; games/activities include video games, foosball, ping pong, company bikes, frisbee, golf course, office razr scooters
Facebook	Amenities in office include 50% reimbursement for monthly gym fees, laundry service, weekly lectures by entrepreneurs, photo processing, leather repair; games/activities include foosball, ping pong, annual game day
LinkedIn	Amenities in office include always-open onsite gym, afternoon yoga/pilates, running trails, chair massages, weekly lectures by entrepreneurs, morning boot camp, beanbag lounge; games/activities include foosball, ping pong, guitar hero, rock band, softball team, basketball team, soccer, hackday
Twitter	Amenities in office include free gym membership, yoga/pilates classes, rock climbing wall, dry cleaning, laundry service; games/activities include video games, foosball, ping pong, soccer team, wine making for charity
Tagged	Amenities in office include free gym membership, yoga room, regular massage days, quiet room, wellness allowance; games/activities include video games, foosball, ping pong, billiards, hacknight, monthly wine tastings, field trips
Eventbrite	Amenities in office include Zen room, monthly stipend; games/activities include foosball, ping pong, bike rides, regular outings, tours to trampoline park
Gaia online	Amenities in office include gym; games/activities include video games, foosball

spa to dry cleaning, restaurants, cafes, espresso stands, and fully stocked kitchenettes; social clubs from dodge ball to photography to theater; wi-fi and power outfitted coaches transporting workers between home and work and between office buildings; and health benefits ranging from lifetime health coverage to free on-site health screening and physician house calls 24/7 in Seattle (Microsoft, n.d.).

Verizon Wireless is also among companies that provide onsite fitness centers and discounts to other gyms (http://www.vzwcareers.com). In addition to its onsite exercise center, Nike has playing fields and running trails (Millennial Leaders, 2010). KPMG's flexible scheduling includes allowing workers to train for extracurricular interests including sports (Hira, 2007). And Recreational Equipment has a Challenge Grant program giving $500 of gear to employees participating in a challenging outdoor experience (*Fortune*, 2011).

Still others are delivering an array of perks at the workplace. At Dreamworks Animation, free breakfast and lunch pave the way for afternoon yoga, onsite art classes, and movie screenings. Zappos.com has a full-time onsite life coach, as well as free lunches and no-charge vending machines (*Fortune*, 2011). IBM brings in financial coaches to advise its younger workers (Gerdes, 2008). Cisco's perks include a car care company on-site twice a week with services like oil changes for workers. SAS provides workers with on-site healthcare, fitness center, quality childcare, summer camp for children, and beauty salon, in addition to car cleaning (*Fortune*, 2011). At Progressive Group of Insurance Companies, perks include dry cleaning services, massage, quiet rooms, and on-site media centers, as well as fitness centers (Experience.com, 2009). And some companies are giving longer paid time off after fewer years of service, conversion of health benefits into deferred compensation, and change of unused earned administrative leave to cash (Southard & Lewis, 2004).

Some companies are offering an array of benefits so inclusive as to be titled by them as "Total Reward." Ernst & Young's website, for instance, describes a Total Reward Connection company-sponsored website providing round-the-clock information on benefits and programs for its workers (http://www.ey.com/Careers). And Verizon Wireless' website describes a Total Reward program including comprehensive health care benefits and $10,000 adoption expense reimbursement for each adopted child (http://www.vzwcareers.com).

Acknowledge and Celebrate

Recognizing positive behaviors and milestones is likely to help humanize and personalize the workforce in ways attractive to Gen Y workers.

They are responsive to positivity so sharing all good news, including contributions they are making, should resonate well with these workers (Cal State Fullerton Career Center & Spectrum Knowledge, 2010) and further illustrate and reinforce cultural and performance norms. Providing a Gen Y worker with a business card, for instance, should help demonstrate that s/he is valued, as can remembering personal occasions like birthdays and noting career achievements (Hira, 2007). To reinforce the high performance described above, positive work-related recognition should be given only when it has been earned and as soon as possible after achievement merits it (Martin, 2008).

Halleland is among companies whose practices illustrate this. Its senior employees e-mail junior ones when the newer staffer's career has a milestone (Hira, 2007). FactSet Research Systems sends gifts during exams with a "thinking of you," "see you soon" note to those who have accepted jobs and are completing undergraduate study (Flander, 2008). InterContinental Hotel Groups annually presents an award to employees who have helped others achieve (Bryant, 2010e), and YuMe gives such an award every 2 months (Bryant, 2010g). Scottrade's Above and Beyond program lets any worker nominate another to be recognized; earned points are traded in for gift cards, IPods, or other merchandise (*Fortune*, 2011).

At DPR Construction, birthdays, engagements, and anniversaries are among personal occasions celebrated (*Fortune*, 2011). At Frog Design, a weekly Monday morning meeting at every studio includes noting worker birthdays and anniversaries, along with sharing information about projects being worked on (Bryant, 2011c). And recognition at Ernst & Young includes service anniversary awards (http://www.ey.com/Careers).

Facilitate Making a Difference

Gen Y's interest in being contributors is multidimensional and long documented. Knowing that they with peers have positively imprinted the company, that they can be "heroes" (Kogan, 2001), coexists with their interest in working for a socially responsible company (Loughlin & Barling, 2001) that benefits workers, community, and broader society. Formulating, communicating, and actualizing company values should be well received by Gen Y workers, as should expressing where the company is going and how each worker fits into that (Hansford, 2002). Describing each worker's role and why s/he is in the job should help each understand the contribution s/he is making to the whole (Cal State Fullerton Career Center & Spectrum Knowledge, 2010).

Teach for America is an organization closely aligned with this. Its website says:

> Teach for America looks for exceptional leaders who will have an immediate, positive impact on their students' achievements. However, we also know that transformational change will not be achieved unless our corps member's impact continues well beyond the 2-year teaching commitment. Realizing our mission relies on corps members becoming lifelong leaders ... Teach for America's more than 24,000 alumni are part of a growing force of leaders ... During those 2 years (as a corps member), you'll develop the skills, insights, and personal commitment needed to help drive lasting, systemic change. (http://www.teachforamerica.org/careers)

UBS is among for-profit companies that appear to recognize and support Gen Y's desire to make a difference. Through its graduate deferral program, newly hired workers can postpone their start date for a year devoted to serving community or acquiring skills. During that year, UBS pays half the accepted position's salary, gives a stipend for health insurance, and reserves the job for that worker (Hewlett et al., 2009). Workers at BCG can spend up to a year working at a nonprofit organization at two-thirds regular pay; the nonprofit and BCG split the cost of that salary (*Fortune*, 2010). At Salesforce.com, 1% of its profits are donated to its Foundation. The Foundation then pays for employees to volunteer 1% of their work time (Trunk, 2007). Northrop Grumman's active community outreach program includes giving workers every other Friday off to perform philanthropic activities. And Target gives some three million dollars weekly to social causes, and encourages its workers to actively serve the community (Experience.com, 2009).

The positive resonance to a company that facilitates making a difference is indicated by the extent to which such activities are publicly claimed on websites. Verizon Wireless's website, for example, declares it has a "culture of giving." Its socially responsive practices include an annual "Summer of Community Service" (http://www.vzwcareer.com). And Liberty Mutual's website has a "Working with Us" page that begins:

> There's nothing more satisfying than knowing you've made a difference in the life of another. When you work at Liberty Mutual, that's exactly what you'll do. For more than 95 years, our purpose has been to help people live safer, more secure lives ... and you can help us make that happen with your drive, commitment and passion. (http://www.libertymutualgroup.com)

Google's website describes extensive philanthropic activity ranging from in-kind product donations to volunteerism. The company sponsors an annual "GoogleServe" event, and many of its offices around the world have

"Google Cares" programs through which its workers volunteer in their own communities. Through Google Grants, the company gives pro bono AdWords to charitable organizations. Google's YouTube for nonprofits promotes nonprofit fundraising and awareness on a designated, branded channel, and its Video Volunteers links nonprofits with volunteers to help the nonprofits produce audiovisuals (http://www.google.org/googlers.html).

Microsoft's website states that, like many other U.S. companies, it provides a dollar to dollar match for its workers' charitable contribution. But, in addition, its Volunteer Matching program matches donated time at $17 per hour up to $12,000 per worker per year. Microsoft's international workers are given paid days off to volunteer in their own communities. Microsoft employees are also encouraged to fill lead roles for nonprofit agencies, and to give "high-value business and technology consulting" to communities. Moreover, team-based volunteering events partner with nonprofits to support activities like the United Way's annual Day of Caring and promote long-term relationships. And Microsoft's disaster and humanitarian aid programs respond to crises in the wake of hurricanes and earthquakes with financial, software, and expert resources (http://www.microsoft.com/about/corporatecitizenship).

LOOKING FORWARD

This review of practices at companies being recognized for their implementation reveals a contemporary workplace where what Gen Y wants and expects to find tends to parallel what these forward-looking companies are implementing, but also to be somewhat ahead of overall policy and programmatic changes made. The positive return for companies that do transition to a new normal reflective of Gen Y's presence is summarized in a recent *HR Magazine* article. It says, "Companies that selectively and effectively embrace Net Gen (Gen Y) norms perform better than those that don't" (Wright, 2011, p. 40). Gen Y expert Bruce Tulgan advises that the attendant transitional effort will be well worth it. He says, "Generation Y is the most high-maintenance workforce in history, but they also have the potential to be the most high-performing if they are managed the right way" (2009).

Current economic conditions may provide a new set of challenges for companies answerable to cost-consciousness at this time when their Gen Y workers tend to consider compensation a "first filter" and "threshold issue" (Cal State Fullerton Career Center & Spectrum Knowledge, 2010). But findings in two recent articles project a downside to companies that neglect the interests and needs of these employees. A Gallup study describes that given tight labor markets workers may be staying in jobs that do not satisfy them, and that employers who cut back on practices meaningful to their

Table 11.7.   Recommended Best Practices for Managing Generation Y

Create a contemporary culture

Flatten and wire the organization

Trigger high performance

Stimulate and support innovation

Lead by example and transparency

Create career paths and opportunity to advance

Mentor, coach, and train

Operationalize work-life balance

Deliver perks

Acknowledge and celebrate

Facilitate making a difference

workers are likely to increase that dissatisfaction (Morales, 2011). The implication for Gen Y employers is described by Orell this way: "(Gen Y workers) have a lower tolerance threshold than generations before them. A Boomer may put up with a job for 5 years even if he or she is bored or doesn't feel valued, but a Millennial may only tolerate it for 5 months ... or until the current job market improves" (2011).

As a result the 11 recommended best practices that emerged from this study, summarized in Table 11.7, appear all the more salient for companies seeking an optimal way forward. These practices were recently shared with a 19-year old Gen Y college sophomore who is majoring in Video Game design at a top-ranked U.S. college. He said, "A company who does these things will have a gold standard business plan." His mother, a Baby Boomer professor who has spent her entire career working at one academic institution, said, "But most companies aren't like that." The Gen Y young man replied, "Then they will fail."

NOTES

1.   Experience.com's top 20 best places to work for recent college grads (2009), ranked alphabetically as published, are: Accenture, Computer Sciences Corporation, Electronic Arts, Enterprise Rent-A-Car, GEICO, Hyatt Hotels & Resorts, Liberty Mutual, McBee Associates, Inc., North Star Resource Group, Northrop Grumman, Peace Corps, Qualcomm, Schlumberger, Sherwin-Williams, Sodexo, Target, The Progressive Group of Insurance Companies, The TJX Companies, Inc., Wachovia, and ZS Associates. Accenture and Liberty Mutual were the only companies to remain on this Experience.com list for 2010 and 2011.

2. Collegegrad.com's top 8 employers of college grads (2011), ranked first to last, are: Enterprise Rent-A-Car, Teach for America, Verizon Wireless, Hertz, PricewaterhouseCoopers, KPMG LLP, Target, and Ernst & Young (http://www.collegegrad.com).

3. *Fortune's* top 25 "Best Companies to Work For" (2011) ranked first to last, are: SAS, Boston Consulting Group, Wegmans Food Markets, Google, NetApp, Zappos.com, Camden Property Trust, Nugget Market, Recreational Equipment, Dreamworks Animation SKG, Edward Jones, Scottrade, Alston & Bird, Robert W. Baird, Mercedes-Benz USA, JM Family Enterprises, USAA, Stew Leonard's, The Methodist Hospital System, Cisco, Container Store, DPR Construction, Goldman Sachs, Whole Foods Market, and Umpqua Bank (Fortune, 2011).

4. The "Corner Office" series is an ongoing weekly feature of *The New York Times* Sunday Business section. Each week's article presents an interview conducted by author Adam Bryant with a top company executive. The companies are from various industries and are of different sizes. For currency, the articles consulted for this chapter were published between 2009 and 2011.

5. *Fortune's* top 25 "Best Companies to Work For" (2011) ranked first to last, are: SAS, Boston Consulting Group, Wegmans Food Markets, Google, NetApp, Zappos.com, Camden Property Trust, Nugget Market, Recreational Equipment, Dreamworks Animation SKG, Edward Jones, Scottrade, Alston & Bird, Robert W. Baird, Mercedes-Benz USA, JM Family Enterprises, USAA, Stew Leonard's, The Methodist Hospital System, Cisco, Container Store, DPR Construction, Goldman Sachs, Whole Foods Market, and Umpqua Bank (*Fortune*, 2011).

6. The companies among *Fortune's* top 25 "Best Companies to Work For" (2011) offering these practices are identified here; 1 indicates telecommuting, 2 indicates onsite fitness center, 3 indicates subsidized gym membership, 4 indicates job sharing, 5 indicates compressed work week, and 0 indicates none: SAS (1, 2, 3, 4, 5), Boston Consulting Group (1, 4, 5), Wegmans Food Markets (1, 3, 4, 5), Google (1, 2, 3, 4), NetApp (1, 2, 4, 5), Zappos.com (1, 5), Camden Property Trust (2, 3), Nugget Market (0), Recreational Equipment (1, 2, 5), Dreamworks Animation SKG (1, 2, 3, 4, 5), Edward Jones (1, 3, 4, 5), Scottrade (2, 3, 5), Alston & Bird (1, 2, 3, 4, 5), Robert W. Baird (1, 3, 4, 5), Mercedes-Benz USA (1, 2, 3, 5), JM Family Enterprises (1, 2, 3, 5), USAA (1, 2, 5), Stew Leonard's (3), The Methodist Hospital System (1, 2, 3, 4, 5), Cisco (1, 2, 3, 4), Container Store (0), DPR Construction (1, 2, 3, 5), Goldman Sachs (1, 2, 3, 4, 5), Whole Foods Market (3, 5), and Umpqua Bank (0) (*Fortune*, 2011).

REFERENCES

Allen, P. (2004, September). Welcoming y. *Benefits Canada, 28*(9), 51-53.

Brusman, M. (2009, August 26). Managing the millennial generation: Strategies to select and develop gen y leadership talent. Briefings Media Group Audio Conference. Retrieved from http://www.slideshare.net/drbrusman/managing-millennial-generation-future-leaders

Bryant, A. (2009a, April 12). Knock-knock: It's the CEO. Interview with T. Lundgreen, Macy's. *The New York Times*. Retrieved from http://projects.nytimes.com/corner-office

Bryant, A. (2009b, November 15). Are you a Tigger, or an Eeyore? Interview with M. Grossman, HSN. *The New York Times*. Retrieved from http://projects.nytimes.com/corner-office

Bryant, A. (2010a, January 3). Remember to share the stage. Interview with G. Bethune, Continental Airlines. *The New York Times*. Retrieved from http://projects.nytimes.com/corner-office

Bryant, A. (2010b, January 10). On a scale of 1 to 10, how weird are you? Interview with T. Hsieth, Zappos.com. *The New York Times*. Retrieved from http://projects.nytimes.com/corner-office

Bryant, A. (2010c, March 7). An office? She'll pass on that. Interview with M. Moore, Watershed Asset Management. *The New York Times*. Retrieved from http://projects.nytimes.com/corner-office

Bryant, A. (2010d, March 14). Three good hires? He'll pay more for one who's great. Interview with K. Tindell, Container Store. *The New York Times*. Retrieved from http://projects.nytimes.com/corner-office

Bryant, A. (2010e, April 4). Where are you when the going gets tough? Interview with A. Cosslett, InterContinental Hotel Groups. *The New York Times*. Retrieved from http://projects.nytimes.com/corner-office

Bryant, A. (2010f, May 2). The C.E.O. with the portable desk. Interview with O. Hamoui, AdMob. *The New York Times*. Retrieved from http://projects.nytimes.com/corner-office

Bryant, A. (2010g, June 20). Want the job? Tell him the meaning of life. Interview with M. Mathieu, YuMe. *The New York Times*. Retrieved from http://projects.nytimes.com/corner-office

Bryant, A. (2010h, October 10). Good C.E.O.'s are insecure (and know it). Interview with H. Schultz, Starbucks. *The New York Times*. Retrieved from http://projects.nytimes.com/corner-office

Bryant, A. (2010i, November 28). Defensive? It leads to destructive. Interview with B. Brennan, Iron Mountain. *The New York Times*. Retrieved from http://projects.nytimes.com/corner-office

Bryant, A. (2011a, January 1). Got an idea? Sell it to me in 30 seconds. Interview with C. Winder, Rainmaker Entertainment. *The New York Times*. Retrieved from http://projects.nytimes.com/corner-office

Bryant, A. (2011b, February 6). Meeting space? In her eyes less is more. Interview with J. Greenwald, Atlantic Records. *The New York Times*. Retrieved from http://projects.nytimes.com/corner-office

Bryant, A. (2011c, March 27). It's showtime. So take that deep breath. Interview with D. Lorenzo, Frog Design. *The New York Times*. Retrieved from http://projects.nytimes.com/corner-office

Bryant, A. (2011d, July 17). Fostering a culture of dissent. Interview with D. Sacks, Yammer. *The New York Times*. Retrieved from http://projects.nytimes.com/corner-office

Bryant, A. (2011e, September 4). Want to lead? Ask Tennyson and Shakespeare. Interview with E. Salem, Symantec. *The New York Times*. Retrieved from http://projects.nytimes.com/corner-office

Bryant, A. (2011f, September 18). Speak frankly, but don't go "over the net." Interview with A. Thompson, Proteus. *The New York Times*. Retrieved from http://projects.nytimes.com/corner-office

Bryant, A. (2011g, September 25). Early access as a fast track to learning. Interview with D. Barger, JetBlue. *The New York Times*. Retrieved from http://projects.nytimes.com/corner-office

Bryant, A. (2011h, October 9). Fix the problem, and not just the symptoms. Interview with J. Jimenez, Novartis. *The New York Times*. Retrieved from http://projects.nytimes.com/corner-office

Cal State Fullerton Career Center & Spectrum Knowledge. (2008). The gen y perceptions study. Fullerton, CA: Author. Retrieved from http://campusapps2.fullerton.edu/career/pdf/Gen_Y.pdf

Cal State Fullerton Career Center & Spectrum Knowledge. (2010). The guide to managing and developing young professionals. Fullerton, CA: Author. Retrieved from http://campusapps2.fullerton.edu/career/pdf/Guide_to_Managing_Young_Professionals_March_2010.pdf

CareerBuilder. (2007). Connecting with generation y workers. Retrieved from http://www.careerbuilder.com

Dealing with your new generation mix. (2004, August). *Accounting Office Management & Administrative Report, 4*(8), 5-7+(4).

Drell, L. (2011, October 17). The perks of working at Google, Facebook, Twitter, and more. *Mashable Business*. Retrieved from http://mashable.com/2011/10/17/google-facebook-twitter-linkin-persk/infographi/

Experience.com. (2009). Top 20 best places to work for recent college grads. Retrieved from http://www.experience.com

Experience.com. (2010). 2010 best places to work for recent grads. Retrieved from http://www.experience.com

Experience.com. (2011). 2011 best places to work for recent grads. Retrieved from http://www.experience.com

Flander, S. (2008). Millenial magnets. *Human Resource Executive Online*. Retrieved from http://www.hreonline.com

Focused on the future: Survey shows financial security tops list of Gen Y career concerns. (2008, February). *U.S. Newswire*. Retrieved from ProQuest database

Fortune. (2010). 100 best companies to work for 2010—The top 25 and other all stars. Retrieved from http://money.cnn.com/magazines/fortune/bestcompanies/2010

Fortune. (2011). 100 best companies to work for 2011—The top 25 and other all stars. Retrieved from http://money.cnn.com/magazines/fortune/bestcompanies/2011

Gerdes, L. (2006, September 18). The best places to launch a career. *BusinessWeek*. Retrieved from http://www.businessweek.com

Gerdes, L. (2007, September 13). The best places to launch a career. *BusinessWeek*. Retrieved from http://www.businessweek.com

Gerdes, L. (2008, September 4). The best places to launch a career. *Bloomberg Business Week*. Retrieved from http://www.businessweek.com

Google. (n.d.). The Google culture—Company. Retrieved from http://www.google.com

Hansford, D. (2002, June). Insights into managing an age-diverse workforce. *Workspan, 45*(6), 48-54.

Hewlett, S. A., Sherbin, L., & Sumberg, K. (2009, July-August). How gen y & baby-boomers will reshape your agenda. *Harvard Business Review*. (Reprint R0907G).

Hira, N. A. (2007, May 28). You raised them, now manage them. *Fortune, 155*(10), 38-44.

Kogan, M. (2001, September 1). Talkin' 'bout four generations. *Govexec*. Retrieved from http://www.govexec.com.

Kropp, B. (2010, June 8). Gen y at work: Not so different after all. *Bloomberg Business Week*. Retrieved from http://www.businessweek.com

Loughlin, C., & Barling, J. (2001, November). Young workers' work values, attitudes, and behaviors. *Journal of Occupational and Organizational Psychology, 74*(4), 543-558.

Lowe, D., Levitt K. J., & Wilson, T. (2008, Fall). Solutions for retaining generation y employees in the workplace. *Business Renaissance Quarterly, 3*(3), 43-57.

Lynch, L. (2011). CollegeGrad.com 2011 top entry-level employers survey — Executive summary. Retrieved from http://www.collegegrad.com

Martin, C. A. (2008, Fall). Getting high on gen y: How to engage the entitlement generation. *Career Planning and Adult Development Journal, 24*(E), 19-22.

Microsoft. (n.d.). Microsoft University careers—benefits & perks. Retrieved from http://careers.microsoft.com

Millennial Leaders. (2010). The generation y attraction and retention strategies of 10 top companies. Retrieved from http://millenialleaders.com

Morales, L. (2011). More U.S. workers unhappy with health benefits, promotions. *The Gallup Organization*. Retrieved from http://www.galluip.com/poll

Orell, L. (2011). 6 ways to retain your generation y future leaders. Retrieved from http://thehiringsite.careerbuilder.com

Piktialis, D. (2004, August). Bridging generational divides to increase innovation, creativity, and productivity. *Workspan, 47*(8), 26-41.

Raines, C. (2002). Managing millenials. *Generations at Work*. Retrieved from http://www.generationsatwork.com

Robert Half International & Yahoo!hot jobs. (2008). Generation y: What millennial workers want: How to attract and retain gen y employees. Retrieved from http://www.accountingweb-cgi.com/whitepapers/generationy_robert_half.pdf

Southard, G., & Lewis, J. (2004, April). Building a workplace that recognizes generational diversity. *Public Management, 86*(3), 8(5).

Sujansky, J. (2002, May). The critical care and feeding of generation y. *Workforce, 81*(5), 15.

Tips for managing gen y. (2006, October). *BusinessWeek*. Retrieved from http://images.businessweek.com/ss/10/06/0608_geny_workers/

Trunk, P. (2007, July 5). What gen y really wants. *Time*.

Tulgan, B. (2009). *Not everyone gets a trophy: How to manage generation y*. San Francisco: CA: Jossey-Bass.

CHAPTER 12

A NEW TALENT AGENDA

Milano Reyna and Rishap Malhotra

THE CHALLENGE: INSPIRING OUR FUTURE

A fresh wave of workforce debuted over a decade ago—the Millennials. These hires are equipped with skills and resources that are unprecedented. They are fueled with a nonstop flow of information and knowledge that allows them to get their work done faster and with ample time to query solutions or concepts along the way. They are challenging business models, and they are reimagining ways of working and how we define productivity and happiness in the workplace.

While we focus this chapter on Millennials, we start off with a quote that is as every bit relevant today as it was 40 years ago:

"He not busy being born is busy dying."

—Bob Dylan

In the midst of the societal and technological changes we are experiencing, the employer-employee relationship is evolving more than ever too; it is becoming more fluid, and as organizations see the need to become more creative, they immediately realize that creativity is a scarce

Managing Human Resources for the Millennial Generation, pp. 279–300
Copyright © 2012 by Information Age Publishing
All rights of reproduction in any form reserved.

resource. Controlled information silos are breaking apart, if not already, and employees just entering the workforce today are more empowered when compared to other generations only a decade ago.

Millennials are optimistic about their future and choices; they are also realists and often mistaken as cynics, entitlement focused or me-oriented employees.

In our industry, advertising, we are experiencing the positive impact of Millennials. This also coincides with the evolution of consumers and brands. Our communication media started off in print, then radio, television, and now it includes anything with a screen. Millennials have been students and teachers in the new work we work. Our industry had to embrace these technologies and the way people use them everyday or fade from relevancy. As Talent Professionals our challenge is similar. Our renaissance is now.

This chapter is about Talent Professionals and Millennials. It is also about inspiring all of us in the workforce. Like most sustainable things, success depends on how well the past, present and future are connected.

We believe radical optimism—the condition whereby you not only feel positive but actively work to inspire others—is what Talent Professionals need to provide business today. It is what the Millennial generation desires. In fact, it is what we hear across every generation. The reality check though is that many corporations generally have lost the trust of the workforce. There have been too many scams and there is a sense that companies cannot be relied on for building one's future. For many places, the focus has shifted from product, service, talent, earnings, to pure greed—"ugh." Business models have been fractured. This is not a pretty picture, no matter how true, and it does not have to remain that way, and indeed many corporations are now Purpose Inspired (Gilson, Pratt, Roberts, & Weymes, 2000). One of Saatchi & Saatchi's clients, Procter & Gamble, believes in "Touching Lives, Improving Lives," and they do this several billion times a day throughout the world with their products developed over 175 years.

We found that Millennials want and care about similar things as other generations: Liberation, Authenticity, Transparency, Doing Good. This is where the power of what business can be for people comes into focus. Within business, this is where Talent Leadership has an opportunity to rebirth itself. Those of us that have a career in human resources have the limelight in shaping organizational performance—because of the vital role of people as the prime productive resource in business. This involves "*Intellectual*" and "*Emotional*" capital, ideas and innovation, management and marketing, operating and educating—all soft power factors that are important beyond financial capital, technology, raw materials, and so forth. Human resource professionals can lead from the front with CEOs and business leaders. This idea of leading from the front was a talent partnership dream for many and reality for a precious few; we believe it is now a necessity for all.

WHO ARE WE?

We are an ideas company, Saatchi & Saatchi. We were founded in 1970 in London. We are now headquartered in New York City, and have been led by Worldwide CEO Kevin Roberts since 1997. We work with the world's largest companies on their brands, advertising, social media, shopper marketing and sustainability.

In our kind of industry, *"Everyday should feel like a Saturday"*—achievement, celebration, community, family, competition, doing good. We thrive on optimism, innovation and each other.

Our halls are filled with connected, restless, passionate, ambitious, accountable, inspirational, and transformative people with a dream to help us *"Create A Hothouse For World Changing Ideas That Transform Our Clients' Business, Brands and Reputations."* This is our Inspirational Dream and the characteristics that make us who we are is called our "Spirit Ladder."

We employ people with different education levels and from a variety of backgrounds: anthropologists, MBAs, artists, designers, writers, musicians, strategists, social and community mavens, psychologists and the occasional "all but dissertation" graduate or drop out. Our common link is ideas and the hunger and ability to make things happen with an attitude of *Nothing is Impossible.*

Our bench is 6000 people representing every nationality, religion, age, gender and orientation. We celebrate each other's diversity in every way. We can be found in every major market. We embrace each other as individuals and perform like a team. We call this *One Team, One Dream.*

Talent is our biggest asset. We lease most of our buildings, contract out most of what is not core to our business and rely on the newest technology and people's input to get ideas out the door. Talent is core to our business strategy. It is at the heart of our Worldwide CEO and a priority in every monthly global business review.

GETTING OUR NOTES TOGETHER

In the summer of 2011, we began collecting our learnings and insights on Millennials formally through a study. Since then we also followed up on things that matter to Millennials and other generations in the workplace through a talent lens. We commenced this study with a hundred plus direct interviews of Millennials—group and individual—across the Americas, Europe, and Asia Pacific. A sample of the questions we explored can be found in Table 12.1. These were built on the Four Pillars of our Talent Strategy, about which we will explain and share Millennial verbatims later: Responsibility, Learning, Recognition and Joy.

We also reviewed what we already did, what we are saying to our people, and relied on some common sense. We researched journals, on-line materials and corroborated many of our own insights—there's plenty to be found.

To complete our study, we listened to high performers across generations, to see where there were similarities or not. Our in house development programs were a great source of learning from all generations. This last piece was important to us so that we represent what we find to be a common link in inspiring high potential employees and high performers across generations.

Our review for this chapter made us think, *"What are we really hearing from the new talent we are attracting? Are we also hearing this from our highest level performers, no matter what generation they represent? Are we retrofitting existing talent tools, or are we transforming our practices and tools to create experiences for our people that matter? Do our talent offerings bring our people responsibility, recognition, learning and joy?"*

OUR FIRST OBSERVATIONS: SIMILARITIES BETWEEN GENERATIONS

We found more in common with Millennials than we did differences: Liberation, Authenticity, Transparency, and Doing Good were common themes across geographies, departments and ages (See Table 12. 2).

While our revelations in this chapter may not be a proxy for all industries, this is what we heard. Yes, the voice was louder on all these points with Millennials; however we also heard an audible voice from other generations on these themes. Only a decade ago, there was a more noticeable gap between generations; one thing for sure is that we are now all connected and regardless of position in the company have felt the effects of the economy not experienced by any of us in the workplace today. We are facing these challenges and learning to solve problems together.

- **Liberation.** Many of the policies and rules in the workplace were written for a different era and no longer apply. Technology has changed the way we communicate and work. Our employees want to explore, innovate, and contribute to making the company productive. We believe our priority is to inspire them. Employees also

Table 12.1. Focus Group Discussion Guide

Dimension		Questions
Career Dream State—To identify patterns in the type of roles, responsibilities and tasks that millennials incline towards	Q1.	If there are no constraints, what would be your dream job right now? (Probe: Money, social pressure, external environment)
	Q2.	What do you like about that career? What day-to-day aspects excite you the most? And why?
	Q3.	What are the constraints that are keeping you away from your dream job?
	Q4.	What perceived or real threats do you see standing in the way of realizing your dream job? (Probe: what fears do you have)
Responsibility—Gain insights into how millennials perceive responsibility at work and their expectations from the company	Q5.	What does responsibility mean to you at workplace?
	Q6.	How important it is to know your job description? How detailed would you like it?
	Q7.	To what extent do you personally identify with the company purpose; does it motivate you? Is it important that your job is contributing or linked to the organizational vision and success?
	Q8.	How open are you to varied experiences at work; why and why not? (probe: cross functional, geographic, different teams)
	Q9.	If you had 20% time to devote to anything at work, what would you do?
	Q10.	Do you think about career planning?
	Q11.	What career planning tools are you currently using and what kind of tools would you use in the future to plan your career? (probe: mentoring, career assessment tools, career coaching, online tools)
Learning—Investigate how millennials are adopting innovative self learning tools and are making traditional training programs irrelevant	Q12.	What is the most inspirational learning experience you have had?
	Q13.	How important is to personally develop yourself? Is it your responsibility? (Probe: Is it company's responsibility, view on formal training programs)
	Q14.	How do you assess your learning needs? (probe: peer driven, industry standards, company requirements)
	Q15.	What will be the best way for you to acquire new skills and knowledge? (Probe: cohort development, learning groups, on-job training, professional development, formal and informal mentoring initiatives)
	Q16.	What level of understanding and knowledge (proficiency level) do you want to establish in each training course? (basic, mastery or whatever gets the job done)
	Q17.	How can the organization contribute to your personal development and learning?

(Table 12.1 continued on next page.)

Table 12.1. (continued)

Dimension	Questions
Recognition—Find out the types of recognition and feedback that millennials want from employers and coworkers	Q18. What is the best way to recognize your work and contribution? (probe: company level, manager, peers, financial and non-financial)
	Q19. Should recognition be only based on performance?
	Q20. How important is a performance evaluation? How frequently do you prefer to be evaluated?
	Q21. How often would you like to receive feedback? (Probe: negative, positive, constructive)
	Q22. How would you like to receive positive and negative feedback? Why? (Probe: formal or informal, oral or written, brief or detailed)
	Q23. Are formal and structured communication skills (art of communication) important in this new digital world?
Joy—Spot trends and patterns in what makes millennials happy at work. Is happiness the glue between personal and professional life?	Q24. When have you been the happiest in your current job? (Probe: project, assignment, location, team members, culture)
	Q25. What aspects of your work made you feel happy?
	Q26. What will make you happier at work? (Probe: Flexibility in work, company/team events, community work)
	Q27. Which companies do you think have the happiest employees, and why?

284

Table 12.2.   Common Themes Across Generations

Common Themes Across Generations
Liberation
Authenticity
Transparency
Doing Good

expressed the desire for freedom of choice. Where they work and what time they work are the most common themes we hear from employees, in particular with Millennials. They seek the company focus to be more on completing assignments without being tied to specific hours or a venue. We reckon this voice will only become louder with technology improvement and on-line security more available. Employees make it clear that they understand the guidelines and want to be trusted to do the right thing. It is a leap for many leaders to let go of work practices that control where and how work gets done; those that do let go, seem to have the most loyalty and productivity.

- **Authenticity.** Truth is a mandatory. Too many companies and leaders have misrepresented themselves, and we have all been bombarded by iconic companies and leaders gone bad. Employees are no longer passive. They have become active observers, willing to question and call out anything that seems off brand. Nothing is forgiven easily. There are chat rooms for everything. There is a higher standard for leaders. Employees seek to match a company's values to their own. The employees we know desire companies with an inspirational Purpose that leaders live up to. Happiness is defined by many things beyond monetary rewards, development opportunities and workplace flexibility. Happiness, we found, has migrated to the company's authenticity and to those that lead the company. Perhaps this is one reason we see companies fast to act when a company's values and a leader's actions no longer match.

- **Transparency.** Employees expect to be well informed and to be able to question the company. They do not want to read about or hear it in the media first. They want timely feedback on their performance too. If something is not going well in the company, they expect to be informed quickly and with facts. Tolerance for delayed news or clouded communication is not negotiable. Being upfront with challenges and plans that may impact the workforce is seen as progressive. When the global financial crisis hit hard across all business in 2009 and 2010, our communication was direct and strongly sign-posted for our employees: "Winning Ugly," referencing the gritty performances of the hardest won sport victories, were tag lines we used on our communication templates for letters and memorandums, inside and outside our company. In 2012 our theme is "Wanting to Win" driving at the motivating factors of peak performance.

- **Doing Good**. Sustainability, social responsibility, and community action are current passion topics. Companies are expected to contribute to communities, charities and causes. Millennials, in particular, were brought up with a positive focus on volunteering and giving back. In almost all our agencies, we have employees engaged pro bono, using their unique creative skills to campaign for political freedoms, stopping abuse of women and children and encouraging diversity. A few years ago we partnered with *Act Now*, a Sustainability Organization in San Francisco; they have now become part of our family, known as *Saatchi S* and are focused on delivering cultural, social, economic and environmental sustainability to our clients and our own brand and holding company. Many of our clients also have corporate social responsibility programs, such as Tide's acclaimed "Loads of Hope," that doing good is an everyday part of their work. Our people report being more attracted to and more loyal to companies and leaders that prioritize and participate in these efforts personally.

Our study of Millennials and other generations revealed that our spirit and attitude as an organization and what we stand for is positive; our structure, practices, tools and our way of working, however, was the elephant in the room. The challenge we faced was matching intentions with actions. We are on our journey today to delivering an inspirational talent agenda, addressing the challenges we learned from Millennials and the rest of the workforce. The remainder of this chapter shares with you our milestones and learnings along the way.

THE SIX E'S TO INSPIRING MILLENNIALS AND BEYOND

Over the last year, 2011, we focused on Six Es to understanding and inspiring a talent agenda that would fit all generations. The process, while not sequential after we started, looks like this (Table 12.3).

1. **Explore.** We invited and continue to involve our highest performing Millennials to walk in our shoes and us in theirs. We encourage

Table 12.3.   Six Es to Inspiring Millennials

Six Es to Inspiring Millennials
1.   Explore
2.   Engage
3.   Excite
4.   Eliminate
5.   Educate
6.   Empower

them to join and participate in our business meetings, leadership sessions, and reviews, and to create new tools and ways of working. We are light on traditional human resource language in our environment; however for many of us who have been around a couple of decades, we were surprised by the power of reverse mentoring. As we will share later, we added Millennial nonhuman resources specialists to our talent teams globally. They have expedited the development of our current human resource teams in new technology and have given us a montage of programs that not only inspire Millennials but the rest of our workforce too. This exploration has led to insights both ways. It has broken down the barriers between our talent departments and the rest of the agency. It has helped us rebrand our way of working. The downsides and watchouts were few. The biggest challenge we encountered was how to speed up our approvals and processes to make things happen before our Millennials got bored. What turned out to be an exploration by inviting Millennials into our talent departments and talent agenda sessions has now become part of our talent structure. We found that the Millennials were able to make things happen with minimum experience and less concerned about getting the minutia done. At the end of the day, this elimination of minutia transformed our talent agenda. Another way to look at this is that Millennials are well equipped to focus their efforts on putting scores on the board that matter versus getting wrapped up in activity and energy that does not count much at the end of the day.

2. **Engage.** Now this seems like a no-brainer. Leaders should be engaged with their people. There is nothing new here. What we learned in our practice and study is that engagement is now a valued currency in the workplace, over the traditional journey of recruit, train, operate and command. In actuality, every generation

we found expects engagement and appreciates it. Attraction is now an essential ingredient of staffing our company. We found that for Millennials, engagement is also a behavior that encourages *Loyalty Beyond Reason* (Roberts, 2005). They seek an emotional connection with your company's brand and leaders.

From other studies, we learned that many Millennials are referred to as the "Trophy Kids." They were brought up in an environment where not only achievement was celebrated but also participation. In our world, we learn that engaging our new workforce at a personal level is wanted. It is not only about being connected on-line; being connected in real time in the workplace helps the transition from home, where many are still attached, to independence in the workplace. We found Millennials to be team oriented, naturally social, and great multitaskers.

Curiously, we found that Millennials expect more structure in the workplace than we have seen with other generations and at the same time much more autonomy to pursue a challenge with people they chose along the way. A key tool we use is RASCI, which sets five clear roles to achieve any task:

o   R = The one person Responsible; the assignment owner
o   A= The Approver; generally the top leader or finance officer
o   S = The Supporter(s); the person or team who carry out what needs to be done
o   C = The Consult; those individuals who are in the loop and provide advice
o   I = The Informed; those who need to need to be communicated to on what happened

We have been using RASCI since our Worldwide CEO took the helm 15 years ago. It has given people at all levels in our agency a tool to lead projects, sort out role conflict and inspire performance. In our experience, RASCI is tailor made for collaborative Millennials and eliminates petty organizational squabbling. It is a nonthreating, liberating way to make things happen and has become part of our agency language: "What is the RASCI?" "Who is the R?" "Who has the A?"

3. **Excite.** Joy is an expectation in our industry. In the last decade or so, we also saw the birth of the psychology of joy. Much of what we refer to as Joy is similar to Mark Seligman's (2011) work on Flourishing. "Employer of the Year," "CEO of the Year" type awards now

include metrics on flexibility and how far companies will go to accommodate Millennials' needs for example, cafés, concierge service, laundromats, office-less environments. Joy in the workplace is not a taboo. Millennials are helping our other generations assess their work and life values. Do we live to work or work to live? Joy has now become mandatory, no matter what kind of business, in particular to Millennials, although there is little push back from other generations who have been rewarded differently over the years. Attracting the best talent to your business means also knowing what attracts them in life. What **Purpose** do they seek? We saw this a few decades ago with Southwest Airlines. Now Google ("Do No Evil"), Starbucks ("Your Third Life") and others have taken the helm on taking Joy to a whole new level. Ideally we believe Joy is every agency's CEO's responsibility. We made delivering it a part of our Global Talent Agenda.

4. **Eliminate.** One of the biggest revelations we had on our talent journey is the need to eliminate what is no longer relevant. We used the Blue Ocean Strategy (Kim & Mauborgne, 2005), as a starter. We put all our Talent Practices on a four-block grid: Create, Increase, Decrease, Eliminate. The challenge was to "Inspire our Peak Performers"—people who could sustain top performance year-in and out delivering highly effective marketing and communications programs. We invited high performers across all generations to participate. Outside of creating some inspirational tools, we eliminated what is no longer core or meaningful to our talent practices. For example we replaced our stodgy international transfer program with an on-line, self-select and driven "*Switch*" program. Millennials eliminated the command and control aspect of our earlier transfer programs and replaced it with something akin to Match.com. We are constructing *Switch 2.0*, taking on board the learning our participants faced, while holding true to the original intent of making it easy for anyone to get an international assignment. To make these kinds of initiatives happen, we had to accommodate the social media in our IT policies, as well as eliminate policies that stood in the way of using technology or how transfers were funded. Elimination is now an annual spring cleaning agenda item for our global talent meetings. We identify early in the year what needs to be eliminated so that we can focus on the important the rest of the year.

5. **Educate.** Our Global Talent Agenda is built on Four Pillars: Responsibility, Learning, Recognition, and Joy. While much has been shared in the literature about not investing in Millennials because they are viewed as less loyal, we decided to increase learn-

ing opportunities for Millennials. They are hungry and remarkably well equipped to take on ideas and apply them. They are also educating the rest of our workforce through application of technologies and innovation. We are seeing a new set of jobs also emerging in the workplace—social media directors, participation and community planners. These new directors are teaching other generations. Likewise our other generations are developing them in how to use insights and our tools; it is difficult to tell who is learning more. It does not matter because everyone is getting better. We found that Millennials seek learning opportunities, especially in how internet-enabled social media are changing the marketing landscape, and favor applied learning. They seek to improve their performance and expect transparency immediately on how well they are doing or what they need to improve.

6. **Empower.** Millennials want meaningful work and challenges; high performers across generations expect the same. We will talk later about our Four Pillars in more detail. We refer to this empowerment as "Responsibility." Like many companies, we streamlined our agencies too. Where we used to have six or more layers of professionals on an account, we now have less than five. We find ourselves promoting high performers well ahead of proven capability.

We experience firsthand the ability and passion of candidates for other opportunities in our agency during our in-house development programs and new business pitches. We do this through discussing the participants' desires and experiences, as part of the program and follow-up. In leadership meetings our Worldwide CEO takes an active role in this process and conducts personal coaching sessions (approximately 8 people at a time, 4 times a year at his home). It is an intimate learning experience and value for our people and involves our Worldwide CEO in the early identification of top talent across all levels of the company. The result has been more than remarkable. Our success ratio on these internal promotions, which we sometimes refer to as "one or two-step" promotable candidates, is better than we have seen in previous generations.

Millennials have been groomed and educated in the internet world. They did not know what it was like before the internet, chat rooms, and blogs. Our latest new graduate hires do not know what it is like not to belong to some on-line social community or what it is like to be without information on almost any subject a key stroke away. There is no trepidation to seek answers on-line. And we are seeing that they are quick to sift out the relevant from the irrelevant, the genuine from the not to be trusted content and in sharing credit or where they picked up the information. Responsibility gives meaning, and we believe it is needed in every role. At Saatchi & Saatchi we are linked by a common **Purpose** to be a hothouse for world-changing creative ideas that transform clients' businesses, brands and reputations from whatever role they have in our agency.

OUR TALENT STRATEGY AND THE MILLENNIALS' VOICE

Our Talent Strategy is based on Four Pillars (see Table 12.4). These Pillars have existed for us in the context of inspiring all our people. The interviews we conducted for this chapter also validated the relevancy of the Four Pillars of our Talent Agenda for all generations.

We use these pillars and the insights we capture throughout the year to build our annual talent agenda. To keep our message on track for Millenials, we invite them to identify and create tools, practices and programs linked to each pillar with our Talent Directors.

Many of our Millennials are now coarchitects of the talent ideas with our more seasoned operational and talent leaders. Our business thrives on relevancy and simplicity; staying focused on these pillars has transformed the way we share and implement our Talent Agenda for everyone.

1. **Responsibility.** We view this through many lenses: mobility, assignment, being given an opportunity to own a part or whole of the idea (or in your case it may be the product or service your company provides). Ownership is key. The best way we find to inspire Millennials is to give them a meaningful challenge—and our clients provide a continuous stream of them—that provides Millennials the opportunity to stretch themselves and see that they can impact. As people who have not lived in a world without internet, they respond well to deadlines and some structure. We refer to this moment we live in as the "Age of Now," the always-on world of social connectivity, continuous commerce and opinion forming. In this context our people need to be in the "Lifestream," with the requisite skills as marketing communicators.

Table 12.4.   Four Pillars of Talent

Four Pillars of Talent
Responsibility
Learning
Recognition
Joy

The Millennials we meet live to innovate, create and collaborate. They are natural team players and flourish by being *Inspired* versus *Managed*. They seem to struggle with authority, especially overbearing controlling leaders. The impact on the rest of the agency has also been far greater than any single talent program we have to boost morale.

We also increased our internal promotions, appointing high potential Millennials to roles that have a steep learning curve. We refer to them as one or two-step promotable. Our success on these placements exceeds our external hires at upper levels.

Employees we found perform better and are happier when they know how they add value to our business. One way we accomplish this is through *100 Day Plans* versus fixed job descriptions—everyone is encouraged to have one. It is a simple set of actions (less than five ideally at a time) that moves the individual and team (for example, *collect insights on what motivates the purchase of sustainable goods in urban settings*). The actions are reviewed continuously during the 100 days, so that barriers can be removed or support added to ensure completion. After 100 days, a new 100 day plan is agreed. Sometimes the new plan may include something to eliminate a barrier encountered earlier. This process has also become part of our language, for example, *"What's on your 100 day plan?"* vs *"What do you do here?"*

Responsibility needs to go further than what happens in the workplace we learned. Millennials also desire that 100 day plans be able to include things where they can explore and achieve things that will accelerate their career, both locally and abroad, personally or professionally, for example as music is a key element to our work, they may wish to explore music trends in developing markets.

From our Millennials' Perspective

The agency needs to create room to participate in more than one job, both inside and outside of work. We would be better if we could also pursue our outside passions that will inspire ideas back at work.

I define myself by many things I do. I see myself having more than one career path. I'm account executive, a blogger, and a chef. I prefer not to be pegged to one thing.

I need challenges. I need to know how I contribute. I need to see how I make a difference.

2. **Learning.** As digital natives, Millennials want to keep developing their skills and knowledge. They thrive for challenges and expect opportunities to work across more geographic borders than their

parents, which supports much of the research we also see in this area. They also expressed desire to work in different departments and across multiple clients. Diversity of experiences outweighs the traditional "career planning." Much of what we heard was familiar except it was voiced with a louder sense of urgency and passion than previous generations. Neglect learning needs, as expressed by digital experiences, conferences, travel, cross-team and pan-regional work, and Millennials become bored and easily lured by other employers.

By the time Millennials get into the workforce, many of them we interview have travelled abroad. They expect collaboration. They believe anyone can be a star. Hierarchy is not revered like it used to be. Being heard, challenged and learning are the highly valued practices companies can provide. They want to be part of a community. Providing opportunities to network and socialize helps them with their jobs and their happiness.

From our Millennials' Perspective

I see myself as having many careers, not just one. Career Planning Tools and Tracks feel suffocating. I can see myself as having more than one career at a time. I'd like to see this as a part-time job, and if possible get full benefits and pay. In our kind of work, it's about what you accomplish and what you contribute to an idea, not how many hours you take to get it done.

I'm constantly connected. I can get answers to questions I don't know quickly. I want more information to do my job better, and I want the latest technology available to help me. How is this company performing? What are the challenges our company is facing? I want to be engaged and involved in making it better. I don't just want to be defined by my job title. I want to be defined by what I can contribute and coached to help.

Traditional employers may blanch at such a seemingly self-centered attitude as expressed by this respondent, but this is reality. The challenges of previous generations, from the Cold War to the preinternet rigidity, have dissipated and do not constrain Millennials. They are serious about key world issues such as sustainability, and see themselves as making an effective contribution, and do not see corporations as the solution to world peace. This is a key alignment corporations must make.

3. **Recognition.** Millennials are conditioned to expect and get instant feedback. The Age of Now is pervasive. This includes anything to let employees know their contribution is valued or what they can be doing better. It can be monetary, or it could be something that

enables them to integrate work and pursue their other passions or help them do their job better. The value of this we learned is how relevant the recognition is to the individual. Does it somehow help them fulfill a dream or perform better? Timeliness and relevancy are important, and clearly knowing your employees' dreams makes all the difference in creating an emotional connection that matters to them. A metaphor is keeping a partner in love—loyalty beyond reason. What would *you* do to keep the passion burning?

Millennials expect feedback. Lots of it! They expect the similar recognition they were brought up on. They believe that their effort in keeping the team running is as integral to the company's success as achieving something outstanding. They want affirmation and recognition that the company values the work they do. While monetary recognition is desired, our Millennials also expressed the need for intangible recognition like getting extra time-off or just applause at a company meeting.

Another perspective we learned was the importance of rewarding a team versus an individual—today so much work is done in collaboration. Highlighting who was involved and recognizing the team is a reality check that the company knows what is going on. The one big difference we found in the generations was that frequency of recognition is much more needed for Millennials.

From our Millennials' Perspective

At our level, we are still at the bottom of everything. Leaders need to share what achievement is for someone just starting. Maybe we should be recognized for how we collaborate or how we facilitate and hold everything together.

I want my team to be recognized. It's not always about one person. Recognize the team and celebrate small success steps too. Freedom to do other things is also valued, especially when companies are strapped for cash. We understand the economics.

Constant feedback is important. Don't wait till an annual review time to set new targets or to tell me how well or not I have been performing. I need real time reviews, nothing fancy or anything that requires a form. I get it.

4. **Joy.** Psychologists over the last decade increased research in the area of happiness. This is a relief, since during previous decades most analyses were spent on what is wrong with people. Our Company's most simple manifestation of Joy is through creating happi-

ness in the workplace through inspiration and delivering the four pillars of our talent strategy: responsibility, recognition, learning and joy. Our kind of industry thrives on being positively engaged on these, and those who succeed well promote it and make it happen for their teams too.

The Millennials that we met have been encouraged to travel and to pursue their own interests—singing, photography, and travel appear frequently. Few of them are willing to give up their passions and lifestyle for a career in a place they know that they will likely move on from within a few years. They seek out careers and agencies that enable them to pursue personal interests too. The opportunities for our agency include providing more temporary assignments abroad, secondments and job exchanges. This will broaden their skills and continue to diversify our work teams and up our engagement in the workplace.

From our Millennials' Perspective

Happiness on the job comes from: teamwork, creating ideas, seeing the company implement ideas (especially if not yet proven), the freedom to choose where and how to work, being challenged, having the latest technology to do my job and stay connected.

I live in a social world on-line and off-line. I value respect, authenticity and privacy. I don't want to be imposed on or lied to. If the agency is genuine and authentic to a positive cause, then ok. If it's about making them money only, or promoting something I don't believe in, then I'll let others know to stay away.

If something doesn't fit for me, I'm an easy flight risk. Lack of transparency, boredom and stress will make me leave. Work is one part of my life. It's not about balance for me. It's about working in a place that will give me the opportunity to bring my life to the company and live life outside the company. Work is one thing I do. I see it as an enabler or a life style or both.

IMPLICATIONS FOR OUR TALENT AGENDA

Talent Practices From Earlier
Generations is the new Base Camp

A few years ago a talent director in Europe shared a tiny piece of paper with some tips on how to get the most from your employees. He said he received this paper from a member of his agency and that it was something that was passed down to an employee (See Figure 12. 1).

The paper was something a father of this employee used to carry with him in looking after his teams for about 30 years. It is called the "Worker's Plea." It's our guess that this piece of paper has been around since the 1970s. It is an amazing reminder that talent professionals have been at this business for a long time.

It is also warming to see the message board notes this employee received after he posted it on the internet. This note can be found at:

http://www.adliterate.com/archives/2008/02/the_workers_ple_1.html

Share this note with your Millennials. We expect you will see that they want it too! As we learned from our Millennials, this *Worker's Plea* represents a simplicity they appreciate.

We also learned that it is not about stopping with the Worker's Plea. It is about starting here, as the new base camp to bring total fulfillment.

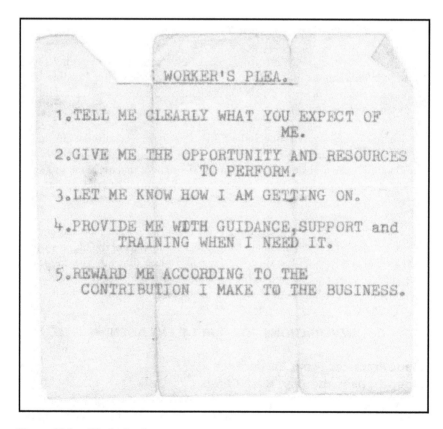

Figure 12.1. Worker's plea.

Leaders still have a mountain to climb, if they want the positive attention and performance from the Millennial generation. Leaders need to emotionally embrace your talent strategy and the parts that make it work for your people, as attitude cannot be line managed or delegated. Our interviews provided a large number of examples that Millennials learned from friends on what other companies are doing to entice them and keep them and get them productive.

We are Competing for the Same Talent

We learned that for the most part, regardless of industry, that we are all competing for the same talent. This is particularly true in larger industry groups. For example, in Advertising, we are now competing with Internet, Digital, Media, consultants and start-ups. We are no longer competing with the Top 4 Agencies—the smaller ones are fierce competitors. Moreover, no matter what industry we are in, we are being held to higher standards of what to do to keep the best talent with us. We are seeing more Millennials willing to cross any industry sector to fulfill their ambition. If you do not have a mechanism to keep them inspired, they are likely to wander. In a 2011 4As study of Advertising Millennials, 70% of them felt they needed to take care of themselves first. Seventy percent said they would call a recruiter back. Ninety-six percent felt confident that they would get a job easily.

Small Things Matter as Much as the Big Things

We noticed much respect from the Millennials on the challenges organizations face in these tough economic times. Remuneration is expected to be fair and competitive. The freedom to pursue other activities and have flexible working schedules is a priority. Emotional currency is as important as monetary reward, and we found that this generation understands the business economics well. The critics say it is all about entitlement for this generation. We learned in our meetings it is about being able to continue to play hard and work hard. From a talent perspective, cracking this challenge ends up being a reward for everyone and something many of us have been pursuing for years with various programs; now something more permanent is needed.

It is Okay to Admit you are Learning too

We found that giving Millennials the opportunity to design and define their dreams and how the company can make them true is a big inspirer in tough times (and probably good ones too).

Companies that admit that they are learning or willing to learn seem more respected. Rational and emotional needs in this area are real. As one Millennial shared from our survey mentioned earlier, "I believe that employees who are unhappy with their agency are more likely to look for another job and also share their frustration with future recruits on-line. Engage us to fix. We're equipped to connect with others who may be able to help faster and in an impactful way." In our industry there are many successful start-ups with Millennials, who believe starting from scratch is easier than joining a bigger company.

We have begun infusing Millennials on everything from the **Purpose** of our Company to business pitches, to even running our Talent Centers globally. We have put in learning opportunities where our highest potential Millennials now get personal mentorship from our Global CEO and his trusted operational leaders as coaches and talent guides.

Eight Millennial Ideas for Talent Practitioners

Our Millennials shared what they would do if they were Talent Director. This starts our action list. The implementation for the most part will be done by Millennials, both in our Talent Centers globally and from within the agencies across our network. We reckon these ideas fit us all. See Figure 12.2.

TALENT CHALLENGES FOR MILLENNIALS AND BEYOND

Millennials were brought up in a time where mobile phones, internet, social networks and reality TV is the norm. They have witnessed a world

---

Top 8 Talent Millennial Ideas

1. Coach
2. Infuse Experiences and Global Connections
3. Communicate and Engage
4. Encourage Bottom Up Innovation
5. Tell Me Like It Is - Feedback
6. Recognize and Reward Effort As Well As Achievement
7. Enable Opportunities To Develop Personal Interests
8. Bring Fun Into The Workplace – Make Everyday Feel Like Saturday

Figure 12.2.   Top 8 talent millennial ideas.

of terror and have seen repeatedly the scandal on iconic people and companies. They have a deep conscience about what is right, wrong or somewhere in the middle. They are critical thinkers. They are in enormous demand. They are a generation that has learned that work-life balance is not a request of employers; it is a condition that needs to be met for them. They investigate employers and the leaders of those companies as much as employers interview them.

- They are looking at how their values match the company and when they arrive how genuine leaders live up to them.
- They are not leaving their parents home sooner; they are leaving when they are ready.
- They have built a network of friends and contacts that surpasses any generation before. They are used to being recognized for progress not only achievement.
- They seek challenges and expect recognition along the way, for their team and themselves.
- They bring a different set of perspectives and capabilities to companies different than previous generations.
- Their media, social, technology savvy is immediate value for companies.
- They can tap into answers, ideas and each other instantaneously and globally 24-7.
- They grew up in a culture of acceptance and were taught to appreciate differences among people; their immersion in the workplace will revolutionize our current diversity programs and become inherent.
- Many of them are better travelled at their age than previous generations, and those who have not, are equally sensitive and knowledgeable about the world and cultures through their on-line experiences.

And now they are entering the workforce equipped for a challenge, small or big, and seeking an employer who gets them and is willing to embrace new ways of working.

We started this chapter by saying it is time for a New Talent Agenda. The refreshing outcome of conducting our research and study on Millennials was that there are more positive things to read, say and learn about this generation than other talent challenges we are faced with today. It was this optimism and the nature of our own business that made us decide it is time for us to Create a New Talent Agenda, for our Millennials and the rest of us.

One Last Anecdote

On a 2,400 mile road trip to Florida from New York, one of the authors' seven-year-old grumbled from the back seat of our SUV, "Dad ...." If we rolled back the years, it would have been followed by "Are we there yet?" He said, "When are you going to stop for a Starbucks?" I replied, "Why?" thinking what a great kid for keeping dad alert and caffeinated. He then answered, "I want to download some new Apps for my Nook, and I need a hotspot."

Later, when I turned on the On-Board concierge system, I asked for hotels in the next 100 miles. My son perked up again, "Dad, make sure you get us a room with Wi-fi." He is about 13 or so years from entering the workforce. We better get busy getting on the Talent Agenda for this generation, ... and somehow we believe the Worker's Plea will remain relevant, with a few tweaks.

REFERENCES

Gilson, C., Pratt, M., Roberts, K., & Weymes, E. (2000). *Peak performance: Inspirational business lessons from the world's top sports organizations,* London, England: HarperCollins.

Kim, W. C., & Mauborgne, R. (2005). *Blue ocean strategy: How to create uncontested market space and make competition irrelevant.* Boston, MA: Harvard Business School Press.

Roberts, K. (2005). *Lovemarks: The future beyond brands.* New York, NY: powerHouse Books.

Seligman, M. (2011). *Flourish: A visionary new understanding of happiness and well-being.* New York, NY: Free Press.

Worker's Plea. (1971). Retrieved from http://www.adliterate.com/archives/2008/02/the_workers_ple_1.html

CHAPTER 13

IMPLICATIONS OF VALUES OF THE MILLENNIAL GENERATION ON HR INFRASTRUCTURE

Sheri K. Bias and Donna L. Phillips

INTRODUCTION

Personal values are the beliefs that serve to influence and guide behaviors of individuals. These values develop over time and through interaction with an individual's environment. While values can vary by individual, there is typically a collective that can be seen within generations. According to Fox (2011), "People's attitudes are influenced by the familial and cultural experiences of their childhood. Whether you grew up during wartime or peacetime, in heady economic times or financial uncertainty, or in periods of profound change such as the civil rights era or the Internet era—all these factors help define your generation's values. And those values are brought into the workplace" (para. 2). It is important to keep in mind that individuals' values can heavily influence their perspectives, as well as their interactions with others within the workplace.

The different generations bring their own perspectives and set of values into the workplace. These values can, and do, have implications on the human resources (HR) infrastructure within an organization which

Managing Human Resources for the Millennial Generation, pp. 301–321
Copyright © 2012 by Information Age Publishing

can be seen in processes such as staffing and recruiting, training and employee development, and performance assessments just to name a few. When there is alignment with the individual values system and what the organization values, there can be a synergy in the employer/employee relationship that serves to guide and motivate behavior.

One may wonder: Could an organization exclusively focus on a particular generation in the operation of its business and still be successful? The answer to this question is more than likely not. There are many variables involved in creating and sustaining effective infrastructure conducive to organizational success. However, when the organization is able to embrace the values of the generations, such as those considered important by the Millennials, the organization can then craft processes and infrastructure to best tap into the needs of the various generations.

With regard to the Millennials, it is critical to keep in mind the influences of parents on the development of an individual, and this is particularly so with the Millennial generation. This generation is a product of the environment in which they were raised. Typically, their parents are Boomers, and the Millennials experienced households where both parents worked. Millennials are products of dual-career families and these parents had a tendency to indulge their children (Lee, 2011). This generation witnessed the hard work of their parents and saw the impacts of economic downsizing by large corporations (Lee, 2011). According to Fox (2011), Millennials also experienced parents who desired more peer-like relationships with their children above and beyond the typical parent-child relationship.

With respect to the Millennial generation, given our research and experiences with these individuals within various organizations, we are defining the values for this generation in terms of categories of immediacy, teaming, and recognition that are mainly influencing behaviors. We will expand on each of these areas to provide further insight and definition for these values. In the discussion that follows, we will use examples from two distinct organizations: (1) the National Aeronautics and Space Administration (NASA), a Federal Government organization, from a broad perspective of activities from NASA at-large as well as specific examples from NASA Langley Research Center, operating in Hampton Roads, Virginia; and (2) Jaderlund Casting, a privately owned organization that provides casting for films and television productions and talent management services; to describe the alignment of the values important to Millennials with HR infrastructure and practices utilized by these organizations.

VALUES DEFINED

It is noteworthy to discuss the difficulty in solidifying the values of the Millennial generation. At first glance, Millennials' values and behaviors appear to be contradictory to one another. For example, Millennials appear to prefer working in teams and enjoy collaboration; however, they also are said to value independence in their working arrangements. In consideration of this dichotomy, one reason for the contradiction could be due to the overall changing of our society and the values system in operation. It could be that Millennials do value the collaborative process of bouncing ideas off one another and then working independently to complete the task. In Jayson's (2010) article entitled "Study: Millennial generation more educated, less employed," she references the Pew Research Center's comment that "there is no one-size-fits-all description of the individual within a generation, … (however, Pew's) findings show clear, distinctive traits for this group" (para. 6). This indicates the need to define Millennials' values in order to better clarify and understand the implications on HR infrastructure.

Immediacy

One of the primary categories, or core values, that can be attributed to the Millennial generation is that of immediacy. Those in the Millennial generation have come to expect a quick response to everything they do. They seem to have a desire to do everything and want everything almost at once. There seems to be a never-ending sense of urgency associated with task accomplishment. This category is defined using terms such as spontaneity, expedience, expectancy, balance, and high energy.

A key premise of this need for immediacy can be seen in the reliance on technology for facilitation of communications and interactions. Fox (2011) also supports the early reference to Millennials and their interaction with technology. She notes that this generation, numbering nearly 80 million, grew up with technology at their fingertips. They have had access to computers since an early age and quickly became adept at using the Internet. These individuals have been termed to be "comfortable texting, talking, typing, Skyping, Googling and Facebooking simultaneously—and feel anxious and disconnected when they aren't" (Hughes, 2011, para. 1). The Pew Research Center, which conducts research on the Millennial generation, released a report in 2010 regarding its Pew Internet Project stating, "Millennials are increasingly connecting to the internet wirelessly, and nearly three in four of those online use social networking sites" (Media & Digital Life, para. 1; Pew Research Center, 2011). Additionally, in an interview with Don Tapscott conducted by Aliah Wright (2010), it was noted that this generation has been surrounded by digital technology, and this has had a profound effect on these individuals in the work environment.

Millennials exhibit a strong sense of commitment to ensuring their performance is exemplary and fulfilling their obligations to the organization. Yet, this generation also values balance. According to Hughes (2011), "the youngest generation of workers seeks balance, meaning and purpose so they can live and work" (para. 1). Balance can be defined as ensuring time is left for activities beyond work such as maintaining equilibrium between personal and professional endeavors. This generation appears to have a strong work ethic; yet, they also make time for family and friends outside of the working environment. Rizzo (2009) notes this generation often replaces family with friends. Seeking work/life balance is important to Millennials.

Teaming

Another of the categories of values which defines this generation is teaming. This category of values can be defined with such terms as belonging, acceptance, camaraderie, and collaboration. Essentially, it means working together on a highly functioning group toward a common end or goal. While the Millennials tend to be achievement oriented, this can often be overshadowed by the importance of being able to collaborate effectively with others within the working environment. Wright (2010) in an interview with Don Tapscott, author of *Grown Up Digital: How the Net Generation Is Changing Your World* (McGraw-Hill, 2009), noted that Millennials are natural collaborators who value conversation and do not want to be lectured. This is a unique identifier as they derive much enjoyment from working on a team which aligns with the value of relationships. Rizzo (2009) notes one of the work paradigms for this generation is that of virtual teaming which can be facilitated through the use of technology. Teaming or networking such as this often serves multiple needs for Millennials in the use of technology to build camaraderie which is important to this generation.

There is a direct connection with being effective on a team and the establishment of relationships. Yet, we do have to consider that the traditional face-to-face interactions that were previously typically experienced within the workplace are now expanded to include other channels such as social media which provide expanded opportunities to build relationships. Fox (2011) discusses the fact that Millennials highly value relationships, but they do not need to have face-to-face encounters in order to build these relationships. Millennials are in a unique position, given the influence of technology on this group, to be fluid in their interactions utilizing technology to establish relationships with others. According to Rizzo (2009) in her work "Creating Synergy in a Four-Generation Workplace," Millennials value information and research that brings about answers which can be had through the use of technology. There is a wealth of information readily available at a moment's notice given the technology currently at their disposal. In this new world, people and machine become one (Rizzo, 2009).

While the Millennials ultimately value working on teams, there is also a perceived need for independence and being able to control the process to get the job done. As previously described, this seems to be a misalignment in terms of these values. This generation exhibits a tendency to have the mentality of being able to complete tasks by themselves (Rizzo, 2009). Thus, this should not be seen as a dichotomy to working on teams as the alignment is in the infrastructure provided for the team and then allowing the individuals to work independently within those parameters. Setting the parameters of the work space and enabling them to operate within this space will allow them to utilize their creativity in order to best accomplish the job.

Recognition

The Millennial generation seems to have a need for achievement and pursues a sense of accomplishment. We have termed this category as recognition which includes the aforementioned variables along with achievement, encouragement, challenging work, and being able to make a difference. This is supported by Rizzo's (2009) description of Millennials displaying the notion that "life is fragile" and they intend to "save the planet" (p. 6). Millennials portray a sense of confidence in their approach to work and are not afraid of working hard in order to get a job done. Their ideal working environment seems to be one where they can make a meaningful contribution to a job or project while working in concert with others on a team which allows them to establish and maintain key relationships. Lipkin and Perrymore (2009) note that organizations need to understand this value embraced by Millennials as their expectation is for their employer to be socially conscious in the conduct of business and this generation will easily look for other job opportunities if this value is disregarded.

Another value that is important to the Millennials is achievement. Achievement is essentially the success of being able to accomplish goals. This generation embraces achievement through their performance and has the mentality that "nothing is impossible" (Rizzo, 2009, p. 6). Further, a recent survey conducted by the Society for Human Resources Management noted that Millennials desire interesting and challenging work as being important to them as this particular factor saw a positive increase in those affirming this importance (Society for Human Resources Management, 2011).

Overall, the values of the Millennial generation operate in concert to enable them to be effective contributing members in the workplace. The challenge for the HR community is to incorporate the knowledge of these values into the objectives and goals of the HR infrastructure. HR also needs to realize that these values are not etched in stone but are drawn in sand as these will continue to evolve and change as societal parameters continue to change.

ORGANIZATIONAL CONTEXT

In the following paragraphs, we will set the context for the organizations from which we draw examples for the innovative pieces of HR infrastructure that are being employed to reach the Millennial generation and tap into what this generation most values.

National Aeronautics and Space Administration (NASA)

NASA is a Federal agency established in 1958 by President Dwight D. Eisenhower in response to satellites launched by the Soviet Union. NASA was a spinoff of the National Advisory Committee on Aeronautics, which was responsible for researching flight technology for 40 years (NASA, 2011). In the 1960's, NASA became a household name when it was given the charge by President John F. Kennedy to develop the technology needed to send a man to the moon by the end of the decade. The first man walked on the moon in 1969.

Today, NASA is an organization composed of 10 Centers across the United States (U.S.) with Langley Research Center being its founding Center. NASA's Headquarters is located in Washington, DC. It conducts work in three principal organizations: Aeronautics; Human Exploration and Operations; and Science (NASA, 2011). Over NASA's 50-year history thousands of people have worked for the agency to accomplish its mission: "To reach for new heights and reveal the unknown so that what we do and learn will benefit all humankind" (NASA, 2011, About NASA, para. 1). As of November 2011, NASA had an estimated 1,462 Millennial generation employees out of a total of 18,637 agencywide. NASA has been mired with an aging workforce and has continued hiring individuals within its mean age for years. The average age for the past decade has been in the 40s and is currently 48 years. This can partly be attributed to a hiring freeze lasting through most of the 1990s (Open NASA, 2011).

However, in 2009 NASA's Strategic Management Council implemented an initiative to rebalance its aging workforce and adopted a policy and goal that 50% of all new civil servants be "fresh-out." "Fresh-outs" are defined as individuals who have just completed a degree whether they are 23 or 40 years of age. NASA anticipates that using this strategy will allow them to double the number of Millennials within their workforce over the next few years (Open NASA, 2011).

The focus for NASA's future is human space flight to explore the solar system and potentially landing on Mars; continuing to staff the International Space Station; using commercial companies to provide crew flights to the International Space Station; researching ways to design safer, quieter, and more fuel-efficient aircraft; conducting science missions to understand the Earth, the solar system and the universe (www.NASA.gov). To accomplish these future challenges, NASA will need to continue its understanding of Millennials and further explore methods to recruit, hire, and retain this generation of potential employees.

One of the 10 Centers that will serve as a focal point for this chapter will be Langley Research Center. NASA Langley Research Center (LaRC) began as a civilian laboratory in 1917, and at the time, concentrated solely on aviation. Later in 1958, it transitioned to performing space exploration work and became a major player in the space race. Even in the mid-2000s Langley continued to adapt by diversifying its portfolio of activity to continue being an integral part of NASA's future (Langley History, 2011).

Jaderlund Casting

Jaderlund Casting is a privately owned company that provides casting and talent management services to organizations as well as individuals. Jaderlund Casting has a variety of clients from Corporate to Government and Nongovernment organizations and serves the population along the Eastern seaboard from Georgia to New York City. Henry Jaderlund, who is a member of the Casting Director's Guild of America, is the owner of the organization and has over a decade of experience in the industry. Through his efforts and involvement in the industry, the Jaderlund Casting organization has participated for 3 consecutive years in projects gaining recognition from some of the world's most prestigious Film Festivals such as Sundance Film Festival, Cannes Film Festival, Tribecca Film Festival and the Berlin Film Festival (Jaderlund Casting, 2011).

The goal of the organization is to ensure the appropriate atmosphere is created for clients to ensure success in achieving the vision for their production. This means understanding and aligning the people needs for the production and securing talent who will be a good fit for the designated roles. Over the company's history, Jaderlund Casting has auditioned and hired over 15,000 people for a variety of projects in National broadcast television commercials for clients such as Walmart, as well as film productions including feature films such as "The Box," "Evan Almighty," and a miniseries—HBO's "John Adams"—which was awarded four Golden Globes and 13 Emmy wins.

Talent demographics are an important part of the business operation for Jaderlund Casting. Clients specify, based on bona-fide occupational qualifications, the atmosphere necessary for their particular treatment (or project). Therefore, the demographic variables of the talent in Jaderlund Casting are closely scrutinized to ensure that the vision of the client is brought to fruition on the project. At the present time, approximately 45% of talent resources available within the Jaderlund Casting infrastructure fall in the Millennial generation demographic. Therefore, it is important for Jaderlund Casting to understand the values of this generation and apply these concepts to its business operation.

CONNECTING MILLENNIAL VALUES TO HR PRACTICES

In this section we describe how the values we have defined for this generation appear in leading-edge HR practices.

Immediacy

NASA

Imagine a Millennial showing up on her first day of work eager and ready to take on the next great challenge in her field of choice only to find the tools she needs are not available. This would not make for a very good first impression of the organization. There was a time when it was not uncommon for new NASA employees to show up their first day of work and not have the equipment needed to perform their duties for up to 2 weeks. This did not bode well with Gen Y individuals, who value expedience. NASA has restructured its on-boarding process within the last several years. Now each employee has a desk, telephone and computer the first day she or he reports for duty. New Employee Orientation programs have been improved too. Langley Research Center's orientation now includes a quarterly "New Employee Center Tour" that concludes with lunch with the Center Director. The Center Director provides an overview of the Center's strategic direction and its alignment with the agency's mission. The significance of the Center tour is it allows individuals to meet and interact with senior leadership early in their career.

Another part of the on-boarding process NASA modified to address Millennials' need for immediacy was to assign new employees a mentor when they come on-board to help them quickly integrate into the culture and community of the organization. The mentor also addresses questions regarding career development and progression. With regard to mentoring, NASA has begun utilizing a developmental tool known as "speed mentoring" or "flash mentoring." Speed mentoring is a high energy activity that puts senior leaders and employees together to allow the employees to ask questions about career management, technical questions or anything they want to ask of the leaders. The process can take up to 2 hours. Two to three senior leaders are placed at six or eight tables depending on the number of employees attending. For example, if you have six tables and want to place two leaders at each table you would need 12 senior leaders to mentor. The employees are divided among the tables with the leaders. A timekeeper allows 10 to 15 minutes of discussion at the table before having the participants rotate to another table. This process continues until participants have had the opportunity to speak with each of the senior leaders. This mentoring process has been a very favorable method among employees for gaining a lot of information from senior leaders in a short amount of time. It can also be used to target specific topics and demographic groups.

As outlined previously in the "Organization Context" section regarding NASA, the mean age of its workforce is currently 48. It is little wonder that the agency is behind the curve in adopting many of the technologies Millennials utilize for the facilitation of communications and interactions. NASA is now striving to catch up. Approximately 2 years ago NASA began using "Yammer" which is a microblog that allows individuals to make brief text updates to anyone who chooses to follow another individual's updates (Other NASA News, 2011). It is similar to Twitter; however, it is more for professional exchange. About the same time, NASA Langley Research Center established a Facebook page for Center employees to meet and interact with one another. However, in 2011 Langley's Facebook page moved to a fan page in order to increase capacity. This change was made due to the overwhelming response Langley received on its Facebook. In just a few years Langley's profile page met the 5,000 friend limit. The fan page allows unlimited growth. Several other NASA Centers have established Facebook pages too. This initiative has brought together individuals that may not otherwise have ever met across Centers and the agency. It is a wonderful mechanism for individuals to share information, generate ideas and collaborate on projects and other work. Other internal NASA technical capabilities include:

- **INSIDENASA.GOV**: An internal NASA portal that provides information to NASA employees on everything from missions and projects to employee benefits.
- **Wikis (inwiki and Confluence)**: Collaborative internal wiki and blog applications used for projects. This allows individuals to share information regarding the research they are performing or projects being worked. The software can be set up so it is open to all NASA employees or restricted to specific users
- **Blogs (blogs.nasa.gov)**: This specific blog site allows NASA employees to share updates and insights to their work with individuals across the agency. It is an efficient tool for keeping abreast of what is going on within NASA.
- **Broadcast messaging (e-mail, RSS, Jabber, LCS)**: Broadcast messaging is used to communicate one-on-one with individuals or groups of individuals. For example, Jabber is an instant message service that can be used in a teaming capacity whether it is with one individual on the team or the entire team. RSS (Rich Site Summary) is used to reduce the amount of time to research information from several websites by receiving regularly changing web content from the sites in which an individual is most interested.
- **Team workspace (Sharepoint, eRoom, NX)**: The team workspace software makes it easier for people to share information with team members, manage documents and publish reports. It allows easy access for everyone on a team to obtain the most current data.

Another tool being used by Langley Research Center for idea generation is Mind Sprints. Mind Sprints provide an opportunity for individuals to provide input to specific topics. The process starts with a sponsor identifying the topic about which they desire to gain creative ideas and presenting it to a facilitator appointed to facilitate the process. Volunteers are solicited using social media like Yammer, Facebook, or an internal electronic publication, which informs them of the Mind Sprint topic. Those who are interested notify the facilitator. The volunteers meet with the sponsor and facilitator to brainstorm ideas, which the sponsor may or may not choose to use.

While having challenging work, performing successfully, and receiving timely feedback is important to Millennials, just as important is work/life balance. The matter of work/life balance has positively been addressed by NASA. Having a family friendly environment is one of the highest scored areas on the Federal Employee Viewpoint Survey by NASA employees. Like other NASA Centers, Langley Research Center has instituted an alternative work schedule which allows employees to flex their schedules each pay period. An alternative schedule also allows individuals to work their hours of duty so they can have a day off every other week. For example, an employee may work 50 hours the first week of a 2-week pay period and 30 the second week and take off the second Friday. Employees are also given flexibility in start and stop times for work each day. This allows employees to report for duty later or come in earlier if they need to run an errand and make up the time at the end or beginning of the day or sometime within the pay period. Taking personal leave time is only required if the employee is absent during "core hours," which are specifically set hours an employee is required to be at work each day, such as 9 am to 3 pm. This approach to work scheduling has had a very positive impact on the workforce at NASA Langley Research Center. Telecommuting has also won high marks from the NASA community due to the flexibility it provides. Employees who telecommute are able to take care of family responsibilities such as putting their children on the school bus in the morning and being there when the bus drops them off in the afternoon. However, it should be noted that these individuals are still held accountable for meeting deadlines and delivering results. For the average telecommuter productivity is not a problem. Having the flexibility an alternative work schedule offers and ability to telecommute fits into the Millennial generation's value set in that it provides them with a balance of work and life.

Jaderlund Casting

In order to tap into the need for immediacy as valued by this generation, Jaderlund Casting has integrated the use of technology as part of the business infrastructure. For example, Jaderlund Casting relies on Facebook in its business processes as a mechanism for recruiting and communication to reach Millennials. As previously noted, this generation has grown up with technology at their disposal which has facilitated this need for immediacy. Often times, Jaderlund Casting is tasked by clients to recruit and book talent for assignments with quick turnaround times, which can be less than 24 hours notice. Prior to the use of Facebook as a means of recruiting, Jaderlund would telephonically contact each individual as well as utilize e-mail as the main method for communication. Utilizing Facebook in this capacity affords the Casting organization the ability to communicate with talent in real time and facilitates the expediting of messages to the target audience as well as increases the reach within the talent network given the number of individuals utilizing this infrastructure. It should be noted that the use of Facebook is for business purposes in communicating externally with talent and clients. E-mail and other communication infrastructure are used by casting directors to interact regarding business matters.

Jaderlund Casting also utilizes its own business website to relay information regarding projects and bookings to talent simultaneously. Using technology in this manner has allowed the Jaderlund organization to achieve cost savings in hours and resource usage in that the individual communications associated with telephone conversations is saved. Further, the delay in communications, such as could be experienced when utilizing e-mail and waiting for responses, is minimized through the use of Facebook and business website simultaneous communications with talent. Given that over 45% of the talent resources of Jaderlund Casting are Millennials, and these Millennials have embraced technology, this proves to be a conducive process for recruiting.

Another component of being successful in the Casting business is being able to provide information to clients in an expedited manner which aligns with the value under discussion. Executives who contract with Jaderlund Casting are also part of this Millennial generation, and therefore expect information requested to be supplied to them in an expeditious manner. Thus, Jaderlund Casting has developed infrastructure to allow them quickly to turn around talent options to the client after gaining an understanding of the vision for the project. Using an electronic format similar to a database infrastructure, Jaderlund Casting can quickly store, retrieve and customize "packages" of talent options for client review and selection. This has doubled the efficiency of the Casting organization by not having to recreate and customize these packages for each new client and minimized the turn-around time of the request from the client.

Teaming

As stated earlier, being a member of a team is an important value to Millennials. These types of relationships can be facilitated by an organization's infrastructure and the way it engages in business operations. Below are several examples of embracing the importance of teaming as it relates to this generation.

NASA

In 2008 NASA's Strategic Management Council, composed of the Directors of each Center and agency leadership, began focusing on the "long-term strategic effects on the NASA mission of current hiring practices and the upcoming gap in U.S. human space flight, and specific actions that the Strategic Management Council and the next generation community could each take" (NASA, 2009, para. 1). One action to address this issue was to provide the NASA workforce with an infusion of fresh ideas, methodologies and technologies. This was accomplished by developing Agency and Center Next Generation and/or Cross-Generation Project Teams, focus groups, and/or inclusion and innovation councils to work on issues. Eventually, the Next Generation Teams at each Center established themselves as formal groups and continue to work issues as well as serve as a networking community. The teams also provide a sense of camaraderie among the NASA Millennials' peers.

NASA Langley Research Center has also adopted an open concept work environment in newly constructed buildings to encourage collaboration. The majority of employees no longer have offices. In fact, offices are a rare commodity in this environment. Individuals reside in cubicles. The openness makes it easy for individuals to share ideas, learn from one another, and keep abreast of the work occurring within their work environment. Some buildings have "teaming" rooms, which are small work rooms used to accommodate ad hoc meetings for task completion. Initially, the open concept was met with resistance and it was difficult for many employees to give up their office for a cubicle. However, as time has progressed, individuals are beginning to see the advantages of an open work environment. It truly lends itself to Millennial values and increases spontaneity, creativity and innovation.

Because much of the work performed by NASA is done within a team environment most of the agency developmental programs have a team project component. The agency has a series of leadership development programs to address all levels of employees. One that specifically fits Milliennials is the NASA FIRST (Foundations of Influence, Relationships, Success, and Teamwork) program. NASA FIRST is a 1-year part-time program that provides participants the opportunity to develop their professional and personal effectiveness by learning about their personality, communication and leadership styles. It is composed of 4 week-long training modules, coaching, shadowing of senior leaders and a group team project. The participants from each Center are given the charge to identify a project that would benefit their Center. This project teaches individuals the dynamics of working in a team, leadership skills, conflict resolution, and communication skills. The program outcomes include (Leadership NASA, 2011):

- having an increased awareness of self, others, and the agency;
- having a broader understanding of what it means to be a fully functioning team member and leader;
- having a greater understanding of personal influence skills and how to use those skills effectively for NASA; and
- being part of a cadre of future NASA leaders who will be inspired, motivated, and eager to play a vital role in the future of NASA.

Jaderlund Casting

In the industry that Jaderlund Casting serves, teaming is not a part of the official infrastructure necessary for success. Given that individuals are not always afforded the opportunity to choose with whom they work on teams, Jaderlund Casting assigns talent to projects based on client specifications. These specifications are the primary driver for staffing projects; it is difficult to create solid work teams on a regular basis as the needs frequently change. Observations of talent cast on assignments reveal that the Millennials, even though they are not officially assigned to teams, quickly form relationships and bonds with each other that carry forward from assignment to assignment. The talent who are a part of the Jaderlund Casting network also often spread the word regarding other casting opportunities within their own network of relationships to other potential talent who may be interested in this line of work. These communications have also assisted Jaderlund Casting with recruiting efforts.

Recognition

NASA

The ability for a company or organization to attract and retain a Millennial as an employee may be a tough sell for any organization. When we consider NASA, the name brand might capture the attention of a Gen Y, but would its bureaucratic and management driven culture and its aging workforce entice them to stay? While the bureaucracy and culture appear to be frustrating for its Millennial workforce, the same could be said for other generational workers within the agency. What appears to attract Millennials to work for NASA is the challenging work and the belief that what they are doing can make a difference for humankind, which is something this generation values. It is not just the ability to travel in space that is appealing, but the technology that is developed to get there and implications it has for use here on earth. A prime example of this is the technical advice NASA employees were able to provide the Chilean government in the 2010 rescue of the Chilean miners who were trapped in a collapsed copper mine 2,300 feet below the Earth's surface for 69 days. The advice they provided was based on the agency's experience in protecting humans in the hostile environment of space, like giving the miners too much food too quickly could be fatal, providing sunglasses for the miners to protect their eyes as they were pulled up from below the Earth's surface after being underground for 2 months, and making recommendations to the design of the capsule constructed to retrieve the trapped men (NASA Innovations, 2011).

It is also interesting to note that the Millennial workers tend to move through the ranks at a more rapid pace than their Baby Boomer counterparts of 20 to 30 years ago. This can especially be seen in the mission support organizations such as procurement, finance, human resources and information technology, where it may have taken someone 50 years of age today, 15 to 20 years to reach their promotion potential, it is not unusual for a Millennial to reach their full potential within 10 years or less. While this addresses the immediacy need of the Millennial, it does present another challenge for the organization. What carrot do you dangle to retain the Millennial who has reached his or her career potential so quickly? However, it should be noted based on a 2008 briefing to the NASA Strategic Management Council that while Millennials progress quickly, "today's workforce needs 10 years more time in NASA to get management experience compared to the workforce just 15 years ago" (Open NASA, 2009, Chart 13). As previously discussed this presents the need for training and development programs focused on professional and personal effectiveness and leadership capabilities, for example, NASA FIRST Program.

NASA must be doing something right. For the past 2 years (2010-2011) it has ranked 5th out of 308 in the Best Places to Work in the Federal Government survey. Over 266,000 employee responses were considered in analyzing the survey data, which measured employee satisfaction and commitment to the Federal Government (Partnership for Public Service, 2011). The areas receiving the highest ratings on the survey include employee engagement, overall quality of work, climate for innovation, employee safety, and selected supervisory practices (NASA 2011 Annual Employee Survey Results, 2011). Some of the related items indicative of these results include:

- When needed I am willing to put in the extra effort to get a job done.
- My work gives me a feeling of personal accomplishment.
- I am constantly looking for ways to do my job better.
- Creativity and innovation are rewarded.
- I feel encouraged to come up with new and better ways of doing things.
- My supervisor supports my need to balance work and other life issues.
- My supervisor/team leader listens to what I have to say.
- My supervisor/team leader treats me with respect.

The modification of NASA's on-boarding process has been discussed throughout this chapter; however, one key area remaining is performance standards. It is imperative for new employees to meet with their supervisor and be assigned performance standards soon after reporting for duty. Performance standards set the direction of the duties the employee should perform in the job and identify management expectations. Not having a performance plan in place creates difficulties later for both the employee and manager. A manager is unable to evaluate an employee's performance if the employee does know what work he or she is to be evaluated for performing. In the Federal Government an employee must have a performance rating before any form of recognition can be awarded. NASA has built into its on-boarding process a mechanism for reminding supervisors to develop performance plans prior to the new employee's start date. Follow up reminders are sent periodically to ensure the new employee is assigned a plan. This has aided in eliminating some of the frustration experienced by new employees in not understanding or knowing what work they should be performing. Getting supervisors to implement performance standards in a timely fashion for new employees continues to be a work in progress for NASA.

In 2011 interviews were conducted with new employees hired between October 2010 and July 2011 at NASA Langley Research Center. In conjunction with performance standards another area cited for improvement during the on-boarding process was the inability for new employees to understand where they fit within the organization. Employees would like to have more information about how their position and organization fits into the center and agency mission. It was recommended that when supervisors meet with the new employees during their first week of employment to review the performance plan, an organization chart with a brief description of the organization tying it to the agency mission be presented. One would think this is an obvious step in the on-boarding process; however, it is evidence that all HR functions need rekindling at times. For the Millennials this step is key to providing the structure they need to begin performing. Often when left to their own devices they get frustrated and move to organizations that can better provide what they need.

Jaderlund Casting

As previously mentioned, Jaderlund Casting utilizes multiple technologies in its business operations. Another source of technology infrastructure that taps into meeting the need for immediacy as well as the ability to provide recognition and encouragement to talent is the use of Skype. Jaderlund Casting utilizes Skype to facilitate meetings and interactions with both talent and producers. This allows the organization to communicate over the Skype infrastructure as needed without concern to time zones or geographical barriers as this service is available to bring the parties together in a format conducive for conducting business meetings. Skype has also been used in training interventions as well as performance assessments to close geographic distances between Jaderlund Casting representatives and talent. Talent is afforded the opportunity to audition immediately for the Casting Directors utilizing Skype versus having to videotape themselves and submit the tapes. Skype also provides the opportunity for the talent to get feedback on their performance in real time since there is a two-way connection between the Jaderlund Casting organization and the candidate who is auditioning. Using Skype has also resulted in cost savings for the Jaderlund Casting organization as there are lesser expenses which are incurred related to travel expenditures as well as a lower number of hours spent by the Casting Directors given that the necessity to travel is minimized. While costs are easier to determine, it is difficult to ascertain the benefits achieved by the talent being auditioned as it is hard to put a price on the encouragement provided to these individuals through this feedback mechanism as typically there may be no feedback provided with the submission of a videotape.

IDEAS FOR FUTURE HR PRACTICES TO TAP INTO MILLENNIALS

NASA

Millennial employees at NASA Langley Research Center were interviewed to gain insight into what they would see as beneficial to them and their career from an HR infrastructure perspective. One individual spoke of the ability to have more interaction with senior leaders in the context of a mentoring role. The desired goal would be to have a structured time, for example, once a month to sit with the leader and have an interchange of knowledge sharing. This seemed to be more appealing than attending an "Open Door" session held by the senior leader. The mentoring session would be less intimidating and would have a specific purpose. This aligns with the Millennial's need for structure and inclusion.

Another recommendation focused on development. The idea was to provide new employees an action learning opportunity. It would involve allowing them to work on a project where they could jump in feet first with the support of a mentor to "prove" themselves. Having support and guidance in the project would be a key factor, especially when given a lead role in the project. The individual providing this idea believed this would help in eliminating some of the prejudices that exist in the workplace surrounding the idea that younger employees are "just kids, who don't know anything." The action learning project would be a mechanism for proving they can contribute early in their career and in a meaningful way.

An important function the HR community should address in the near future is performance and how it is measured. In the past managers viewed a productive employee as one who was in his seat everyday producing something. With work-life balance initiatives now in play, this is not an accurate measure for performance. In addition to producing something employees should also be measured for the impact they make in the workplace. Maybe the measure is not the number of widgets the individual in the factory makes, but it is the value an individual adds by identifying a way to eliminate waste. The impact of how the individual streamlined the process allowing more widgets to be produced becomes what is valued rather than peers believing the individual is not pulling his weight because he is not building widgets. Having this paradigm shift would be huge in making Millennials feel empowered to make greater contributions in the workplace.

Jaderlund Casting

Jaderlund Casting recognizes the needs of the Millennial generation and has tapped into these various needs given the examples previously provided. One area that Jaderlund is exploring is the use of Twitter to reach its current constituents as well as expand interaction with other potential clients and talent. Use of this medium would allow for the Casting Directors quickly to disseminate information or hold impromptu meetings as necessary. Given that Millennials are adept at the use of technology this might be a good next step for interacting with this generation and increasing the reach of Casting messages.

Another potential area for exploration is that of using a blog to promote Jaderlund Casting activities as well as spotlight talent. Casting previously used an e-mail to distribute this type of information; however, by using a blog, the information could simply be put on the company's website to facilitate communications. Updates could be made frequently and expeditiously and would not inundate users with unnecessary information. Additionally, unlike the utilization of e-mail, previous information discussed on the blog would remain in reverse chronological order so that users of the blog could easily access the information as necessary.

An added innovative practice that Jaderlund Casting is employing is the use of Quick Response codes (QR codes) on business cards and other marketing materials. QR codes are two-dimensional matrix bar codes. Korhan (2011) describes these codes as being similar to barcodes used in inventory tracking and product placement with the key difference being that a QR code can hold thousands of characters of information. These QR codes can be scanned with a camera-enabled Smartphone or other such device, and this serves to link back to digital content on the Internet. Korhan (2011) noted that the QR codes are useful in being able to "connect people with each other and to multimedia digital content" (QR Codes 101, para. 5). Jaderlund Casting's QR code is linked back to the company website where scanners can access company information, a trailer with the casting promotional information, as well as the latest media and press coverage. This will also allow Jaderlund Casting to expand its reach to multiple constituents of the Millennial generation through the use of print combined with electronic media.

CONCLUSION

In this chapter we have defined the values of the Millennial generation which serve as the basis for our discussion. An individual's values do have a significant impact and influence on behaviors and thus interactions both personally and professionally in all facets of life. Collectively, we have defined the values for the Millennial generation in terms of the broad categories of immediacy, teaming, and recognition. As we have noted, values can, and do, change over time, so it will be incumbent upon organizations to stay in tune with to the ebbs and flows within society.

An individual's values system can have an impact on the way HR operates within the organizational infrastructure. The various HR processes should be aligned with these values systems, as we showed when we explored the importance of the use of technology when communicating with the Millennial generation. Communications are an important part of our societal network. We must also keep in mind, however, that the organization has to recognize that there needs to be service to multiple generations that are employed within the workplace so as not to inadvertently overlook the larger potential for synergy between the employer and employees.

In this chapter we have provided examples from two organizations' HR practices that tap into the value systems for Millennials. The National Aeronautics and Space Administration (NASA) and Jaderlund Casting are distinctly different organizations; however, one thing they have in common is that they currently employ Millennials and will continue to do so for many years. These organizations are embracing this generation's values as seen in the examples provided regarding the employment of HR infrastructure to cultivate relationships with these individuals. It stands to reason that these organizations will continue to evolve their processes as they strive to fulfill their missions and conduct their business.

Overall, much can be gleaned from having an understanding of this generation's values system and what this means for HR and the organization at large. It is not beyond expectation that organizations will have to employ leading-edge practices, such as those described above, to attract and retain Millennials. Overall, we recommend that further research be conducted on what Millennials want and how organizations can best craft an experience that will exceed their expectations.

REFERENCES

Fox, A. (2011). Mixing it up. Society for Human Resource Management. Retrieved from http://www.weknownext.com/workforce/mixing-it-up

Hughes, K. (2011). What does Generation "Why?" really want? Society for Human Resource Management. Retrieved from http://www.weknownext.com/workforce/what-does-generation-why-really-want

Jaderlund Casting Website (2011). Retrieved from http://jaderlundcasting.com/cmi/?page_id=55

Jayson, S. (2010, February 23). Study: Millennial generation more educated, less employed. *USA TODAY*. Retrieved from http://www.usatoday.com/news/education/2010-02-24-millennials24_ST_N.htm

Korhan, J. (2011). How QR codes can grow your business. Retrieved from: http://www.socialmediaexaminer.com/how-qr-codes-can-grow-your-business/

Langley History. (2011). NASA Langley—On the leading edge since 1917. Retrieved from http://www.nasa.gov/centers/langley/about/history.html

Leadership NASA. (2011). Retrieved from http://leadership.nasa.gov/nasa_first/home.htm

Lee, J. (2011). Managing the Millennial generation. Newsletter for Small Business Owners. *Small Business Review*. Retrieved from http://smallbusinessreview.com/human_resources/managing-millennial-generation/

Lipkin, N., & Perrymore, A. (2009). *Y in the workplace: Managing the me-first generation*. Pompton Place, NJ:Career Press.

NASA. (2011). Retrieved from www.NASA.gov

NASA 2011 Annual Employee Survey Results. (2011, September). Retrieved from https://searchbus.nssc.nasa.gov/servlet/sm.web.Fetch/NASA_2011_AES_Reportpdf

NASA Innovations. (2011). President honors NASA's role in Chilean mine rescue. Retrieved from www.nasa.gov/news/chile

Open NASA (2009). Rebalancing NASA's workforce. Retrieved from www.open.NASA.gov

Open NASA (2011). The Next Gen space workforce. Retrieved from www.open.NASA.gov

Other NASA News. (2011). Retrieved from http://www.open.NASA.gov

Partnership for Public Service. (2011). Best places to work rankings 2011. Retrieved from http://bestplacestowork.org

PEW Research Center. (2011). Retrieved from www.Pewresearch.org/pubs/1501/millennials-new-survey-generational-upbeat-open-new-ideas-technology-bound

Rizzo, R. (2009). Creating synergy in a four-generation workplace. Society for Human Resource Management, SHRM Academic Initiatives. Alexandria, VA.

Society for Human Resources Management. (2011). *Generation Y goes directly to source in job hunt.* Retrieved from http://www.weknownext.com/workforce/generation-y-goes-directly-to-source-in-job-hunt

Wright, A. (2010). Millennials: "Bathed in bits." Society for Human Resource Management. Retrieved from http://www.weknownext.com/workforce/millenials-bathed-in-bits

CHAPTER 14

MILLENNIAL-CENTRIC STRATEGIC HR

Key Practices for Attracting, Developing, and Retaining Millennials

Scott A. Quatro

THE GENERATIONAL CULTURE REVOLUTION IS UNDERWAY!

The Millennials are coming. And understanding the uniqueness of the Millennial Generation is critical to on-going business success (Hershatter & Epstein, 2010; Walmsley, 2007). The current situation at one of my long-term client organizations clearly demonstrates these truths. Chattem is over 130 years old. Several of its brands (Gold Bond, Pamprin, Bull-Frog) have been market leaders for many decades. The company has enjoyed a stable workforce, a stable management team, and steady growth throughout its history. It's not uncommon to meet a Chattem employee that has been with the company for over 25 years (current Chief Executive Officer [CEO] Zan Guerry has led Chattem since 1990). In fact, I recently shared in the retirement celebrations of two departing employees, each of

Managing Human Resources for the Millennial Generation, pp. 323–333
Copyright © 2012 by Information Age Publishing
All rights of reproduction in any form reserved.

which left behind a legacy of over 50 years of service to the company. To be sure, for most of Chattem's history, "slow and steady" has won the race.

But in December of 2010 the pace picked up considerably. Chattem was acquired by Sanofi-Aventis (a $41 B global healthcare company) as their growth vehicle for the North American OTC pharmaceutical and personal care product markets. In less than 2 years the revenue base of the company has increased by almost 50%, with multiple new product offerings fueling the growth. The faithful, and "aged" (more on this somewhat bemusing observation in my concluding remarks) Chattem employee base has been pushed to its limits. Put simply, a revolution of sorts is underway at Chattem. As the human capital-related demands multiply, more Millennials (by very necessity) are being hired. And the generational "culture-war" is being waged. Chattem will truly never be the same.

MILLENNIALS ARE DIFFERENT

The simple fact is that Millennials are different from the other three generations they now work alongside, and most current executives simply don't understand them (Barzilai-Nahon & Mason, 2010; Espinoza, Ukleja, & Rusch, 2010). The fact that for the first time in history U.S. companies are managing four generations of workers (Atkinson, 2008; Jenkins, 2008) only magnifies the uniqueness of this new generation of employees, as conveyed by Table 14.1.

The Millennial Generation is the first to grow up in a truly connected global community. The technology with which they are very comfortable ensures this connectivity, which leads and empowers them to seamlessly transition from personal to professional life at any moment. In that sense, Millennials lead a very integrated life. All of this culminates in Millennials being most motivated by meaningfulness. A great example of this is TOMS Shoes. The company sells shoes, primarily as a means of then contributing shoes to under-privileged children around the world on a one-for-one basis. For every pair of shoes sold by TOMS, a pair is donated by TOMS to a needy child. Millennials are compelled by this meaningfulness, and the globalism and integration behind it. Virtually all of TOMS customers are Millennials, most of which (I suspect) would clamor to secure a job with the company if given the opportunity.

ATTRACTING, DEVELOPING, AND RETAINING MILLENNIALS

Clearly not every company can have a purpose as compelling or altruistic as that of TOMS. But I am convinced that all employers can be more

Table 14.1. Comparing Four Generations of U.S. Employees as of 2012

Generation	Years Born	Primary Age of Current Employees	Population	Core Work-Related Values	Core Work Motivation
Silents	1925-1945	mid 60s to mid 70s	21.6MM	Nationalism, loyalty	Security
Baby Boomers	1946-1964	50s to mid 60s	58.8MM	Meritocracy, industriousness	Prosperity
Generation X-ers	1965-1980	mid 30s to 40s	64.8MM	Individualism, balance	Autonomy
Millennials	1980-2000	20s to mid 30s	62.7MM	Globalism, integration	Meaningfulness

Millennial-centric in their efforts to attract, develop, and retain employees. That is, all employers can be more like TOMS. It begins with understanding the uniqueness of Millennials as global-minded employees leading integrated lives in search of higher-order purpose, and then building key strategic HR practices that reflect this understanding. To that end, I outline the following as key Millennial-centric, strategic HR practices (juxtaposed against their traditional HR practice manifestations)

Employer Branding Versus Job Advertising

Traditionally, HR has emphasized job advertising as the primary means of attracting candidates for a particular role. But Millennials are more compelled by the larger employer context than they are by the specifics of the job itself. As a result, employer branding is critical for organizations intent on successfully attracting and hiring Millennials.

Organizational Purpose Versus Shareholder Wealth Maximization

Historically, shareholder wealth maximization has been at the center of organizational purpose for most companies. While this may be compelling to other generations, it is much less so for Millennials. Thus, HR must have a voice in the articulation of the mission and core values statements that delineate strategic purpose and philosophy, and these statements of purpose must go beyond articulating employees as "assets." This is challenging on two distinct levels. First, HR has traditionally not had the opportunity to have a voice in the shaping of such strategic statements/frameworks. Second, HR will have to overcome the powerfully shared assumption that business purpose is centrally about shareholder wealth maximization.

Personal and Peer Coaching Versus Performance Appraisal

Traditionally, HR has emphasized performance appraisals as summative, annual events. While this transactional approach to managing employee performance has been largely acceptable to older employees (while still not optimal), Millennials find it simply untenable. Rather, Millennials expect performance feedback to be both relationally based and concurrent with observed behavior, consistent with a personal coaching approach to evaluating and shaping employee behavior.

Work-Life Integration Versus Work-Life Balance

HR has long been a proponent of work-life balance, espousing the merits of paid time off and flexible work hours. While this is admirable in its goal of encouraging employee balance, Millennials expect a subtle but important shift toward work-life integration. Thus, the traditional boundaries between "work" and "life" become blurred, and even what constitutes "on the clock time" versus "personal time" becomes more fluid. In short, Millennials are remarkably adept at integrating work priorities and life priorities, and getting things done regardless of where and when they get them done. "Face time" at the office or "personal time" away from the office are not priorities for them at all. Having the flexibility to get things done, on-site or remotely, synchronously or asynchronously, is what they expect.

One company that seems to really get all of this is Google, currently the 17th most valuable company in the U.S. based on market capitalization ($147.2B), and 10th most valuable in terms of market capitalization per employee ($6.03MM). For illustrative purposes, the story of Google's strategic HR practices is woven through the remainder of the chapter.

Build an Employer Brand

The days of generic brands are over. Consumers are no longer satisfied with the prospect of purchasing Citrus Soda or Lemon-Lime soda. Instead, they insist on Mountain Dew, or Mello Yello, or at least Mountain Lightning (the Wal-Mart private label brand offering in the same product category). The same is true for employer brands, especially in regards to Millennials. As employees, Millennials desire to psychologically and emotionally identify with the brand identity of their employer organization. They desire for their employer's brand identity to be an extension and expression of their personhood. This is one of the many ways Millennials foster integration and meaningfulness in their lives.

The implications here for strategic HR staffing practices are significant, and far reaching:

1. *Dedicate budgetary resources to employer branding and related marketing activities*. This is a must for employers in order to attract Millennials into their workforce. Google's corporate website is dominated

by employer branding content and messaging, galvanized by the campaign theme "Let's Work Together."

2. *Commit to continuous recruitment.* Just as PepsiCo never stops advertising Mountain Dew, employers must never stop selling their employer brand. The lack of current openings must never be an excuse for pulling out of the employment market. Google's corporate website includes multiple links designed to pull potential employees into their candidate pool. It's Google's version of "banner ads" for marketing themselves as an employer of choice, and they don't want to lose any potential "sales." Granted, Google currently has significant on-going hiring needs. But I'm convinced that if and when the company confronts a "hiring freeze" or even a reduction in force, Google will still be actively marketing to potential "Googlers."

3. *Maintain an active presence on college campuses.* Aggressively seek to build brand equity with Millennials before they ever enter the workforce. Tailor the brand messaging and positioning to a college student demographic. Google's current brand campaign theme for college students is "Google Your Future. Awesome Starts Here." The days of simply posting an opening with the college career development office are over.

4. *Sell the employer brand, not the job.* Millennials are less compelled by the specifics of the job than the purpose and meaningfulness of the employer as conveyed via the employer brand. The job posting area of Google's corporate website focuses primarily on selling employee candidates the opportunity to "change the world" and "impact millions of people's lives," and only secondarily on the more technical role description and qualifications associated with particular job openings.

Taking all of these employer-branding steps accomplishes two key things. It provides a compelling message to Millennials to attract them into your workforce, and it continually energizes your incumbent workforce of Millennials (as well as others).

Emphasize Higher Order Organizational Purpose

A surefire way to lose the interest of Millennials is to espouse the importance of maximizing shareholder return. This is simply not a core interest of Millennials, and it's certainly not the reason they want to work for your company. Rather, promulgate and aggressively celebrate the mis-

PART IV

SPECIAL ISSUES AND CONTEXTS

CHAPTER 15

PROMISES OF TELECOMMUTING AND PREFERENCES OF MILLENNIALS

Exploring the Nexus

**Ajantha S. Dharmasiri, Danielle Beu Ammeter,
John E. Baur and M. Ronald Buckley**

INTRODUCTION

There are currently four generations in the workforce—Traditionalists/
Silent Generation (born between 1909 and 1945), Baby Boomers (born
between 1946 and 1964), Generation Xers (born between 1965 and 1979)
and Millennials (born between 1980 and 1999). In the U.S., there are
approximately 30 million Traditionalists/Silent Generation, 79 million
Baby Boomers, 51 million Generation Xers and 75 million Millennials
(half of which are already in the workforce). Each generation brings a
unique historical perspective that shapes interpersonal and business
biases. In order to be successful, leaders need to understand each generation and how best to work with them. Most executives and managers are
Baby Boomers, who evaluate themselves and others based on hours spent

Managing Human Resources for the Millennial Generation, pp. 337–354
Copyright © 2012 by Information Age Publishing
All rights of reproduction in any form reserved.

on the job—and that means face time. The term "workaholic" was coined to describe the Baby Boomers' work ethic. But over the next 15 years, this generation will be retiring—replaced by Generation Xers and Millennials. Those in Generation X are more interested in balance and less concerned about hierarchy—and they embrace technology. Millennials have never known a world without laptops, cell phones, and remote controls. This generation is also well networked and used to open, constant communication. These four generations, with different historical perspectives, different priorities, and different ways of interacting with the world, need to be managed in a way that accommodates their preferences and meets the goals of the organization.

From this brief introduction, it is clear that the generational differences we are witnessing in the workforce have been partially spurred by the interaction of technology and individual difference variables. In this chapter, we will illustrate how this interaction is leading to the nexus of telecommuting and Millennials.

Millennials in Focus

Who are the Millennials, also known as Nexters, Generation Net and Generation Y? What makes Millennials, as a generation, unique? The popular press has many adjectives to describe them ... open-minded, diverse, sociable, outgoing, assertive, optimistic, confident, collaborative, well connected, brash, outspoken, bold thinkers, highly educated, mobile, flexible, environmentally sensitive and unconventional (Pew Research Center, 2012). But the number one descriptor of this generation is "tech savvy." The Millennials were brought up with internet connectivity to the world and now they are the first "always connected" generation. They use their handheld smart phones as an extension of who they are. It allows them to connect 24 hours a day by text, e-mail, and phone calls. It is normal for Millennials to check in by smart device all weekend, as long as they have flexibility during the week. They can use these devices for internet searches, songs, videos, news, games and more. They thrive in this multitasking environment. They also embrace multiple modes of self expression using social networking sites, blogs, and YouTube. As such, they believe technology actually connects people. They have a sense of community fostered by relationships with an extensive network of colleagues and friends established and maintained over the internet. Whereas a Baby Boomer might expect a phone call or a face to face meeting, a Millennial may prefer working with virtual teams and virtual problem solving. This generation relies on technology to perform their jobs better and in an unconventional working environment, making physical location less important.

This generation respects and appreciates the moral values and work ethic of older generations. However, they are the first generation that did not use "work ethic" as one of its principal claims to distinctiveness (Pew Research Center, 2010). Millennials are much more concerned with a desire to balance work and family life, have meaningful work and autonomy (Buckley, Beu, Novicevic, & Sigerstad, 2001). They grew up with school shootings, 9/11, terrorism as a real threat, and wars in several parts of the world, so they tend to have a sense that life really is short and they place a high value on self-fulfillment. They do want to work, but they do not want work to be their lives. Again, they have always had the internet, which allows us to get information quickly and efficiently. This has made them accustomed to efficiency, which they seek in all aspects of life. They pay attention to their own peak efficiency times and they like to work when they are most productive, not necessarily 8 to 5. Instead, Millennials like to work on a schedule that fits their personality and at a time of day where they feel most energized to do what they have to do. As such, they are very interested in and are asking for more flexible work arrangements. According to Nicholas and Guzman (2009), autonomy, work-life balance and computer competence are the key drivers for Millennials to opt for telecommuting.

This is also a generation that is much more conscious of ecological issues and the need to go green. In 2006, the movie *An Inconvenient Truth* won both critical and box office success, including two Academy Awards, and has been credited with helping to promote a very environmentally aware generation. One emerging trend associated with Millennials is their preference toward eco-friendly work patterns (Boroff, 2011). According to Boroff, the Millennials are frontrunners in the "Going Green" movement, which is adopting and developing technologies intended to conserve energy. Such a movement can reduce carbon footprints, which can be caused by many variables. The Millennials' preferences for an environmentally focused work environment are very strong, not only in the physical aspects of the workplace, but also in their way of working such as flexible working, travel, etcetera. For instance, driving to and from work every day can be both exhausting for the person working and harmful to the planet. As Boroff (2011) comments, the "average [commute time] is fairly large, as many people will spend approximately 60 minutes or more per day traveling to and from work." Also, the green technologies that are associated with telecommuting, like cloud computing and the increased use of web conferencing, have brought the workplace to a new and even more competitive level. Any company that does not consider its effects on the planet will have a hard time attracting this new generation of green workers.

As we move forward in our discussion of telecommuting, we will make the argument that the technology savvy Millennials with a preference for work-life balance and green employers will continue to change the working environment to one more focused on results and less on face time.

THE NATURE OF TELECOMMUTING

Telecommuting or telework is considered as working outside the conventional workplace and communicating with it by way of telecommunications or computer-based technology (Nilles, 1994; Olson & Primps, 1984). As one of several forms of "work-at-home," this chapter uses the term "telecommuting" to refer to work carried out by employees of organizations in which the employees experience significant flexibility in working location and hours of work.

Certain factors in the last couple of decades have led toward the reliance on, and adoption of, telecommuting in the workplace. The first major factor contributing to more organizations considering telecommuting has been the recent financial crisis in America and elsewhere. Organizations can save money by reducing the amount of work space and other work environment enhancers in the organization's office. Campbell (2007) makes the point that less money is spent on workstations, maintenance, utility bills, common office space, and insurance. Both the organization and the individual employee can benefit financially from telecommuting. Ransom (2010) suggests that thanks to improved technology and the high price of gasoline (i.e., transportation) working remotely has become an increasingly popular—and less expensive— option for both large and small workforces. This is particularly important to Millennials just starting out. While the Millennials are on track to become the most educated generation in American history, their entry into the job market during the Great Recession has been difficult and 67% of college graduates carry an average debt of $23,200 (Project on Student Debt, Quick Facts January, 2010). Approximately a third of Millennials depend on financial support from their families, live with their parents, are uninsured and cannot pay their bills (AFL-CIO Young Workers: A Lost Decade, 2009; Pew Research Center, 2010). Organizations that support telecommuting for their employees help reduce those employees' work-related costs, such as work clothing, dry cleaning, transportation/fuel, lunches out, child care, and so on.

Organizations that use telecommuting have more potential to succeed in the event of a natural disaster, terrorist attack, or epidemic. Caine

(2009) has suggested that there may be advantages to telecommuting during the traditional height of flu season, not to mention winter blizzards and weather calamities. Some experts are advising that businesses prepare for the worst by planning to allow employees to telecommute when these types of events occur. For example, in the immediate aftermath of the terrorist attacks of 9/11, preestablished telework practices at American Express helped ensure that the business could continue functioning. By decentralizing the workforce, organizations can still maintain operational readiness under almost any unforeseen and unanticipated situation.

Organizations may also implement telecommuting in order to retain geographical freedom in the ever-changing work environment. Some organizations do not have a static geographical base. Instead they rely solely on telecommuting. Organizations can maintain an employee pool worldwide with employees in many time zones, and each person can work at hours convenient for himself or herself and conducive to one's optimal performance level. Millennials in particular like the concept of being location independent.

By allowing employees to work anywhere and anytime, telecommuting offers employees greater opportunity to balance work and personal life. With flexible schedules and mobile technology, employees are no longer tied down to one specific location during the work day in order to accomplish their responsibilities. As employer-employee relationships are becoming less hierarchical and more transactional, workers are able to choose their own method of work, which allows them to pay attention to desired results instead of prescriptive processes. The increased scheduling flexibility gives the employees the opportunity to provide more care to their families; an absolute necessity for single parents taking care of their children (a significantly large worldwide demographic).

Millennials prioritize family and lifestyle over physical presence in the office, and they value the ability to control when they are on and off the job. Another personal benefit of telecommuting is improved wellness because the stress related to travel to and from work can be nearly eliminated, thus producing a happier worker. Employees also save time by eliminating the commute to and from work. These hours can be used for personal pursuits or as additional hours in the work week, thus creating more efficiency and job satisfaction among employees. Millennials' preferences for elastic schedules and multitasking mean their workday may span longer hours or pack more activity. By controlling their schedules, they are able to manage their work to satisfy their needs for work-life balance.

The factors mentioned above have led to many workers in myriad locations replacing their commute to an office with a walk from their bedroom to their living room. Telecommuting to work is trending upward all over the world. A recent survey in *PCworld* (Kanaracus, 2007) indicates that approximately 23% of all workers regularly do their work from some place other than the office, and approximately 27.5% of the US workforce telecommutes. What is more, 84 of *Fortune*'s 100 Best Companies to Work For list allow employees to work from home at least 20% of the time. In 2010, the amount of employers who encourage or allow telecommuting was 44%, up from 19% in 2007 (2010 survey by the National Small Business Association). Millennials account for 42% of the telecommuting population according to a 2009 study by the Telework Advisory Group.

Between new technology and a global workforce, organizations are implementing flexible work arrangements for everyone. It is perceived as a cost-effective, flexible and eco-friendly alternative to traditional work. Millennials are leading the charge for this change because they do not want to work in the same environment as their parents. According to Schwabel (2011), this is important since Millennials will represent 75% of the workforce in 2025. In such a context, telecommuting emerges as one way organizations can help staff be more productive, as well as improve retention by increasing employee engagement.

It must be noted, though, that telecommuting—while desired by most Millennials—is not always the best arrangement for individual and organizational productivity. In the pages that follow, we present a model and discussion of critical success factors for telecommuting. We then show how this model can guide decision making with respect to its use not only with Millennials, but with all members of an organization's workforce.

Critical Success Factors for Telecommuting

The popular press tends to talk about telecommuting as though it is a perfect way to demonstrate a trusting work environment and create more loyal employees. However, telecommuting is not always successful. When a telecommuting experience is unsuccessful, an organization may decide that it should do away with the entire program because they believe the type of organization or type of job is not conducive to telecommuting. However, this conclusion may be premature, as they are overlooking another important variable—the suitability of an individual for a telecommuting experience. The model that follows shows that it is the confluence of a number of individual and organizational issues that will contribute to the appropriateness of the telecommuting experience.

A critical look at both the organization and the talents of the available workforce will provide a gross yardstick for considering the potential for the implementation of telecommuting. The two most important factors are (see Figure 15.1): (1) The organizational and individual capacity

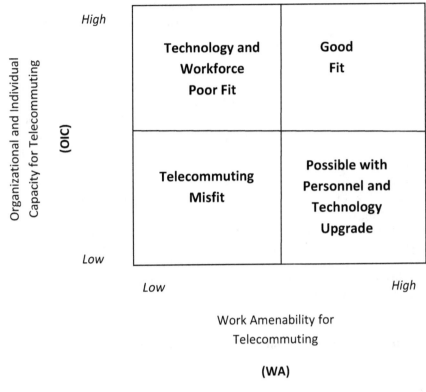

Figure 15.1.   Telecommuting typologies.

(OIC) for telecommuting, and (2) The amenability of the work (WA) to telecommuting.

If the OIC and the WA are both high then the situation appears to be a good fit for telecommuting. In a situation where OIC is high and WA is low there appears to be a situation in which there is a poor level of fit between the well prepared workforce and the type of work not appropriate for telecommuting. If OIC is low but the WA is high, telecommuting may be possible if an organization makes an attempt to upgrade both technology and the level of personnel employed by the organization. If WA and OIC are both low, then it can be concluded that telecommuting is a poor fit in this situation. This is just a first step an organization should take in evaluating the decision of implementing a telecommuting option. If organizational and individual capacities are high and the work is amenable to telecommuting, then the organization should move on to other, more detailed, considerations which influence this decision.

There are several research studies that can be cited in support of the above model. Ellison (1999), in describing the social impacts of telework, stressed the importance of a fit between organizational and individual factors. Garrett and Danziger (2007) discuss individual characteristics, organizational and technological contexts in their proposed taxonomy of technology-mediated work at a distance. Telework impacting occupational health (Montreuil & Lippel, 2003), effect of telecommuting on worker performance (de Croon, Sluiter, Kuijer, & Fringsdresen, 2005), work performance and location significance (Redman, Snape, & Ashurst, 2009), telecommuting in a changing workplace (Thatcher & Zhu, 2006), managing emotions at telework (Marsh & Musson, 2008), flexible work and turnover (Stavrou & Kilaniotis, 2010), telecommuting and work-life balance (Eikhof, Warhurst, & Haunschild, 2007), job satisfaction in telecommuting (Ilozor, Ilozor, & Carr, 2001), meaning of telework (Illegems & Verbeke, 2004), collaborative technologies in telework (Belanger & Allport, 2008), effects of cognitive styles on telework (Workman, Kahnweiler, & Bommer, 2003), workers' propensity to telecommute (Belanger, 1999), and justice and control in telecommuting (Kurland & Egan, 1999) can be cited as other related research.

Factors Influencing Ability and Desire for Telecommuting

The literature clearly shows the influence of *Job-related/Work Amenability* factors and *Organizational/Individual Capacity* factors on the individual's ability and desire to telecommute. Focusing on amenability of the work, idiosyncratic details of individual jobs, rather than general job traits, are more likely to determine whether a specific individual can telecommute (Mokhtarian, 1998). Perceptions of job suitability based on intimate knowledge of specific jobs, rather than global job categories, may better predict who can telecommute (Bailey & Kurland, 2002).

Telecommuting is not necessary, or even possible, in all situations. Organizational leadership needs to exercise rational decision-making to determine what positions, as well as how many employees, they can offer telecommuting to. Organizations must maintain a delicate balance of what needs to happen in person and what can be done with telework. In determining whether telecommuting will work for a company, one factor to consider is the amenability of the work.

- Review the business and customer requirements of the job, independent of scheduling considerations.
- Evaluate the impact of telecommuting on the ability to meet customers' needs, as well as those of teammates.

- Identify potential problems or obstacles to meeting customer and other business requirements.
- Consider what communication techniques will most effectively support the telecommuting arrangement.
- Assess the impact on compensation and benefits, safety and security, taxes, workers compensation and liability.

Based on this evaluation, the employee and the organization can determine if the specific job role can be accomplished successfully by telecommuting. While most jobs can accommodate some degree of flexibility, independent, task-based work is a particularly good match for telecommuting.

The second factor to consider is organizational and individual capacity. Organizational capacity is not just about the technology available, but also includes the ability of the manager or supervisor to support the employee's telecommuting arrangement. A key to successful teleworking is the ongoing commitment and involvement from the manager/supervisor. This person must be able to manage or supervise for results by working with the employee to develop shared, measureable goals. The manager/supervisor must give timely, clear feedback, be open and flexible, and be able to effectively manage the entire team of both office and teleworking staff. A study based on samples of more than 500 workers in public agencies in the United States reflected that organizational factors are most predictive of an individual's choice to work remotely (Mannering & Mokhtarian, 1995). As Mannering & Mokhtarian reported, these organizational factors included the manager's willingness, workplace interaction, and self-perceived job suitability. If the manager is willing, the employee and manager will assess the needs, work habits, and performance of the employee requesting a telecommuting arrangement. Those who succeed in telecommuting tend to have solid, successful job experience, are highly self-motivated, independent/self-directed, strong team players, effective communicators across a variety of media, and able to work well with limited or no supervision.

In addition to individual characteristics, family-related issues need to be taken into consideration. A number of individual and family attributes, such as lack of personal discipline, household distractions, preference to work with a team, family orientation, and workaholism affect the suitability of telecommuting (Mannering & Mokhtarian, 1997). With respect to other family related factors, maintaining a healthy work-life balance (e.g. Shamir & Salamon, 1985) has been identified as a factor influencing an individual's choice for telecommuting. A job involving telecommuting was found to attract candidates who seek a higher work-life balance and thereby influences the job choice (Thompson, 2009). A study involving public sector employees in Germany found that lower family-work conflict was a psychological influencer for home-based telecommuting (Hornung, 2009). Employees expect greater autonomy and flexibility with telecommuting that could lead to better balancing of private and professional duties (Taskin & Devos, 2005).

Employee and Employer Responsibilities With Telecommuting

Organizational leadership has certain responsibilities toward employees who telecommute. Ransom (2010) offers organizations guidance in managing telecommuting by suggesting they start off slow, utilize probationary periods, set expectations, use appropriate technology, do not "stalk" employees, and establish clear performance measurements. Leaders must assign specific responsibility and guidelines to the employee. They should work with the employee to establish reasonable expectations for quality and quantity of work. Furthermore, performance-based results should be valued over number of hours spent behind a desk. Organizations display trust when they empower employees, as well as increase employee autonomy with work-related tasks and responsibilities, when they allow employees to telecommute. With increased trust toward employees, equity theory would predict that companies can expect to gain a return of trust toward the organization from telecommuting employees.

Telecommuting may not be offered to every employee, so it is very important to have a telecommuting policy that clearly explains who can and cannot participate. Human resources professionals are deeply involved in setting policies and procedures, ensuring technical support, providing training and development for off-site workers, and establishing work/life balance guidelines that ensure the success of virtual working (Schramm, 2010). Organizations must perform appropriate risk and screening processes prior to implementing telecommuting into an employee's work schedule. One option is to offer telecommuting to an employee after s/he has earned trust and shown responsibility in a traditional work climate. Because employees may be in different time zones, time synchronization is another responsibility of the employer. Time differences present certain constraints on project deadlines, company meetings, or simply timely responses to e-mail. As you can see, any organization considering telecommuting must understand the large amount of planning and preparation to set up this type of program for their staff.

To earn the privilege of telecommuting, employees must demonstrate responsibility to the organization. The employee is expected to meet goals and deadlines, perhaps even display an increase of performance with the increased responsibility and independence. They must also be available for meetings and respond to inquiries, just as if they were in an office. Regardless of what the organization may task an employee, it is the ultimate responsibility of the employee to delineate work from personal life. However, organizations and employees generally work together to determine guidelines for work hours and circumstances when an employee can be called during nonwork hours.

Essentially, the employee and the employer must exhibit trust and responsibility toward one another in telecommuting situations. Although they both have increased responsibility and communication requirements, the employer is ultimately responsible for the success or failure of the telecommuting worker. The employer has to provide the same standards of an office environment to an employee's at-home workstation. Because the employee has increased autonomy, organizational leadership must provide appropriate performance measures to ensure the employee understands what needs to be done to be successful—both with telecommuting and with the organization.

Telecommuting and Social Interaction

A serious consideration that accompanies telecommuting is based upon the time and place model of social interaction, which is a two-by-two matrix with time zone on one axis and place/location on the other. When people are in the same physical location, and thus the same time zone, it is easy for staff to get together to discuss business. Once telecommuting is introduced, so too are different place/same time and different place/different time situations. Each of these combinations has serious considerations associated with it.

For any different place situation, regular telecommuting may make some workers feel isolated from the informal networks and opportunities to socialize with others that those in the office enjoy. They may also believe they do not have the same opportunities to interact with influential others, which may be important in certain growth or advancement opportunities. Congruent with the lost opportunity to interact is the inability to share information through informal communications and the inability to seek and receive concurrent feedback upon issues at work. With respect to the different time/different place interactions, individuals experience a temporal asynchrony, the result of which is, from a learning perspective, the ineffectiveness of receiving feedback that is not temporally contiguous with performance. Furthermore, telecommuting may be hindered by four key biases:

1. *The temporal synchrony bias:* Since employees are working at different times, when a misunderstanding occurs, it is accompanied by an inability to correct these misunderstandings in a timely fashion. A misunderstanding uncorrected may result in the expending of significant effort toward goals that are incorrect.

2. *The squeaky wheel bias:* People have a tendency to become rude and impulsive when communicating electronically, becoming more adversarial than when communicating face-to-face. Factors that usually suppress negative emotions in person are absent when communicating electronically.

3. *The sinister attribution bias:* Individuals have a tendency to misattribute the behavior of others and this is exacerbated when the only communication with individuals is via computer. Similarly, some are likely to ascribe diabolical intentions to those they do not know and they are more likely to mistrust and suspect the other party of lying when contact with them is via a computer. In fact, people are more likely to attempt to deceive others over the computer.

4. *The burned bridge bias:* When interacting over a computer, individuals have a tendency to engage in more risky behavior in terms of threats and demands. They neglect many of the "politeness rituals" that are so important from a business perspective. They may ignore the "social lubricant" which is important in managing and directing others. Many of these issues can be minimized by building in face-to-face time with telecommuters—establishing strong, trusting relationships. This is especially true with Millennials. According to the OXYGENZ project by Johnson Controls (2012), Millennials are not seeking a home based work environment—they want a place to go to work. There does need to be a legitimate reason for requiring office hours or face time, but once they understand, Millennials are eager to learn and collaborate at the office. They value a healthy mix of face to face and flexible work from home schedules.

Repercussions

Despite its many advantages, telecommuting has potential hazards to the specific employee, and thus to the effectiveness of the organization. Individuals are vulnerable to merging work and personal life when they work from home. Employees may be motivated to work more diligently and efficiently during the day when they do not feel tied down to their "workspace" from 9 A.M. to 5 P.M. Genova (2010) opines that the more situational freedom employees enjoy, the more liability follows their natural proclivity to blend business and personal activities. Some people need the separation, as well as the commute to and from work in order to transition between work and home. There is also the potential for more distractions at home than at the workplace. Family, pets, and other at-home comforts may present challenges in focusing on work. The office environment is a more fostering and work supportive atmosphere for some. However, this blending of home and office is not much of an issue with Millennials because they are used to being connected all day, every day and they routinely blend work and personal life.

An office has all of the physical, emotional, and interpersonal resources readily available to support an employee in difficult situations. With the advanced use of webcams, phone calls, e-mail and instant messaging to replace face to face conversations, a "lost in translation" dilemma becomes possible during telecommuting. The proliferation of e-mail and instant messaging has made communicating at a distance much easier; however, e-mail blunders can lead to missed opportunities, inaction, misunderstandings, damaged relationships, erroneous decisions, and legal liability. Digital messages need to be clear with guidance and detail. They cannot be left open for interpretation by the reader. Companies can utilize telecommuting only if they are aware of the risks and disadvantages and are prepared to mitigate possible misuse and the pitfalls telecommuting presents to the modern employee.

WHERE WE STAND NOW: THE NECESSITY OF TELECOMMUTING FOR MILLENNIALS

Millennials grew up pampered, nurtured and programmed with activities. They have received constant feedback and recognition from teachers, parents and coaches. Now they expect the same from their bosses and they will become resentful or lost if they are not getting regular input on their performance. They want a structured, supportive work environment, personalized work and interactive relationships where they can make a difference and be recognized for their contributions. It was always normal for them to question their parents, now it seems normal to question their bosses. They believe in their self worth and speak their minds. They are not afraid to challenge the status quo and want to work where creativity and independent thinking are appreciated. They value work environments that allow them to express themselves, offer their points of view, learn from others and share their ideas both virtually and face to face. They want to work where they can access social media sites so they can remain connected to family, friends and coworkers throughout the day. They are tech-savvy, well educated and eco-friendly. Indeed, this is a generation of potentially high maintenance, high performers.

To make matters even worse, Millennials tend to change careers quickly, frustrating employers struggling to recruit and retain talented high performers. Empirical evidence suggests that young workers do not actually change jobs any more than older generations, but they do it for less concrete reasons (Deal, 2007). They change jobs, or even careers, just to try something else as they seek out self-fulfillment in the workplace. And because many of them receive financial support from their parents, they feel more free to do so. A recent Conference Board report shows that less than 37% of Millennials report job satisfaction—much lower than any other generation (Pew Research Center, 2010).

So, what can organizations do to attract and retain members of this generation? Many will say "Nothing—they need to conform to the way we work—what has already been shown to be successful." However, this would be a mistake. Again, Baby Boomers number approximately 79 million and there are only 51 million Generation Xers to take their place. In the U.S., 28% of managerial positions are already held by Millennials (U.S. Bureau of Labor Statistics, 2011). That means this new generation will have considerable influence in the world of work within the next decade. This chapter argues that Millennials have the individual capacity and the desire to telecommute … not every day, but in a way that allows them flexibility. In addition, the technology and business practices necessary to allow workers to telecommute have advanced a great deal in recent years. E-mails, smart phones, instant messaging, webcams and other electronic communication tools are used more and more as means of communication at work. The remaining ingredient is management of this new cadre of workers.

Millennials distrust corporations as a whole, yet we know that a trusting work environment breeds more loyal employees and increases efficiency. Millennials consider work as a social element in their lives and they like to collaborate with others. They are very productive workers if managers can keep them stimulated and feeling like they are valued. They want emotional engagement and a sense of community. They choose employers for meaningful work, opportunities for learning, quality of life and strong work colleagues. Based on this discussion, organizations are challenged to create a workplace that is structured enough to get the work done, but flexible enough to accommodate employees of various cultures and backgrounds. It is up to the organization and manager to find role models Millennials can trust and follow, provide challenging opportunities, realize the importance of social networks (exploit virtual water coolers, online cafes, etc.) and provide flexible job environments. Both the individuals who are available for work and the type of work are changing significantly and we suggest that telecommuting is one tool companies can use to incorporate existing technology with the flexibility demanded by today's (and tomorrow's) workforce. By adopting a telecommuting program, employers will be more likely to attract and retain high performing Millennials.

CONCLUSION

The decision concerning whether to engage in telecommuting is an important one. As we have demonstrated, this decision is not one to be taken lightly by organizations. There are myriad factors which must be considered in order to ensure that telecommuting is the optimal path toward organizational effectiveness. While telecommuting holds many potential advantages for Millennials and the organization, the disadvantages must be taken into account as well. We would suggest that consideration of the above mentioned issues will facilitate an examination of the appropriateness of telecommuting based on organizational/individual capacity and work amenability.

Strategically, organizations need to engage in those practices which will facilitate their efficiency and effectiveness based upon the variables that exist in that organization. These strategies may include a component of situational leadership in which new employees are assimilated into the culture of the organization through training and on-site responsibilities. As the employees are able to prove their abilities, they are rewarded with autonomy and more flexibility to telecommute. Failure to consider the myriad factors suggested above may have an unintended result—an incongruous situation where an intervention meant to enhance work actually has an opposite and deleterious effect. However, if both parties work together to set standards of reasonable behavior regarding the use of telecommunication, we believe it can be managed successfully and the promises of telecommuting can be properly matched to the preferences of Millennials. Such an endeavor will shed more light into the exploration of telecommuting, in highlighting new vistas of work arrangements for Millennials, potentially resulting in a better fit between employee and organization.

REFERENCES

AFL-CIO. (2009). Young workers: A lost decade. Retrieved from http://www.afl-cio.org/aboutus/laborday/upload/laborday2009_report.pdf

Bailey, D. E., & Kurland, N. B. (2002). A review of telework research: Findings, new directions, and lessons for the study of modern work. *Journal of Organizational Behavior, 23*(4), 383-400.

Bélanger, F. (1999). Workers' propensity to telecommute: An empirical study. *Information & Management, 35*(3), 139-153.

Bélanger, F., & Allport, C. D. (2008). Collaborative technologies in knowledge telework: An exploratory study. *Information Systems Journal, 18*(1), 101-121.

Boroff, R. (2011). *Managing the new and improved virtual office.* Retrieved from http://www.sooperarticles.com/business-articles/management-articles/managing-new-improved-virtual-office-377036.html

Buckley, M. R., Beau, D. S., Novicevic, M. M., & Sigerstad, T. D. (2001). Managing generation NeXt: Individual and organizational perspectives. *Review of Business, 22*, 81-85.

Caine, E. (2009). Turning to telework in times of disaster. *Workspan Magazine, 52*(11), 55-58.

Campbell, S. J. (2007). *Collaborative technologies lead to increase in virtual workers/telecommuters.* Retrieved from http://www.tmcnet.com/voip/ip-communications/articles/7231-collaborative-technologies-lead-increase-virtual-workerstelecommuters.htm

De Croon, F., Sluiter, J. K., Kuijer, P. F. M., & Fringsdresen, M. H. W. (2005). The effect of office concepts on worker health and performance: A systematic review of the literature. *Ergonomics, 48*(2), 119-134.

Deal, J. J. (2007). *Retiring the generation gap: How employees young and old can find common ground.* San Francisco, CA: Jossey-Bass.

Eikhof, D. R., Warhurst, C., & Haunschild, A. (2007). Introduction: What work? What life? What balance?: Critical reflections on the work-life balance debate. *Employee Relations, 29*(4), 325-333.

Ellison, N. B. (1999). Social impacts: New perspectives on telework. *Social Science Computer Review, 17*(3), 338-356.

Garrett, R. K., & Danziger, J. N. (2007). Which telework? Defining and testing a taxonomy of technology-mediated work at a distance. *Social Science Computer Review, 25*(1), 27-47.

Genova, G. L. (2010). The anywhere office = anywhere liability. *Business Communication Quarterly, 73*(1), 26-31.

Hornung, S. (2009). Home-based telecommuting and quality of life: Further evidence on an employee oriented human resource practice. *Psychological Reports, 104*(2), 395-402.

Illegems, V., & Verbeke, A. (2004). Telework: What does it mean for management? *Long Range Planning, 37*(4), 319-334.

Ilozor, D. B., Ilozor, B., & Carr, J. (2001). Management communication strategies determine job satisfaction in telecommuting. *Journal of Management Development, 20*(6), 495-507.

Johnson Controls. (2012). *OXYGENZ project.* Retrieved from http://www.johnson-controls.com/publish/us/en/products/building_efficiency/gws/gwi/projects_workplace_innovation/workplace_innovation/future_generation_y_workplace_innovation.html

Kanaracus, C. (2007). Telecommuting: A quarter of U.S. workers do it regularly, *PCWorld*. Retrieved from http://www.pcworld.com/article/140003/telecommuting_a_quarter_of_us_ workers_do_it_regularly.html

Kurland, N. B., & Egan, T. (1999). Telecommuting: Justice and control in the virtual organization. *Organizational Science, 10*(4), 500-513.

Mannering J. S., & Mokhtarian P. L. (1995). Modeling the choice of telecommuting frequency in California: An exploratory analysis. *Technological Forecasting and Social Change, 49*(1), 49-73.

Marsh, K., & Musson, G. (2008). Men at work and at home: Managing emotion in telework. *Work & Organization, 15*(1), 31-48.

Mokhtarian, P. L. (1998). A synthetic approach to estimating the impacts of telecommuting on travel. *Urban Studies, 35*, 215-241.

Montreuil, S., & Lippel, K. (2003). Telework and occupational health: A Quebec empirical study and regulatory implications. *Safety Science, 41*(4), 339-358.

National Small Business Association. (2010). 2010 small business technology survey. Retrieved from http://www.nsba.biz/docs/nsba_2010_technology _survey.pdf.

Nicholas, A. J., & Guzman, I. R. (2009). Proceedings from the SIGMIS-CPR '09: *Is teleworking for the millennials?* Thousand Oaks, CA: SAGE.

Nilles, J. M. (1994). *Making telecommuting happen: A guide for telemanagers and telecommuters*. New York, NY: Van Nostrand Reinhold.

Olson, M. H., & Primps, S. B. (1984). Working at home with computers: Work and nonwork issues. *Journal of Social Issues, 40*, 97-112.

Pew Research Center. (2010) Millennials: A portrait of Generation Next. Retrieved from http://pewsocialtrends.org/files/2010/10/millennials-confident-connected-open-to-change.pdf

Pew Research Center. (2012). Millennials: A portrait of Generation Next. Retrieved from http://pewresearch.org/millennials/

Project on Student Debt. (2010). Quick facts about student debt. Retrieved from http://projectonstudentdebt.org/files/File/Debt_Facts_and_Sources.pdf

Ransom, D. (2010). Six ways to manage a virtual workforce, *SmartMoney*. Retrieved from http://www.entrepreneur.com/humanresources/managingemployees/article206214.html

Redman, T., Snape, E., & Ashurst, C. (2009). Location, location, location: Does place of work really matter? *British Journal of Management, 20*(1), 171-181.

Schramm, J. (2010). At work in a virtual world. *HR Magazine, 55*(6), 11.

Schwabel, D. (2011). *The beginning of the end of the 9-to-5 workday?* Retrieved from http://moneyland.time.com/2011/12/21/the-beginning-of-the-end-of-the-9-to-5-workday

Shamir, B., & Salomon, I. (1985). Work-at-home and the quality of working life. *Academy of Management Review, 10*(3), 455-464.

Stavrou, E., & Kilaniotis, C. (2010). Flexible work and turnover: An empirical investigation across cultures. *British Journal of Management, 21*(2), 541-554.

Taskin, L., & Devos, V. (2005). Paradoxes from the individualization of human resource management: The case of telework. *Journal of Business Ethics, 62*(1), 13-24.

Thatcher, S. M. B., & Zhu, X. (2006). Changing identities in a changing workplace: Identification, identity enactment, self-verification, and telecommuting. *Academy of Management Review, 31*(4), 1076-1088.

Thompson, L. F. (2009). The recruitment value of work/life benefits. *Personnel Review, 38*(2), 195-210.

U.S. Bureau of Labor Statistics. (2011). *Labor force statistics*. Retrieved from http://www.bls.gov/cps/home.htm

Workman, M., Kahnweiler, W., & Bommer, W. (2003). The effects of cognitive style and media richness on commitment to telework and virtual teams. *Journal of Vocational Behavior, 63*(2), 199-219.

CHAPTER 16

MILLENNIALS IN THE WORKFORCE

Unions and Management Battle for the Soul of a Generation

Marcia A. Beck and Jonathan P. West

INTRODUCTION

The tumultuous battles between unions and cash-strapped state governments in Wisconsin, Ohio, and Indiana during the "great recession" in 2011 have put into sharp relief the dilemma of collective bargaining in an era of fiscal restraint and high unemployment. In what may well be an historical crossroads in union strength and influence, Generation Y will be a key player in determining the fate of America's private and public sector unions. Will members of the Millennial Generation turn to traditional or reformed union structures to pursue their collective interests in the workforce, or will they ignore calls to unionize in the name of increased flexibility, individualist meritocracy, and professional independence?

Managing Human Resources for the Millennial Generation, pp. 355–397
Copyright © 2012 by Information Age Publishing
All rights of reproduction in any form reserved.

While public service membership has remained steady since the 1970s, private union membership has declined sharply. One effect is that Generation Y has had little exposure to either union activism or union lore, since unions have not been a part of the Millennials' family, educational, or workplace experiences (Fontes & Margolies, 2010). Many unions and prounion think tanks identify positive attitudes among Millennials toward unions based on survey materials and the extrapolation of values such as the desire for equality, fairness, a legal minimum wage, health care, environmental standards, and empowerment as support for unions (AFL-CIO, 2009; Madland & Teixeira, 2009). This is countered by some Millennials themselves, who write that while Generation Y holds these values, they do not consider unions the way to attain them in the workplace (Greenberg & Weber, 2008, pp. 93-94), and sometimes even view unions as obstacles to attaining their professional goals (Alsop, 2008,p. 30).

Unions are seeking to encourage prounion attitudes among Millennials and to translate attitudes into membership and activism. Richard Trumka, AFL-CIO president, has prioritized the challenge of reaching out to a new generation of workers who have no experience of labor-management struggles and whose workforce values of flexibility, transferability, independence, and disdain for bureaucratic structures differentiate them from the union "old guard" (Trumka, 2009). Emphasizing the economic plight of young workers in a prolonged recession, and arguing that "the majority (of them) know they can not rely on their employers to make (improvements on the job)," unions are calling for this "lost generation" to revitalize the union movement (AFL-CIO, 2009). Labor activists are developing innovative ways to attract Millennials based on their cultural, financial, and employment orientations (Goldstein, 2008).

Employers, at the same time, have devoted much energy to researching, understanding, and appealing to the Millennial Generation as they compete for talent in a rapidly changing, technologically fueled, knowledge-based global economy (Alsop, 2008; Lancaster & Stillman, 2010; Lipkin & Perrymore, 2009). Companies try to engage Millennials by facilitating individual and collective lines of employee-employer communication, encouraging and rewarding high performance, offering opportunities for value-based volunteer work, and promoting professional development that transcends a specific workplace. Human resource policies designed to involve Millennials in all aspects of workplace operations will appeal to this generation of workers, who are eager to interact and collaborate with managers, leaders, and colleagues to make their professional mark.

In the highly charged atmosphere of employer-union competition to engage Millennials and foster commitment to their organizations and goals, some union advocates label any attempt by employers that is viewed as undercutting the influence of unions as "union bashing." The charge is misplaced if employer strategies to establish more productive employee-employer relationships are directed toward promoting the health of the organization and the well-being of the organization's employees, only indirectly undercutting the influence of unions by convincing employees that collective action is not necessary to make their voices heard. Union *avoidance* as a strategy to weaken unions for the sole purpose of reducing their power and influence is unethical. Union *substitution*, in contrast, whereby employers "(emphasize) programs that positively impact employee attitudes ... through effective implementation of many HR best practices ... to build a high performance culture that is characterized by high morale, organization commitment, and employee involvement" (McClendon, 2006, pp. 274-275) is ethically justifiable. If employers recognize employee rights to join or form unions, and follow the letter and spirit of union-related legislation, rulings, and executive orders, then employers can legitimately engage employees in ways that may make unionization redundant.

Research shows, for example, that employers who introduce employee involvement strategies, to give employees a voice in company policy, and variable pay structures (VPS), such as profit-sharing and merit pay, are more concerned with encouraging employee commitment than discouraging union representation (Butler, 2009; Marginson, Arrowsmith, & Gray, 2008). Employers articulate aims such as "breaking down traditional 'them' and 'us' attitudes among the workforce" (Marginson et al., 2008, p. 339) to create a commonality of purpose with employees. While some employers may introduce employee involvement policies as a form of "defensive union avoidance," the motivation evolves into "more proactive and creative concerns relating to the decision-making process and a desire to stave off employee exit" (Butler, 2009, p. 189).

Employers increasingly realize the "real-world impact of an engaged and satisfied workforce on an organization's bottom line" (Van Rooy, Whitman, Hart, & Caleo, 2011, p. 147). Attempts to discourage the unionization of the workforce or to engage in tough negotiations with existing unions are unlikely to take place for the sole purpose of "union bashing" if this would alienate prounion employees. Employers attempt to engage and satisfy their workforce without the intermediaries of unions when direct interaction proves more cost-effective and better fosters employee satisfaction and commitment. Exchange theory suggests that employees who perceive that their employers are not committed to their best interests will lack commitment to the organization (Farndale, Van Ruiten, Kelliher, & Hope-Hailey, 2011). Employers who fail to address Millennials' interests and values will either lose them to competitors or drive them into the arms of unions eager to revitalize their ranks with motivated and skilled young activists (Tyler, 2009). Employers thus have an incentive to actively engage employees, either directly in nonunion settings, or through union representation, when employees decide this is in their best interest.

Employers seek to attract and retain Millennials to gain a competitive edge; unions call on young workers to revitalize the union movement. Employers and unions may ethically vie to engage Millennials when the letter and spirit of laws are followed and employees decide for themselves how best to engage with management. If Millennials believe their interests are being served by employers, they are likely to shun union representation. If they see the need for a collective voice, as in low paying service jobs or freelancing tech fields, they may well seek union representation. When employees freely decide that unions are necessary to provide collective voice, protection from arbitrary policies, employment security, organizational trust and commitment, and transparent performance measures, unions may prove to be an asset to employers by streamlining communication, fostering employee commitment, and preventing excessive turnover (Masters, Merchant, & Tobias, 2010, p. 20). In environments where unions are firmly established, employers and unions can prevent their relationship from turning adversarial by cooperating to engage young workers in labor-management partnerships based on mutual goals. Constructive partnerships speak directly to Millennials' penchant for active involvement in workplace activities and teamwork to improve performance.

After detailing Generation Y demographics and work-related attitudes and orientations, this chapter examines Millennials' attitudes toward and involvement in unions in the context of declining union influence. The analysis then turns to a battle and a truce. The mutually exclusive battle is between unions and employers to appeal to Millennials' interests and values to capture their loyalty and commitment; it will be fought over the "rules of engagement." Both unions and employers understand that engaging Millennials in organizational causes, goals, operations, and reorientations is crucial for the longevity, effectiveness, and influence of their organizations; several of these engagement strategies are examined here. A truce emerges when employers and unions, compelled to work together by employee choice, develop labor-management partnerships based on mutual goals and common commitments. As the adversarial battle between employers and unions in the private and public sectors rages on, a series of truces has emerged under the radar, providing palpable hope that Millennials will be able exercise their talents and realize their goals in an arena where partnership trumps partisanship.

DEMOGRAPHICS, WORKPLACE ORIENTATIONS, EMPLOYMENT TRENDS

Millennials, born between 1979 and 1997, number about 86 million (U.S. Bureau of the Census, 2011) and comprise up to 35% of the current work-force (Toland, 2011). Almost half of them work in corporations (Sujansky & Ferry-Reed, 2009, pp. 3-4); 26% are employed in leisure, hospitality, and food service industries and 21% are employed in retail trade. (U.S. BLS, 2011b). A core group of these Millennials display life and work values that are instructive for human resource management in both union and nonunion settings (see Table 16.1).

Table 16.1. Millennial Generation Workplace Values

Millennials:

- Value communication and interaction with colleagues and managers;
- Seek to engage their employers as colleagues;
- Value transparency and trust in workplace relations;
- Value teamwork;
- Value talent over tenure and expect to be rewarded for high performance;
- Are self-confident and want to show off their skills and advance quickly;
- Are even more interested in work-life balance than their older cohorts;
- Expect employers to act on socially-conscious values and support employee volunteer activities based on these values;
- Are not wedded to a particular job or career;
- Consider fulfillment as important as wages in employment;
- Value higher learning and are "on track to become the most educated generation in American history;" (Pew 2010c: 1-2)
- Are technologically savvy and value the use of technology in the workplace;
- Have more confidence than older generations that "business corporations generally strike a fair balance between making profits and serving the public interest" (Pew, 2010c: 74);
- React positively when asked about unions, but they tend not to know much about them and are less likely to join than their elders;
- Lean toward the Democratic Party, have more confidence in an active government, and are more socially liberal than their older cohorts; voted overwhelmingly Democratic in the 2008 presidential election.

Note: Compiled from: AFL-CIO (2009); Alsop (2008); Gray (2007); Hershatter & Epstein (2010); Kahmann (2002); Keene & Handrich (2010); Lancaster & Stillman (2010); Levenson (2010); Lipkin & Perrymore (2009); Meister & Willyard (2010); Myers & Sadaghiani (2010); Pew (2010c); SBR Consulting (2011); Singer, Messera, & Orino (2011); Sujansky & Ferry-Reed (2009).

Millennial Employment Trends

Full-time employment has fallen by 9 percentage points for Millennial workers since 2006, the largest drop for any age group since that time (Pew, 2010c). Millennials aged 16 to 29 had an employment rate of 55.3% in 2010; a 12-point percentage drop from 2000 and the lowest rate since the end of the second World War (AP, 2011). The youngest of the Millennials, those aged 16-24, maintained a labor force participation rate hovering around 66% in the 1990s. By 2009, however, the rate was only 56.7%, a drop the Pew Research Center labels "precipitous" (Pew, 2009, pp. 8-9). The participation rate in July 2011 gives a snapshot illustration of the bleak situation confronting this age group: "The share of young people who were employed in July was 48.8%; .... the labor force participation rate (for youth ages 16-24) was 59.5% in July (2011), the lowest July rate on record" (U.S. BLS, 2011b).

The unemployment rate for young workers under the age of 35 increased from 6.2% in 1999, to 12.9% in 2009, to 13.1% in 2010 (AFL-CIO, 2010). In 2011, Millennials' unemployment rate was much higher than that of older workers: 14% compared with 9.1% (Navarette, 2011). For the lower age tier of Generation Y, 16 to 24, the unemployment rate in 2010 was far higher at 18.4%—the highest rate of unemployment for this age group since records began in 1950 (Shierholz & Edwards, 2011, p. 1). In the 4-month period from April to July 2011, the number of Millennials aged 16 to 24 who were unemployed increased to 18.6 million, a rise of 1.7 million (U.S. BLS, 2011b). Within this age group, the rates vary markedly based on education level and race. The overall unemployment rate for high school graduates was 22.5%; for college graduates 9.3%. For African American high school graduates, 31.8% and college graduates, 19.0%. For Hispanic high school graduates 22% and college graduates 13.8%. There are clear generational differences as well: The 22.5% unemployment rate for high school graduates of all races in the under-25 age group compares to a 10.3% rate for all high school graduates over the age of 25. The 9.3% unemployment rate of all college graduates under 25 compares with a 4.7% unemployment rate for college graduates 25 and older (Shierholz & Edwards, 2011).

The term "lost generation" has come into widespread use to characterize a Millennial generation coming of age and entering the workforce in the midst of a long-lasting and economically deep recession (AFL-CIO, 2010; AP, 2011). Millennials have suffered greatly from the current economic situation in terms of overall employment trends, especially the youngest part of the group. Many of those who do have jobs are underemployed, as they are compelled for financial reasons to seek employment below their skill levels. This high rate of Millennial un- and under-employment means that increasingly the U.S. labor force will be deprived of future employees who have the skills and training to tackle the challenges of a rapidly changing and demanding economy and workplace environment. This makes it even more important that Millennials have the opportunity and impetus to take part in job training and skill development programs, either before they enter the job market or between jobs and during short periods of unemployment. Human resource strategies, both in nonunionized and unionized environments, should focus on both organizational-specific and transferable professional development skills that prepare young workers for lateral as well as vertical moves within an organization, and during periods of unemployment.

The Declining Power of Unions

Unions have gone through "profound changes" since the National Labor Relations Act gave employees the right to form unions in 1935 and states started passing collective bargaining laws giving state and local government employees the right to public union representation in the late 1950s (Whorisky & Gardner, 2011). In 1960, 10.8% of public sector workers belonged to a union, compared with 31.9% of private sector workers ("A Union Education," 2011). By 2010, the membership trends reversed dramatically: the union membership rate for those aged 16 and above in the public sector was 36.2% (7.6 million employees), compared with 6.9% (7.1 million employees) in the private sector, for a total of 11.9% in both sectors (down from 12.3% in 2009 and 20.9% in 1983, the first year for which comparable data is available). About 1.6 million workers are covered by union contracts but do not belong to unions, with the percentage of workers covered at 7.7% in the private sector and 40% in the public sector, for a total of 13.1% in both sectors (Hirsch & Macpherson, 2011; U.S. BLS, 2011a). The average total union membership rates for U.S. states is 11.9%; 31 states fall below that average and 19 states are above. New York has the highest unionization rate at 24.2%; and North Carolina the lowest, at 3.2% (U.S. BLS, 2011a). There has also been a marked decline in Americans' approval of unions as measured by regular Gallup polls. Approval fell from a high of 75% in 1957 to a low of 48% in 2009, the first time since 1937, when polling began, that the rate fell beneath 50% (Saad, 2009).

Changes in the economic structure, including an increase in service jobs at the expense of the manufacturing sector and globalization, whereby companies can outsource production for lower costs, go a long way toward explaining the dramatic decrease in union density and influence in the private sector in recent decades (Riccucci, 2007). A softening of class-based identities has also undermined the "movement" nature of unionism, where class solidarity was a rallying cry in the struggle to make blue collar workers a permanent part of the American middle class. In addition to these structural and sociological factors, the policy environment influences the relative strength and weakness of unions in both the public and private sectors. In the private sector, the most divisive issue is that of "right to work" legislation in 22 states that prevents closed shops and mandates that conditions of employment cannot depend on union membership in any given workplace. As companies increasingly move production to these areas, more and more states are looking to introduce or further institutionalize measures to limit unionization campaigns (Maher & Belkin, 2011, p. A3). The National Labor Relations Board under the Obama Administration has introduced counter-policies to give unions more power to prevent companies' relocation to right-to-work states, compel employers to inform employees about unionization rights, and shorten the time it takes for unionization efforts at the workplace (Trottman, 2011).

In the public sector, the most contentious policy issue is collective bargaining, protected in the private sector but subject to the vagaries of legislation in the public sector. As elected state officials encounter pressure to balance budgets, reduce debt, and increase employment, many have attempted to weaken existing collective bargaining rights or eliminate them altogether. Federal policies to influence the state and local policy environment depend to a large extent on politics and lead to expected outcries from labor or management, depending on their orientation. State "right-to-work" laws are considered to stem from ideologically motivated hostility to unions by some prounion activists (Goldstein, 2008), while others emphasize the deeper job losses and slower personal income growth in nonright-to-work states. (Burton, James, Hagerty, & Douglas, 2011, p. A4). Similarly, some consider collective bargaining laws as an inherent right of workers that requires state protection (Ogle & Wheeler, 2001); others view it as practically equivalent to meet-and-confer rights that do not obligate the employer to treat worker representatives as an equal partner (Kearney, 2010, p. 106, fn.4), while others see collective bargaining as constraining the ability of employers, especially in the public sector, to make decisions based on fiscal constraints (Barro, 2011).

The policy environment, while not the sole cause of union fortunes, certainly has an impact on both union membership levels and union strength in negotiating, especially in the public sector. There is a distinct correlation between collective bargaining laws and union density (Kearney, 2010, p. 95), as there is between right-to-work laws and union strength (Vedder, 2010, p. 176). One thing remains constant in the ever-changing landscape of a policy environment shaped by political orientations and politicking: union-related policies tend to promote or exacerbate adversarial relationships between union and management (Berman, Bowman, West, & Van Wart, 2012).

Unions themselves are in part responsible for their own decline, as disputes within their organizations have led to very public dissension, leading to fractionalization and rebellion in the ranks (Greenhouse, 2009a; MacGillis, 2010; Raine, 2005). More polemical accounts argue that union avoidance on the part of managers has been responsible for the deliberate weakening of unions (Reuss, 2011) or that workers who do not see the need for unions suffer from a "false consciousness" that prevents them from realizing their own exploitation (Kleis, 2008).

Whatever the reasons, Millennials encounter an environment of weakened private sector unions. They are unlikely to have heard about unions in their families, studied them in school, or to have developed opinions about their role in the economy and society. Millennials are more likely than older generations, in a 2010 survey, to have a favorable opinion of unions, although the percentage has been declining in recent years: In 2007, 66% of respondents under 30 had a favorable view; 24% unfavorable. By 2010, the favorable to unfavorable ratio was 53% to 33%, a differential of -13 in the period from 2007 to 2010 (the differentials ranged from -5 to -31 for older generations) (Pew, 2010b, p. 2).

Despite relatively favorable ratings, members of the Millennial generation are far less likely than older cohorts to belong to a union (Goldstein, 2008; Kahmann, 2002; Schmitt, 2008; Tannock & Flocks, 2002). "Over 70% of those ages 16-34 are part of the civilian labor force, but only 8.2% of them belong to unions" (Firestine, 2010, p. 1); in 1983 16% of young workers aged 18-29 were union members (Schmitt, 2008, p. 2). An even smaller proportion of the youngest end of the Millennial spectrum belong to unions (Tannock & Flocks, 2002, p. 17). In 2003, 14.7% of workers aged 45-64 belonged to unions; 11.3% of those aged 25-44; and 5% of those aged 16-24 (Mayer, 2004). In 2010, 15.7% of those aged 55-64 belong to unions; 4.3% of those aged 16-24 (U.S. BLS, 2011a). The union membership rate of young workers is also declining faster than that of older workers (Kahmann, 2002) (See Table 16.2).

Given this relatively low level of union membership, conflicts that result when states attempt to limit or eliminate collective bargaining rights might have a different impact on Millennial generation workers than on their older cohorts who are more heavily represented in unions. Older union members will see a decrease in collective bargaining rights as undermining their wage and benefits packages and will thus likely come out in force, as they have in Wisconsin and Ohio, to fight any changes. Millennial generation workers, either those looking for work or

Table 16.2.   2009/2010 Union Membership/Union Representation in Two Millennial Age Groups

	2009	2009	2010	2010
Age group	% members	% represented	% members	% represented
16-24	3.7	4.4	3.6	4.3
25-34	10.0	11.3	9.5	10.7

Note: Compiled from U.S. BLS, (2011a).

having less seniority in unions, will not experience the same sharp decreases in wages and benefits. Since Millennials "don't always equate experience with being qualified for a job" (Lancaster & Stillman, 2010, pp. 56-57), they may also perceive the wave of early retirements of older union members resulting from less lucrative wage and benefits packages (Khadaroo, 2011) as beneficial to them. While unions may succeed in mobilizing the Millennial Generation's support for strikes and opposition to legislation that limits collective bargaining, it is open to question whether nonunion Generation Y members will commit themselves to a cause that may negatively affect their ability to find a job or advance quickly in their profession.

UNION STRATEGIES TO ATTRACT GENERATION Y WORKERS

Unions have recognized that they must attract Millennials if they are to grow their ranks, revitalize their membership, and reinvigorate their strategies. While unions, especially in the United States, have been relatively slow to recognize this need in contrast to private companies (Tannock & Flocks, 2002), once unions identified the need to attract Millennials, they approached this goal with great purpose and vigor. For an overview of union strategies, see Table 16.3).

After years of complaints that older union members simply "talked down" to young members or treated them like children who had a lot to learn from their elders (Fontes & Margolies, 2010, p. 28) unions recognized the necessity of giving young workers a voice in union policies. Activists realized throughout the 1990s that social networking could be effective in making Millennials aware of unions and their activities, but was not enough to get these young workers invested in unions. Unions began to encourage Millennials to assume leading positions on union committees and projects and started incorporating them into their consultation and decision-making processes (Tannock & Flocks, 2002). This is part of a broader trend of "diversity unionism," which "emphasizes the

Table 16.3.   Union Strategies to Attract Millennial Generation Workers

1. Outreach through social networking to inform and energize non-union and union Millennials;

2. Merge union culture with Millennials' culture;

3. Offer training and educational programs geared to union and non-union Millennial workers and students;

4. Apply "diversity unionism" to incorporate diverse Millennial members into existing union structures;

5. Re-structure unions to appeal to Millennials' financial and social interests;

6. Appeal to the movement, class struggle, and solidarity nature of unionism;

7. Organize low-wage service workers and high-tech freelancers across workplaces;

8. Use "community unionism" based on social justice, environmental, and political activism;

9. Promote tangible benefits of union membership, such as higher wages and better health care;

10. Work with foreign unions to organize Millennial employees of global companies that do business in the United States.

Note: Compiled from: AFL-CIO (2009); AFL-CIO (2011); Bunkley (2011); Carter (2006); Cunningham & James (2010); Fontes & Margolies (2010); Greenhouse (2009); Healy et al. (2004); Heery & Adler (2004); Higgins & Naughton (2011); Hurd (2004); Kahmann (2002); Pare (2011); Schmitt (2008); Tannock & Flocks (2002).

need to adapt governing structures of unions to ensure that the views and interests of underrepresented groups, such as women, young people and ethnic minorities, are adequately represented and acted upon" (Cunningham & James, 2010, p. 37).

This is necessary to educate young workers about unions and the potential benefits of union membership, but not sufficient to compel Millennials to join unions or assume leadership roles addressing the specific interests of Millennial union members. To appeal to Millennials unions must make structural changes in union organization that allow young workers to assume leadership positions in specific professional development projects, directly interact with employers, and engage in discussions about performance evaluations and alternative compensation schemes. This process has been slow, as senior officials are reluctant to relinquish power and influence they have acquired in existing union structures (Bach & Givan, 2008; Cunningham & James, 2010).

Richard Trumka, President of the AFL-CIO since 2009, highlighted the need to attract members of Generation Y to the union movement and recognized that simply incorporating Millennials into existing union structures will not suffice:

(I)t will not matter how many unions are in the AFL-CIO if we fail to capture the imagination of Millennials.... The problem is not that they dislike unions. They think we do a lot of good things for our members; the problem is that they do not think we have much to offer them.... And you can not blame them because we have not really focused on the way they work. Well, we can not ask Millennials to change the way they earn their living to meet our model for unionism; we have to change our approach to unionism to meet their needs. (Trumka, 2009)

Trumka had learned the lesson that workplace-oriented organizing campaigns to attract new members were not successful in appealing to a Millennial generation that was more educated, more likely to be employed in white collar positions, and more willing to change jobs and careers than older workers (Cunningham & James, 2010; Hurd, 2006). The AFL-CIO leader thus called for direct union efforts to recognize the changing economy and the role of Millennials in it. Trumka turned to "community unionism" to engage Millennials—students, workers, and the unemployed—in a wide range of ever-expanding union services. Community unionism advocates complain that "unions remain entrenched in a paradigm based on negotiating bread and butter issues, and continue to be averse to taking on social issues" (Firestine et al., 2010. P. 17). They argue that "the way in which membership can be increased is through unions addressing external labor market and social concerns of relevance to potential members in collaboration with other interest groups" (Cunningham & James, 2010, p. 37). One strategy is to appeal to a new cohort of workers by redirecting efforts from wages and benefits to programs that speak to young employee demands for a greater work/life balance through family leave programs, flextime, and opportunities for employees to pursue their interests outside of the workplace (Firestine et al., 2010).

Trumka spoke directly to the interests of Millennials in calling for union efforts to organize telecommuters, freelancers, and temporary workers in white collar jobs, such as computer technology, to pursue goals such as commitment to professional standards and portable health care insurance. This call may very well resonate with itinerant highly educated Millennials working in technology industries (Blain, 2001; Dunn 2011). Trumka also called for unions to go beyond their traditional mandates to, for example, get involved in efforts to make college more affordable so that Generation Y members do not start their working lives struggling to pay off mountains of debt. Trumka's appeal is directed toward revitalizing the union movement by identifying with Millennials' concerns and reorienting union organizing strategies and service provisions to speak to them directly.

The AFL-CIO's "Union Summer" internship program recruits students on college campuses to participate in union organizing projects in an effort to combine student activism with union activities (Tannock & Flocks, 2002). This 10-week internship assigns students to work in union organizing drives throughout the U.S. by getting involved in state legislation debates, visiting workers at home to assess their needs, taking part in demonstrations, and "assisting in building community, labor and religious organizations" (AFL-CIO, 2011). Internships expanded into activism when unions called on students to participate in protests with public sector unions against state reduction of benefits and limits on collective bargaining in Wisconsin in February 2011 (Stripling, 2011). A critique of this approach is that by focusing on college students in their training and organizational drives, unions may be devoting resources to groups of middle-class youth who will not have the motivation to join unions, rather than focusing their efforts on lower class working youth in areas such as service jobs and retail trade (Tannock & Flocks, 2002). Just as in the Wisconsin union strikes in 2011, Millennial generation participation in union internship programs may reflect short-term interest rather than long-term commitment to union engagement and membership.

The AFL-CIO's "Working America" organization of nonunionized workers who either lack a union at their place of work or are unemployed seeks to appeal to young workers who are suffering from the effects of the economic downtown in the millennium's second decade (Goldstein, 2008). Working America, which by its own assessment has 3 million members as of 2011 (http://www.workingamerica.org/issues/), combines diversity and community unionism, a restructuring of union organization and service provision, and activism to foster new union identities, with a special appeal to Millennials. This type of union organizing campaign may appeal to young workers in low-wage service industries with little job security, especially health care services, who feel that they have no voice in improving their working and living conditions without some form of collective action.

The "Change to Win" coalition of unions, spearheaded by the Service Employees International Union (SEIU) that broke with the AFL-CIO in 2005 over a disagreement in union strategies, moved from organization to mobilization to attract new union members. Then-president of the SEIU, Andrew Stern, applied a mobilization strategy of organizing workers in low-wage service industries on an industry-wide basis, rather than at individual workplaces. Stern reenergized the SEIU's "Justice for Janitors" campaign, begun in 1990 to reverse the decline in janitors' wages and health care benefits, as well as petition for paid vacation time, by introducing "name and shame" tactics against employers, supporting strikes, demonstrations and sit-ins in front of shopping malls, and negotiating with the corporate owners of buildings in addition to cleaning service contractors (Greenhouse, 2006). The SEIU continued its efforts to organize low-wage workers in home health care, nursing care, and hotel industries.

The organization's social mobilization approach, which seeks "to achieve social and economic justice and earn broad-based support from the public, as well as religious, political, and community leaders" (SEIU, 2011), was hailed by union advocates and foreign observers alike as ushering in a new era of union organizing that could be used as a model for efforts in Great Britain, Australia, and Canada (Carter, 2006, p. 420; Kahmann, 2002, p. 36). Initial enthusiasm for Stern's mobilizing efforts, however, turned sour when it emerged that the SEIU's tactics centralized union hierarchies by consolidating local branches, drained union finances, and actually disempowered workers by making deals with managers and government officials that precluded rank-and-file input (MacGillis, 2010). While union members and officials criticize Stern for the tactics he employed, the SEIU's success in organizing low-wage workers on an industry-wide basis illustrates the potential gains for unions to attract low-wage Millennial workers if they believe they lack a voice in determining work conditions. But to be successful at this, unions will have to show that they will give Millennials' a voice in strategy and decision making, rather than speak in their stead (Hurd, 2006, Moore & Read, 2006).

Community unionism and mobilization expands into political activism when organizing efforts are combined with building "supportive community and political alliances" (Cunningham & James, 2010, p. 39), as they were in efforts to organize migrant workers in California and janitorial staff throughout the U.S. in the SEIU's "Justice for Janitors" campaign. The AFL-CIO emphasizes political activism as part of its community unionism approach to attract Millennials: "Union and other advocacy groups have a vital role to play in maintaining and growing young people's political involvement to help transform their vision into reality" (AFL-CIO, 2009:, p. 40). Millennials' overwhelming support for Obama in the 2008 presidential election, as well as their socially liberal and active-government orientations, convinced some labor leaders and prolabor observers that this was part of a realignment of the electorate (Madland & Teixeira, 2009, pp. 1, 32-33) based on the merging of union and Millennials' progressive values (AFL-CIO, 2009, p. 37). Some posit a connection between Millennial union involvement and political orientation: "Getting involved with a union can foster a real commitment to progressive politics" (Goldstein, 2008).

Political trends since 2008, however, indicate that Millennials are no different from the general population in reduced confidence in and support of the Democratic Party's policies and leadership based on economic trends. Millennials remain more socially liberal and progovernment than older generations, but the 2008 elections likely have not caused a realignment of the electorate, as Millennials increasingly moved away from Democratic Party identification after 2008 (Pew, 2010a, pp. 1-2; Pew, 2010c, p. 63). Some Generation Y members may be uncomfortable with the political partisanship promulgated by unions (Goldstein, 2008), especially as efforts such as those by Democratic Governors in New York and California to moderate union demands in the face of fiscal constraints may weaken any inherent union-Democratic Party connection (Samuelson, 2011; Whoriskey & Gardner, 2011). Millennials tend to concur with all age cohorts that economic conditions are primarily responsible for their political orientations; their attitudes toward unions will most likely correspond to the overall economic environment rather than to political ideology.

Trumka's and Stern's strategies correspond to theories that dynamic leadership (Francia, 2006) and community unionism (Bach & Givan, 2008) should be directed toward reinvigorating the "movement" orientation of unions, one built on class and social solidarity. This approach is not likely to be an effective union strategy for attracting Millennials given this generation's tendency to value individual skill development and their strongly developed sense of being a "meritocratic elite" (Hershatter & Epstein, 2010, p. 215). Not only do Millennials have a variety of technologically-fueled opportunities to expand their social networks, providing them with alternatives to worker-based identity groups, but they lack a clear class identity, are less likely to join collective movements, and tend to view unions in terms of instrumentality rather than identity (Kahmann, 2002, p. 23).

Educated Millennials also have a very well-developed sense of their own professional interests and will not hesitate to shun existing unions or create alternative groups to speak to these interests. A group of young public school teachers in New York City, for example, was dissatisfied with the absence of skill-based performance indicators in teachers' unions and broke off to form E4E—"Educators for Excellence," an organization dedicated to improving teaching standards, promoting legislation to institutionalize those standards in practice, and providing teachers the necessary supports to perform well (Morris & Stone, 2011). Some committed young teachers devoted to improving performance standards gravitate more toward E4E than teachers' unions that emphasize more traditional union goals of rewarding seniority and protecting union members from layoffs (Santos, 2011).

The tendency of Millennials to view unions instrumentally in terms of economic, work/life balance, and professional standards, rather than in terms of identity or as a complement to political activism, may weaken or prevent a long-term attachment to unions on the part of those Millennials who change jobs or careers on their own volition. Millennials who are dissatisfied with working conditions at one place of employment are likely to seek other employment rather than turn to union representation:

> If the job is not working out for (Generation Y employees), they are very comfortable leaving for a new opportunity. This generational dynamic requires a union to overcome a significant barrier by trying to sell more complex social justice ideas rather than focus on traditional employee concerns. This generational shift is clear and is likely to cause further diminishment of the perceived benefit of unions in the workplace as Generation Y becomes a more dominant percentage of the workforce. (Haeberle, 2011)

This assessment, however, will apply only to those Millennials who have the luxury to change jobs without worrying about periods of unemployment, uprooting families, or disruption of wages and benefits. If lower-wage earning Millennials feel that they are being exploited by employers and unable to affect change on their own, they may well turn to unions that strive to organize across workplaces and engage whole communities.

HUMAN RESOURCE MANAGEMENT STRATEGIES: THE "RULES OF ENGAGEMENT"

While some employers may view workers as simply items on a balance sheet, savvy managers realize that workers must be invested in the companies and agencies for which they work if levels of retention, performance, and productivity are to remain high. This is especially the case with Millennials, who expect to be respected, valued, and rewarded for skills they bring to work. Characterizations of the ways employees relate to their work environment are varied, their definitions inconsistent, and their applications subject to different interpretations. The most common concepts used to define this relationship are *employee satisfaction, voice, commitment, involvement,* and *engagement.*

The extent to which employees are satisfied in their work environment is usually gauged through surveys and interviews; it is predominantly passive, requiring no active participation on the part of workers in revising workplace policies. Employees can offer suggestions for improving satisfaction and HR departments can revise policies to enhance satisfaction based on these suggestions, but the employees' role is limited to responding to employer overtures. "Voice" refers to employees' ability to respond to organizational decisions that affect them individually (Farndale et al., 2011, p. 114). It allows employees more active involvement in responding directly to organizational decisions and gives them greater input into specific policies than provided by satisfaction surveys, but it is still a reactive approach to assessing employee attitudes. "Commitment" is understood as employees' loyalty to the organization and the stake they have in promoting organizational goals and missions. Exchange theory posits that the cognitive and emotional orientations of employees toward all aspects of their workplace environment, including perception of employers' treatment of them, determine levels of commitment (Farndale et al., 2011, pp. 113-115).

Employee involvement is often equated with employee engagement (EE) in the popular literature, though a more systematic overview of academic usage illuminates differences between the two. Involvement indicates the degree of employees' psychological investment in their work and working environment; engagement includes a whole panorama of cognitive beliefs, emotional attitudes, and behavioral characteristics, such as the amount of energy and discretionary effort devoted to work (Kular, Gatenby, Rees, Soane, & Truss, 2008, pp. 3-4; Van Rooy et al., 2011, p. 149). Involvement refers to individual attachment and takes place within existing hierarchical and power structures in terms of accountability and performance. Engagement includes participation in teamwork and communication across organizational and power structures (Schulte, n.d.), and emphasizes workplace culture (Wright, n.d., pp. 17-20). Companies now have positions entitled "Global Engagement Director" and hold "Employee Engagement Conferences," working closely with HR departments to promote retention, enhance commitment, and improve employee and organizational performance (Schulte, n.d.). A survey of the EE literature reveals engagement methods that are very much in sync with the life and workplace values articulated by Millennials (Table 16.4).

Gallup polling over a 30-year period of both a swath of working Americans and employees at specific companies indicates that engaged employees are more satisfied and that there is a direct correlation between employee engagement and organizational performance (Tyler, 2009). Nonunion employees tend to consider themselves more engaged than unionized workers (ibid.); this could be because union members delegate their "voice" to union representatives (Benson & Brown, 2010) or because employers use strategies to engage more directly with individual employees in nonunion workplaces (U.S. MSPB, 2010). The important lesson is that engaged workers in both categories perform better than those who feel no engagement.

The seriousness of purpose underlying employee engagement strategies is evident by the rich literature dedicated to the field in the private and public sectors, where the concept has been integrated into all components of the federal workforce (U.S. GAO, 2005; U.S.MBPS, 2008). The

Table 16.4.   Employee Engagement Strategies

1. Involve employers and managers in teamwork activities;

2. Generate collective knowledge, as in "cloud computing;"

3. Base regular individual and team performance evaluations on interactive feedback;

4. Establish regular communication between managers and employees and among colleagues;

5. Eliminate "command and control" decisionmaking; encourage employee input into all aspects of company policy;

6. Encourage employees to act as company advocates for products, service, and talent recruitment;

7. Encourage employee networking for ideas and contacts;

8. Remove communication, technology, and generational barriers to create an integrated workforce;

9. Introduce reverse mentoring between Millennials and older workers;

10. Reward creativity, risk, and innovation to enhance performance;

11. Provide opportunities for portable training and professional development;

12. Coordinate organizational mission and goals with employee beliefs;

13. Integrate state-of-the-art technology into workplace activities;

14. Support employee volunteer activities to highlight organizational values;

15. Institutionalize transparency in pay, policies, and performance;

16. Create an organizational culture that fosters mutual trust and support.

Note: Compiled from: Alsop (2008); AARP (2007); Butler (2009); Haeberle (n.d.); Keene & Handrich (2010); Schulte (n.d.); Shellenberger (2011); Tyler (2009); U.S. GAO (2005); U.S.MPSB (2008); Wright (n.d.).

aim of these strategies is clearly to attract top talent, promote employee well-being, and enhance organizational performance (Butler, 2009; Riordan, Vandenburg, & Richardson, 2005, p. 475; U.S. MSPB, 2008). Yet some observers and union activists claim that employee engagement strategies are problematic if they result in union substitution. Employee focus group responses in one study, for example, indicating that some employees liked the "existence of a familial culture where people are committed to a cause and accept lower wages" and enjoyed the "benefits of working in a small organization (such as) mutuality and the ability to discuss problems openly with managers," were labeled as "attitude problems." These "problems," the authors wrote, "were seen by a number of interviewees to be compounded by a shortage of workplace activists who would challenge them" (Cunningham & James, 2010, p, 50). The only way these attitudes, most of which refer to engagement, could be described as "problems" is if observers believe that employees do not know what is in their own interest or if union presence were desirable not for the purpose of improving employee wellbeing but to promote the power of unions in the absence of specific employee complaints (Bunkley, 2011b; Higgins & Naughton, 2011).

In like fashion, a regional AFL-CIO official in Alabama, where Hyundai built an auto factory that pays high wages and encourages employer-employee engagement, complained that employees have shunned unionization because "these car companies know what they are doing. They come in and pay the best wages in town ... to convince employees that they do not need representation" (Higgens & Naughton, 2011). Since complaining about high wages did not encourage workers to unionize, UAW chief Bob King reverted to calling Hyundai "human rights violators" (Bunkley, 2011a). This approach will not capture the imagination of Millennials, who value workplace conditions, skill-based performance pay, and cooperative employer-employee relations. Millennials, the most highly educated, connected, and socially-oriented generation, are also not likely to respond well to the idea that they do not know what is in their own interest. More than any other generation, they have had the opportunity to test their perceptions and interests in the marketplace of ideas on social and professional networking internet sites; they enter the marketplace "with eyes wide open" and are not likely to take well to the assertion that they need unions or any other group to tell them where their interests lie. At the end of the day, only Millennial employees will decide if they are genuinely engaged in their workplaces or merely being manipulated. Decisions to join unions will be theirs based on their own assessment of the facts.

This analysis is corroborated by auto industry workers, including those in Generation Y, who have shunned unionization in southern "right-to-work" states, where foreign automakers have increasingly set up shop in order to enhance their competitiveness (Hirsch, 2011). Company engagement strategies to create productive and trust-based employer-employee relationships appear to be successful in obviating the perceived need for union representation among workers, many of whom "have an intense loyalty to the automakers who brought high-paying blue-collar employment to these small towns and cities starved for jobs" and see no need to join a union (Higgins & Naughton, 2011; Hirsch, 2011). The words of one worker, "I don't need someone talking to the boss for me," sum up employee comments when asked about unionization at a Kia plant in Georgia and a Nissan factory in Tennessee (Hirsch, 2011), indicating that good communication with management, employee "voice," high wages, and job satisfaction convince workers that they do not need union representation. The attempt by the president of the UAW, Bob King, to "expand (the union's) reach by courting new political constituencies such as environmentalists and human-rights activists" is unlikely to appeal to a blue-collar working class constituency making good wages and encountering positive working conditions (Higgins & Naughton, 2011).

Two specific components of EE are most likely to succeed in pairing up employers with ambitious, white-collar Millennials: LiLAs and career-pathing, both of which speak to Generation Y's desire for skill-oriented training and professional development. LiLAs are worker-owned accounts to fund employee education and training through matching employer-employee contributions, some of which are tax-deductible; further funding is potentially available through government or educational foundations. LiLAs are an innovative tool to merge three strategic goals: skill development, economic productivity in the public and private sectors, and a matching of worker skills to the needs of a rapidly changing economy ("Lifelong Learning Accounts," 2011).

LiLAs differ from existing educational programs in that, like 401(k) retirement funds, they belong to the employee and are not tied to a particular employer or place of employment. The LiLA project was introduced by the Council for Adult and Experiential Learning in 2001 and tested in three states and four industries: restaurant service, health care, manufacturing, and the public sector (Mullane, 2006). The success of the pilot program motivated a group of bipartisan politicians, educators, and employers to spearhead legislation in several states to institutionalize LiLA accounts ("Overview of LiLA State Legislation," n.d.); as of 2011, Washington State, California, and Maine have introduced different forms of LiLAs. In 2011 a bipartisan group of U.S. Congressmen introduced The Lifelong Learning Accounts Act (H.R. 1869) to provide federal support and funding for LiLA accounts. LiLAs speak to the particular needs and interests of the Millennials: they are targeted to this generation's hunger for further education, skill development, and training. Their portability accommodates Millennials' propensity to switch jobs and careers. They also address the economy's skills gap, which creates a mis-match between a high number of unemployed young job seekers and employers' hiring needs, and enhance productivity for employers by increasing retention and cutting the cost of hiring new employees.

LiLAs are a boon to employers and employees alike, with the additional benefit of addressing a rapidly changing and globalized economy that continually demands new skills (Olson, 2010). Perhaps even more importantly in a polarized environment, LiLAs enjoy bipartisan support from politicians and employers in the private and public sectors and engender enthusiasm among workers and employers alike (Mullane, 2006). Employers should encourage and support state and federal legislation to make LiLA programs a permanent workforce fixture. In Britain, trade unions have taken up the cause of lifelong learning projects. While the benefit in terms of skill development for employees may be similar, placing the accounts within trade union structures may consolidate the "worker solidarity" approach to employers and reinforce employer-union tensions rather than encourage employer-employer mutual interests (Payne, 2001, pp. 382, 386). By devoting resources to employee lifelong learning and training, employers in both the public and private sectors can create mutually beneficial interests in a nonconfrontational environment.

Career-pathing establishes a series of goals and support systems within an organization to guide young workers through the hoops of career advancement. Career pathing—defined skill-based strategies to provide employees with a clear path to professional advancement—has been around for decades. It initially focused on an individual's attempt to chart career goals based on a self-assessment of a composite of skills and experience (Burack & Mathys, 1979, p. 7) and evolved into "an organizational process identifying promotional possibilities and sequencing" (Simonsen, 1986. p. 70). In the 1990s, more sophisticated techniques, focusing on knowledge, skill, and ability data and centered on a "job analytic approach" have been developed to "identify previously hidden career paths which could aid an organization in its internal manpower planning efforts" (Wooten, 1993, p. 561). Such efforts speak directly to the goals of Millennials, who "place a premium on self-determination, want to be in charge of their careers ... (aim to develop) as many marketable skills as possible and ... expect companies to help them with their resume-building mission" (Alsop, 2008, pp. 32-33). Career pathing is thus a mutually beneficial skill-centered exercise that speaks both to Millennials' desire for well-defined performance criteria and employers' goals of productivity and retention.

Research on Millennials indicates that they value clear structures and guidelines when it comes to attaining their goals (Keene & Handrich, 2010). Career-pathing techniques can encourage Millennials to develop and refine skills that help them advance vertically within an organization or laterally across different agencies in the civil service. Career-pathing entails performance development planning, mentoring during planning and implementation stages, performance appraisals, and employer-employee collaboration to successfully merge employee and employer goals. In nonunion workplaces, employers can speak directly to the interests of Millennials by offering institutionalized professional development through career-pathing to enhance employee retention, productivity, and the commitment of employees to organizational mission. Employers may engage Millennial Generation workers directly by offering skill-based guidelines and support structures to enhance young workers' career goals. In unionized environments, unions can work with employers to establish performance measures that promote organizational goals while promoting employee skill development. Potential tensions, especially in teachers' unions, can develop over "seniority versus talent" as the major criterion for career advancement. Unions have to navigate between Millennials' focus on skill-based talent, and older members' arguments that seniority rules reward valuable experience and are central to employee security (Coggshall, Behrstock-Sherratt, & Drill, 2011, p. 15; Greenberg & Weber, 2008, pp. 71-72). Unions have begun to address this "tenure versus talent" debate (Kearney, 2011), which will result either in fractious union debates or creative ways to balance the two.

THE TRUCE: MILLENIALS
AND LABOR-MANAGEMENT PARTNERSHIPS

Concession Truces

In the midst of economic downturns, employers engage in concession bargaining and variable pay strategies (Dougherty & Slobin, 2011). In private sector unionized environments, managers must appeal to mutual employer-employee goals (e.g., the financial viability of a company and its plants in a harsh economy, job retention, long-term wage and benefit equalization, and education and training opportunities) in order to compel unionized young workers to accept lower wages and benefits packages than their older cohorts. Both company management and unions have a common goal in protecting the financial viability of the company and saving jobs, which has resulted in unions eventually relinquishing some of the gains in wages and benefits negotiated during flush economic times, compelling them to adapt to financial realities that lessened their negotiating power (Samuelson, 2011).

In public sector unionized environments, government employers and managers face a more complicated situation: in an era of fiscal crisis, they are now caught between two constituencies: taxpayers who vote them in or out of office and unions that can direct considerable financial resources toward supporting or opposing their candidacies. Public sector managers must navigate between shrinking state and local budgets, on the one hand, and union opposition to reduction in wages, benefits, and workplace resources, on the other. In addition to having to reconcile the interests of two constituencies, government employers at all levels, including school boards, must deal with a polarized environment, where attitudes toward unionization transcend benefits and take place on a level of political philosophy (the role of the state), sociology (social movements and class conflicts), and political rights (collective bargaining versus "the right to work").

Starting in 2006, private companies such as Caterpillar, Kohler, and Harley-Davidson engaged in concession bargaining, compelling unions to accept concessions with the threat of moving their operations to right-to-work states where unions are not as strong and unionization drives less successful (Romell, 2010; Uchitelle, 2006). Companies argued that the concessions were necessary in light of higher production costs and decreasing sales. Unions balked but eventually relented, in large part because job security assumed priority over all other considerations; high unemployment rates meant that the companies would likely be successful in hiring new workers at lower wage and benefit structures. In 2011, concession bargaining caused an uproar in Wisconsin, Indiana, and Ohio, as public unions fought tooth and nail against state officials' attempts to limit collective bargaining rights and increase employee contributions to health care and pension funds (Maher & Belkin, 2011). Whereas private sector concession bargaining is usually limited to individual companies or sectors, public sector concession bargaining captivated the nation as it addressed fundamental questions of the government's role in the economy, class, conflicts, and workers' rights.

Even in the context of concession bargaining, unions can take an active role in mitigating some of the concessions and agreeing with employers on ways to make a reduction in wages and benefits less painful to both established and incoming workers (Bennett, 2011, p. B2). One component of concession bargaining that applies most directly to Millennials working in the manufacturing sector, and that is likely to be successful with the sometimes grudging consent of unions, is the introduction of a two-tier wage structure and other components of a variable pay system (VPS).

Variable Pay Systems

Variable pay systems allow employers to compensate employees in different ways based on performance, company profitability, or seniority. Variable pay includes employee performance-based merit wage increases and bonuses, company performance-based profit sharing, and two-tier wage structures. Critics argue that VPS undermines the legitimacy of unions in representing their workers' interests (Chaison, 2008), while some analysts counter that union involvement over variable pay structures can enhance union legitimacy and give unions more voice in deciding the nature of VPS and control over its implementation (Marginson et al., 2008).

Unions are especially averse to merit pay increases, fearing that they come at the expense of across-the-board wage increases for employees. The most divisive component of VPS is the two-tier wage system, by which companies pay either new workers or workers with little seniority less than they pay current workers with a certain amount of seniority. Two-tier wage structures can be either permanent or temporary. Permanent two-tier wage systems institutionalize lower wages for all incoming hires and standardize the lower tier on a company-wide basis through retirements, buyouts, and resignations. The airline industry tried this in the 1980s and it failed because of the bitter divisions it caused. Temporary two-tier wage structures, whereby lower-tier workers know that they will have the opportunity to catch up to a higher tier of wages and benefits in the foreseeable future, have been more successful and look to become a core feature of contract negotiations in the midst of the new millennium's prolonged recession (Cappelli, 2011).

While unions have traditionally based their wage negotiations on the principle of "equal pay for equal work," a bad economy, high unemployment, and companies' attempts to insulate themselves against a fluctuating economy have made two-tier wage structures an increasingly prominent part of new union contracts in recent years. Managers view two-tier wage structures as a strategy to save costs for mutual employer-employee gain, maintain or increase employment, resuscitate failing industries, and adjust wage and benefit packages to market conditions in order to avoid peaks and valleys in economic vigor and union strength (Uchitelle, 2006). Some union activists, in contrast, view the strategy as weakening unions by setting members against each other, undermining past wage and benefit gains, and violating an implicit "social contract" that guarantees a solid middle-class lifestyle for reliable workers who enhance company performance in the long term (Romell, 2010).

In 2007, the UAW accepted proposals by America's big three auto makers to institute a two-tier wage structure, offering lower wages to new hires, because of wage competition from foreign automakers that was hurting U.S. auto sales (Dziczek, 2011). The ensuing contract meant that about 12% of Chrysler's 23,000 union workers received lower tier wages and benefits, including reduced vacation time and lower pensions (Vlasic, 2011). Workers at GM plants in Orion, Michigan and Indianapolis, Indiana rebelled against UAW concessions on pay structures, basing their protests on traditional "equal work for equal pay principles" (Chen, 2011) and balking against a deal that would have workers with 10 years seniority or less taking a significant cut in pay. Workers were angry that union representatives accepted the two-tier wage structure without the input of the union rank-and-file and said that they would rather see plants shut down than accept concessions on the pay structure ("GM workers protest,"

2010). Antiunion critics have different reasons for opposing tiered wages: they argue that union negotiators distort the job market by creating a "cartel" for higher wage workers when they prevent across-the-board lowered wage adjustments (Sherk, 2011). Nevertheless, two-tier wage structures are becoming a permanent feature of the economic landscape.

Despite push-back from some rank-and-file workers, the UAW accepted temporary two-tier pay systems as it negotiated new contracts with the big three American auto manufacturers in the autumn of 2011 (Dolan, Bennett, & Ramsey, 2011, p. B1). In September of that year, the UAW signed a new 4-year contract with General Motors covering 48,000 workers, whereby about 6,400 new or existing union members will receive lower wages than longer-term employees. GM also made use of other components of the VPS: to avoid increasing fixed-costs, UAW accepted worker signing bonuses and profit-sharing disbursements in lieu of wage and benefit increases, as a way to ensure company solvency and save jobs. In return, GM agreed to increase base wage and health benefits for entry-level workers. Key to the deal was GM's agreement to hire more workers at its U.S. plants and to allow unions to organize and represent them (Woodall & Bailey, 2011).

Companies' attempts to connect a two-tier wage structure to limitations on union organizing of new hires prove to be more contentious. The Kohler Company, for example, tried to introduce a two-tier wage structure linked to a hiring strategy based on "flexible" workers, a move that led to much union antipathy and cries of union-busting (Romell, 2010). One reason union representatives give for their acceptance of two-tier wage structures is management's willingness to allow unions to continue organizing new lower-paid workers (Eaton, Kochan, & McKersie, 2003). The same is true for the September 2011 GM-UAW contract: UAW Vice President Joe Ashton said that "the biggest win for the union was the pledge of new factory jobs at GM ... the union aspires to have as many as 60,000 UAW-represented GM workers in 4 years" (Woodall & Bailey, 2011). Unions are more likely to accept two-tier pay structures if they are de-linked from union organizing campaigns and viewed in the context of mutual employer-employee gains to increase employment and retain employees, rather than seen as underhanded company attempts to foment dissension within unions or marginalize unions by creating a permanent tier of lower-wage workers hired on a temporary basis.

The important issue for young workers is that they be given the chance to catch up to a higher wage and benefit tier in the near future. Younger workers are likely to be more accepting of lower tier wages when they are just starting out than older workers who have been laid off and are reentering the workforce. Whereas the older workers see a palpable decline in wages and benefits in terms of their skill levels and past experience, Millennials are inclined to think that if they work hard, even for relatively lower pay, they are bound to do well and eventually start earning what they believe their work is worth (SBR Consulting, 2011). The results of one study and internet discussion with employed Millennials indicate that this generation is willing to accept reduced benefits if it means retaining more workers: "[I]t is less about the company needing to lay off workers but more about how companies come to that decision and the manner in which they do so. Many Millennials feel ... that companies should first cut back on hours, benefits, and refocus on company strategy first" (SBR Consulting, 2011, p. 9). Whereas some unions prefer to protect established wage and benefits packages for senior employees over existing jobs when there is the need for a tradeoff, Millennials appear to be more interested in job retention and creation.

Some companies are addressing this issue head on, by telling young workers that they will make up for lower wages with increased educational and training opportunities, career-pathing, and better workplace conditions (Uchitelle, 2006). In a depressed job market, opportunities for continued educational and professional advancement are likely to outweigh depressed wages, especially given Millennials' long-term perspective and belief that hard work will eventually pay off. Millennial workers are more likely to accept two-tier wage structures if they are temporary and if they are given other opportunities for professional development within the company. But they will have to be convinced that the motivation for the two-tier wage structure derives from the mutual interest of unions and employers to save existing jobs and add new ones (SBR Consulting, 2011). If young workers perceive that companies are earning huge profits that benefit upper-level executives at the cost of profit-sharing or raising wages for employees, this could drive young workers into the arms of unions, and set them against union leaders who support temporary two-tier wage structures (Uchitelle, 2006).

Experience suggests that variable pay systems neither promote adversarial relationships between management and unions nor decrease union legitimacy in representing worker interests. If management engages unions in an atmosphere of transparency and trust, explaining the need for the bifurcated wage structure, unions can enhance their legitimacy and voice by taking an active role in negotiating the VPS terms. What is important is that both sides agree on the necessity of the strategy, management is trusted to be acting out of concern for performance and profitability, and unions have a say in determining the conditions under which the two-tier structure is introduced. Agreement on the total amount of money set aside for merit pay increases or bonuses, for example, can assuage unions' concerns that this type of VPS limits wage and benefit increases (Marginson et al, 2008). Agreement on a phasing out of the two-tier structure can help convince rank-and-file union members at the lower end of the two tiers that it is better to be employed at lower wages than to be unemployed with no wages and that they can eventually work themselves up the wage ladder once economic times are better (Dziczek, 2011; Vlasic, 2011).

The potential tensions between management and unions over two-tier wage structures and between senior and junior workers within unions can be mitigated by union involvement in determining the specific components of the tiering agreement. By making two-tier wage structures temporary; replacing base wage increases with sign-up, performance, and profit-sharing bonuses; reopening closed plants; hiring new workers; and negotiating the continued organization and representation of new hires, unions and management can address common goals while compromising on issues important to each side (Bennett, 2011, p. B2). Variable pay systems, including two-tier wage structures, give companies the flexibility they need to control costs in an economic downturn. While some young workers may be angry at older union members for accepting a two-tier wage structure, high unemployment rates, the chance to advance to a higher wage and benefit category, and opportunities for professional development are likely to compel them to accept concessions. Millennials, disadvantaged not only by prolonged high levels of unemployment but also by intense competition for jobs with long-term unemployed older workers, large education debts, and few chances to practice or develop skills, are likely accept two-tier wage structures, believing that the future is theirs.

Partnership Truce: Labor-Management Cooperation Based on Interest-Based Bargaining

An alternative to concession bargaining is interest-based bargaining (IBB) carried out within the context of labor-management partnerships. These partnerships occur on a formal or informal basis in the private sector, and at the local, state, and federal levels of the public sector. Private sector partnerships are most likely to succeed given the commitment of labor and management leaders to make them work, the presence of a third-party negotiator, and mutual employer-employee interest in company profitability, job retention, and high performance standards. State and local informal partnerships can also succeed if based on the long-term, bipartisan commitment of both parties to make the partnership work, especially since both government managers and union members are constrained by financial realities, taxpayer pressure, and threats of layoffs. Federal labor-management partnerships have the most hurdles to overcome because they emerge from presidential executive orders mandating that agency heads accept partnerships, which may compel them to follow the letter of the law but lack commitment to its spirit, thus undermining actual practice. In addition, while agency heads may encounter budgetary constraints, neither they nor union members are under immediate pressure from state and local taxpayers or the threat of layoffs—pressure that might induce them to cooperate with each other.

Labor-management partnerships seek to bring labor unions and employers together in a framework that emphasizes mutual goals, common commitment, and open dialogue. These partnerships are founded on interest-based bargaining, also called integrative or principled bargaining, an alternative or complement to adversarial collective bargaining. IBB addresses specific issues in a working environment and provides employers and unions the tools, techniques, and training to identify mutual interests and cooperatively solve problems by relying on objective data as much as possible (FMCS, n.d.). By de-emphasizing institutional power struggles, entrenched bargaining stances, confrontational positioning, personalities, and past animosities, IBB "utilizes problem-solving tools as a way of avoiding positional conflicts and ... achieving better outcomes for all stakeholders" (O'Dowd & Barrett, 2005, p. 6).

The critical question underlying interest-based bargaining is whether or not there is an inherent tension involved in the employer-union relationship that creates a structural "us versus them" dichotomy that does not lend itself to consensual decision-making. Some union leaders and members involved in both public and private labor-management partnerships have questioned the consensual approach based on the assumption that there are antagonistic stances built into the employer-worker relationship. IBB is sometimes viewed as a front for employer dominance; some union members criticize union representatives engaged in IBB for developing close relationships with managers that call into question their commitment to union objectives (Eaton et al., 2010). Nevertheless, labor-management partnerships based on IBB have quietly taken hold in the private sector and come into prominence once again in the public sector during the Obama Administration. Given the problems that IBB was designed to address, as well as the work-related orientations of Millennials, it can be argued that labor-union partnerships based on this form of bargaining will appeal to this generation more than adversarial bargaining techniques that structurally set employer against employee (O'Dowd & Barrett, 2005). Following are examples of labor-management partnerships in the private sector and local and federal levels of the public sector.

Private Sector Partnership: Kaiser Permanente

Kaiser Permanente is a nonprofit foundation, that provides health care to more than 8 million customers in nine states. The Kaiser Permanente labor-management partnership was formed in 1997 "after years of labor turmoil … and competitive pressures within the health care industry" ("History of Partnership," 2010, n.p.), when concession bargaining on the part of Kaiser and adversarial negotiation on the part of unions had seriously undermined workplace morale, negatively affected company performance and customer satisfaction, and created tensions between management and unions. Both union and management leaders turned to a labor-management partnership approach to find a way out of the impasse that had developed. After three years of framework preparation and the training of more than 400 managers and union representatives, the two sides signed a 5-year agreement with 26 local AFL-CIO unions. This contract replaced a series of separate contracts with different expiration dates negotiated by more than 50 bargaining units (Eaton et al., 2010). Two more 5-year contracts were signed in 2005 and 2010, and the partnership now encompasses 30 local unions and 90,000 Kaiser Permanente employees. These partnership employees work in function-oriented unit-based teams with managers and doctors to improve performance, increase efficiency, create a better workplace environment, and support regional business priorities ("History of Partnership," 2010).

Observers attribute the relative success of Kaiser's partnership model to management and union leader commitment to make the partnership work, ongoing training in interest-based negotiation techniques, the involvement of a third party negotiation specialist to facilitate IBB, the emphasis on performance improvement, a UBT-centered performance-based award system, and transparency. IBB was based on explicit agreement on the topics open for negotiation: "The issue of scope is inextricably tied to decision making. Scope sets the boundaries for the Partnership: what is in play, what is not" ("LMP Founding Agreement," 1997). Especially critical in 1997 was the leadership role of both new Kaiser CEO David Lawrence and union negotiators who proved willing to rethink a formerly adversarial union-management relationship and steer it in a more cooperative direction. Lawrence rallied skeptical managers around the idea of partnership and union leaders fended off accusations that they were renouncing traditional union goals and getting too close to management. Without this shared commitment, it is unlikely that the Partnership would have gotten off the ground. There are still thorny problems that dog negotiation, most notably employment security (Eaton et al., 2010) and disagreement among participating unions (Maher, 2011). The willingness of some unions to go outside the Partnership agreement to take part in a solidarity strike illustrates the potential structural problem of overcoming an "us versus them" mentality in union-employer relationships (Sklueff, 2011).

Local Public Sector Partnerships

In a context where teachers' unions are fighting divisive battles with school boards and government officials over performance evaluations, wages, benefits, and working conditions, the American Federation of Teachers has identified three cases in which local AFT affiliates have developed productive relations with local school boards and government officials. The common goal is to establish professional development programs, alternative compensation systems, skill-based performance evaluations, performance reviews, and the "leveraging (of) technology to enhance performance" directed at Generation Y workers to improve both the quality of education for students and retention trends among young teachers (Coggshall et al., 2011, p. 2). In St. Francis, MN, Philadelphia, and Austin, Texas, AFT affiliates have collaborated with administrators, school boards, and local officials to improve student performance, create alternative salary schedules based on performance rather than seniority, introduce teacher evaluation and feedback systems, and install professional development programs. There have been marked improvements in teacher morale and retention, performance criteria development, and feedback mechanisms. Crucial to the success of these measures is the collaboration between unions and public employers:

> collaboration between unions and management (is) beginning to build sustainable high-performing workplaces—from St. Francis, which upended traditional ways teachers are supported, evaluated, and compensated, to Philadelphia, where the union and management together made some bold initial steps toward transformation.... [T]hese transformative changes to teachers' work would not have been possible if union and district officials had not joined forces. (Coggshall et al., 2011, pp. 31, 11)

Instructive here is that one of the AFT's cooperative partnerships is in Austin, Texas, where collective bargaining is prohibited (Coggshall et al., 2011, p. 18, fn. 5). Union-management collaboration based on the will to work together to pursue common goals that serve the needs of management, consumers, and employees may even lead to more collaborative bargaining than that encouraged by mandated collective bargaining, which can exacerbate a confrontational culture. Former UFT union leader Albert Shanker's proclamation that, "When schoolchildren start paying union dues, that's when I'll start representing the interests of schoolchildren" (Klein, 2011, p. A15), is unlikely to appeal to Millennial teachers, who value service, education, and skill-based performance more than institutional power, seniority, and loyalty. The AFT's cooperative strategy is far more likely to capture the imagination of dedicated Millennial teachers.

Federal Public Sector Partnerships

The U.S. federal government has a big stake in promoting productive employer-employee relations, especially with 60% of its workforce unionized (Masters et al., 2010, p. 2). President Clinton, arguing that union-based labor-management partnerships are the best way to attain that goal, issued an executive order in 1993 that created a Labor-Management Partnership Council to formally engage unions in agency processes. President George Bush, countering that "managing for success" would be served best by direct employer-employee relations, issued his own executive order in 2002, making federal-level labor-management partnerships optional, but obviously discouraging them. Bush's Labor Secretary, Elaine Chao, argued: "The best way to protect workers is to help employers understand their legal obligations and promote collaborative working relationships between employers and workers on safety and other issues" (Fund, 2010).

President Obama issued Executive Order 13522 in December 2009, reinstituting the National Labor-Management Council to oversee mandated labor-management partnerships in all federal agencies (U.S. Federal Register, 2009). It includes the Clinton-era requirement for extensive training of partnership participants and adds the factor of "predecisional involvement," which gives unions the right to participate in decisions that go beyond the scope of those delineated in negotiation agreements (Parker, 2009). These would include annual budget process decisions (U.S. OMB, 2011), freezes on federal employee pay, and possible government shutdowns (Dougan, 2011). Proponents argue that partnerships facilitate agency missions, improve operations, promote consensual labor-management relations, entice talent to the federal civil service, and enrich employee engagement (Rosenberg 2007). Critics argue that they may hamper the budget process, constrain managerial flexibility, increase bureaucratic wrangling, and give unions too much influence in budgetary decisions that undermine transparency (Tapscott, 2011).

A white paper for the National Labor-Management Council noted that the partnerships will prove productive only if both management and union leaders are committed to their success; both sides recognize the legitimacy of each other's goals; participants receive adequate training in

IBB and prove committed to making cooperation work; and predecisional involvement is actively pursued in a measureable way (Masters et al., 2010, p. 2). The problem is that none of these requirements will be easy to attain; in fact, some of the factors that have made the Kaiser Permanente and AFT labor-management partnerships successful are missing in the federal case.

It is far from given, for example, that agency managers and union leaders will be committed to a structure that has been mandated by executive order rather than voluntarily agreed to. Agency heads may balk at the limitations on decision-making involving budget and pay and some union leaders may be averse to partnerships based on IBB when they believe that unions and management have fundamentally different interests. John Gage, the President of the American Federation of Government Employees, for example, criticized "'the philosophy (behind all the rules on consensus)' ... because (it) often forces labor and management to pretend they have more in common than they did and ignored the fact that each side had different interests at stake during negotiation" (Rosenberg, 2009). Gage also advocated eliminating both the training requirements of the Clinton-era partnerships and throwing out the whole notion of IBB (Rosenberg, 2009). Though the AFGE and other federal unions have since come out to actively support the Obama administration partnerships (AFGE, 2011), attitudes such as these would undermine the very foundation of the cooperation and the whole concept behind proactive engagement. Unions strongly support the predecisional involvement component of the Obama Administration partnerships; Kaiser Permanente officials, in contrast, claim that one reason their labor-management partnership works so well is because of the well-defined "scope" factor, referring to clearly articulated issues open for labor-management negotiation ("History of Partnership," 2010).

Based on the aforementioned orientations of the Millennial generation, it is likely that labor-management partnerships in the private sector will appeal more to the Generation Y mindset than traditional adversarial approaches. Millennials like to work in teams, seek communication and open dialogue with employers, desire skill-based performance measures for which they are adequately trained and rewarded, advocate for better work-life balance, and want to participate in workplace decisions. Private sector labor-management partnerships based on IBB speak to these Millennial orientations. The Kaiser Partnership, for example, is structured on integrated teamwork that emphasizes and rewards performance: regional partnership teams address work-life balance issues and career transitions, and strategy groups develop ongoing education, training, and performance-measuring metrics (Eaton et al., 2010, p. 22). Interest-based bargaining will appeal to Millennials more than adversarial zero-sum negotiations based on irreconcilable conflicts or identities because it encourages cooperation with employers and colleagues to attain specific goals. By providing Millennials with a constructive voice in workplace policies (O'Dowd & Barrett, 2005), IBB-based partnerships can tap into the skills and creativity of a new generation interested more in performing than protesting.

CONCLUSION

Millennials exhibit characteristics that make them open to cooperative management-employee relations as long as employers make employees the company's most important asset (SBR Consulting, 2011, p. 9). Employee engagement strategies have proven to increase not only employee satisfaction but also to benefit the company's bottom line (Van Rooy et al., 2011, p. 147). It thus behooves companies to foster productive employer-employee relations. Creative EE strategies may then indirectly obviate the need for unions in the minds of employees.

In environments where employers fail to address basic employee needs, unions have a role in organizing workers who otherwise would not have a voice or any leverage vis-à-vis their employers. In workplace environments where unions have a strong and long-term presence, employers can appeal to Millennial workers by cooperating with unions on skill development, evaluation practices, and employee advancement. The battle for the soul of Millennial Generation workers will leave scars only if employers value profit over employee satisfaction and unions value power over employee benefits in light of a realistic assessment of the current economic situation. Millennials have many skills to offer; the extent to which these skills can be positively exploited and developed by employers and unions alike depends on how employees are treated at the workplace. In nonunionized settings, the more effectively employers engage Millennials, the less likely young workers will be compelled to join unions. The more tenuous the job situation, as with temporary workers and freelancers, and the lower and less stable the wage and benefit packages, as with low-skilled blue-collar jobs and piecemeal tech jobs, the more likely Millennials, like their older cohorts, will seek to address "representation gaps" through union participation (Healy, Heery, Taylor, & Brown, 2004). In unionized settings, Millennials will likely prefer IBB over adversarial relationships with employers, such as participating in solidarity strikes, if employers are willing to work with union representatives to attain mutual goals and engage employees in the process. Union and management leaders agree that employee engagement is the way to attract, retain, and energize employees (Haeberle, 2011; Levi, Olson, Agnone, & Kelly, 2009;

Masters et al., 2010). Engagement policies will have a special appeal to Millennials who expect to have their voices heard and their skills recognized. If the competition between employers and unions to attract Millennials is based on engagement, those most likely to emerge victorious are the Millennials themselves, as they will gravitate to whichever group offers the most opportunities for them to practice their skills in a teamwork setting. "Members of the (Millennial) generation envision symbiotic relationships with the organizations that employ them—they are loyal to organizations that are loyal to them" (Hershatter & Epstein, 2010, pp. 219-220).

Millennials have a healthy distrust of institutions, though a willingness to believe that they can be made better through engagement. This distrust extends from corporations to unions. Corporations that seek to improve the bottom line for the sake of corporate power defined as high stock prices or enormous CEO salaries will alienate Millennials as much as unions that seek to exacerbate class tensions or engage in adversarial bargaining for the sake of enhancing union power for power's sake. Millennials are interested in developing, employing, and improving their skills to do well for themselves and to do good in the world. They devote their energies to those people and organizations that allow them to do this best, whether it be creative employers who seek to tap the wealth of talent in the Millennial Generation by engaging its members and investing in their skills and performance, or unions that strive to revitalize their ranks by offering Millennials support structures and opportunities for professional development lacking in their workplaces.

Millennials are savvy enough to know what is good for them and are not likely to bow to any institutional attempts to define their interests, whether on the part of employers or labor unions. Both employers and labor unions will have to appeal to the interests of young workers as highlighted here to attract and retain members of Generation Y. The battle between employers and unions for the soul of Millennials will be resolved either by a truce based on labor-management partnerships or by one side or the other better understanding the "rules of engagement."

REFERENCES

A union education. (2011, March 1). *The Wall Street Journal*, A14.

AFL-CIO. (2009). Young workers: A lost decade. *Working America*. Retrieved from http://www.aflcio.org/aboutus/laborday/upload/laborday2009_report.pdf

AFL-CIO. (2010). Young workers: A lost decade. One year later. Retrieved from http://www.aflcio.org/aboutus/youthsummit/upload/young_workers_100810.pdf

AFL-CIO. (2011). Union summer internship: Description. Retrieved from http://www.aflcio.org/aboutus/unionsummer/qapage.cfm

Alsop, R. (2008). *The trophy kids grow up. How the millennial generation is shaking up the workplace*. San Francisco, CA: Jossey-Bass.

American Association of Retired People. (2007). Leading a multi-generational workforce. Retrieved from http://assets.aarp.org/www.aarp.org_/cs/misc/leading_a_multigenerational_workforce.pdf

American Federation of Government Employees. (2011). Working hard to implement management partner forums. Retrieved from http://www.afge.org/Index.cfm?Page=LaborManagementForums&from=home

Associated Press. (2011, September 22). Recession's lost generation: Census finds new low in mobility, jobs, wedlock for young adults. *The Washington Post*. Retrieved from http://www.washingtonpost.com/politics/recessions-lost-generation-census-finds-new-lows-in-mobility-jobs-wedlock-for-young-adults/2011/09/22/gIQArTYDoK_story.html

Bach, S., & Givan, R. K. (2008). Public service modernization and trade union reform: Towards managerial-led renewal? *Public Administration, 86*, 523-539.

Barro, R. (2011, February 28). Unions versus the right to work. *The Wall Street Journal*, A19.

Bennett, J. (2011, September 26). UAW talks run into detours, delays. *The Wall Street Journal*, p. B2.

Benson, J., & Brown, M. (2010). Employee voice: Does union membership matter? *Human Resource Management Journal, 20*, 80-99.

Berman, E., Bowman, J., West, J., & Van Wart, M. (2012). *Human resources management in public service* (4th ed.). Thousand Oaks, CA: SAGE.

Blain, M. (2001). IT workers need a union. *Network World*. Retrieved from http://www.networkworld.com/forum/2001/0604faceoffyes.html

Bunkley, N. (2011a, February 18). Hyundai's swift growth lift's Alabama's economy. *The New York Times*. Retrieved from http://www.nytimes.com/2011/02/19/business/19hyundai.html?pagewanted=all

Bunkley, N. (2011b, January 12). UAW to renew organizing efforts at foreign-owned plants. *The New York Times*. Retrieved from http://www.nytimes.com/2011/01/13/business/global/13uaw.html

Burack, E. H., & Mathys, N. (1979). Career ladders, pathing and planning. *Human Resource Management, 18*, 2-8.

Burton, T., James, M., Hagerty, R., & Douglas, B. (2011, February 23). Two-track economy. *The Wall Street Journal*, A4.

Butler, P. (2009). Riding along on the crest of a wave: Tracking the shifting rationale for nonunion consultation at Finance Co. *Human Resource Management Journal, 19*, 176-193.

Cappelli, P. (2011, September 18). A tenable position for unions. *The New York Times, Opinion*. Retrieved from http://www.nytimes.com/roomfordebate/2011/09/18/can-detroit-sustain-its-two-tier-pay/unions-can-get-behind-two-tier-wages

Carter, B. (2006). Trade union organizing and renewal: A response to Turberville. *Work, Employment, Society, 20*, 415-426.

Chaison, G. (2008, December). Two-tier wage settlements and the legitimacy of American unions. Unpublished paper. Retrieved from http://www.

ilera-online.org/15thworldcongress/files/papers/Track_4/Wed_P4
_CHAISON.pdf

Chen, L. (2011, September 18). A crucial system, likely to evolve. *The New York Times, Opinion*. Retrieved from http://www.nytimes.com/roomfordebate/2011/09/18/can-detroit-sustain-its-two-tier-pay/two-tier-wages-are-likely-to-evolve

Coggshall, J. G., Behrstock-Sherratt, E., & Drill, K. (2011, April). Workplaces that support high-performing teaching and learning: Insights from Generation Y teachers. *American Federation of Teachers and American Institutes for Research*. Retrieved from http://www.aft.org/pdfs/teachers/genyreport0411.pdf

Cunningham, I., & James, P. (2010). Strategies for union renewal in the context of public sector outsourcing. *Economic and Industrial Democracy, 31*, 34-61.

Dolan, M., Bennett, J., & Ramsey, M. (2011, October 5). Auto makers now import jobs. *The Wall Street Journal*, B1.

Dougan, W. R. (2011, March 6). Federal labor management partnerships can solve problems. *Federal Times, White Paper*. Retrieved from http://www.federal-times.com/article/20110306/ADOP06/103060302/1037/ADOP00

Dougherty, C., & Slobin, S. (2011, February 25). Budget battles roil straitened states. *The Wall Street Journal*, A6.

Dunn, K. (2011, June 14). Your employee happiness argument is invalid. *HR Capitalist*. Retrieved from http://www.careerdigital.com/union/united-states/wage/

Dziczek, K. (2011, September 18). Win-win for workers and employers. *The New York Times, Opinion*. Retrieved from http://www.nytimes.com/roomfordebate/2011/09/18/can-detroit-sustain-its-two-tier-pay/win-win-for-workers-and-employers

Eaton, S. C., Kochan, T. A., & McKersie, R. B. (2003). The Kaiser Permanente labor management partnership: The first five years. *Institute for Work & Employment Research*. Harvard University John F. Kennedy School of Government. Retrieved from http://www.lmpartnership.org/sites/default/files/lmp_first_five_years.pdf

Farndale, E., Van Ruiten, J., Kelliher, C., & Hope-Hailey, V. (2011). The influence of perceived employee voice on organizational commitment: An exchange perspective. *Human Resource Management, 50*, 113-129.

Federal Mediation and Consultation Service. (n.d.). Interest-based bargaining. Retrieved from http://www.fmcs.gov/internet/itemDetail.asp?categoryID=140&itemID=15950

Federal Register. (2009, December 14). The President. Executive order 13522. Retrieved from http://edocket.access.gpo.gov/2009/pdf/E9-29781.pdf

Firestine, N., King, D., & Quan, K. (2010, July). New approaches to organizing women and young workers. Social media and work-family issues. Labor Project for Working Families. Cornell ILR Labor Programs, UC Berkeley Labor Center. Retrieved from http://laborcenter.berkeley.edu/workingwomen/newapproaches10.pdf

Fontes, M., & Margolies, K. (2010). Youth and unions. Cornell University ILR School. Working Papers #104. Retrieved from http://digitalcommons.ilr.cornell.edu/cgi/viewcontent.cgi?article=1103&context=workingpapers

Francia, P. F. (2006). *The future of organized labor in American politics*. New York, NY: Columbia University Press.

Fund, J. (2011, December 3). Government by executive order. *The Wall Street Journal* Retrieved from http://online.wsj.com/article/SB100014240527487033775 04575650700370696396.html

GM workers protest two-tier pay deal at Orion. (2010). Justauto.com. Retrieved from http://www.just-auto.com/news/gm-workers-protest-two-tier-pay-deal-at-orion_id106441.aspx

Goldstein, D. (2008, February 25). Another kind of youth movement. *The American Prospect.* Retrieved from http://prospect.org/cs/articles?article=another_kind_of_youth_movement

Gray, R. (2007). Working practices—Bite-sized generation. *Human Resources Management International Digest, 15*, 37-38.

Greenberg, E. H., & Weber, K. (2008). *Generation we: How millennial youth are taking over America.* Emoryville, CA.: Pachatusan.

Greenhouse, S. (November 21). Cleaning companies in accord with striking Houston janitors. *The New York Times.* Retrieved from http://www.nytimes.com/2006/11/21/us/21janitor.html

Greenhouse, S. (2009b, September 16). Promising a new day, again. *The New York Times.* Retrieved from http://www.nytimes.com/2009/09/16/business/16labor.html

Haeberle, K. (2011). Labor unions are dead, or at least on life support. *Becker's Hospital Review.* Retrieved from http://www.beckershospitalreview.com/news-analysis/labor-unions-are-deador-at-least-on-life-support.htmlHealy,

Healy, G., Heery, E., Taylor, P., & Brown, W. (Eds.). (2004). *The future of worker representation,* London, England: Palgrave.

Heery, E., & Adler, L. (2004). Organising the unorganized. In C. Frege & J. Kelly (Eds.), *Varieties of unionism: Strategies for union revitalization in a globalizing economy.* Oxford, England: Oxford University Press.

Hershatter, A., & Epstein, M. (2010). Millennials and the world of work: An organization and management perspective. *Journal of Business Psychology, 25*, 211-223.

Higgins, T., & Naughton, K. (2011). Hyundai teaches UAW best factory job doesn't need a union. Bloomberg. Retrieved from http://www.bloomberg.com/news/2011-06-22/hyundai-teaches-uaw-best-factory-job-doesn-t-need-a-union-cars.html

Hirsch, B. T., & Macpherson, D. A. (2011). Union membership and coverage database. Retrieved from http://unionstats.gsu.edu/

Hirsch, J. (2011, March 29). Who wants a union? Not southern autoworkers, it seems. *LA Times.* Retrieved from http://articles.latimes.com/2011/mar/29/business/la-fi-0329-autos-unions-20110329

History of Partnership. (2010). Kaiser Permanente, Labor-Management Partnership. Retrieved from http://www.lmpartnership.org/what-is-partnership/history-partnership

H.R. 1869. Lifelong Learning Accounts Act of 2011. (2011, September 14). *The New York Times.* Retrieved from http://politics.nytimes.com/congress/bills/112/hr1869

Hurd, R. (2006). The rise and fall of the organizing model in the U.S. In M. Harcourt & G. Wood (Eds.), *Trade unions and democracy: Strategies and perspectives* (pp. 191-210). New Brunswick, NJ: Transaction.

Kahmann, M. (2002). Trade unions and young people: Challenges of the changing age composition of unions. *European Trade Union Institute, Discussion Paper*, 1-41.

Kearney, R. (2010). Public sector labor-management relations: Change or status quo? *Review of Public Personnel Administration, 30*, 89-111.

Kearney, R. (2011). Randi Weingarten, the American Federation of Teachers and the challenges of policy leadership in a hostile environment. *Public Administration Review, 71*, 772-781.

Keene, D. L., & Handrich. R. R. (2010, September). Between coddling and contempt: Managing and mentoring millennials. *The Jury Expert, 22*, 1-14. Retrieved from http://www.thejuryexpert.com/wp-ontent/uploads/KeeneHandrichTJESept2010Vol22Num51.pdf

Khadaroo, S. T. (2011, September 16). Wisconsin teachers retire in droves after union loss in bargaining fight. *The Christian Science Monitor*. Retrieved from http://www.csmonitor.com/USA/Education/2011/0916/Wisconsin-teachers-retire-in-droves-after-union-loss-in-bargaining-fight

Klein. J. (2011, May 10). Scenes from the New York education wars. *The Wall Street Journal*, A15.

Kleis, J. (2008). Generation Y: Perceptions and views on labor unions. M.A. Thesis, California State University, Dominguez Hills, #1456064 (MAI 46/06), i-61.

Kular, S., Gatenby, M., Rees, C., Soane, E., & Truss, K. (2008, October). Employee engagement: A literature review. Kingston University Business School, *Working Paper Series 19*, 1-33. Retrieved from http://eprints.kingston.ac.uk/4192/1/19wempen.pdf

Lancaster, L. C., & Stillman, D. (2010). *The M factor. How the millennial generation is rocking the workplace.* New York, NY: Harper Business.

Levenson, A. R. (2010). Millennials and the world of work: An economist's perspective. *Journal of Business Psychology 25*, 257-264.

Levi, M., Olson, D., Agnone, J., & Kelly, D. (2009). Union democracy re-examined. *Politics and Society, 37*, 203-228.

Lifelong Learning Accounts. (2011, August). Indiana Institute for Working Families, Policy Brief. Retrieved from http://www.incap.org/documents/iiwf/2011/FINAL%20LiLAs.pdf

Lipkin, N., & Perrymore, A. (2009). *Y in the workplace. Managing the "me first" generation.* Pompton Plains, NJ: Career Press.

LMP Founding Agreement. (1997). Labor-Management Partnership, Kaiser Permanente. Retrieved at http://www.lmpartnership.org/what-is-partnership/national-agreements/lmp-agreement

MacGillis, A. (2010, April 4). At the peak of his influence, SIEU chief set to leave a mixed legacy. *The Washington Post*. Retrieved from http://www.washingtonpost.com/wp-dyn/content/article/2010/04/13/AR2010041304659.html?sid=ST2010041304683

Madland, D., & Teixeira, R. (2000, May). New progressive America: The millennial generation. Center for American Progress, Progressive Studies Program.

Maher, K. (2011, August 17). Unions set for new battle in turf war. *The Wall Street Journal.*   Retrieved   from   http://online.wsj.com/article/ SB10001424053111904253204576512570301621088.html

Maher, K., & Belkin, D. (2011, February 16). State cuts rattle unions. *The Wall Street Journal*, p. A3.

Marginson, P., Arrowsmith, J., & Gray, M. (2008): Undermining or reframing collective bargaining? Variable pay in two sectors compared. *Human Resource Management Journal, 18*, 327-346.

Masters, M. F., Merchant, C. S., & Tobias, R. (2010, February 2). Engaging federal employees through their union representatives to improve agency performance. *Labor Management Resource Council*, White Paper. Retrieved from http:/ /www.lmrcouncil.gov/meetings/handouts/EngagingFederalEmployees ThroughTheirUnionRepresentativesToImproveAgencyPerformance.pdf

Mayer, G. (2004, August 31). Union membership trends in the U.S. *Congressional Research Service. Domestic Social Policy Division.* Retrieved from http: //digitalcommons.ilr.cornell.edu/cgi/viewcontent.cgi?article=1176 &context=key_workplace&sei-redir=1#search=%22United%20States %20Bureau%20Labor%20Statistics%20Union%20Affiliation%22

McClendon, J. (2006). The consequences and challenges of union decline. In J. R. Deckop (Ed.), *Human resource management ethics* (pp. 261-281). Greenwich, CT: Information Age.

Meister, J., & Willyard, K. (2010, May). Mentoring millennials: Delivering the feedback Gen Y craves is easier than you think. *Harvard Business Review, 8*(5), 68-72. Retrieved from http://epowerment.eqmentor.com/docs /Mentoring%20Millenials.pdf

Moore, S., & Read, I. (2006). Collective organisation in small- and medium-sized enterprises—An application of mobilization theory. *Human Resources Management Journal, 16*, 357-375.

Morris, S., & Stone, E. (2011, May 18). Yes, judge teachers using tests. *New York Daily News, Opinion.* Retrieved from http://articles.nydailynews.com/2011-05-18/news/29572619_1_judge-teachers-highest-rating-classroom-teachers

Mullane, L. (2006, November 28). On the cusp: LiLA pilot project winds down as support gears up. *American Council on Education.* Retrieved from http:// www.acenet.edu/AM/Template.cfm?Section=Home&TEMPLATE=/CM/Con- tentDisplay.cfm&CONTENTID=20014

Myers, K., & Sadaghiani, K. (2010). Millennials in the workplace: A communication perspective on millennials' organization relationships and performance. *Journal of Business Psychology, 25*, 225-238.

Navarette, Jr., R., (2011, August 5). Are millennials cut out for this job market? CNN Opinion. Retrieved from http://www.cnn.com/2011/OPINION/08/05/ navarrette.millennials.jobs/index.html

O'Dowd, J., & Barrett, J. T. (2005). *Interest based bargaining. A user's guide.* Victoria, British Columbia, Canada: Trafford.

Ogle, G., & Wheeler, H. (2001, January). Collective bargaining as a fundamental human right. Unpublished paper, prepared for presentation at the 53rd annual meeting of the Industrial Relations Research Association, Columbia, SC.

Olson, E. (2010, March 3). Education on the company's dime. *The New York Times.* Retrieved from http://www.nytimes.com/2010/03/04/business/retirementspecial/04LEARN.html

Overview of lifelong learning account state legislation. (n.d.). *The Learning Group.* Retrieved from https://www.learningfunds.com/uploads/Legislative_Overview.pdf

Pare, M. (2011, August 19). VW labor exec won't promote UAW in city. *Chattanooga Times Free Press.* Retrieved from http://www.timesfreepress.com/news/2011/aug/19/c1-vw-labor-exec-wont-promote-uaw-in-city/

Parker, A. M. (2009, December 9). Obama creates labor-management council. *Government Executive.com.* Retrieved from http://www.govexec.com/dailyfed/1209/120909p1.htm

Payne, J. (2001). Lifelong learning: A national trade union strategy in a global economy. *International Journal of Lifelong Education, 20,* 378- 392.

Pew Research Center. (2009, September 3). *Recession turns a graying office grayer.* Retrieved from http://pewsocialtrends.org/files/2010/10/americas-changing-workforce.pdf

Pew Research Center. (2010a, February 18)). *Democrats' edge among millennials slips.* Retrieved from http://pewresearch.org/assets/pdf/1497.pdf

Pew Research Center. (2010b, February 23). *Favorable ratings of labor unions fall sharply.* Retrieved from http://people-press.org/files/legacy-pdf/591.pdf

Pew Research Center. (2010c, February). *Millennials: A portrait of Generation Next.* Retrieved from http://pewresearch.org/millennials/

Raine, G. (2005, July). 2 big unions break from AFL-CIO. SFGate.com (*San Francisco Chronicle* online). Retrieved from http://www.sfgate.com/default/article/2-big-unions-break-from-AFL-CIO-Teamsters-and-2620528.php

Reuss, A. (2011, March 31). What's behind union decline in the United States? *Dollars and Sense: Real World Economics.* Retrieved from http://www.dollarsandsense.org/archives/2011/0311reuss.html

Riccucci, N. M. (2007). The changing face of public employee unionism. *Review of Public Personnel Administration, 27,* 71-78.

Riordan, C. M., Vandenburg, R. J., & Richardson, H. A. (2005). Employee involvement climate and organizational effectiveness. *Human Resource Management, 44,* 471-488.

Romell, R. (2010, October 4) Kohler seeks two-tier wage system, more use of "flexible" workers. *Milwaukee Journal Sentinel.* Retrieved from http://www.jsonline.com/business/104284268.html

Rosenberg, A. (2007, October 19). Lawmakers push labor-management partnerships. *GovernmentExecutive.com.* Retrieved from http://www.govexec.com/dailyfed/1007/101907ar1.htm?oref=rellink

Rosenberg, A. (2009, February 5). Unions differ on how to revive labor-management partnerships. *Government Executive.com.* Retrieved from http://www.govexec.com/story_page_pf.cfm?articleid=41984&printerfriendlyvers=1

Saad, L. (2009, September 3). Labor unions see sharp slide in U.S. public support. *Gallup, Inc.* Retrieved from http://www.gallup.com/poll/122744/Labor-Unions-Sharp-Slide-Public-Support.aspx#1

Samuelson, R. J. (2011, February 28). Big labor's big decline. *The Washington Post.* Retrieved from http://www.washingtonpost.com/wpdyn/content/article/2011/02/27/AR2011022702873.html

Santos, F. (2011, May 10). New to teaching, idealistic, a risk for layoff. *The New York Times.* Retrieved from http://www.nytimes.com/2011/05/11/nyregion/new-idealistic-teachers-face-layoffs-in-bloomberg-budget.html?partner=rss&emc=rss&pagewanted=print

SBR Consulting. (2011). Millennial generation today: Impact of the economic environment on recruitment, retention, and engagement. Retrieved from http://randallresearch.com/pr/SBR_Millennial_Generation_Today_white_paper.pdf

Schmitt, J. (2008, October). Unions and upward mobility for young workers. *Center for Economic Policy Research.* Retrieved from http://www.cepr.net/documents/publications/unions_and_upward_mobility_for_young_workers.pdf

Schulte, J. (n.d.) Strategies to impact engagement across an organization. In D. Zinger (Ed.), *The Employee Engagement Network Top Tens* (pp. 8-10). Retrieved from http://api.ning.com/files/NckfCD1NOq6n1F2Lx1MtnZiE8vRS0n85UkvkPggObmVxfbLPufSfmIZJPc5kOu52Kajy4HBRCo0XXiuGcOuXAQ6XemgbTPnd/TopTensofEmployeeEngagement.pdf

Service Employees International Union. (2011). Justice for janitors. Retrieved from http://www.seiu.org/a/justice-for-janitors/justice-for-janitors-20-years-of-organizing.php

Sherk, J. (2011, September 18). Blame the UAW cartel. *The New York Times, Opinion.* Retrieved from http://www.nytimes.com/roomfordebate/2011/09/18/can-detroit-sustain-its-two-tier-pay/win-win-for-workers-and-employers

Shierholz, H., & Edwards, K. A. (2011, April 20). The class of 2011. Young workers face a dire labor market without a safety net. *Economic Policy Institute, Briefing Paper 300.* Retrieved from http://docs.google.com/viewer?url=http://www.epi.org/page/-/BriefingPaper306.pdf&hl=en_US&chrome=true

Simonsen, P. (1986, November). Concepts of career development. *Training and Development Journal*, 70-74.

Singer, P. W., Messera, H., & Orino, B. (2011, February 2). D.C.'s new guard: What does the next generation of American leaders think? Retrieved from http://www.brookings.edu/~/media/Files/rc/reports/2011/02_young_leaders_singer/02_young_leaders_singer.pdf

Sklueff, A. (2011, September 20). Area nurses to join thousands of other nurses in statewide strike. *The Daily Californian.* Retrieved from http://www.dailycal.org/2011/09/20/area-nurses-to-join-thousands-of-other-nurses-in-statwide-strike/

Stripling, J. (2011, February 15). With unions under threat, academics join huge rally in Wisconsin. *The Chronicle of Higher Education.* Retrieved from: http://chronicle.com/article/With-Unions-Under-Threat/126379/

Sujanski, J., & Ferri-Reed, J. (2009). *Keeping the millennials. Why companies are losing billions in turnover to this generation.* Hoboken, NJ: Wiley.

Tapscott, M. (2011, January 1). Obama put union bosses in charge of federal agencies, then exempted them from FOIA. *The Washington Examiner.* Retrieved from http://dev.washingtonexaminer.com/blogs/beltway

-confidential/2011/01/obama-put-union-bosses-charge-federal-agencies-then-exempted-them

Tannock, S., & Flocks, S. (2002). The Canadian labor movement's big youth turn. *UC Berkeley Labor Center.* Retrieved from http://laborcenter.berkeley.edu/youngworkers/canadian.pdf

Toland, C. (2011, May 31) Tips to position millennial employees for career success. *Diversity Executive Newsletter.* Retrieved from http://diversity-executive.com/article.php?article=1187

Trottman, M. (2011, August 31). Business irked as labor board backs unions. *The Wall Street Journal.* Retrieved from http://online.wsj.com/article/SB10001424053111904199404576540883245332752.html

Trumka, R. L. (2009, August 31). Remarks, Center for American Progress. Retrieved from http://www.aflcio.org/mediacenter/prsptm/sp08312009.cfm

Tyler, J. (2009, September 10). Employee engagement and labor relations. *Gallup-Management Journal.* Retrieved from http://gmj.gallup.com/content/122849/employee-engagement-labor-relations.aspx

Uchitelle, L. (2010, November 19). Unions yield on wage scales to preserve jobs. *The New York Times.* Retrieved from http://www.nytimes.com/2010/11/20/business/20wages.html?pagewanted=all

U.S. Bureau of the Census. (2011, May). Age and sex composition: 2010. *2010 Census Briefs.* Retrieved from http://www.census.gov/prod/cen2010/briefs/c2010br-03.pdf

U.S. Bureau of Labor Statistics. (2011a, January 21). Union membership annual news release, union members 2010. *Economic News Release.* Retrieved from http://www.bls.gov/news.release/union2.htm

U.S. Bureau of Labor Statistics. (2011b, August 24). Employment and unemployment among youth – summer 2011. Retrieved from http://www.bls.gov/news.release/youth.htm.

U.S. Government Accountability Office. (2005, July). Human Capital Symposium. Retrieved from http://www.gao.gov/new.items/d051048t.pdf

U.S. Merit Systems Protection Board. (2008, September). The power of federal employee engagement. A Report to the President and Congress of the United States. Retrieved from http://www.mspb.gov/netsearch/viewdocs.aspx?docnumber=379024&version=379721&application=ACROBAT

U.S. Merit Systems Protection Board. (2010, April). Partnership forums and employee engagement. *Issues of Merit.* Retrieved from http://www.mspb.gov/netsearch/viewdocs.aspx?docnumber=491200&version=492557&application=ACROBAT

U.S. Office of Management and Budget. (2011, January 19). Memorandum for heads of executive departments/agencies and labor-management forums. Retrieved from http://www.actnat.com/docs/Predecisional_letter_Labor_Management_Forums.pdf

Van Rooy, D. L., Whitman D. S., Hart, D., & Caleo, S. (2011). Measuring employee engagement during a financial downturn: Business imperative or nuisance? *Journal of Business Psychology, 26,* 147-152.

Vedder, R. (2010). Right to work laws. *Cato Journal, 30,* 171-180. Retrieved from http://www.cato.org/pubs/journal/cj30n1/cj30n1-9.pdf

Vlasic, B. (2011, September 12). Detroit sets its future on a foundation of two-tier wages. *The New York Times*. Retrieved from http://www.nytimes.com/2011/09/13/business/in-detroit-two-wage-levels-are-the-new-way-of-work.html?pagewanted=all

Whoriskey, P., & Gardner, A. (2011, February 8). As unions' dynamic shifts, so does fight. *The Washington Post*. Retrieved from http://www.washingtonpost.com/wp-dyn/content/article/2011/02/27/AR2011022704038.html

Woodall, B., & Bailey, D. (2011, September 20). GM labor deal creates jobs, holds line on costs. *Reuters*. Retrieved from http://www.reuters.com/article/2011/09/20/us-autos-uaw-idUSTRE78J0QA20110920

Wooten, W. (1993). Using knowledge, skill and ability (KSA) data to identify career pathing opportunities. *Public Personnel Management, 22*, 551-563.

Wright, T. (n.d.). Ten ways to define and refine your culture to engage. In D. Zinger (Ed.), *The employee engagement network top tens* (pp. 17-20). The Employee Engagement Network. Retrieved from http://api.ning.com/files/NckfCD1NOq6n1F2Lx1MtnZiE8vRS0n85UkvkPggObmVxfbLPufSfmIZJPc5kOu52Kajy4HBRCo0XXiuGcOuXAQ6XemgbTPnd/TopTensofEmployeeEngagement.pdf

CHAPTER 17

SMALL BUSINESSES, VALUE ADDED, AND THE MILLENNIALS

Jackie A. DiPofi and Margaret Fitch-Hauser

INTRODUCTION

As the number of Millennials—young people that graduated high school in the year 2000 to present—entering the workforce increases, small business owners face new challenges. They must integrate Millennials into the workplace dominated by two older generations and identify ways to keep them engaged and maximize their contributions. This challenge is particularly important to small business owners who operate with very small if any training and development budgets. In addition, small business owners are often skilled in the focus area of the business but often not in the area of people management skills. This chapter will help small business owners broaden their understanding of critical human resource topics related to identifying and maximizing the value of the Millennial Generation of workers.

UNDERSTANDING THE MILLENNIAL GENERATION

While we know you have already read a great deal about Millennials we will talk a bit about the mind-set Millennials bring into small business

Managing Human Resources for the Millennial Generation, pp. 399–418

work settings. This discussion will focus on technology, work ethics, personalities, locus of control, trophy kids and praise.

Technology

The Millennial Generation is the most technologically savvy group ever to enter the workforce. Their entire lives have been lived in a world with technological means of communicating. A recent Pew Foundation survey indicates that Millennials feel that their use of technology is the number one distinction that sets their generation apart from others (Pew Research Center, 2010a). In order to maximize the contribution of members of this group in the workplace, it is important to realize that Millennials not only have technological gadgets, they fully embrace the use of these gadgets to expand key elements of their lives, social networks and entertainment. Not surprisingly, Millennials also embrace the use of technology in the workplace. Unfortunately, many small business owners have not quite embraced the use of technology as deeply. The embracing of technology is not the only factor that businesses have noticed about Millennials.

Work Ethics

A recent survey of executives reveals that executives perceive Millennials to have a different work ethic, blurred boundaries between work and personal lives, a lack of focus and a tendency to change jobs often (Barzilai-Nahon & Mason, 2010). Are these perceptions accurate or do they merely represent a lack of understanding of the Millennial work force?

Other research has found that fundamentally the attitudes toward work ethics and job values differ only slightly from those of older generations (Real, Mitnick, & Maloney, 2010). Work ethics focus on attitudes and beliefs toward work, self-reliance, leisure, wasted time, morality/ethics, and delayed gratification. Interestingly, one study found only small differences on the elements of work ethics between Millennials and older generations. The study found that Millennials expressed stronger values than Boomers in the centrality of work and the importance of hard work as well as self-reliance and delayed gratification (Real, Mitnick, & Maloney, 2010). While the study did find some differences in work related attitudes between generations, these differences were small. Of course, not all business people agree as we found out when we asked a small business expert to read over an early draft of this chapter.

Personalities

Research has revealed that Millennials seem to exhibit higher levels of narcissism, anxiety, and depression (Twenge & Campbell, 2008). They also seem to have a lower need for the approval of their peers and supervisors and have a stronger external locus of control than prior generations. The latter findings are particularly relevant to businesses for understanding some of the workplace behaviors that have been reported about Millennials.

Locus of Control

Locus of control is an expectation that "outcomes in life are controlled either by one's own actions or by other forces" (Spector, 1988, p. 335). Individuals who exhibit external locus of control tend to be less satisfied with their jobs, view their supervisors as less considerate and see the job as more stressful largely because they feel no sense of control over what is happening or will happen (Spector, 1988). One Millennial, a small business entrepreneur and internet expert, observed in his agreement with the previous statement that young employees "are detached from their job and … do not care about the quality of their work. They feel as though they are entitled to a good job regardless of how qualified they are and in their delusional minds, they are doing the boss a favor by showing up to work every morning regardless of how much work is accomplished that day" (Denaburg, personal communication, March 9, 2012).

The feeling of external locus of control may also be seen in the belief that many Millennials have that technology, not them, can improve the workplace. A manifestation of this attitude can be seen in the observation that many new workers fresh out of college have few privacy concerns when it comes to the use of computers. After all, if something gets out, it is technologys' fault, not theirs.

Trophy Kids and Praise

In addition to wanting to feel they are contributing to the workplace, Millennials also want to be recognized for their contributions. As one source stated, most Millennials have received a great deal of positive feedback and encouragement throughout their lives. They have even been called "trophy kids" because of the number of awards they have received (Denaburg, personal communication, March 9, 2012).

Subsegments of the Millennial Generation

As we continue to research the changes taking place in the business world due to rapid technological advancements, subsegments of the Millennial Generation emerge. Within the Millennial segment of the total population, employers will find basic personalities or ranges in characteristics similarly described by the Myers-Briggs Personality Inventory, or other assessment tools used in discussing traditional team dynamics. Through such approaches, strengths and weaknesses of individual team members and how they impact the whole team are explored. The following discussion focuses on three spectrums of characteristics that are highly relevant to the discussion of small businesses, value added and Millennials (see Figure 17.1).

1. Micro—Multi spectrum: "Microworkers" have the ability to focus on a single task, whereas "multitaskers" perform a number of value-added tasks simultaneously with the capacity to juggle the various tasks in order to reach goals.
2. Solitary—Social spectrum: "Solitary Players" are those individuals who have the desire and self-discipline to work alone, whereas "Social Players" desire personal interaction with others, and seek social opportunities within the work place.
3. New school—Old school spectrum. New school communicators are also known as "Emerging Media Communicators" who actively embrace a lifestyle that incorporates current and future technology, whereas "Old School Communicators" hold on to past communication practices with fervor.

At a minimum, business owners (O) need to assess the relevance of these characteristics to their particular business needs, and determine where each potential employee (E) falls on the characteristic spectrum to make the best staffing decisions. The need to hire anyone from one extreme or the other is probably rare, but in some cases, could be the very kind of person desired. Employers are more likely to be seeking an individual located in "the middle ground." But the point remains, the small business owner needs to start the staffing process by determining what the needs of the business are in terms of "value added" activities to find the individual most capable of performing those activities. A discussion of each of the spectrum continua will help clarify the complexity of the decisions.

Microworkers and Multitaskers

Microworkers fit the scenario of lean office or lean manufacturing, where there has been a return to scientific management approaches in an

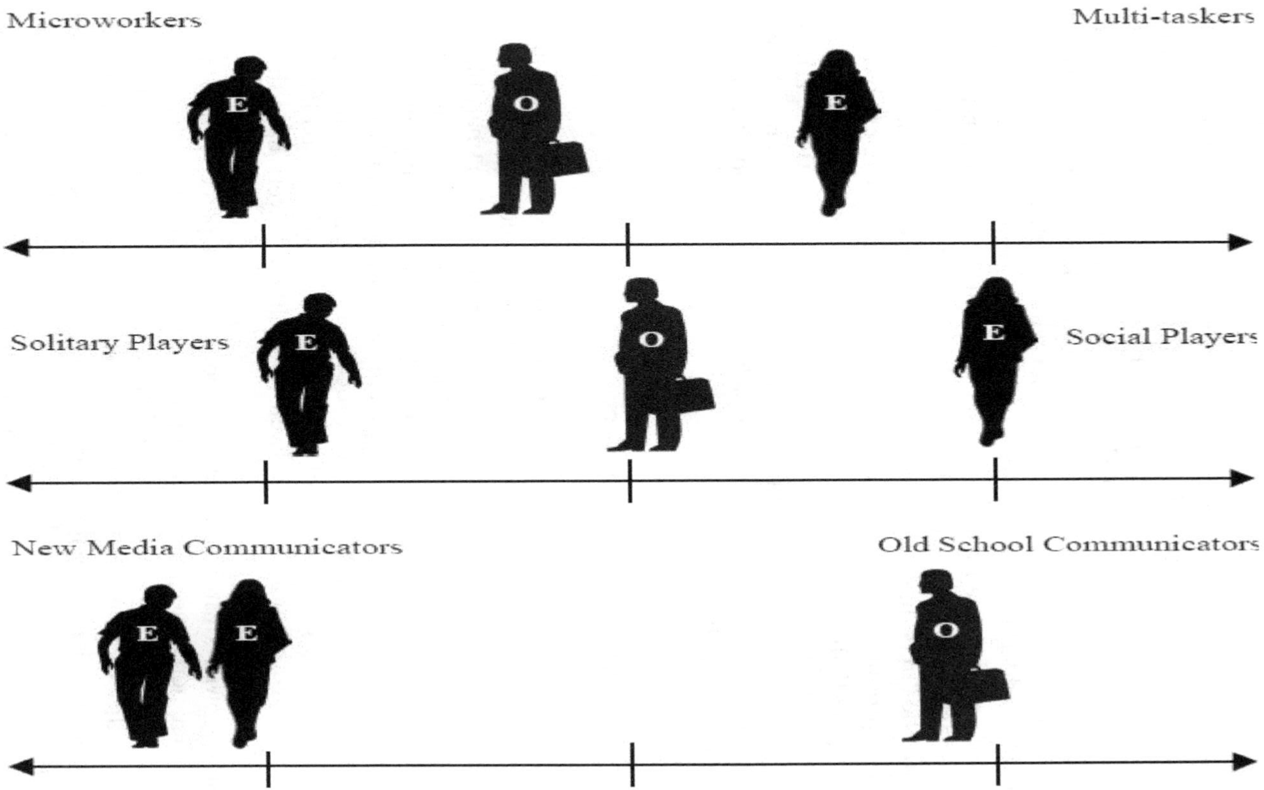

Figure 17.1. The three characteristic spectrums that impact employment situations.

attempt to improve efficiencies. Total activity is broken into as many small steps as possible and efficiency studies are conducted to see which steps can be handled by one individual before moving to the next step in the business process. This approach is grounded in the "piecemeal" approach, where one step is done over and over and over by the same person, day after day after day. At the other end of the Microworker characteristic spectrum are the Multitaskers who perform many different value added activities. Initial value added of a microworker comes from freeing up *specific* time of the small business owner who can then do other tasks. Initial value added from a multitasker employee may come from freeing up *any* time of the small business owner who can then do other, possibly more important or more difficult, tasks. What the small business owner does with the "freed up" time can add value to the business, as well as the increased productivity added by the employee. Small business owners have so many demands on their time that to alleviate any of the pressure is added value by reducing stress. Microworkers may experience a high level of job satisfaction performing very specialized tasks, whereas Multitaskers may be more satisfied being a part of the total product development process from beginning to end.

Solitary Players and Social Players

Another characteristics of the Millennials hypothesized is illustrated with the Solitary Player representing one end of the spectrum and Social Player representing the other end. With the invention of the smart phone and other communications technology that facilitates work activities anywhere, anytime, employees can more readily structure their own best work environment. Some workers enjoy working alone while others cannot tolerate the loneliness and actively seek social interactions with coworkers. The Millennials live in a world of constant information overload, always "connected" to the global world. Even the Solitary Players have this in common with the Social Players.

Business owners will also want to remember that perceptions, either self or other perception, are sometimes inaccurate. For example, a small business expert suggests that many Millennials think they work best alone when in reality they need very strict direction. He also suggests that many employees who claim to enjoy working alone let their social lives, often accessed through mobile technology, interfere with their work. The challenge for the business owners is to determine how accurate their read of the Millennial hire is and how accurate the self-report of the employee is, as well (Denaburg, personal communication, March 9, 2012).

New Media Communicators and Old School Communicators

The old business mantra "location, location, location" has been replaced with a new one, "technology, technology, technology." The traditional means of getting information out to the customers and employees are not sufficient in contemporary business times. Not only does the business owner need to identify the key messages that need to be communicated, he/she must now contend with the challenge of how to send out that information. Millennials want to receive information electronically, digitally. They want it on demand. They are used to the world's knowledge being at their fingertips or in the palm of their hands. Using the latest technology is part of the Millennial Generation's "cool" factor, and they take for granted that their employment environment will have the latest communication gadgets or progressive communication advancements on a regular basis. In just a very few years, technology has changed the problem solving and business decision making process completely as illustrated in the following example.

Small Business Example 1. Witness to Impact of Technology Change:

When Stephen J. Kapurch (NASA scientist and book author) was asked what he felt the biggest change in business he had witnessed in his career with the space program had been, his reply focused on the method of problem solving and communicating among the scientists and others. Paraphrasing, he said, "When I first joined the space program in the early 1960's, whenever there was a problem, we would all gather in a large room with one giant computer, talking, brainstorming, playing devil's advocate as programmers entered our data. Then around 1982, with the invention of the personal computer, we would all gather in a large room with everyone having their own computer, talking, brainstorming, playing devil's advocate as we entered our own data. Now, when there is a problem, we all go to our own computers, in our own offices or homes or wherever, and communicate around the world, possibly never meeting some of the individuals on our team."

The Millennial Generation is accustomed to having access to computers and the internet and they use it for a multitude of reasons related to work and play: interactively receiving and sending information, building and maintaining relationships. A 2010 conference at the Newseum in Washington, D.C. featured Pew Research Center analysts and other experts (Pew Research Center, 2010b). One of the topics discussed at the conference was the Millennial affinity for media. Here are some of the observations from that panel of experts that can give a business person insight into this employee pool. Danah Boyd, a Fellow with Harvard University's Berkman Center for Internet and Society, suggests that the world in which this young generation grew up is much, much different than the one in which Boomers and even Xer's grew up. While those of us who are older grew up in a time when we could ride bikes all day with our friends and come home by dark, the Millennial Generation grew up in a time of fear and structured activities. The concept of "stranger danger" plus the idea that parents felt children should be involved in structured activities, and the lack of mobility as youngsters forced this generation to look for "a place to hang out." That place became "online" with activities such as web based gaming and social media available to most all socioeconomic groups. Millennials learned to use the internet or other technology to stay connected with friends, family, and in the workplace, fellow workers. However, when Millennials have the option of face-to-face communications, they still enjoy and prefer that over electronic means. But, Millennials do not hesitate to use digital means of communicating for convenience, even if the person is in the next room. Electronic media is a tool that Millennials can not remember not having.

To make use of new technology in their own ways, Millennials have even adopted a new language, of sorts, called texting. Abbreviations and codes mixed with slang provide a strange world for the older generations trying to keep up. But, Millennials are as comfortable, if not more comfortable, texting to maintain social contacts as they are actually talking with the other party.

ACTIVITY CHAIN OF A SMALL BUSINESS

The environment of the small business owner is complex and exponentially complicates the communication process which is then compounded by emerging media pressures. The diagram below, Activity Chain of a Small Business Owner, illustrates the mindset and environment of the small business owner and the gravity-like force that defines the small business management process.

The functioning of a business is akin to a "marble works" toy that has pipes put together in an assortment of ways, but regardless of the design, all marbles travel down. The illustration below demonstrates this complex process. In this illustration, five stages of management: planning, organizing, budgeting, staffing, controlling, are applied to five key functions of a business: operations, marketing, finance, accounting and human resources. All of these activities together create the activity chain of a small business.

The illustration shows two time periods (see Figure 17.2). In time one there is only the Owner who does everything. The internal communication challenges are minimal. In time two, an employee is hired and a

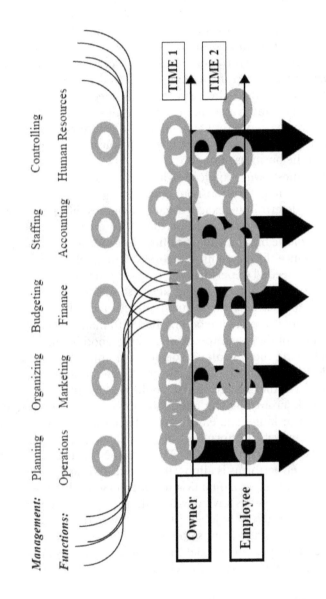

Figure 17.2.   Activity chain of a small business.

407

transfer of value added responsibilities or some type of training must occur if the employee is to function maximally.

Unless this transfer of activities is well managed, the employee training process becomes random and out of control. In the world of business, some transfers are successful and some are not. When the transfer of activities is effective and efficient, the owner has more time to do what he or she does best. Often owners favor the operations of the business, that is, the art or science, craft or skill, manifested in the product or service offered by the business. The owner may also need to keep certain tasks in order to remain motivated to stay in business over the long haul. For example, creative entrepreneurs may lose interests in one business as other ideas develop, if not for some inspiration keeping the owner focused on the business at hand.

Small business owners typically transfer activities to newly hired individuals in person. To get the most out of the hiring process, owners need to be proactive in determining exactly what capabilities they need from the new hire. The specific areas of need may arise from either quantity or quality constraints of the organization. Staffing decisions to meet those needs is a challenge. Once the capabilities are identified, a job description delineating the skills needed to perform the necessary activities should be written. As always, owners or their hiring agent should test interviewees on the needed capabilities so the best qualified person can be objectively hired.

Small business owners are bombarded with many needs, wants, desires, and demands of the marketplace, so making good hiring decisions is critical to achieving those goals. A constructive approach to take in making hiring decisions is to ask the question: What routine activities does the owner perform that someone else could do? Examples of specific tasks could include answering the telephone to cut down on interruptions to operations, checking mail, emptying garbage cans, checking in inventory, greeting customers, performing sales activities, processing information, and researching target markets. The number of activities that a small business owner performs is almost unlimited. To manage all the functions of a business is a monumental task for one person. That is why, eventually, if the small business has any growth goals, the owner will employ someone else. At this critical step in job creation, how well the small business owner manages the transition from solo owner to being an employer and manager of another person will determine long term business success. The following example illustrates this challenge.

Small Business Example 2. Sad Reality:

In many small business situations the number of tasks is so overwhelming to the owner, he/she gives up before ever getting to the hiring stage, as one small business owner explains about the decision to close her business after only one year: "I didn't realize before I started the business that I would never be able to escape it; that at the end of each work day, I take the business home with me and I wake up with it each morning. I have learned I am not able to cope with the constant pressure. I want a job now that I can turn off at 5:00 and have a personal life again."

Some of the activities and time required to manage human resources may be one of the first functions in a small business to be transferred to another person or agent. For example, tasks like keeping books and screening applicants can be outsourced to a bookkeeper or employment agency.

The Cleaning Company example below illustrates a significant transfer of activities from the owner to another individual. Although this example is with a transfer to an employment agency, rather than an employee, the transfer of activities is the same. The employment agency method of staffing has the merit of freeing up time for the owner, and probably costs in the range of 3% of gross payroll. This cost is balanced against the benefit of time to focus on things that keep the owner engaged in the business.

Small Business Example 3. Outsourcing Business Activities:

An owner of a growing Commercial Cleaning Company proactively switched to an employment agency when the number of his employees reached five, the point at which Workmen's Compensation has to be paid, which increased the transaction cost of payroll with a further drain on his time. Until that point the owner prepared the payroll, calculating total pay, tax withholding, check writing, tax payments, and W-2's, etc.

The transferring of tasks from owner to employee involves psychological processes as well as financial processes. For some individuals, delegating comes naturally and letting go of responsibilities to others is not overly wrought with worry. On the other end of this characteristic spectrum are some individuals who cannot delegate due to fear of outcomes and the belief that only they can do the task correctly. Those who are the business owner, founder, and creator, may find handing over responsibilities for any part of the business to be excruciating. This situation is compounded in family business and well documented in succession research. The emotional toll on the owner needs to be recognized by the owner prior to the hiring process otherwise the transfer of responsibilities will not be successful and may be a very costly lesson. Only by recognizing and facing their own personality quirks are business owners and managers able to manipulate their own behavior to reach desired results in human resources development.

The challenges discussed so far apply regardless of the age of the potential hire or employee. The focus of this book, however, is working with Millennials. At this point we will focus on how to delegate tasks to younger employees in such a way they feel valued and motivated to continue their employment with the organization.

What the above finding suggests is that the real challenge for business people, particularly small business owners, is how to work effectively with the new generation of employees. The key may well be in how best to communicate the needs of both the task and the business to the young worker. The next section will present a schema for doing just that.

INCORPORATING MILLENNIALS INTO AN ORGANIZATION

The multicommunication channel comfort of the Millennials may be preparing them for the workplace where they will have to interact with customers and fellow employees via many communication channels. As mentioned earlier, because they have grown up with technology, younger employees' concerns about business headaches such as information security may not match those of the business owner (Havenstein, 2008). Consequently, business owners should include any restrictions on media usage in an employee orientation. Clearly technology is an integral part of the communication world of the Millennial Generation. If small business owners are uncomfortable or lack confidence in using current communication technology, then they should get help. That help may well come in the form of hiring a Millennial employee who can take on the emerging media responsibilities and relieve the owner from that task.

Understanding the behavior patterns of the Millennial Generation will help a small business owner understand which employee has the knowledge, skills and abilities desired and which does not. *What* the business owner needs to communicate to potential employees has already been discussed: value added activities that will be transferred from owner to employee. A greater challenge may be *how* to communicate the desired behaviors or activities. Once value added activities are identified, how does the business owner communicate effectively with the Millennial segment? The first step may be to understand how the world of getting tasks done has changed and then fitting those changes to the communication needs of the Millennial worker.

A look at current news publications highlights the transformation of the work world as the Millennial Generation claims a decade of work experience. "Meet the Microworkers," a 2011 Bloomberg *Businessweek* article, reveals radical change taking place that impacts small business owners, and gives further insight into how the Millennial Generation works.

Employers can break a job into small pieces and use the internet to find workers to do those tasks for as little as 50 cents for quick jobs like checking Web pages for errors or transcribing audio recordings. Tasks outsourced might require a few minutes or a few days to complete but enable in-house employees to focus on higher value work. Freelancer.com reports 2.1 million registered workers, and predicts, "The whole industry has only just begun—this is going to go mainstream" (King, 2011, p. 1).

Contemporary businesses will contend with many human resource issues related to emerging media and the Millennial Generation. Concepts like Open Source Programming, Global Virtual Teams, crowdsourcing, and cloud computing are thriving in today's media and can be capitalized on by small business owners as they create jobs that individuals in the Millennial Generation will fill.

Maximizing Value Added Work

A persistent challenge for any business, but particularly for small businesses, is maximizing the talents and skills of a new hire in such a way as to get a positive return on the investment of training the new hire and having a positive impact on the bottom line. Addressing these challenges takes skillful communication on the part of the manager or business owner as he or she communicates with the new employee about the nature and priority of work as well as identifying how the specific tasks fit into the big picture of the organization. The traditional approach of simply telling or showing the employee how to do something probably is not the best way to incorporate a Millennial into the organization. This generation needs to be approached in a different way.

The *new* challenge to business owners and the focus of this book is to effectively and efficiently communicate with a particular segment of the population, Millennials, in a world of constantly changing emerging media. The *old* challenge of defining the nature of work, priority of the work and value added of the work are all long-standing challenges of small business owners.

Just as the business owner cannot do all things, neither can the employee, so the owner must clearly define the most desired behavior pattern which adds greatest value to the business, and communicate that to employees in a way they understand. As the example below illustrates, making decisions about how to communicate with the Millennial Generation can determine whether the employer maximizes the benefit of the hire's talent or keeps the employee long enough to recoup the cost of hiring the individual in the first place.

Small Business Example 4. Restaurant Owner and Employee Coach

An owner of a college town family-style restaurant, celebrating 20 years of success with a second location on a lake front location, employing over 80 young workers, says, "I must explain everything to my staff," for example:

1. Everything is your job. "It's not my job" is an unacceptable excuse not to do something at work.

2. If you see it needs done, do it. "If there is trash on the ground, pick it up, throw it away. Empty the garbage can when full, put new garbage bag in container."

3. Do it exactly as instructed. "Put each table along this mark on the wall. Keep the music volume exactly on this setting as marked on the dial." She further explains, "Young workers today do not have the same work ethics or skills as the prior generation; some of them do not even know how to hold a broom and sweep."

A swimmer in her college days, she adds, "I am their coach. What I teach them is important. The skills they learn in my business will be with them throughout their careers. I enjoy that aspect of my job, but the challenge is greater than ever when it comes to hiring from this breed of new young workers."

Identifying the desired behavior pattern, or job tasks to be accomplished, occurs at the beginning of the staffing process. How this information is presented can impact how well the new hire integrates into the organization. This is particularly important when working with a Millennial hire. Certainly all new employees need to learn about the company culture, history, and operating procedures. Unfortunately, much of this information is presented at one time in some type of orientation package. To have greater impact on a Millennial hire, the information should be spread out over a longer period of time allowing the new hire to truly absorb it and develop a picture of how his/her work contributes to the big picture of the business (Ferri-Reed, 2010). Like all employees, Millennials want to feel their efforts are important and contributing to the overall effort. An added benefit of spreading the orientation information over a longer period may be that older employees get a reminder and consequently, a motivational boost.

To create an opportunity for a young employee to earn recognition, a small business person might consider giving that employee a challenge in the form of a special assignment. Of course, successful completion of the assignment would garner recognition that should motivate the employee to truly engage with the project and consequently the organization.

Another aspect that seems to motivate Millennials in the workplace is learning how they can advance within the organization. This generation expects to do well in their jobs and to advance quickly. Laying out a career path is one way to help a young employee learn what type of effort is necessary to reach the top. This type of approach addresses the Millennials' strong need for regular feedback and reinforcement (Hu, Herrick, & Hodgin, 2004). While giving this feedback, employers will want to include a frank look at how the employee's efforts contribute to the mission of the organization (Hu et al., 2004).

Another important characteristic of the Millennial Generation is that they have been rewarded more than any other generation. Consequently, they are generally *not* accustomed to receiving negative feedback. A business person may, therefore, want to take a coaching approach (as illustrated in the example below) when delivering corrective feedback (Hu et al., 2004). As a coach, the business person will want to include praise along with the corrective elements of the message. During this type of session, the information should be specific and objective. It should also include information that shows how changing the undesired behavior will increase chances of success. The following model provides a guideline for such a discussion.

Small Business Example 5. Coaching Approach for Corrective Feedback:

Describe what behaviors are problematic. Include positive points as well as fair and objective descriptions of the problematic behaviors. Be specific and deal with concrete behaviors that can be changed.

Explain why the above behaviors are problematic. Include how these behaviors will negatively impact the employee's progress in the organization.

Specify both what changes are needed and how these changes will positively impact the employee's progress in the company.

Clearly emphasize the consequences and benefits of making the changes. This information should focus on the benefits to the individual, the work place, and the organization.

Millennials also seem to be motivated by the atmosphere of the workplace. Workplaces with a high "cool" factor tend to motivate this generation more than others (Hu et al., 2004). The cool factor can be created by such things as creative communications, open workspaces, technology, flexibility in the work schedule, and social networking opportunities. A challenge that comes with workplace "cool" may be keeping younger employees engaged in the work rather than the "coolness" of the workplace. Small businesses may in particular be challenged by the technological expectations of this generation who has never known a world without the internet. However, this demand can also bring an opportunity to delegate certain tasks to a technologically savvy employee. If a small business is lucky enough to employ such a person, finding special tasks to move the company forward technologically will be a great challenge for the employee.

Employers may be uncomfortable with some communication methods, as they grapple with new technology along with managing a business. This technological skill of the younger set may be one of the value added activities a small business owner needs.

RECOMMENDATIONS

What does this all mean to the small business owner? It means owners should rely on proven techniques to determine human resource needs of the business; identify value added activities required to be transferred from the owner to the employee; and capitalize on the knowledge, skills and abilities of the Millennial segment from which they will hire. Business owners should rely on ever changing communication technologies to facilitate the hiring, training, and rewarding needed to facilitate the transfer of activities to the Millennial segment. Owners must set a goal for all to focus on, conduct a strengths, weaknesses, opportunities, and threats analysis, hire to enhance strengths and take advantage of opportunities, as well as hire to shore up weaknesses and neutralize threats. If done correctly, the burden of small business ownership may be lessened.

But how does a small business owner make best decisions for staffing the business when he or she is already overwhelmed by the amount of work that demands they get help? Because owners need it now and need it cheap, they make quick and often hasty decisions hiring by happenstance from whoever crosses their path. Few small business owners conduct skills or aptitude testing to guide them in hiring positions neatly described in detail in employee handbooks. Most small business owners may not feel as though they have the time, energy, money, or know-how to develop and implement a staffing plan, but they must learn to do so in order to grow.

In view of the rapid changes in technology and the mindsets of Millennials, small business owners may need to embrace a strategy of "positive turbulence." Positive Turbulence is a plan for developing climates for creativity, innovation, and renewal (Gryskiewicz, 1999). This is the environment of the Millennial, fast-paced, on the cutting edge, born during a technological revolution. They do not know the work week as 9-to-5; their world is 24/7. In 1999, just as the future Millennials were entering their senior year of high school, Stanley Gryskiewicz, wrote of focusing on the periphery, inviting multiple perspectives, and actively practicing receptivity to "become fully committed to seeking a constant flow of creative ideas and new products and processes" (p. xviii).

In summary, to manage the Millennial Generation requires certain reliance on core principles of management that enables us to develop human resource strategies for small business owners. However, adaptation to new methods of communication based on ever changing technology will make the ultimate difference. Below is a checklist to help:

1. Determine value added tasks performed by the owner that can be transferred to another individual.

2. Write a job description and activity tests for skills, knowledge and abilities needed to perform those tasks identified as transferrable. For industry specific ideas, see Small Business Example 6 Test for Value Added Activities.

3. Prepare digital "How to Guides" including templates saved on Shared Drives detailing how the tasks are performed as the tasks are transferred from owner to employee.

4. Develop a digital employee weekly reporting procedure giving key benchmarks of activity.

5. Review digital employee weekly reports to determine if desired tasks have been transferred effectively and efficiently, acknowledging receipt of the employee report, commenting on level or quality of output with digital communication feedback.

6. Fine tune the process over time, transferring additional tasks to employee, or removing tasks, as necessary. Communicate changes digitally.

7. Revise procedures and update the electronic version as each value added activity is clearly defined.

8. Review the job description quarterly in the first year.

9. Make changes when necessary. Reward as possible.

10. Stay focused on the goal of an effective and efficient workforce to share the burden of the small business owner.

If these recommendations are achieved, the small business owner will have more time to follow the entrepreneurial passion that created the small business, and grow the business by improving the company's abilities to fill the needs of its prospects and customers, with a dedicated Millennial employee at his/her side. That is quite an accomplishment.

Small Business Example 6. Tests for Value Added Activities:

An owner should develop activity tests relevant to the business to use in screening applicants. For an office position, Microsoft Office proficiency skills may be needed. Test for knowledge of business taxes, laws, and compliance requirements of industry. Test for abilities for preparing or securing written confirmation of orders or deliveries. For a manufacturing position, knowledge of safety requirements and materials functionality of industry should be tested. Test for ability to focus on and perform routine welding activities and maintain Six Sigma quality standards in output. Test for a proficiency in Excel software skills. Test knowledge of project scheduling and compliance requirements of industry. Test for ability to talk at ease with clients and vendors to determine their needs and respond by preparing or securing written confirmation of orders or deliveries. Employee candidates can be asked to alphabetize files, add up columns of numbers, call someone to place an order, pick up items with tweezers, or distinguish colors, to provide evidence of the knowledge, skills, and abilities related to performing specific, desired job duties. The industry in which the business competes dictates the type of activity testing for best results.

If the recommendations are followed, the transfer of activities is more orderly and effective, as illustrated in Figure 17.3. There is not the usual chaos and randomness as illustrated in Figure 17.2. Figure 17.3 represents a well-managed plan for employing a Millennial with defined outcomes, using technology to facilitate the transfer of activity from owner to employee. With the Millennial employee, information is flowing in both directions, very rapidly, resulting in instant 2-way communication. This information exchange should lead to better decision making concerning the knowledge, skills and abilities of the new hire and capabilities to perform desired value added activities.

In Figure 17.3, movement of defined value added activity is planned, strengthening the link between owner and employee like a chain, with activity circles going from "operations" and from "marketing" down to the employee. For all the other categories, a single activity circle is shown in the employee area. In this particular case, Figure 17.3 represents how the owner decided he needed most help with operations and with marketing, selecting specific activities that the owner needs the employee to do, in those two categories. The one circle in each of the other areas represents how the owner has to provide an overview of the entire company to the new employee, but that the employee has limited responsibilities in the other areas. Figure 17.3 thus represents a desired outcome.

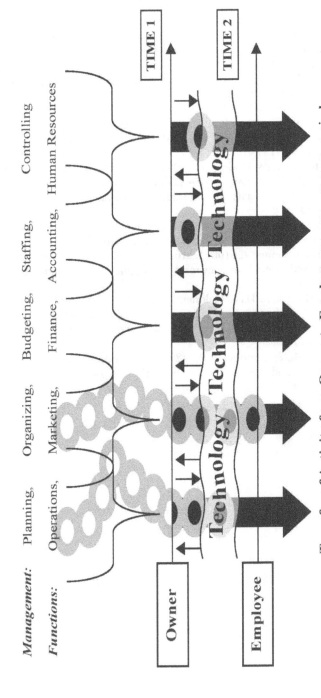

Figure 17.3. Activity chain of a small business incorporating technology.

REFERENCES

Barzilai-Nahon, K., & Mason, R. (2010, April). How executives perceive the Net generation. *Information, Communication & Society, 13*(3), 396-418.

Denaburg, J. (2012, March 9). Personal communication on millennial employees.

Ferri-Reed, J. (2010, April). The keys to engaging millennials. *Journal for Quality & Participation, 33*(1), 31-33.

Gryskiewicz, S. S. (1999). *Positive turbulence, developing climates for creativity, innovation, and renewal.* San Francisco, CA: Jossey-Bass.

Havenstein, H. (2008, September). Millennials demand changes in information technology (IT) strategy. *Computerworld,* 13.

Hu, J., Herrick C., & Hodgin, K. (2004). Managing the multigenerational nursing team. *The Health Care Manager, 23*(4), 334-340.

King, R. (2011, February 1). CEO guide to the micro workforce. *Bloomberg Businessweek,* 1-2.

Pew Research Center. (2010a). Millennials: A portrait of generation next. Retrieved from http://pewresearch.org/millennials/

Pew Research Center. (2010b, February 24). Millennials, media and information. Retrieved from http://pewresearch.org/pubs/1516/millennials-panel-two-millennials

Real, K., Mitnick, A. D., & Maloney, W. F. (2010). More similar than different: Millennials in the U.S. building trades. *Journal of Business Psychology, 25,* 303-313.

Spector, P. (1988). Development of the work locus of control scale. *Journal of Occupational Psychology, 61,* 335-340.

Twenge, J. M., & Campbel, S. M. (2008). Generational differences in psychological traits and their impact in the workplace. *Journal of Managerial Psychology, 23,* 862-877.

PART V

CONCLUDING THOUGHTS

CHAPTER 18

BUILDING BRIDGES BETWEEN THE MILLENNIALS AND OTHER GENERATIONS

Ronald R. Sims

INTRODUCTION

The 21st century workplace is continuing to become more diverse. The magnitude of this phenomenon can be witnessed in all types of organizations (i.e. public, private, not-for-profit). Diversity is defined as a fact or quality of being diverse; difference. A point or aspect in which things differ. A diverse workforce continues to be a necessity for organizational success as the idea of diversity spreads. The difficult challenge that organizations face today is finding a way for all of its employees, top to bottom, to realize the importance of diversity in the workforce and performing best in such an environment.

Many organizations appear to be more receptive to workforce diversity as we move further into the second decade of the 21st century. Workforce diversity is referred to as the differences among people based on gender, race, ethnicity, age, religion, physical or mental disability, sexual orientation, and socioeconomic class. As diversity is seen everywhere, it continues

Managing Human Resources for the Millennial Generation, pp. 421–444
Copyright © 2012 by Information Age Publishing

to be debated everywhere from corporations to governments, K-12 to higher educational institutions, and domestic to global organizations.

We live in an age of knowledge and innovation. For organizations to be successful in today's competitive market, they must be able to harness the collective knowledge of their own employees. An individual's knowledge is limited, and those who are similar to an individual will tend to be limited to the knowledge that they share. Diversity brings together individuals from diverse backgrounds that will help organizations generate new, innovative ideas. Organizational leaders want a heterogeneous group of employees working together with different minds rather than a homogenous group consisting of the same type of people. Effectively managing diversity can help organizations attract the individual talent to work for the organization.

Over the past few decades, leaders and human resources management (HRM) professionals have recognized that they must be tuned in to the many facets of diversity in today's workplace. It is not only the right thing to do, but "just makes sense" for the organization's bottom line or success. In reality, it is getting harder to have discussions in organizations with leaders, managers and HRM professionals without the issue of age differences arising. Age, or more appropriately generational, diversity is affecting the workplace like never before and is increasingly getting quite a lot of attention these days (as evidenced by this book). And with the oldest Baby Boomers turning 65, it seems that everyone has an opinion! Clearly, an effective "HRM or people strategy" built around diversity includes many dimensions, some we can see and others we cannot.

Today's workforce is aging and we are beginning to see some major changes that will definitely impact all sizes and types of organizations— the exodus of the Traditionalists and Baby Boomers, postretirement/early retirement second careers, the focus on quality of life issues, and the number of organizational leaders under 40. We are becoming more and more aware of the complexities of today's workforce and their impact on the organization's results.

The workplace environment organizations and HRM professionals set in place impacts employee morale, productivity and *engagement*—both positively and negatively. One cannot lose sight of the reality that employees (of four generations) are driving today's organization's results. In order to bring out the best in each generation, organizational leaders and HRM professionals need to understand not only what motivates them, but what motivates each employee. Understanding, appreciating and leverage the various employee styles (i.e. learning, decision making, problem-solving, work, and so on) is critical in creating a positive and supportive environment and in forging the all important employee partnerships so critical to organizational success.

This chapter first takes a brief look at the different generations at work. The discussion then turns to the concepts of generationalism and generational consciousness which are offered as critical components necessary for managing and leveraging the positive interactions between generations in the workplace. Next, the chapter offers some solutions (i.e. dialogue, good conversation and conversational learning) available to HRM professionals to develop connections or bridges among Millennials and other generations in their organizations. The next section discusses the importance of organizational culture, culture shock and valuing to the creation of a work environment where Millennials and others are successful. Before concluding the chapter, the next section takes a look at the importance of assessment and evaluation of how well an organization is doing in their efforts to recruit and retain Millennials (i.e. create generational consciousness and generationalism).

A BRIEF LOOK AT THE DIFFERENT GENERATIONS AT WORK

As introduced earlier, one of the more apparent diversity issues currently prevalent in the world of work is age diversity, which is partially created because of the multiple generations present in the workplace. To recruit and retain the cream of the crop from today's and tomorrow's worker pool, human resource management (HRM) professionals and other organizational leaders must understand

> what it means to "treat people respectfully" [which] varies from generation to generation. The members of the previous generation would say that respectful treatment means being direct and straightforward, while a member of the WWII generation might define "respectful" as using good grammar, "Sir" or "Ma'am," and "please" and "thank you." (Raines, 2008)

As the members of the World War II generation, or the Traditionalist generation, continue to retire and leave behind massive amounts of job vacancies, employers are turning to the current generation, also known as Generation Y or for the purposes of this book, Millennials, to hire the best talent to fill in the vacancies (Trunk, 2007). To effectively recruit and retain the "cream of the crop" Millennials, organizational leaders and HRM professionals must ensure that their organizations understand what makes the generation unique in comparison with the other generations present in the current workforce.

So, what are the four generations represented in today's workforce [i.e., Traditionalists, (1900-1945); Baby Boomers (1946-1964); Generation X (1965-1980); Millennials (1981-2000)?] Given that the other contributors in this book have done a thorough job in describing the different generations at work I will offer a brief look at the generations so as not to rehash the differences or definitions as articulated by other contributors in this book.

As noted earlier, it seems that there is no shortage of opinions on how generational diversity is affecting the workplace. The controversy has clearly been generated from Millennials, Gen Xers, and Baby Boomers (there are fewer and fewer Traditionalists in the workplace) mixing in the workplace—and trying to learn how to get along. The primary point of conflict: work ethic. Baby Boomers believe the Millennials are not hard working and are too "entitled." Baby Boomers value hard work, professional dress, long hours, and paying their dues—earning their stripes slowly (Mithers, 2009). Millennials believe Baby Boomers and Gen Xers are more concerned about the hours they work than what they produce. Millennials value flexibility, fun, the chance to do meaningful work right away, and "customized" careers that allow them the choice to go at the pace they want.

Each generation brings its own view of the world and work to an organization along with its experiences, perspectives, ethics, and values. And each generation forces society and organizations to look at life and work with a different focus, resulting in changes in workplace policies and procedures. It is not just coincidence that new HRM programs addressing lifestyle changes, work/life balance, health and fitness—previously not always considered key benefits—are now primary considerations of potential Millennial employees and employees from other generations, and common practices among the most admired organizations (e.g., "Employers of Choice").

"Employers of Choice" recognize that Baby Boomers like the Traditionalists will increasingly use their skills in new careers as they approach their 70s. Many organizations continue to review their retirement policies and offer these seasoned workers part-time jobs. Baby Boomers are not only impacting the way we look at health and wellness, they are also reintroducing spirituality into the workplace. Much smaller in numbers than the Baby Boomers, Generation Xers are keeping up their concern about maintaining balance in their lives. We have yet to see the full impact of the largest generation to date, Millennials. They relate more to the seniors in their values and ethics, are the most diverse of any generation, and are considered to be the biggest influence since the Baby Boomers. Studies show that Generation X and Millennial individuals combined now make up a majority of the workforce and that majority will grow. Recently there has been increased discussion about yet another generation to watch, labeled Generation Z, also known as "generation 9/11" that includes everyone born between 2001-2021 (*The Sydney Morning Herald*, 2011; Reidling, 2007). It is important that HRM professionals and their organizations recognize that being an "Employer of Choice" requires going beyond having a basic understanding of the generational labels to actively creating a culture of generationalism built upon generational consciousness as discussed in the next section.

GENERATIONALISM AND GENERATIONAL CONSCIOUSNESS

HRM professionals play a major role in the recruitment of employees like Millennials into an organization and an even stronger role in preparing Millennials—and others—to live, cope, and succeed in today's generationalistic or multigenerational organizations. In this regard, HRM professionals, organizational leaders, and employees throughout the organization must be actively engaged in creating an organizational culture and work environment that not only tolerates but welcomes the many differences found among employees. Operationalization of this message requires that HRM professionals and others in the organization avoid blaming one another for any crossgenerational issues, problems or tensions like previous workforce diversity initiatives. HRM professionals have to help their organizations develop connections or bridges among individuals from the Millennial and other generations.

As noted by other contributors in this book there are four generations working together in today's organizations. And, at a minimum it is important that HRM professionals and others understand what we do and do not know about the different groups (e.g., Traditionalists, Baby Boomers, Generation X, or Millennials) before one can begin to embrace the diversity that comes with the overlap of multiple generations and do the work necessary to create generationalism or a generational consciousness within the organization. For purposes of this chapter, generationalism is defined as "an organizational condition in which several distinct generations successfully work side by side, willing to respect and affirm each other's uniqueness, ready to benefit from each other's experiences, and quick to acknowledge each other's contribution to the organization's success."

Before we discuss in more detail the concept of "generational consciousness" let us briefly look at the word consciousness. The word "consciousness" refers to one's thoughts and motivations; the word refers to a state of awareness (Collins Dictionary, 2011). For our purposes, consciousness refers to an individual's awareness of self, environment and mental activity. If we take key components of this definition and connect them to the word "generations" (e.g. cohorts of people who were born in the same date range and share similar experience), HRM professionals can realize that:

1. The word "generations" can provide some context and scope of individual motivations for those in a particular cohort. And the goodness of such information can be used to help test and better understand the individuals within a cohort and to bear good fruit in building bridges across generations and designing HRM policies and practices to maximize performance and productivity throughout the organization.

2. An individual and generation's sense of awareness has got to be broadened beyond their immediate generation to include the state of other generations. In a sense HRM professionals must work to help individual employees, like the Millennials, to overcome the "blind-side effect" in all human interactions. This blind-side effect makes us unable to see the uniqueness, values and contributions of others (i.e., individuals or generations).

3. Collins Dictionary (2011) also mentions that consciousness is about self-awareness and so therefore consciousness is about identity. The word "generations," as evidenced by the discussions of contributors throughout this book, can better help HRM professionals define the scope of an individual's or generation's identity, and recognize that if one's identity cannot incorporate or effectively interact (i.e. work) with individuals from other generations in the organization the individuals will be disconnected from others and in fact, will likely be a stumbling block to the individuals' and organizations' success (i.e. generationalism). Further, such information will help HRM and the organization invent and implement policies and procedures that lead to good results hopefully instead of crises between individuals and generations; and will not parent a passive-reactive mode, but more importantly help all spend time establishing a value system respectful of all generations.

Generational consciousness deals with a process of (firstly) understanding one's own and other generations and (secondly) producing generationalism within the organization for Millennials and others through a vigorous process of orientation, learning, training, development and empowerment. As a process generational consciousness compels individuals throughout the organization, regardless of their generational label, to view and interpret the state of organizational success beyond their own and others' perceived limitations, to include historical and environmental conditions and the emerging future.

Clearly, organizational success cannot result from HRM policies or procedures that treat one generation "different" than another (introducing a single-generation framework), where say, there is an overemphasis on Millennials as the most or more important keys to such success. Celebrating organizational success because of the contributions of only one generation as such an emphasis is both unfounded and most likely becomes a burden and a curse for say, those in the Millennial Generation. A word of caution is in order for HRM professionals, and others who are recently overly emphasizing the benefits of the newest "in-generation"—the Millennials while ignoring or deemphasizing the Traditionalists, Baby Boomers and Generation Xers.

Secondly, generational consciousness can be an anchor to any HRM or organizational processes intended to create generationalism through concerted efforts to enhance understanding of the positive relationships that can and must exist between the various overlapping generations. In the end, generational consciousness serves as the foundation for building bridges between generations. These should be bridges that are not simply based on mere generational data analysis and sharing but on building organizational success on the collective efforts of employees regardless of their generation. So the organizational commitment to a culture of generationalism becomes the portal for its operations. An organization cannot project stability when one generation is in conflict with another. HRM and other leaders cannot project a strong culture when there is a constant collapse of the value system, sense of relationship, respect and the "value-added" by each individual employee and generation. While HRM professionals cannot predict the future they can rely on historical experiences with diversity and on current organizational-systemic efforts to manage multiple-generations.

Generational consciousness implies the need for the HRM professionals and their organizations to craft an intelligence system that has the ability to keep track of and understand the ever evolving information or data on Millennials, for example, and other generations in the workplace. Again, this is not unlike previous efforts over the past several decades to understand diversity and globalization. All organizations and their HRM professionals must have viable intelligence systems that are preoccupied with foretelling future implications of any forms of or changes in diversity. In the end, generational consciousness brings a demand for the crafting of organizational systems that bring solutions not only to present conditions of a multigenerational workplace but also to future generational overlaps.

Some solutions available to HRM professionals to develop connections or bridges among Millennials and other generations in their organizations are through dialogue, good conversation, and conversational learning to enhance action and learning among the various generations. Such bridge-building would shift the focus from differences among the generations to understanding and acceptance as each individual finds ways to make personal connections and build communication bridges between self and others around him or her.

BUILDING BRIDGES BETWEEN THE GENERATIONS THROUGH DIALOGUE AND GOOD CONVERSATION

Building upon the discussion so far in this chapter generational consciousness and generationalism are important to organizational success. In my experience, creating formal opportunities for dialogue, good conversation and conversational learning is one of the most proactive interventions HRM professionals and their organizations can use to build bridges between Millennials and other individuals and generations. Without dialogue generational consciousness and a culture of generationalism will not come to fruition. Good dialogue and conversation is a means for Millennials and others to acquire understanding and learning of themselves and others in an organization. Ideal-speech, ideal-listening, discourse in relationships, and the promotion of the different voices that exist within an organization, are necessary components of dialogue and a good conversation between Millennials who are learning about themselves, others and their organizations.

Dialogue

The merit of a dialogue is its practicality. Dialogue, however, must subscribe to what is termed "the new decorum," which requires Millennials and other individuals to listen to others and engage in a moderate tone of conversation. Dialogue plays a role in identity formation. Self-awareness is facilitated by self-disclosure and interaction with others (Jourard, 1971). When in the process of dialogue, each party recognizes the identity of the other, both then will become able to understand better their individual selves and where possible generational identities can develop. Through dialogue we create a broader horizon that serves as the backdrop against which we operate in the world. This broader horizon results from the "fusion of horizons"—situating one possibility, our usual standard, alongside other possibilities, new and unfamiliar standards (Taylor, 1992).

Experiential learning theory insists that genuine learning occurs only when individuals are engaged in "praxis"—political action informed by reflection (Friere, 1973). A fundamental aspect of praxis is the process of "naming the world." Naming the world is achieved through dialogue among equals regardless of generation, a dual process of inquiry and learning. In my experience, an organization committed to instilling generational consciousness among its employees and a culture of generartionalism rejects the notion of pitting generations against each other, and is not passive in its efforts to maximize the benefits of the Millennials and other generations collectively. The idea is to instill "critical generational consciousness" in each employee in the organization where generational differences and similarities, for example, are explored through dialogue among equals (i.e. peers and others regardless of their generation).

HRM professionals must champion the view that dialogue is good conversation. Such a view adheres to rules of the new decorum. Dialogue has the potential to serve many purposes in today's and tomorrow's organizations. It facilitates self-awareness and awareness of others. It is a source of learning. It is liberating, and leads to the creation of a climate of inclusion and psychological safety within an organization. Psychological safety opens the door for good conversation among Millennials and other employees within an organization.

Striving for Good Conversation

HRM professionals have an obligation to help create a culture of generationalism within their organizations. This means a culture where Millennials and others talk freely and understand the importance of taking risks, listening and sharing their experiences and views within the organization. According to Nash (1996), a conversation is literally a manner of living whereby people keep company with each other, and talk together; in good faith, in order to exchange sometimes agreeable, sometimes opposing, ideas. A conversation is not an argument, although it can get heated. A conversation is at its best when the participants are not impatient to conclude their business, but wish instead to spend their time together in order to deepen and enrich their understanding of an idea, or, in our case, the differences and similarities that may exist, say between Millennials and any other individuals or generations.

A conversation that is genuine is one whose conventions emphasize the fundamental worth and dignity of each individual in the organization despite their generational label. To date, it has been my experience that using this view of conversation is a useful way for HRM professionals to get an employee to talk openly about generational issues, views, beliefs, values or other concerns. This means that HRM professionals must ensure that Traditionalists, Baby Boomers, Generation Xers, and Millennials treat each other with utmost respect. It is important for HRM professionals to help facilitate learning and increased generational consciousness with the highest regard in the sense that Millennials and others share and learn from each other. That is, that no generation has a "corner on the market" of organizational impact, value or importance. No single generation inhabits the knowledge or organizational contribution high ground *a priori*. Each member of a generation is made up of travelers with a purpose on a journey to find meaning in the work they do (and in their personal life beyond work), and because this journey is their own, it possesses intrinsic worth and is to be respected.

An important purpose in engaging in conversation in organizations is to test, expand, enrich, and deepen employees' understanding of themselves and others so that each employee can better contribute to the organization regardless of his or her background beliefs, experiences or generational label. With the ideal of conversation in mind, hopefully Millennials (and others) can be genuinely respectful of each other and work to find common language to express their individual similarities and differences, and to take conversational risks in constructing a cogent discourse.

In brief then, good conversation between Millennials and others starts with:

1. an honest effort by all employees to put the organization first;
2. an acute awareness that we all have biases and blind spots;
3. an open-mindedness to the possibility of learning something from others in conversation;
4. a willingness to improve current and future understanding of others;
5. a conscious effort to refrain from advancing one's own self or views as if they were best;
6. an inclination to listen intently in order to grasp the meaning of other people's views or means of expressing their opinions (i.e. suggested solutions);
7. an agreement that clarifying, questioning, challenging, exemplifying, and applying ideas are activities to be done in a self- and other-respecting way;
8. a realization that we will frequently get off course in our conversations because a spirit of charity, intellectual curiosity, and even playfulness will characterize many of our discussions, and because, as David Bromwich (1992) says: "The good conversation is not truth, or right, or anything else that may come out at the end of it, but the activity itself in its constant relation to life" (pp. 131-132); and
9. an appreciation of the reality that it will take time for us to get to know each other, and a realization that eventually we will find ways to engage in robust, candid, and challenging dialogue and conver-

sation without being so "nice" we bore each other to death, or without being so hostile that we cripple each other emotionally and intellectually.

It is one thing to speak of the importance of dialogue and good conversation between generations and another for HRM professionals to bring it to fruition. In my experience, one way HRM professionals can do this is to move to a focus on conversational learning in an organization.

CONVERSATIONAL LEARNING

Addressing potential and existing generational problems, challenges or decisions in today's world of work requires the recognition that conversations among what some believe are vastly differing generations are imperative. According to Alan Webber (1993), formerly a managing editor/editorial director of the *Harvard Business Review* and a founding editor of *Fast Company*, "the most important work in the new economy is creating conversations ... But all depends on the quality of the conversations ... Conversations—not rank, title, or the trappings of power—determine who is literally and figuratively 'in the loop' and who is not" (p. 28). The new economy and world of work are dependent upon the ease, frequency, and quality of conversations within and among organizations and individuals. It is also dependent, in my view, on the success of HRM professionals in helping to create organizational cultures or a climate conducive to dialogue and good conversation and learning between Millennials and others.

Given the continued emphasis on workforce diversity in general and Millennials more specifically I think it is important that we call for a new kind of conversation in organizations–*conversational learning*. Because the quality of conversations is so critical, the nature, intentions, and contexts surrounding conversations need to improve. This leads to the role of HRM professionals vis-à-vis the increasing demands or pressures to get the most out of an organization's workforce and prepare Millennials as the newest entrants in the world of work for the challenges presented by overlapping generations and changes in the global economy.

Given the fears, challenges and opportunities that some believe come with any effort to assimilate Millennials or any new and different group of individuals into an organization, how is conversational learning relevant? How can a conversational learning approach contribute to generational consciousness and generationalism and increase an organization's capacity to possibly reframe Millennial's perceptions of, for example, Baby Boomers in general (and visa versa) and ways of responding to possible workplace tensions or conflicts in particular? What does conversational learning involve in an environment of four overlapping generations? To address these questions, initially I offer a brief conceptual description of conversational learning.

What Is Conversational Learning?

The concept of learning used in this chapter is one that is grounded in experience and is described by David Kolb (1984) as "a process whereby knowledge is created through the transformation of experience" (p. 41). Conversational learning eludes precise definition (Kolb, 1998). Yet, some parameters to guide you, the reader, may be helpful. Much of the spirit of my meaning of conversational learning rests in this message from Howard Stein (1994):

> To listen is to unearth rather than to bury. It is to feel rather than to be compelled to act. It gives us all greater liberty and responsibility in our actions ... The heart of listening deeply ... is attentiveness to others' voices ... the capacity for surprise in the face of any and all planning. Serendipity is readiness and playfulness in the face of surprise ... incorporation of the astonishing into the ordinary, the refusal to hide behind a shield of routine. It is a willingness to be moved, changed ... letting go of control. (p. 111)

To support the kind of listening that Stein is describing in organizations, it is essential as suggested earlier that HRM professionals and others create receptive spaces for conversations to take place throughout the organization. When these safe receptive spaces exist in the organization, in my experience, Millennials like previous generations can learn to self-reflect and listen deeply to their own inner voice and to the voices of others – to listen in the spirit of learning, of being surprised, of being willing to slow down and reflect and share, and of being open to learning about and from others who may be different.

To prepare Millennials for the challenges they will encounter in their work careers, these kinds of conversations are essential to facilitate learning in organizations where individuals may reframe how they conceive of themselves and respond to issues they might encounter in their own work lives. I have found that conversational learning requires many substantial shifts in thinking for most employees including:

- listening to others with the intention of learning with them;
- reflecting intentionally to gain more understanding of the complexities of organizational life using Schon's (1983) model of the reflective practitioner;

- moving away from assuming there is one way of thinking (either/or) toward assuming that there are multiple legitimate and viable perspectives and possibilities of any organizational situation or experience;
- moving away from assuming there is a right answer or a right approach toward placing more value on trying to learn from the multiple perspectives of as many other people as reasonably possible about organizational issues like business ethics and ethical decision making; and
- avoiding reactive behavior by becoming highly proactive in anticipating organizational situations and finding ways to learn from different perspectives.

A conversational learning approach can be especially advantageous when it involves:

- recognition of individual differences as essential for the continuous learning required; and
- collaborative learning among individuals with differing worldviews, skills, areas of expertise, vocabularies, and so on.

In my experience working with HRM professionals on diversity issues in the workplace has convinced me that there are many unexamined assumptions that could limit the capacity for the kind of learning needed among Millennials and other employees. Some of these might include:

- their varying preferences and expectations about, for example, how ethical decisions should be made; appropriate styles for speaking and presenting themselves;
- who—or if anyone in the organization—could be trusted enough to take risks and share one's thoughts, feelings, and/or opinions on complex and sensitive organizational issues;
- whether the organization or individual is responsible for an employee's career or how loyal or committed one should be toward their organization; and
- who has power and who does not have power as well as perceptions about sources of power—i.e., positional, personal, authority, influence, etc.

At this point I hope it is clear to you, the reader, that I believe dialogue, good conversation and conversational learning are critical to building bridges among the generations, generational consciousness and generationalism within organizations as we continue, for example, to identify ways to both recruit, integrate and better manage today's Millennials and other generations. HRM professionals should work with Millennials and others consciously and sincerely to take into account what others have to say. I and many HRM professionals have realized that this is essential to the successful integration of Millennials into their organizations.

One thing that is important to the success of any organization's commitment to the diversity and difference of Millennials is the institutionalization of such a commitment into the organization's culture—generationalism. That is, that the recognition, appreciation, and understanding of Millennials is an accepted part of the organization's culture.

ORGANIZATIONAL CULTURE: CULTURE SHOCK AND VALUING

One of the most important lessons we have learned about Millennials (or any other generation to date) is that their successful integration into the organization occurs when there is a true commitment by senior leadership to diversity and effective management and integration of individuals into the culture of the organization. Practically, culture is defined as "the way we do things here." Every organization has its own culture, values, communication styles, and typical behaviors. The culture of the organization is influenced by the combination of personalities, values, and backgrounds of its members who represent various generations. The organizational dynamics created by this type of diversity directly affect the job satisfaction of Millennials and other workers, as well as group performance and productivity.

Organizations with clearly defined and enforced cultures committed to generationalism (1) empower their members to feel good about themselves in relation to their individual uniqueness (diversity and difference) and work; (2) have employees who are more likely to work hard and produce more; and (3) have clear values and expectations for performance and behavior. In my experience I have found that communicating the organization's "culture" through HRM initiatives like employee orientation, training and development involves transmitting signals, for example, to Millennials about how employees should treat each other. In addition, organizational interventions, like employee training, are based on a clearly defined culture that communicates the rules about available rewards and what the Millennials have to do to get them. Coleman (1990) notes that the members who succeed are those who understand the organization's cultural signals. For Millennials, this means that they understand how to play the organization game and how to overcome its hurdles.

Many of the contributors in this book have provided examples of how organizations are assimilating or integrating Millennials into their organizations. One organization the author is familiar with has committed to institutionalizing such efforts as part of its culture. More specifically, the diversity and difference orientation and training within the organization imparts the corporate philosophy regarding a diverse work force and examines generational differences as well as some generic principles about working with people who are different.

Culture Shock

Another key learning point for the successful integration or management of Millennials is that organizations and their HRM professionals must take responsibility for ensuring that their employees all have the opportunity to be successful within the organization. For example, organizations that recognize the importance of employee orientation training work to see that Millennials understand the unspoken issues, unwritten rules, and expectations of appropriate behavior in the organization. That is, the culture of the organization as discussed in the previous section. These organizations also use experienced HRM professionals and others to conduct the orientation training. The HRM professionals are sensitive to individual differences and the interpersonal and group dynamics of the organization.

When organizations take responsibility for enlightening Millennials about the unwritten and written rules of the organization, they decrease the likelihood that their Millennial employees will experience culture shock. Culture shock occurs when employees are involved in an organizational culture that has rules and practices different from their own. Shock sets in when employees do not know how to function successfully in that culture. They react with anxiety, fear, or withdrawal, and members of the organization's dominant culture usually react with rejection and isolation. These often create an immediate loss of productivity, prolonged frustration, disillusionment, and can result in job termination (Coleman, 1990; Deal & Kennedy, 1982).

I have noticed that the culture shock situation is common but costly to the individual, other group members, and the organization. With the proper planning and implementation of HRM initiatives, however, this cycle of attraction, uncertainty, frustration, withdrawal, and separation can be addressed effectively, for example, to benefit Millennials and their organization. I have also noticed in my work with various organizations that the critical, core element of organizational cultures based on generationalism is the emphasis upon the unique but complementary assets of each individual member of the organization as opposed to her or his generation. That is, for example, in training each person is presented and accepted as a complex mixture of values, beliefs, expectations, attitudes, aptitudes, and work styles that are defined by a unique set of experiences. And such training emphasizes that these combinations result in a unique dynamic interaction in the organization and in the organization's various work groups. In the end, organizational productivity and performance lie partially in recognizing, understanding, and appreciating the differences individuals like Millennials exhibit at work and fostering an attitude of generationalism and optimal performance by all members of the organization.

Efforts by HRM professionals and other organizational decision-makers to minimize the culture shock of Millennials and other employees occurs through bridge-building and generationalism based on inclusion, a spirit of community, and the continuous development of a sense of shared respect and responsibility. HRM professionals, Millennials and others in the organization must share responsibility for ensuring that generational consciousness and generationalism is embraced and managed as an integral part of every employee's experience. This means valuing everyone.

Valuing

One of the most vital, yet elusive, aspects of an organization and its HRM professionals doing a good job of creating and sustaining an environment or culture of success for Millennials, as well as all employees, is the concept of "valuing." Valuing means that the people and the organization have the capacity to appreciate and to utilize the multitude of differences, experiences, and talents that are brought to the organization by each individual or generation. This is important because, in order for an organization to truly value its people, it must have people who are able to express (through dialogue, good conversation and conversational learning) their valuing of one another and organizational processes and procedures that allow all members to contribute their attributes to the productive process (generationalism).

In some organizations this is still an extremely elusive element because, for too long, HRM professionals and other leaders assumed that processes and procedures that have worked for years for one group or generation would automatically work for other groups (i.e. Millennials). It is still believed by some, in error, that once members of the Millennial generation have been hired or recruited into an organization, past orientation or assimilation efforts used with Traditionalists, Baby Boomers and

Generation Xers, will automatically work with this new generation of employees. As alluded to by a number of contributors to this book, the organizations that successfully manage the Millennial experience well do not make this mistake of omission and especially as they emphasize, for example, the importance of developmental and promotional processes so necessary for individual contributions to organizational success.

The well-managed diverse organization has managers (or leaders) and HRM professionals who realize a real sense of being valued comes not from "hearing" but from "feeling." Millennials and other employees are told his or her value and that she or he belongs to the family but, more importantly, the person feels like a member. This feeling comes from processes and procedures of the organizations that are truly receptive of the differences in people. Further, those who are managing the Millennials do not leave this appreciation to chance.

What distinguishes the success of some organizations in enhancing the diversity Millennials are bringing to the world of work depends upon the vision and strength of management. The stronger senior leadership's vision and commitment is to assimilate Millennials into the organization, the greater the chances for generational consciousness and a culture of generationalism to come to fruition. This means, therefore, that organizational leadership plays a significant part in raising the generational consciousness of all employees about the values of others. And it also means that without the support of senior managers, attempting to be an "Employer of Choice" for Millennials will be compromised.

Astute leaders and HRM professionals increasingly perceive the overlapping of four generations as a formidable challenge that must be addressed. And they realize the need to be sensitive to generational differences in the workplace and in the marketplace if their organizations are to be productive and competitive. With this in mind, top executives and HRM professionals at numerous organizations as described throughout this book continue to implement aggressive and successful efforts to increase generational awareness and make differences an asset rather than a liability. What is it that these leaders are doing to encourage generational consciousness and generationalism?

Leaders in organizations that are successfully coming to terms with Millennials as new entrants into their organizations did so through thoughtful deliberations, careful planning, and calculated action that considers obstacles and opportunities and develops opportunities for dialogue, good conversation and HRM interventions throughout the organization. And many are prepared to demonstrate their commitment to enhancing generationalism by selective interventions. A few important steps taken by one such organization were as follows:

1. A careful study was done by an outside group with in-house representation to gather demographic or generational data on Millennials and baseline data about its work force.

2. The study surfaced data revealing the growth and interest of Millennials, a very small representation of Millennials in the organization, and a large percentage of employees—Baby Boomers and Traditionalists—eligible for retirement within the next 5 years.

3. The results of the study were shared with the board of directors.

4. Management decided to share the study with the employees along with its plans to better understand the changing work force.

5. Several in-house and public meetings were held to discuss and to get employee input and suggestions to include in management's eventual plans for action.

6. Finally, once input had been received from different stakeholders, the board of directors approved a plan of action and instructed management (and particularly the HRM professionals) to carry it out.

Recognizing the value of the data, cooperatively planning to address its work force or human capital needs, and operationalizing appropriate action programs (i.e. an increased emphasis on technology in the organization's operations required more technologically savvy and literate employees in the coming years) helped the organization to set quantitative and qualitative goals to recruit and retain an increased number of Millennial employees. Of course, this means that the organization must commit to putting in place assessment procedures to track their progress in this initiative.

ASSESSMENT PROCEDURES

Do most organizations systematically assess how well they are doing after implementing HRM plans like the one alluded to in the previous section? And what if the plan involves a highly sensitive issue like transitioning from a work force with a majority of Traditionalists or Baby Boomers to one predominantly made up of Millennials? The answers most often given are that organizations do not always evaluate their performance in implementing such plans of action, especially when they are trying to make important changes like dramatically increasing their proportion of Millennial employees. It is not surprising, however, that many organizations confuse the term "assessment" with "evaluation." Assessment involves determining effectiveness and/or efficiency of a new plan or policy, and learning about processes. Evaluation, on the other hand, is involved with results and outcomes. While both measure performance, one should focus on process and the other on the bottom line.

After a plan, for example, to increase the number of Millennials into an organization's work force is developed and operationalized, it is important that HRM professionals and the organization's leaders work to determine how it is working. While managers and board members want to know if a plan to increase the number of Millennials into the organization's workforce is successful, the gauge too many organizations fall back upon is a change in numbers—that is, how many more Millennials. What is most important, however, is having reliable information on the impact of a new plan or program on the work force and the organization's performance or productivity. The assessment process should, therefore, be an integral part of any plan of action. And its sensory mechanism(s) to obtain data and gather intelligence must be in place at the inception of a new HRM plan or policy within the organization. In some instances carefully gathered anecdotal information must be factored in with hard data to form a composite. These data and anecdotal sources should be candidly analyzed and serve as feedback to management. Only then will an organization's leaders and HRM professionals know what kind of progress has taken place, and what parts of the plan may require attention and possible modification.

So, what should organizations do to enhance efforts to recruit and retain Millennials? Consider the following approach by one organization. First, management formed a generational strategy task force to define and clarify the concepts of generational consciousness and generationalism, stress their importance for the organization's success, and identify HRM strategies for making progress toward successfully managing an integrated generational work force. Second, the task force included Traditionalists, Baby Boomers, Generation Xers, and Millennials from all parts and levels of the organization. Third, this group was able to learn about, understand, and appreciate the complex nature of the organization and the different elements that would need to be considered to successfully integrate Millennials and other generations. An important by-product of this process was the high visibility the task force provided for a focus on generational consciousness and generationalism, dialogue, good conversation and conversational learning between Traditionalists, Baby Boomers, Generation Xers, and Millennials. Many of the recommendations offered by the task force were accepted by management and served as the foundation for future HRM policies and procedures intended not only to recruit and retain Millennials but to create and institutionalize a culture of generationalism and generational consciousness within the organization.

CONCLUSION AND REFLECTIONS

Managing partner at Deloitte & Touche USA LLP, Barry Salzberg, said "Given the changing demographics in the marketplace and projections about the diversity of future labor pools, it is evident that our success increasingly depends on the full use of the skills, talents, and life experiences of all our people" (Booth, 2007, p. 1). Salzberg added Deloitte's commitment to fostering a high performance culture and developing their talents so every employee can reach their full potential, which will lead to the company's full potential and high productivity level. As Salzberg said, our world is changing and it is important for organizational leaders to recognize the changes and adapt to them in order to be successful. With the growing diversity in the workforce, it is only wise for organizations to use all their employees' diverse characteristics and skills to their advantage and develop those skills further. Increasing workforce diversity will continue to spawn new and innovative organizational responses as is the case with efforts currently being undertaken by numerous organizations related to age diversity and the Millennial generation.

HRM professionals and other leaders must work to build bridges and connect people in the workplace if their organizations are going to be successful. Individuals, regardless of their generation, must rely on one another in the workplace. In a recent report, Deloitte Research, an arm of Deloitte & Touche, put it this way: "Work has always been done through relationships. But as jobs become more complex, people increasingly depend on one another, whether it is to design software, lead a call center, or sell a service (Hitt, Miller, & Colella, 2011, p. 235).

To build bridges and connections among people, Deloitte recommends a number of tactics which others also recognize (Athey, 2004; Fichter, 2005; Hitt et al., 2011; Momberto, 2007):

- Design physical space that fosters connections. Proximity and layout matter. Being located far away from others who have relevant knowledge and insight can be particularly harmful to those with complex jobs. A lack of face-to-face interactions, the richest type, can be harmful to those who have such jobs. Also, an absence of dedicated areas for collaborative discussions as well as areas for quiet contemplation can be detrimental.

- Build an organizational cushion of time and space. Overly busy associates and managers often do not have time to consult with others. With today's leaner organizations and stretched people, connecting to other people in rich ways can be difficult. Yet, those connections can improve productivity and quality in the long run, particularly for those who have complex jobs.

- Cultivate communities. Without a sense of community, associates and managers may not seek out those who have relevant knowledge and insight. Communities revolve around shared interests and goals, and they foster a sense of shared identity and belonging.
- Stimulate rich networks of high-quality relationships. Many associates and managers have limited informal networks of colleagues. Without a rich network that stretches across departments, divisions, and hierarchical levels, individuals are blocked from key sources of information and problem solving. In some organizations, explicit mapping of informal networks is carried out and those with deficient networks are counseled on how to increase them.

When HRM professionals and organizational leaders take responsibility for building bridges between people as Deloitte has done they set the tone for Millennials, Gen Xers, Baby Boomers, and Traditionalists to build positive relationships and a culture of generationalism.

Employees cannot work to their best potential when put in an uncomfortable environment. It is the organization's responsibility to provide a safe, friendly work environment for their employees and to respect individual differences. This can be best done by organizations and their HRM professionals working toward a culture based upon generational consciousness and generationalism. Proper diversity management should provide opportunity for all employees to maximize their potential and fully contribute to the organization's objectives and goals. Also, HRM professionals and organizational managers and leaders must not take advantage or disadvantage of any group and ensure that all employees, regardless of their generational label, treat each other with dignity and respect.

Generationalism will continue to become a crucial part of every organization as workplace populations become more diverse and cross-generational concerns or potential tensions are no longer issues. Ideally, in the future, diversity training that focuses on age, for example, will become unnecessary as employees understand early on that in order to be successful in today's world of work, they must be able to get along and work with other individuals. This means that generational consciousness and generationalism must be cornerstones of the organization.

While it is great that many organizations are practicing and adopting initiatives that focus on issues like age diversity (or the overlapping of the current four generations one finds in some organizations) fitting for their organization, not all of them are able to keep up to their words. Age diversity issues that come with the retirement of Traditionalists and Baby Boomers and the entrance of Millennials, for example, do not exist separately from other organizational and managerial (i.e., HRM) processes. Understanding how people actually behave with respect to diversity, rather than how they say they behave, is necessary for any effective and successful human resources or diversity management policy and interventions. The entrance of Millennial and other diverse individuals into an organization does not mean success in diversity initiatives but is an illustration of attempting to understand diversity in an organizational context and provides insights into what factors influence different constituencies' reactions to diversity.

Some Reflections on the Efforts to Integrate the Millennials

A few key issues regarding the recruitment and assimilation of Millennials into organizations need to be considered. Clearly, leadership throughout the organization and from HRM professionals is absolutely essential to manage organizational change. Any program or plan of action to effectively address the entrance of Millennials into an organization will encounter some resistance. Supportive leadership is often the difference between success and failure.

Every organization has a unique culture that influences change, particularly diversity efforts like the integration of Millennials. Understanding an organization's culture is critical. Only by doing so is it possible to implement successful strategies to enhance the integration of Millennials and other individuals into the workforce. While superficially it may appear that hiring Millennials in an organization may be no different than previous efforts to bring employees from other generations into the organization, there may be more obstacles that HRM professionals and others need to understand and remove given all of the attention we are showering on the Millennial generation. Otherwise they will be formidable barriers to change. The recruitment and deployment of Millennials in an organization require that its leaders and HRM professionals prepare for change by building supporting alliances and creating a hospitable environment for these new employees.

Every HRM initiative intended to recruit, retain and integrate Millennials into the organization must have an assessment mechanism that allows management to determine how effectively and/or efficiently it may be operating. Otherwise, the actual impact of such initiatives may be more superficial than real. Numbers alone may not be a valid indicator of an organization's Millennial recruitment and retention plan's effectiveness. If the organization is constantly recruiting Millennials because of a high turnover, the organization needs to assess itself to determine why this costly revolving door is occurring.

Successfully including Millennials into an organization's talent management strategy requires leaders and especially its HRM professionals to manage, understand and commit to a culture based on a generationalism mind-set. Progress will not be automatic. There will likely be some resistance to change, especially over the increased emphasis and attention on Millennials and their entrance into the workplace. Some of the promising ways to counteract institutionalized preferences for the status quo are focusing attention, goal setting, rewards, and an information flow that provides reliable feedback on how generations can best understand and work with each other. HRM professionals, experts and external consultants who understand Millennials and generational issues can be very useful to an organization as they work to become an "Employer of Choice" for all potential employees.

In the end, it is important for HRM professionals and their organizations to have a strategy or program in place within their organizations for meeting the specific needs of each generation. Given the strong focus on generational differences over the past few years it is important that HRM professionals and other organizational leaders not believe that addressing the distinct sets of values, attitudes and behaviors of four generations is an insurmountable task with no real solution. The key to effectively managing generational differences is to treat employees as *individuals* and not classify them as merely Traditionalists, Baby Boomers, Gen Xers or Millennials with stereotypical needs. While generational characteristics can certainly provide greater insight into specific views and motivators, employees need to be treated as individuals with unique career and life goals, values, expectations and frustrations. Such attention will most often enhance an organization's HRM efforts to attract, motivate and retain top talent.

In conclusion, the generational mix provides an excellent example of diversity in action. For example, as emphasized by a number of contributors to this book, one thing Millennials can bring to the workplace is their appreciation for gender equality and sexual, cultural, and racial diversity—Millennials embrace these concepts more than any previous generation. Millennials also have an appreciation for community and collaboration. They can help create a more relaxed workplace that reduces some of the problems that come from too much focus on status and hierarchy (Mithers, 2009). Traditionalists, Boomers and GenXers bring a wealth of experience, dedication, and commitment that contribute to productivity, and a sense of professionalism that is benefitting their younger counterparts. Together, Millennials and Gen Xers may be able to satisfy the Gen X desire for more flexible scheduling and virtual work. Accomplishing such changes will come when all the generations learn to understand, respect—and maybe even like—one another.

REFERENCES

Athey, R. (2004). *It's 2008: Do you know where your talent is?—Part 1*. New York, NY: Deloitte & Touche.

Athey, R. (2007). *It's 2008: Do you know where your talent is?—Part 2*. New York, NY: Deloitte & Touche.

Booth, J. D. (2007). In celebration of differences—Our salute to diversity. Retrieved from http://corp.dev.biznetis.net/DesktopModules/EngagePublish/printerfriendly.aspx?itemId=108&PortalId=0&TabId=%2054

Bromwich, D. (1992). *Politics by other means: Higher education and group thinking*. New Haven, CT: Yale University Press.

Coleman, T. L. (1990). Managing diversity at work: The new American dilemma. *Public Management, 70*(10), 2-5.

Collins English dictionary. (2011). Retrieved from http://www.collinslanguage.com/collins-english-dictionary-11th-edition-9780007437863

Deal, T. W., & Kennedy, A. A. (1982). *Corporate cultures: The rites and rituals of corporate life*. Reading, MA: Addison-Wesley.

Fichter, D. (2005, July/August). The many forms of E-collaboration. *Online*, 48-50.

Friere, P. (1973). *Education for critical consciousness*. New York, NY: Continuum.

Hitt, M. A., Miller, C. C., & Colella, A. (2011). *Organizational behavior* (3rd ed.). Hoboken, NJ: John Wiley & Sons.

Jourard, S. M. (1971). *The transparent self*. New York, NY: Van Nostrand Reinhold.

Kolb, D. A. (1998). Experiential learning: From discourse model to conversation. *Lifelong Learning in Europe, 3*, 148-153.

Kolb, D. A. (1984). *Experiential learning: Experience as the source of learning and development*. Englewood Cliffs, NJ: Prentice-Hall.

Mithers, C. (2009, May). Workplace wars. *Ladies Home Journal*, 104-109.

Momberto, C. (2007, July 24). Instant messaging invades the office. *Wall Street Journal*, p. B.1. Retrieved from http://online.wsj.com/article/SB118523443717075546.html

Nash, R. J. (1996). *"Real world" ethics: Frameworks for educators and human service professionals*. New York, NY: Teachers College Press.

Raines, C. (2008). 10 most frequently asked questions. Retrieved from http://www.generationsatwork.com/FAQ.htm

Riedling, A. M. (2007). *An educator's guide to information literacy: What every high school senior needs to know*. Westport, CT: Libraries Unlimited.

Schon, D. A. (1983). *The reflective practitioner: How professionals think in action*. London, England: Temple Smith.

Stein, H. F. (1994). *Listening deeply: An approach to understanding and consulting in organizational culture*. Boulder, CO: Westview.

Taylor, C. (1992). *Multiculturalism and "the politics of recognition": An essay by Charles Taylor*. Princeton, NJ: Princeton University Press.

The Sydney Morning Herald. (2011). Generation Z in the workplace. Retrieved from http://blogs.smh.com.au/executivestyle/managementline/2009/08/05/gen-zinthewo.html

Trunk, P. (2007). What Gen Y really wants. Retrieved from http://www.time.com/time/magazine/article/0,9171,1640395,00.html

Webber, A. M. (1993, January-February).What's so new about the new economy? *Harvard Business Review, 71*, 24-42.

ABOUT THE AUTHORS

Danielle Beu Ammeter has a bachelor of arts degree in chemistry from Baylor University, a master of business administration degree from Texas Christian University, and a PhD in human resource management from the University of Oklahoma. Prior to joining the American Heart Association, Danielle was an assistant professor of management at Louisiana Tech and West Virginia University. She taught in the areas of general management, change management, staffing, compensation, leadership, and teams. She also directed organizational change project plans for education, healthcare, and banking organizations and conducted leadership development seminars. She published and presented in the areas of business ethics, human resource management, international human resource management, and management history. Her scholarly credits include 20 peer-reviewed publications, 5 book chapters, 4 additional publications, and 10 professional presentations. Dr. Ammeter joined the American Heart Association in 2006 as an organizational development consultant, and in 2007 she became an instructional designer on the new American Heart University team. In these roles, she facilitated courses in diversity, corporate strategy, customer service, and supervisory skills; managed development of new employment branding materials; was responsible for onboarding new hires; was intimately involved in building the American Heart University; and worked with a variety of people to create American Heart Association-specific curricula available at the American Heart University. In 2010, Danielle became the director of Talent Management, in which role she manages the processes for onboarding, the employee engagement survey, national and local talent reviews, succession management, and leadership development.

John E. Baur is a doctoral student in management in the Price College of Business at the University of Oklahoma, specializing in organizational behavior and human resources management. He received an MBA with a dual focus in management and finance from Creighton University. His current research interests include employee expectations, group dynamics, employee commitment, and organizational power.

Marcia A. Beck received her PhD in comparative politics at the University of Notre Dame. Her research interests focus on comparative civil society development, public administration, and Soviet/Russian politics. She is the author of *Russia's Liberal Project: State-Society Relations in the Transition from Communism* (Pennsylvania State University Press, 2000) and coauthor, with John Donovan, Richard Morgan, and Christian Potholm, of *People, Power, and Politics*, 3rd edition (Littlefield Adams, 1993) and, with James S. Bowman and Jonathan P. West, of *Achieving Competencies in Public Service: The Professional Edge*, 2nd edition (M. E. Sharpe, 2010). Beck has taught courses in comparative politics, Soviet/Russian politics and foreign policy, and European Politics at Bowdoin College, where she was associate professor in the Government Department until 2003, the University of Notre Dame, and the University of Miami. She was a national fellow at the Hoover Institution on War, Revolution, and Peace in 1991/92 and is the recipient of an NEH archival grant for research in postcommunist Russian archives. Beck has contributed articles to the journals *Comparative Politics*, *The Russian Review*, *Demokratizatsiya*, and *The Review of Politics*, among others.

Brian L. Bellenger has extensive experience in the field of employee selection, specializing in high fidelity assessment tools incorporating video technology. Dr. Bellenger has worked with multiple public and private sector organizations, including The Southern Company, Auburn University, DeKalb County, Georgia, and the State of Alabama. Over the course of his career, Dr. Bellenger has served as an expert in several employment discrimination cases and has successfully led project teams in developing valid, nondiscriminatory selection tools under federal court scrutiny. Dr. Bellenger received his doctoral degree in Industrial and Organizational Psychology from Auburn University. He currently serves as the manager of performance measurement with the Personnel Board of Jefferson County in Birmingham, Alabama, and he is a partner and principal consultant in Centrus Personnel Solutions, LLC, a human resources consulting firm specializing in public safety testing.

Sheri Bias, SPHR, is currently the owner of Liquid Talent Agency based in Richmond, VA. She has been involved in the industry for many years with accomplishments of casting for feature films as well as corporate client productions. Dr. Bias has been a senior-level executive in human resources management with over 25 years experience and an extensive background in business. She has previously led human resources initiatives in companies such as Philip Morris USA and Anheuser-Busch. She was a management consultant with PriceWaterhouse Coopers where her primary focus was performance improvement and technology implementations for Fortune 500 companies. Dr. Bias received her PhD from The Fielding Graduate University where she studied a variety of human resources topics focusing specifically on the impacts of diversity and social justice. She possesses an MBA from The College of William and Mary and a Master of Arts in Education and Human Development from The George Washington University. Bias also taught business and human resources courses at The College of William and Mary, University of Virginia, Hampton University, Saint Leo University, and South University.

Kyle Brink is an Assistant Professor in the Haworth College of Business at Western Michigan University. In addition to his academic experience, he has worked for Fortune 100 companies and government organizations providing human resource management solutions. Kyle has also presented and published research in the areas of selection, performance management, career development, diversity and training. He received his PhD in Industrial & Organizational Psychology from the University of Georgia.

M. Ronald Buckley is the JC Penney Company Chair of Business Leadership and a professor of management and a professor of psychology in the Price College of Business at the University of Oklahoma. He received his PhD in industrial/ organizational psychology from Auburn University. He is interested in a variety of topics in human resources management, for example, interview decision making, fairness and bias in selection, and organizational socialization. Buckley has published over 70 peer reviewed articles, many of which have appeared in the *Journal of Management*, *Academy of Management Review*, *Journal of Applied Psychology*, *Personnel Psychology*, *Organizational Behavior and Human Decision Processes*, and the *Journal of Organizational Behavior*.

Daniel D. Butler, PhD, is a Thomas Walter Professor of Technology Management at Auburn University. Dr. Butler earned his doctorate in marketing and international business operations from the University of South Carolina. He holds MBA and Finance degrees from the University of Central Florida. He was a Rotary Fellow to La Universidad Nacional de Cordoba in Argentina studying the impact of monetary inflation on the global economy. Dr. Butler is the recipient of 28 teaching awards including the 2008 Auburn University Leischuck Presidential Teaching Award. Dr. Butler has extensive experience across a range of global and domestic business enterprises. Dr. Butler's core value of treating others as one would like to be treated is the foundation for his interest in customer and employee satisfaction; internal and external to organizations. He has consulted with and presented Executive Development programs across the United States, Europe, and Asia. Dr. Butler has been a frequent speaker at the Blue Ridge Conference on Leadership, the Society for Marketing Advances, and civic organizations. In addition to his other work experience, Dr. Butler has worked as a bank auditor, a government lobbyist, and assistant cruise director for Norwegian Cruise Lines.

Jeffrey Crenshaw is an industrial and organizational psychologist and the deputy director at the Personnel Board of Jefferson County in Birmingham, Alabama. In addition to this position, he has significant experience in human resources and organizational development in internal and external consulting settings for both the public and private sectors. He received his PhD in industrial and organizational Psychology from DePaul University in Chicago, Illinois.

Kristin Cullen, PhD, is a postdoctoral research fellow at the Center for Creative Leadership (CCL). Her current research focuses on individual characteristics that are related to workplace success and leader derailment and also the importance of workplace relationships and social networks for achieving interpersonal influence, leadership, and organizational change. Kristin has published numerous articles and book chapters on topics including political skill, interpersonal conflict, work-family conflict, social support, and personality measurement. Her publications can be found in the *Journal of Management, Journal of Vocational Behavior,* and the *Journal of Personality Research*. Kristin earned an Honors BS in psychology and commerce from the University of Toronto and an MS and PhD in industrial/organizational psychology from Auburn University. Kristin has taught undergraduate courses in psychology and management at Auburn University and the University of North Carolina Greensboro.

Patrick "Pat" Deery is the director of Human Resource Development (HRD) at Auburn University. Pat has a bachelor of arts from Marshall University (1966) and a master of arts from Auburn University (1979). He has the designation of Certified Professional in Learning and Performance (CPLP) from the American Society of Training and Development and was in the pioneer group receiving their CPLP. In addition to his 13 years of experience in the training and development field, Pat has served

25 years in the U.S. Army and spent 12 years teaching composition and literature on the collegiate level. Pat's responsibilities as the director of HRD are principally concerned with the management of training and development for staff and faculty. He is a member of Phi Kappa Phi academic honorary at Auburn University and serves on the City of Auburn's veterans' committee.

Ajantha Dharmasiri is a senior faculty of the Postgraduate Institute of Management (PIM), Colombo, Sri Lanka. He is also an adjunct professor in International HRM at Price College of Business, Oklahoma, USA. He has over 2 decades of private and public sector experience as a consultant on organizational issues, including consulting with numerous multinational organizations. He is a chartered electrical engineer and a member of the Chartered Institute of Management, UK. He engages in consultancies in more than ten countries, and is also an independent director of a development bank. Having a PhD and an MBA from PIM and a BSc in engineering from University of Moratuwa, Sri Lanka, he is a Commonwealth AMDISA Doctoral Fellow and a Fulbright Postdoctoral Fellow as well.

Jackie A. DiPofi, PhD, is director of the Small Business Development Center in the College of Business at Auburn University. The SBDC operates as a partner to the U. S. Small Business Administration through counseling and training to promote start-ups, expansion, innovation, increased productivity, management improvement and profits. Under Dr. DiPofi's direction, the AU SBDC has been recognized as playing a key role in the Auburn-Opelika area receiving national recognition as one of the best places in the country for small business. She began her teaching career at Auburn University at Montgomery in 1989, and served as an adjunct faculty for the College of Veterinary Medicine at Auburn University in 2004. In 2009 she joined the faculty of the Thomas Walter Center of Technology Management in the College of Engineering to coteach Integrating Business and Engineering Theories with Practice. Dr. DiPofi earned her BS in marketing and her MBA from The University of Alabama, and her PhD in management from Auburn University. She is the creator of the *RAMPS Plan to Marketing Success*. Since its inception in 1983, the *RAMPS* model has been used by thousands of individuals and praised for its effectiveness. Dr. DiPofi's interests include entrepreneurship, family business, marketing, strategy, organizational behavior and organizational change. She is a past president of the Greater Peace Community Development Corporation, Opelika, AL.

Susan P. Eisner is a tenured professor of management in the Anisfield School of Business at Ramapo College of NJ. Prior to teaching she held key positions in a leading television station, prominent health care foundation, national political party, and presidential campaign. Her graduate degree is from Harvard's Kennedy School of Government, where she was an administration fellow. Her interests include organizational behavior, leadership, diversity, and entertainment/media management. She has received the *All-Thomases Award for Faculty Excellence* (All-College), and the *Outstanding Teacher Award* (School of Business). She is recognized in prestigious listings including *Who's Who in the World*, *Who's Who in America*, and *Who's Who Among America's Teachers*. She serves on the Society for Advancement of Management's (SAM) Board of Directors and the *SAM Advanced Management Journal* Editorial Review Board.

Margaret Fitch-Hauser has 35 + years of experience as an educator, consultant, trainer and coach. She is a published scholar in the field of listening and information processing and has served as an expert witness in several fraud litigations. Her current research efforts focus on cultural differences in listening related measures and situations as well as listening fidelity. Her coauthored textbook, *Listening: Processes, Functions, & Competency*, was recently published by Allyn & Bacon. She is a life member of the International Listening Association and was inducted into the ILA Hall of Fame in 2004. Margaret's education includes a BA and MA in speech communication from Stephen F. Austin State University in Texas and a PhD in interpersonal communication from the University of Oklahoma. Margaret is currently the Chair of the Department of Communication and Journalism at Auburn University in Auburn, Alabama, USA.

Jared J. Llorens is an assistant professor in the Public Administration Institute at Louisiana State University. Prior to beginning an academic career, he served as a human resources specialist with both the U.S. Office of Personnel Management and the U.S. Department of Labor. His research interests include public sector compensation, human resources automation and civil service reform. He is coauthor of the textbook *Public Personnel Management: Contexts and Strategies, 6th ed.*, and his recent work has appeared in the *Review of Public Personnel Administration* and the *Journal of Public Administration Research and Theory*. He received his PhD in public administration from the University of Georgia in 2007.

Rishap Malhotra is a transdisciplinary strategist who has a particular interest in understanding how business, technology, brands and people, live, grow and coexist. Rishap has a MBA from the College of William & Mary. He has worked abroad and in the United States in advertising and marketing. Most recently Rishap worked with Saatchi & Saatchi in Corporate Development and Shopper Marketing. Rishap is an international cinema buff and is fluent in English, Hindi, Punjabi and Russian. A native of New Delhi, India, Rishap now lives with his wife in New York City.

Donna L. Phillips has 29 years of Federal Government experience and is currently the training officer at NASA Langley Research Center in Hampton, VA. She holds a bachelor of science degree in business administration with an emphasis in management from Christopher Newport University and a master of arts degree in education and human development from George Washington University. She earned a leadership coaching certificate from Georgetown University and completed her organization development certificate at the National Training Laboratory (NTL) Institute. Ms. Phillips' passion is helping individuals tap into their personal power and encouraging them to achieve the unachievable. As an internal coach for NASA, Donna works with young professionals to transform themselves into perceptive leaders.

Scott A. Quatro is professor of management in the Department of Business Administration at Covenant College. Dr. Quatro is an experienced strategic human resource management professional with 18 years of related experience. He has been a senior human resources and organizational development consultant with American Management Systems, then the eleventh largest management consultancy in the world, and a corporate human resource manager for Payless ShoeSource. Since entering academe Dr. Quatro's teaching, consulting, and research work have focused on strategic human resource management, holistic leadership development, and organizational strategy/purpose/spirituality. His consulting clients have included both Fortune 500 firms and small to midsized organizations, including Merrill Lynch, Chattem, Payless ShoeSource, DriveTime, and Southern Champion Tray. He has authored or coauthored over 20 journal articles, chapters, and books, including *Executive Ethics: Ethical Dilemmas and Challenges for the C-Suite* (2008), and *The Praeger Handbook of Human Resource Management* (2009). Dr. Quatro serves on the Peer Review Boards for *Human Resource Development Review* and the *Journal of Business Ethics*. He received a BA in English from Pepperdine University, an MBA from the College of William and Mary, and holds a PhD from Iowa State University. He lives in Lookout Mountain, Georgia with his wife Jamie and their four children.

Milano Reyna started his career in industrial and organizational psychology at the Center for Business and Economic Development at Auburn University at Montgomery. Milano has led several of the Center's clients in both private and public sectors. Focus areas included employee selection, employment law and organizational development. Milano joined the private sector in the 90's as a corporate development director for Weidmuller, Inc, in Richmond, Virginia focused on its business transformation and leading human resources. Milano is currently the global chief talent officer for Saatchi & Saatchi and has been in this position for more than a decade. He is a member of the worldwide executive board and chairs the Global Talent Board. He is also a member of the Publicis Groupe Talent Committee. He works in New York City. Saatchi & Saatchi is an ideas company and works for some of the world's largest companies on their brands, advertising, social media, shopper marketing and sustainability needs.

William I. Sauser, Jr., PhD, is professor of management and higher education at Auburn University. Dr. Sauser earned his BS in management and his MS and PhD in industrial/organizational psychology at the Georgia Institute of Technology, and an MA in business ethics from the University of Wales. He is licensed to practice psychology in Alabama and holds specialty diplomas in industrial/organizational psychology and organizational and business consulting psychology from the American Board of Professional Psychology. Dr. Sauser's interests include organizational development, strategic planning, human relations in the workplace, business ethics, and continuing professional education. He is a fellow of the American Council on Education and the Society for Advancement of Management. Dr. Sauser is also a commissioned lay pastor in the Presbyterian Church (USA) and serves as pastor of the Union Springs (Alabama) Presbyterian Church. He was awarded the 2003 Frederick W. Taylor Key by the Society for Advancement of Management in recognition of his career achievements.

Ronald R. Sims is the Floyd Dewey Gottwald Senior Professor in the Mason School of Business at the College of William and Mary. He received his PhD in organizational behavior from Case Western Reserve University. His research and consultation focuses on a variety of topics to include leadership and change management, HRM, business ethics, employee training, and management and leadership development (i.e. human resource development), learning styles, and experiential learning. Dr. Sims is the author or coauthor of thirty-one books and more than eighty articles that have appeared in a wide variety of scholarly and practitioner journals.

Kyra Leigh Sutton, PhD, is an assistant professor of human resources management in the Department of Management at Auburn University.

She earned her BA degree at Spelman College and her MA and PhD degrees from the Ohio State University. She enjoys teaching human resources management and organizational behavior. Prior to joining the faculty at Auburn, she previously taught at Miami University's Farmer School of Business, and Ohio State University's Fisher College of Business. Dr. Sutton's work has been published in: *Asia Pacific Journal of Management, Journal of STEM Education: Innovations and Research, and Work and Life Integration: Organizational, Cultural and Psychological Perspectives.* Further, multiple peer-reviewed papers have been presented at the Society for Industrial and Organizational Psychology (SIOP), Academy of Management (AMA), and International Association of Conflict Management (IACM). Dr. Sutton's research has received funding from the Ohio State University Graduate School's Alumni Grants for Graduate Research and Scholarship (AGGRS), the Coca-Cola Critical Difference for Women Graduate Studies Grants for Research on Women, Gender, and Gender Equity; she was most recently a Heanon Wilkins Fellow at Miami University. She serves as a reviewer for *Academy of Management Journal* (AMJ). Dr. Sutton also has more than 3 years of work experience as a consultant with AT Kearney and JPMorganChase, and she was a senior economic forecasting analyst for Delta Air Lines. Dr. Sutton is a member of Academy of Management, Society for Industrial and Organizational Psychology, Society of Human Resources Management, and the National Association for African Americans in Human Resources (NAAHR). She also volunteers for the United Way and Big Brother, Big Sister.

Daniel J. Svyantek, PhD, received his degree from the University of Houston in 1987. He was a faculty member in the industrial/organizational psychology PhD program at The University of Akron from 1987 to 2003. He is currently a full professor in the Psychology Department of Auburn University. He served as the program director of the Industrial/Organizational Psychology PhD program from 2003 to 2008. He is currently serving as chair of the Auburn University Psychology Department. He has published in journals such as the *Journal of Applied Psychology, Journal of Vocational Behavior, Journal of Applied Behavioral Sciences,* and *Human Relations.* He has served as editor of the journal, *Organizational Analysis* and is currently series editor for the annual series, *Research in Organizational Sciences.* He has consulted with several organizations on organizational change projects in the areas of problem solving, compensation systems, and implementing work teams. He is particularly interested in the development of new evaluation methods for assessing the practical value of applied research within applied contexts. In addition, his research interest areas include person-organization fit issues and the role of organizational culture and climate as the context for the expression of individual behavior in organizations.

Frances L. H. Svyantek, MA, received her degree from the University of Houston in 1988. She has been a lecturer for the Auburn University College of Business for 4 years. Her research interests include statistical analytic techniques, the development of statistical instructional technologies, and the role of modeling in organizational settings.

Jessica McManus Warnell teaches the undergraduate-level required business ethics course and electives in sustainable business, values-based decision-making, and managing Millennials. She has earned her MA from the University of Chicago and her BA summa cum laude from Saint Mary's College, the Certificate in Executive Management from the ND Executive Education Program, and Global Reporting Initiative (GRI) Sustainability Reporting Certification. Her research explores principled moral reasoning and business ethics curricula, leadership and sustainability education, and managing Millennials toward effective, ethical leadership.

Jonathan P. West, professor, interim chair of the Political Science Department, and director of the Graduate Public Administration Program at the University of Miami, specializes in human resource management, productivity, local government, and ethics. He has published 8 books and more than 100 scholarly articles and book chapters. His most recent books include *Human Resource Management in Public Service*, coauthored with Evan Berman, James Bowman and Monty Van Wart (Sage, 2010, third edition), *Achieving Competencies in Public Service: The Professional Edge*, coauthored with James Bowman and Marcia A. Beck (M. E. Sharpe, 2010, second edition), *American Public Service: Radical Reform of the Merit System*, coedited with James Bowman (Taylor & Francis, 2007), and *The Ethics Edge*, coedited with Evan Berman (International City/County Management Association, 2006, second edition). His coauthored book titled *American Politics and the Environment* (with Glen Sussman and Byron Daynes) was published in 2002. He is managing editor of *Public Integrity* and a member of the editorial board of three other professional journals. He has taught at the University of Houston and the University of Arizona and has worked as a management analyst in the Office of the Surgeon General, Department of the Army.

Alexandrea Wilson is a recent alumna of the public administration institute's master of public administration program at Louisiana State University. Her prior work experience includes nonprofit volunteer recruitment, program management, and educational and training support for the Louisiana banking industry.

Ken Yusko is currently an associate professor of human resources and management in the School of Business Administration at Marymount University and coprincipal of Siena Consulting, a human capital consulting firm. He has authored two books on human resource and human capital management practices and is a frequent contributor to both trade and research journals on the topic of employee selection. Dr. Yusko's research focuses on two areas, including promoting diversity by reducing subgroup differences in employment testing, and in negotiation/conflict management. His doctoral research on attorney negotiation techniques was funded through a grant from the National Science Foundation. Ken and his team were recently awarded the M. Scott Myers Award for Applied Research from the Society of Industrial/Organizational Psychology and the International Personnel Assessment Council's Innovations Award for their work in developing and implementing the Siena Reasoning Test, a cognitive ability test that substantially enhances diversity in hiring.